HOW TO TEACH READING SYSTEMATICALLY

HOW TO TEACH READING SYSTEMATICALLY

SECOND EDITION

GERALD G. DUFFY, GEORGE B. SHERMAN, AND LAURA R. ROEHLER

MICHIGAN STATE UNIVERSITY

HARPER & ROW, PUBLISHERS
New York, Hagerstown, San Francisco, London

Sponsoring Editor: Wayne E. Schotanus
Project Editor: Cynthia Hausdorff
Designer: Gayle Jaeger
Production Supervisor: Will C. Jomarrón
Compositor: Port City Press, Inc.
Printer and Binder: The Murray Printing Company
Art Studio: Vantage Art Inc.

How to Teach Reading Systematically, Second Edition
Copyright © 1977 by Harper & Row

Library of Congress Cataloging in Publication Data

Duffy, Gerald G
    How to teach reading systematically.

    1. Reading.   I.   Sherman, George B., joint author.
II.   Roehler, Laura R., 1937–   joint author.
III.   Title.
LB1050.D75   1977   372.4'1   76–20721
ISBN 0-06-041784-6

CONTENTS

● v

EIGHT

WHERE TO GO FROM HERE   353

PREFACE

This is a book about teaching children to read. It was written to help you become the best possible teacher of reading. It is likely that you have heard the old saying, "Teachers are born, not made." Don't believe it! That statement is based on the popular assumption that teaching is some kind of mystical art that can only be practiced by favored individuals blessed at birth with creative insights hidden from the rest of us. Again, don't believe it! You can learn to be a competent teacher.

This competence is composed of three ingredients. First, teachers of reading *know* something—they know their pupils, they know the content of reading, and they know how to teach it. Second, teachers *do* something—they diagnose, instruct, direct, counsel, create, organize, inspire, and praise. Third, teachers *are* something—they are people who care, who are alternately warm and loving, stern and aloof, and they are people with authentic personalities, who wear masks only on Halloween. In short, this book is based on the belief that the teacher is the single most important influence on the school life of a child. What a teacher knows, what a teacher does, and what a teacher is are what count.

Each chapter of this book deals with one aspect of teaching children to read. Each lesson is followed by a series of activities designed to insure that you have mastered and can apply the information in the chapter. *Test Your Knowledge* recaps the salient terms and concepts discussed in the chapter; *Simulation Activities* sets up hypothetical situations to test your understanding of these concepts and how they can be applied; *Suggested Field Experiences* presents appropriate activities for applying your knowledge in actual teaching; and *For Class Discussion* provides stimulating topics that can be discussed in class. The *Answer Key* that follows these sections is a self-checking device for the *Test Your Knowledge* questions.

Although no single book or course of study can honestly claim to guarantee for you these teaching attributes "or your money back," we sincerely believe that if you expend time and energy in studying, thinking about, and acting on the ideas described in this book—if you actively seek to understand what you are learning and don't just memorize facts for an exam—you will end up with a relatively sophisticated understanding of *what* a teacher does when teaching a child to read and *how* the teacher does it.

Gerald G. Duffy
George B. Sherman
Laura R. Roehler

ONE
AN INTRODUCTION TO
READING INSTRUCTION

DEFINING READING

OVERVIEW

When asked to give a definition of reading, we might assume that teachers would respond uniformly. Comparisons of such definitions would, however, reveal a great diversity of opinion. Published literature on reading reveals a similar dilemma: reading is not consistently defined. From these diverse definitions comes a second debate focusing on how reading should be taught since different definitions lead directly to different views of what reading instruction should be.

This chapter provides you with four general categories of reading definitions, along with the implications these definitions have for reading instruction. The ultimate objective is:

> Given various definitions of the reading process, you will create a definition of reading which reflects elements of the major views of what reading is.

KNOWLEDGE BACKGROUND

Deciding upon your own definition of reading is a crucial first step in learning to teach reading since the definition becomes the foundation from which all teaching techniques arise. The way you define reading will be directly reflected in your reading instruction.

● 3

Definitions of reading can be divided into four general categories. In the first, reading is defined as an interest. Looked at in this way, the reading program tends to emphasize motivation to read through literature appreciation. The program goal would largely be one of providing interesting and stimulating reading material in a supportive atmosphere. If you subscribe to this view, your reading instruction will emphasize the development of the recreational reading habit.

A second view defines reading as a language process and emphasizes experience development. In this view, reading is seen as one of several interrelated language modes for conveying meaning, all of which can best be developed through shared experiences, discussions, vocabulary expansion, and the reading and writing of child-written stories. If you subscribe to this definition, your program will focus on developing the child's awareness of reading as speech in print.

A third view defines reading from a cultural aspect; instruction would emphasize the uniqueness of a child's cultural background by carefully selecting material to enhance that unique aspect. Attention would focus on the relation between dialect differences and the written message, as well as on one's cultural heritage. If you subscribe to this view, you will always attempt to make your instruction relevant to the child's cultural background.

Finally, reading may be defined as a learned system. Viewed in this way, instructional emphasis is placed on controlled development of skills in a structured sequence progressing from the simple to the complex. This view of reading contains several subdivisions according to the kinds of skills emphasized. Basically, these subdivisions are word recognition emphasis, comprehension emphasis, or a combination of these two.

At the word recognition end of the continuum, reading is viewed as the act of decoding print into sound. Though the need for obtaining meaning is not denied, it is not emphasized. Reading is viewed essentially as a decoding experience, a process of verbalizing the printed word. If you share this view, your instruction would emphasize oral pronunciation, oral reading practice as a check on decoding skills and sight-word recognition, and analysis of words through the use of techniques such as phonics.

At the other end of the continuum, decoding is deemphasized and the primary stress is on the need to obtain meaning from the written message. The "whole sentence approach" reflects this subdivision. In this approach, words are never taught in isolation since they obtain their meanings from their contextual environment and since the sentence, not the word, is the meaning-bearing unit. If you share this view, your instruction would stress comprehension exercises and would deemphasize word and sounding skills.

In the combination view, word recognition skills are viewed as the crucial base of the reading process but are not taught to the exclusion of comprehension skills. Both types of skills are mutually supportive, and both are a daily part of the reading program. Viewed in this manner, reading is the meaningful interpretation of the printed symbols. Applying this definition to the classroom, one would find structured teaching and practice of both word recognition and comprehension skills together with a heavy emphasis on the application of learned skills in purposeful silent reading. This is the view emphasized in this book.

SUMMARY OF DEFINING READING

There is considerable difference of opinion about how reading should be defined. Current definitions range from emphasis on cultural heritage, to interests, to language development, to one of several kinds of skill development. The result is that teachers are often confused about what reading really is.

Such confusion is costly because it results in confused instruction. However, the practice of rigidly subscribing to one view to the exclusion of all others is equally costly since it results in narrow instruction which denies the complexity and breadth of the reading act. The trick is to recognize that each of the four general areas have some validity and to develop for yourself a definition which draws elements from each.

Consequently, this book defines reading as a learned process in which the skills of word recognition and comprehension are mutually supportive. Additionally, however, in recognition of the fact that each of the four general definitions possesses strength, the best elements of each are synthesized to form a broad base for a thorough and well-rounded reading program. As you move through this book, you will find attention given to the cultural, motivational, and language elements of reading as well as to the learned aspects.

TEST YOUR KNOWLEDGE

1. _____ is not consistently defined.
2. The way in which a teacher defines reading is reflected in _____.
3. In a classroom where motivation and self-selected materials are largely emphasized, reading is likely to be viewed as an _____.
4. Emphasis on sequential skill development reflects a definition of reading as a _____.
5. Reading may also be defined as a language process and focus on enlarging the child's _____ background.
6. Those who view reading as culturally based emphasize the use of reading materials which reflect a child's _____.
7. The skills taught by those who view reading as a learned process may range from a _____ emphasis to an emphasis on _____.

SIMULATION ACTIVITIES

Examine the following statements from teachers. On the basis of these statements, describe how each teacher defines reading.

> I do not have a separate reading hour. Reading skills are developed as part of a child's total language experience. With equal attention to all modes of communication, the child develops an understanding of reading and its relationship to speaking.

> Reading about Dick and Jane in the country will not help my learners. It is essential to provide materials that are relevant to the children's lives and written in a language that they will be able to understand.

> Reading is not an isolated subject. It is taught throughout the day, at home and at school. Motivation, experience development, effective skill teaching, and application are crucial components of a successful reading program.

SUGGESTED FIELD EXPERIENCES

Observation. When observing in schools, note how teachers teach reading and hypothesize, on the basis of your observation, what their definition of reading might be.

Teaching activities. As you begin teaching reading, explicitly state your own definition of reading. Then keep a checklist of the elements of your reading program. Later, examine your checklist to see if your instruction reflects your stated definition.

Client impact. One's definition of reading formulates the basis of reading instruction. Therefore, an effective reading program rests on a clear, consistent, and open-minded definition of the reading process.

FOR CLASS DISCUSSION

On the basis of the reading definitions described in this chapter, formulate your own definition of reading. Describe what your classroom instruction would be as a result of this definition.

ANSWER KEY
1. reading
2. instruction
3. interest
4. learned system
5. experience
6. cultural heritage
7. word recognition, comprehension

MAJOR APPROACHES TO READING INSTRUCTION

OVERVIEW

As seen in Chapter 1, even "experts" define reading in a variety of ways, which in turn affects the way the teacher approaches instruction. This chapter describes the basic ideas of each approach to familiarize you with their strengths and weaknesses; knowing that, you can make more competent choices and decisions when you are designing and planning reading instruction for your students. The specific objective is:

> Given information about eight different approaches to reading
> instruction, the student can identify specific characteristics of each
> approach and state ways in which the approaches can be used
> most efficiently.

KNOWLEDGE BACKGROUND

This chapter describes eight different approaches to reading instruction: the basal textbook, the linguistic, the phonics, the programmed, the skills monitoring system, the language experience, the psycholinguistic, and the personalized reading approaches. To maintain the relationship between this chapter and the first, these eight approaches will be discussed in terms of three of the four general definition areas discussed in Chapter 1: reading as a learned system, reading as a language process, and reading as an interest. Since none of the eight approaches reflects a cultural definition per se, that one has been omitted.

READING AS A LEARNED SYSTEM

The most prevalently used approaches to reading instruction reflect the definition of reading as a learned system. Included in this category are the basal textbook approach, the linguistic approach, the phonics approach, the programmed approach, and the skills monitoring approach.

THE BASAL TEXTBOOK APPROACH

The most common tool for teaching reading is the basal textbook. Traditionally, basals are books of short stories which are graded to be used sequentially from the first grade, or the readiness, level through the sixth grade level, although a few series continue through the junior high school level. Recently, there has been an effort to make basals appear nongraded by replacing grade level indicators with codes. However, most basal series follow the same general format:

KINDERGARTEN   Readiness workbooks

FIRST GRADE   Preprimer level—three (or more) soft-covered texts with accompanying workbooks

Primer level—hard-covered text with accompanying workbook

First level—hard-covered text with accompanying workbook

SECOND GRADE   Two hard-covered texts and accompanying workbooks
AND ABOVE   at each grade level

While there are many different basal series produced by various publishing houses, the standard basal text lesson follows these steps:

1. BACKGROUND OR MOTIVATION   Pupils are oriented to the story, interest is created, and the story content is related to the pupils' background or experience.
2. VOCABULARY DEVELOPMENT   New words are presented in context and their meanings explained.
3. PURPOSEFUL SILENT READING (guided silent reading)   Pupils are directed to read silently to find answers to specific questions. They may be told to read one page, several pages, or an entire story.
4. DISCUSSION   Pupils and the teacher discuss the story.
5. PURPOSEFUL REREADING   Students are given specific purposes for rereading; for example, to find how a character felt at a particular

point in the story, to find evidence supporting a point, and so on. This may be either oral or silent reading.

6. SKILL INSTRUCTION   Pupils are provided with instruction in a specific word recognition or comprehension skill. This activity usually involves the use of workbooks.

7. ENRICHMENT ACTIVITIES   Pupils are directed to do activities that go beyond the story, such as additional related reading, related art projects, and so on.

Various basals have different kinds of stories depending on the author's views. For instance, some basals strictly control the number of new words introduced, thereby restricting the amount of variety that can be incorporated into stories. Others concentrate on the interest appeal of stories as of primary importance and are less concerned with the number of new words. Some basals reflect the view that words that refer to common home and school experiences which the "average" learners have in common should be used, while others create stories which reflect particular cultural backgrounds or create stories using words that carry a great deal of power and interest, such as **dinosaur, tiger,** and **rocket.** Still other basals include familiar rhymes and chants at the primary levels in an effort to tie the language the learner uses orally with the language that is being read.

Different basal series may also vary greatly in terms of *what* is taught. Some emphasize decoding, others stress comprehension, and still others place a major emphasis on story appeal. Generally, however, most basals attempt to strike a balance between decoding and comprehension.

Skill instruction in the basal text may often be haphazard rather than systematic. This is because the skills to be taught frequently depend on the content of the story. For example, if the word **cars** is being used in a story, skill instruction might focus on the initial **c** sound, **–ar** phonograms, and the **–s** inflectional ending rather than the next skill in a clearly specified sequence of skills.

Basals can be of great help when they are used wisely. The quality and variety of reading material found in the basals is generally good; the teachers' editions provide many suggestions; the workbooks provide practice exercises.

Basals cannot, however, be viewed as *"the* total reading program." There are three disadvantages in relying on a publisher to provide a total reading program. First, the reading instruction often becomes lock-step and teachers tend to move from story to story and book to book without any flexibility. The class is often divided into three groups which go through the series at different rates—an average rate for the fast and average students, a slower rate for students who are having some difficulty, and an extremely slow rate for the students who are really in trouble. The net effect is that some students fail to move as fast as they ought to, while others are moved too fast; a group of elementary children can seldom be neatly divided into three groups. Second, the basals tend to teach decoding and comprehension skills in terms of when the skills fit the content of the story rather than when the learner needs instruction. This weakens instruction since the child's needs in terms of the reading process should be the basis for instructional decisions, not the story to be read. Finally, because of the emphasis placed on the stories in the basals, teachers are led to believe that children will learn how to read simply by reading; as a result, they often "teach" by having children read paragraphs of a story aloud in turn. While such practice may not harm those who already know how to read, it does not teach the child who is having trouble learning how to read.

THE LINGUISTIC APPROACH

Linguistics is not a method of teaching reading but is the science of studying language. The findings from linguists can, however, be applied to reading. Linguists look at reading as recognizing and interpreting graphic symbols representing spoken sounds which have meaning. The first linguistic reading materials placed a major emphasis on decoding and practically ignored comprehension. More recently, there has been a shift of emphasis to reading for meaning.

Linguists teach that *graphemes* (letters) are used to represent speech *phonemes* (sounds); consequently, linguistically based reading materials often stress sound–symbol regularity and systematic exposure to frequently used sounding patterns. The initial vocabulary presented to the learners is controlled by presenting only words fitting the regularity of the sound–symbol patterns, resulting in sentences such as "Dan ran to the tan van." Initial reading instruction using linguistic principles employs the following steps:

1. Mastery of left-to-right orientation, alphabet, and sound–symbol connections.
2. Presentation of two- and/or three-letter words that have short vowels and follow regular patterns (**bat, pen, sit**).
3. Introduction of consonant digraphs, blends, and final double consonants.
4. Discussion of semiregular vowel patterns (**cake, bike**).
5. Introduction of irregular patterns.

In the linguistic approach, comprehension is studied as language patterns, both in terms of grammatical structure and choice of words in sentences. The learners are taught to change or transform sentences by adding words or phrases or by substituting words. Examples of the technique of transforming sentences are:

The boy ran. → The boy ran home.
Mother drove the car. → Father drove the car.

Opponents of the linguistic approach cite two weaknesses. First, there is a lack of meaningful reading material in the initial stages of instruction, and, second, the vocabulary is unnatural and too limited. Both of these criticisms focus on the lack of interesting and meaningful material in the linguistic method. When the language children read does not correspond very closely with their oral language, interest in reading can be lost.

The linguistic approach does have strengths, however. Reading deals with language, and since linguists study language, it is crucial to listen to what they are saying and to incorporate some of their principles in our classroom instruction. Specifically, we should make use of the linguists' ideas regarding sound–symbol regularity, sentence patterns, and transformations when teaching word recognition and comprehension.

THE PHONICS APPROACH

For years, a controversy has raged in the field of reading about the place of phonics instruction. Those who support phonics believe that our English spelling system is essentially regular in its correspondence between letters and speech sounds and that letter sounds can be blended together to form words. The shared focus on sounding is common to the linguistic and phonic approaches; in fact, sometimes the terms appear together in compound form, as in linguistic–phonemic or linguistic–phonetic.

It is not surprising, then, that the phonics approach has the same general weaknesses found in the linguistic approach to reading instruction. Opponents of both approaches say that English spelling is not regular and that it is, therefore, fruitless to teach phonics. Similarly, they point out that heavy emphasis on phonics causes some children to be overanalytical or nonfluent in their reading.

Despite these criticisms, however, most reading teachers recognize that a knowledge of sound–symbol relationships and the ability to apply that knowledge are necessary for successful reading. It is up to the skillful teacher to incorporate elements of the phonics method meaningfully into reading instruction and to balance them with the other skills. While an overemphasis on phonics instruction may hinder a learner in becoming fluent, a total lack of phonics instruction can make it difficult for the learner to become an independent reader.

PROGRAMMED INSTRUCTION

Programmed instruction is more structured than the other reading approaches, but it incorporates principles of learning that contribute to individualized instruction. These include step-by-step learning, immediate knowledge of results, regular and constant review and testing, learning by doing, and individual progress through materials.

In programmed instruction, each task is analyzed into its component parts and arranged into sequential steps which are presented in small increments called "frames." The child provides an answer for each frame and receives immediate feedback on whether the answer is correct or not. By proceeding in small increments and actively producing correct answers, the child learns more readily and the tasks are reinforced. This has been found to be a beneficial technique for some slow readers and remedial readers because the materials can be self-paced.

While programmed approaches seem to help some disabled readers, criticisms of this approach do exist. For instance, many critics point out that the materials are too dull and fragmented, making reading instruction a boring rote. In addition, most current programmed approaches to reading emphasize phonics and neglect other crucial aspects of reading growth.

THE SKILLS MONITORING APPROACH

The final view of reading as a learned system is the skills monitoring approach to instruction. In this program, reading is analyzed in terms of its component skills, which are then arranged in hierarchies. The skills are usually broken down into very small steps, each skill being the direct prerequisite of the next. The basic rationale is that reading ability is the sum of its component parts, and instruction, therefore, should focus on teaching each of these parts in sequence.

Because many skills are usually identified, this approach also specifies a means for systematically determining when a child knows a skill and a record-keeping device for noting the child's progress. The underlying belief is that teachers should know what skills to teach, how to determine when a skill has been learned, and how to keep track of each child's progress through the hierarchy. While various skills monitoring systems differ in terms of the specific selection and ordering of skills, the means for assessing mastery, and the type of record-keeping, all share the belief that reading is composed of a variety of skills which should be taught in an orderly and systematic fashion.

A major strength of this approach is its specificity. Teachers feel that knowledge of the specific skills provides them with a tangible concept of the reading process, while the assessment and record-keeping devices are pragmatic tools immediately applicable in the classroom. The result is that teachers are clear about what they are to do and confident of their ability to do it.

Disadvantages do exist, however. The first is that skills monitoring approaches are only as good as the skills hierarchy upon which they are based. If the skills objectives are not accurate and precise, there will be no growth in reading ability. Second, emphasis on skills is of no value if there is not a concomitant emphasis on using those skills in context—on developing children who *do* read rather than children who can only do skills in isolation. Finally, the skills monitoring approaches require much work, and some teachers are reluctant to put forth the necessary effort.

SUMMARY

Instructional plans which tend to reflect a view of reading as a learned system include the basal approach, the linguistic approach, the phonics approach, the programmed approach, and the skills monitoring approach. Each has its strengths and weaknesses which teachers must take into account. Also, it is important to recognize that there is much spillover among the approaches since the programs combine elements common to all the programs. For instance, it is not unusual to find a basal series which emphasizes linguistics, a skills monitoring system which emphasizes phonics, or other combinations.

READING AS A LANGUAGE PROCESS

There are more and more experts who tend to regard reading as a language process and are, therefore, modifying instruction to accommodate this view. Usually, its proponents recommend either the language experience approach or the psycholinguistic approach.

THE LANGUAGE EXPERIENCE APPROACH

The language experience approach to reading instruction views reading as an extension of speaking. The major ideas behind this approach are summarized in the following statements:

1. What I think about I can talk about.
2. What I can talk about I can express in other ways.
3. What I can write I can read.
4. What I say is important to me.

In other words, reading is part of a communication cycle in which thinking leads to talking which leads to writing which leads to reading.

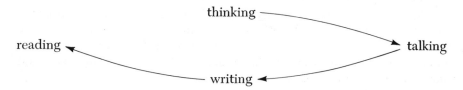

A child's functional vocabulary is the foundation for this approach. When a child enters school at age six, his or her estimated speaking vocabulary is 2500 or 2600 words. Yet, average first grade reading programs teach only approximately 400 words. Through the language experience approach, the learner's own language usage becomes the basis by which vocabulary is selected for instruction. Thus, the entry into reading is theoretically smoother because the learner's own language is the basis for instruction.

The major technique of the language experience approach is taking dictation from the children, from which their stories are "published" and become part of the classroom library. Children are thereby using their langauge as authors and can see their oral language being written down for others to share and admire. Steps in taking dictation are:

1. Discuss a topic with the student to establish a rapport and explore ideas.
2. After investigating several ideas, say to the pupil, "Let's write some of your ideas down on paper."
3. Direct the student to select a title and begin dictating.
4. Copy the exact words in manuscript form.
5. Read the dictated story to the student.
6. Direct the student to read the dictation to you. Underline all the words that he or she remembers.
7. Have the child recopy the dictation; the method depends on the level of the student.
   a. Beginners should trace over the dictation.
   b. Children who have mastered tracing should be directed to recopy the dictation directly below that taken by the teacher.
   c. More advanced students should recopy the dictation on a separate sheet of paper or even use a typewriter.
8. Compile each child's dictation into a booklet and let the children decide if the book should become part of the classroom library.
9. Review the next day.

Theoretically, the dictation and shared reading activities would be followed by appropriate skill development and reading literature. This, however, is where language experience frequently breaks down. Skill instruction often becomes haphazard and incidental rather than systematic and specific, and children tend not to see the relationship between the language and words they have used in dictation and the reading skills they are ultimately expected to use in books.

When used wisely, however, the language experience approach provides a powerful bridge between reading and the other language processes. Reading becomes a vital and meaningful activity which accurately reflects the functions of the language rather than an arbitrary and static set of tasks to be learned.

THE PSYCHOLINGUISTIC APPROACH

There is no true psycholinguistic approach or method, but there is a psycholinguistic *view* of reading which defines reading as the interaction of thought and language. To the psycholinguist, reading is a process of combining psychology and linguistics—the science of the mind and behavior and the science of the study of speech.

Psycholinguists study reading, like listening, as a receptive process used to understand a written message. Reading begins with graphic symbols from which readers must reconstruct the author's meaning in their own minds since there is no meaning in printed symbols. To the psycholinguists, there can only be meaning in the minds of the author and the reader—the sender and the receiver. For the reader, the act of reading becomes a guessing game in which the reader searches for understanding by a sampling–predicting–guessing process and attempts to reconstruct the author's intended meaning. Proficient readers are skilled at rapidly testing and confirming their use of the sampling–predicting–guessing process.

The psycholinguists believe that reading involves the simultaneous use of three types of cues. First, the reader must be able to use the grapho–phonic information, which consists of the letter, spelling, word patterns, sound patterns, intonation patterns, and sound–symbol relationships. Second, the reader must utilize syntactic information, which consists of grammatical sequence, functional words, affixes, and punctuation. Finally, semantic information must be employed by the reader, who brings a unique experiential background, concept acquisition, and vocabulary development to the printed symbols to reconstruct the intended meaning of the author.

Although psycholinguists state that psycholinguistics is not an approach to reading instruction, they suggest strategies to be used in classrooms to promote language usage and increase reading proficiency. Many of these strategies are borrowed from other reading approaches and should be included in any thorough reading program. Strategies to be used to increase reading proficiency include the following:

1. The learners should be able to predict and complete grammatical structure. This is similar to the cloze technique for proficient readers in which words are deleted from written sentences, and the reader is taught to guess the correct word and thus *cloze* the sentence. For less proficient readers, simple sentences such as "The boy swam in the _____" can be used.
2. The learners should be able to see the relationships between thinking, speaking, writing, listening, and reading. The use of dictation and experience charts is recommended.
3. The learners should be exposed to good literature.
4. The relationships that exist should be taught to the learners through word substitution and changing the order of words in sentences. The following sentences are examples of sentence transformation:

    Mary and Bill rode bikes going up the hill.
    They rode bikes going up the hill.
    Going up the hill they rode bikes.

5. Sounds and words should not be studied in isolation but in context for meaning.
6. Reading experiences should be related to the content areas and recreational areas.
7. Context should be used by the learners to build concepts.

8. The learners should be able to classify pertinent information and disregard useless or redundant information.
9. The learners should be able to use context to identify unfamiliar words.
10. From context, the readers should make judgments and draw inferences.
11. The learners should predict events and analyze the theme and plot of the stories that they are reading.

A major criticism of the psycholinguistic view of reading is that psycholinguists have not yet operationalized their thinking—that is, they have not yet been able to demonstrate how their ideas should be put to work on a regular basis in an elementary reading class. Consequently, they are currently operating in the world of theory rather than in the real world of teaching children in classrooms.

Despite this disadvantage, however, it would be foolish to deny the insights that psycholinguists provide. Their view of the interconnectedness of various aspects of the language and their emphasis on the sampling–predicting–guessing process should be incorporated into all reading instruction.

SUMMARY

Both the language experience approach and the psycholinguistic approach reflect the view of reading as a language process. Both place a premium on using the child's oral language and intuitive thinking to build instructional programs. Both suffer, however, from a lack of system, of order, and of logical progression from one instructional activity to another which make their ideas difficult to implement effectively.

READING AS AN INTEREST

There is only one major approach to instruction which reflects a view of reading as an interest. This is the personalized reading approach.

Personalized or individualized reading programs are formed around the concept of self-selection in which children select the books they wish to read and the words they wish to learn. From these selections, the teacher instructs the learner in the skills that are needed to read the chosen material and words. Individual conferences are held with each pupil during which the teacher discusses the book currently being read by the learner and assesses the learner's comprehension and word recognition needs and achievements.

To incorporate personalized reading instruction into a classroom, the teacher would implement the following steps:

1. Start collecting books. For the average classroom, try to collect 100 books, which is at least three different books per pupil. If there are

not enough available in your school, borrow, trade, and ask for donations.

2. Set up an interesting library area with a rug, pillows, and some furniture. Try to arrange the books with the covers facing the students.

3. Teach your children the "Rule of Thumb." Tell them to select a page in the middle of the book and begin reading it silently. Each time they miss a word, they should put up a finger. If all of their fingers are up before the page is finished, the book is too hard. Older children can just count up to five words missed.

4. Teach them to get books quietly.

5. Teach them how to get help with a word. They could go to the dictionary, an aide, experience charts, other books that they know, a friend, the buffer, their teacher; or they could try to figure it out from the context, the pictures, or the sounds.

6. Teach them to prepare for a conference with the teacher by:
   a. selecting a story
   b. reading silently to themselves or reading aloud to a friend
   c. signing up for the conference.

7. During the conference, which should last 5 to 10 minutes, sit side-by-side and ask questions about the main idea, facts, interesting information, author's purpose, and how the story can be applied to other situations; finally, have the learner read a portion of the story aloud in order to check the learner's performance.

8. Meanwhile, the rest of the class is reading its books, practicing skill instruction, or doing an original activity to follow-up something they have read. Examples of creative activities to follow reading are writing for a class newspaper, keeping track of books, choral reading, dramatization, writing letters, and creative writing.

9. After you have had about ten conferences and while other students are busy with number 8, work on skills with the children who need them.

The advantages of the personalized approach to reading are many. It is highly motivating since the children are personally involved in selecting their materials. Vocabulary control is not imposed by an outside source but is expanded by the child as a variety of books is read. It promotes personal interaction between each pupil and the teacher. Finally, and most important, it encourages the reading habit; it promotes reading as reading and not as some esoteric school task which has no relation to the real world.

Opponents of personalized reading, however, question its lack of emphasis on skill instruction. Skills are not taught systematically but are taught when the learner needs them in relation to the self-selected materials. It takes a highly skillful teacher to determine skill needs as quickly and as accurately as is demanded by this approach, and it takes a highly organized teacher to find the time after conferences to teach the skills once the need is recognized. Most teachers feel that they cannot do this adequately and that the lack of structure causes skill instruction to suffer.

SUMMARY OF APPROACHES TO READING INSTRUCTION

The eight approaches to reading instruction tend to reflect the various views of what reading is. If one feels that reading is a learned process, instruction will focus on skill acquisition, and the skills will be taught using a basal text, a skills monitoring system, a linguistic or a phonics approach, a programmed approach, or a combination of all of these. If one feels that reading is primarily a language process, instruction will rely heavily on the child's own oral or natural language using either a language experience or a psycholinguistic approach. If one feels that reading is primarily an interest, instruction will focus on building a love for reading using the personalized reading approach.

However, nothing says that a teacher must adhere to only one or another of the various views of reading and approaches to instruction. In fact, since we have seen that each of the approaches to reading has strengths and weaknesses, it would seem only wise to build an instructional program which draws upon the best of all approaches. This is the purpose of Chapter 3.

TEST YOUR KNOWLEDGE

1. Linguistics is the science of studying _____.
2. Graphemes represent _____.
3. The three strengths of linguistics are in its ideas about
   _____, _____, and _____.
4. Five principles of learning incorporated in programmed reading instruction are:
   a. _____
   b. _____
   c. _____
   d. _____
   e. _____
5. Some slow and remedial learners benefit from programmed instruction because materials are _____.
6. Two major criticisms of programmed instruction are:
   a. _____
   b. _____
7. Basal readers reflect the definition of reading as a _____.
8. A basal series generally starts at _____ grade and goes to _____, although some include material for _____.
9. Proponents of the language experience approach view reading as
   _____
10. The psycholinguistic view looks at reading as _____.
11. Self-selection is the basis for personalized reading instruction because _____.
12. The advantages of personalized instruction are that it promotes
    a. _____
    b. _____

c. _____

d. _____

13. Skill instruction in terms of personalized reading is based on the student's _____.

SIMULATION ACTIVITIES

1. Imagine that you are told that your school operates under the philosophy that the findings from the linguists should be included in the reading program. Unfortunately, no teacher's manual exists! How would you plan your reading instruction if you were:
   a. a first grade teacher?
   b. a fourth grade teacher?
2. Assume that you are teaching in an area where many children speak English as a second language. Which of the approaches to reading might be most effective to use with such children?
3. If you were teaching a third grade composed of children who were average, below average, and above average in reading ability, which might profit most from a programmed approach to reading?
4. The view of reading which focused on cultural background is not reflected in the approaches to reading discussed in this chapter. How would cultural elements of reading be incorporated into basal texts? Into language experience? Into personalized reading?
5. If you were teaching a fifth grade in which almost all your pupils were reading exceptionally well, which approach to reading would make the most sense to you?

SUGGESTED FIELD EXPERIENCES

Observation. Now that you are aware of eight different approaches to reading instruction, you should begin to investigate the implementation of the approaches in the schools. To determine to what extent the approaches are being used, start interviewing school personnel—teachers, aides, administrators, and tutors—observe classroom practices, and examine the materials being utilized. The following activities will give you guidelines for your investigation:

1. Interview a teacher and a pupil who have been involved with each of the various approaches and compare their views to determine the strengths and weaknesses of each approach.
2. Observe classrooms to determine the extent to which they are language centered. Are the children compiling word banks? Are there evidences of the children's own books being utilized, dictation being taken, and opportunities for creative expression?
3. Examine the classroom library to see if it contains no less than three books for each child and includes a representative sample of interests and a wide range of reading levels.
4. By observing reading lessons, attempt to determine the nature of the

groups being taught (flexible or lock-step), the amount of time the teacher spends on word recognition skills and comprehension instruction, and the approach the teacher relies on for reading instruction.

Another way to become familiar with each approach is to attempt to teach reading using all the approaches and relate the activities of each approach to something that you already know.

Teaching activities. As you begin teaching reading, be consciously aware of the approaches, and their respective elements, that you are incorporating into your reading program.

Client impact. Reading instruction should incorporate the strengths of all reading approaches. Awareness of the strength of each approach allows its incorporation into your reading program.

FOR CLASS DISCUSSION

1. We have seen, through an investigation of a variety of approaches to reading instruction, that controversies exist among the proponents of each approach. Discuss possible reasons for the controversies.
2. A teacher must have a balanced reading instructional program which incorporates many elements of instruction. Suggest ways of balancing instruction.
3. Although programmed instruction packages usually include principles of good instruction—step-by-step presentations of content, immediate knowledge of results, active responses, and individually paced materials—they are criticized for being too dull and fragmented. Discuss strategies in which you could wisely and more interestingly use programmed materials.
4. Vocabulary control is an area where each approach to reading instruction varies. The phonics and linguistic approaches both introduce words according to the regularity of sound–symbol relationships. Basal readers introduce words that appear frequently in beginning literature, are common to both school and home, and are functional or service words. The language experience approach and the personalized reading approach put no control on vocabulary since instruction in vocabulary is determined, respectively, by the learners' dictation and by the content of library books. Each view of vocabulary control has merit. Suggest classroom activities that can incorporate each view.
5. You are working in a school that has just spent all of its current reading budget on purchasing a new basal reading series. You were given 30 basals at the grade level for your class. State some problems that might arise with such a purchase.

ANSWER KEY
  1. language
  2. speech phonemes
  3. sound–symbol regularity, sentence patterns, and sentence transformations

4. a. step-by-step learning
   b. immediate knowledge of results
   c. regular and constant review and testing
   d. learning by doing
   e. individual progress through materials
5. self-paced
6. a. materials are dull and fragmented
   b. phonics is overemphasized
7. learned system
8. first, sixth, junior high
9. an extension of speaking
10. a combination of psychology and linguistics
11. it builds interest
12. a. motivation
    b. expansion of vocabulary
    c. personal interaction between teacher and child
    d. reading as a habit
13. need

COMPONENTS
OF A
SYSTEMATIC
READING
PROGRAM

OVERVIEW

You have seen in Chapters 1 and 2 that various educators define reading in different ways. This book attempts to incorporate the strengths of several definitions and approaches to reading. This chapter orients you to that integrated view and provides a framework for the remainder of the book. The ultimate objective is:

> Given the information contained in this and previous chapters, the student incorporates the strengths of several approaches into an instructional program in which reading is viewed primarily as a learned process.

KNOWLEDGE BACKGROUND

While reading can be defined in various ways and instruction can reflect differing emphases, *this* book reflects the view that reading is essentially a learned process which can be analyzed and translated into a sequential list of teachable skills. As will be seen, this view does not necessarily deny that reading is also an interest, a language process, and a reflection of cultural heritage, nor does it mean that instruction cannot include components of the various approaches discussed in the previous chapter. Rather, it is simply the core around which a comprehensive program can be built.

To understand this instructional core and the way it blends the various other definitions and approaches, you must understand our underlying assumptions and what they mean to you as a classroom teacher.

THE BASIC ASSUMPTIONS

The underlying assumptions which form the core of this book include concepts for the reading program, the reading process, the individual child, and the nature of instruction.

THE READING PROGRAM

In this book reading instruction is viewed in terms of a "means-ends" relationship. The ends or goals of reading instruction are that the child should read—library books, textbooks, magazines, comics, recipes, directions, encyclopedias, application forms, letters, and any other written communication he or she encounters.

However, many children do not achieve those ends if you simply surround them with books or wait for them to generalize to reading "naturally." Instead, they must be taught the means by which one reads—they must be taught the individual skills which, when viewed collectively, represent the act of reading. These means, or skills, are the second element of a reading program.

Finally, there should be a bridge between the means of reading and the ends of reading since it is often difficult for children to transfer learned skills to the actual reading act. Consequently, they need a bridge which guides them to apply the learned skills in context.

Graphically, the reading program ought to look like this:

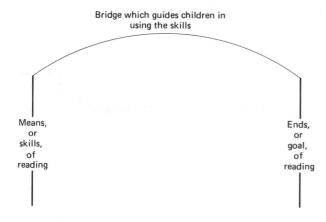

Bridge which guides children in using the skills

Means, or skills, of reading

Ends, or goal, of reading

In operation, a reading program should include instruction in the means or skills that constitute the act of reading, guided assistance in using these skills in contextual settings, and multiple opportunities for using the skills in reading meaningful and exciting material.

This concept of the reading program incorporates several of the views and approaches described in Chapters 1 and 2. First, of course, the emphasis on the means reflects a view of reading as a learned system of hierarchical skills. In addition, however, the emphasis on the ends reflects the view of reading as an interest and encourages the incorporation of approaches such as personalized reading. Also, the inclusion of a bridge to enhance transfer invites the use of basal textbooks since graded basal series can conveniently be used as the place where children put learned skills to work under the teacher's guidance. Finally, none of the above elements precludes the use of either language experience stories which reflect the child's oral language or material which reflects various cultural heritages. For instance, the material the child reads for both guided transfer and for the ends of reading can be stories that were dictated and can reflect cultural elements.

The reading program, then, should include instruction in the basic skills, guided application in using these skills, and a wide variety of opportunities to read for functional and recreational purposes.

THE READING PROCESS

If one of the main emphases of the reading program is on the means or skills of reading, the selection of these skills becomes crucial. Because reading is a complex and lifelong activity, there are many, many skills which could be taught. However, this book emphasizes the beginning stages of reading which are frequently encountered in the elementary school, the development of *functional literacy* or the ability to read material of fifth grade level.

This book views functional literacy as a balance between being able to identify the words and knowing what the words are saying—a balance between *word recognition* and *comprehension*. As such, the means of reading—the skills that are taught—should include an equal emphasis on both word recognition and comprehension; when reading either basal textbooks or recreational reading books, the child should be applying learned skills from both of these major categories.

This broad view of the reading process allows several of the previously described approaches to be incorporated. For instance, the phonics, linguistic, and psycholinguistic approaches to reading emphasize various crucial elements of the reading process, all of which should be reflected in the skills taught in a good reading program. Further, emphasis on systematically teaching the skills which comprise the means of the reading act is consistent with a skills monitoring system. However, this does not mean that "any old skills hierarchy" will do. Rather, the monitoring system should reflect both word identification *and* comprehension, incorporating the many skills emphasized in all the various approaches to reading instruction.

THE INDIVIDUAL CHILD

One cannot work for long as a teacher without facing the reality that children differ dramatically in terms of their interaction with the reading act. Some children learn to read easily and need little systematic instruction, while others find reading a mystery which they desperately need help in unlocking. In any given grade or classroom, some children have achieved the ends of reading (i.e., they can read very difficult books), while others may not be able to read any book at all. In terms of the means or skills of reading, some children seem to learn all the skills almost without any external effort; others need much help in either comprehension or word identification, finding one easier than the other; still others find both difficult.

No reading instruction is effective unless it satisfactorily deals with the reality of individual differences. This book does so—both tangibly and intangibly.

Tangibly, the book offers specific and concrete guidelines for the twin pillars of individualization—diagnosing what the differences are and organizing these differences into manageable classroom routines once they have been discovered. Under the category of diagnosis, the book provides you with directed assistance in determining the rate at which your students are apt to learn, their current reading level, and their specific strengths and weaknesses in terms of the skills of word recognition and comprehension.

In the second category—organizing the classroom to accommodate the differences among children—the book offers specific guidelines on how teachers can organize classrooms, monitor student progress, and simultaneously supervise the multiple classroom activities which accompany any individualization. These are the nitty-gritty routine tasks of classroom management which are often overlooked but which frequently make the difference between success and failure of individualized instruction.

Less tangibly, this book deals with the issue of teacher attitude and sensitivity—a crucial prerequisite to individualization. No program of individualized instruction is effective unless the teacher is particularly sensitive to the unique difficulties associated with being less adept than your peers at learning to read. While this book makes no pretense of knowing how to make you a sensitive and caring teacher, it nevertheless acknowledges the importance of attitude and periodically offers reminders that knowledge of program, process, and instruction is for naught if you don't care enough to take a deep personal interest in the growth and progress of each child.

THE NATURE OF INSTRUCTION

Once the program has been outlined, the skills identified and diagnosed, and the classroom management system established, learning must occur. In this book, learning focuses both on the word recognition and comprehension skills and on using these skills to increase the child's level of reading ability.

Some children learn to read with little or no direct instruction. They possess hereditary and environmental characteristics which make it easy for them to learn. Such children are seldom a problem for most teachers—in fact, teaching these children is often simply a matter of keeping them pointed in the right direction.

For many other children, however, reading is a difficult task, a mysterious process which appears to have no order or system to it. Giving such children a book or a basal text and hoping they will learn to read by reading is fruitless, and providing only incidental instruction in the skills often compounds the problem rather than alleviating it. Instead, such children need a systematic program of both skills instruction and application of these skills in the reading act.

Instruction is systematic if each of several criteria is met. First, the instructor must teach the child the precise skill he or she needs to learn next—not a skill already taught nor one for which the child lacks necessary prerequisites. Second, the teacher must do a task analysis of the skill to be learned and use that analysis in planning instruction. Third, the teacher must guide the child through a series of instructional steps until the task can be performed independently. Fourth, the teacher must insure that the learned task is habituated. Finally, and most important, the teacher must insure that a learned skill is usefully applied to improve the child's reading of contextual material.

SUMMARY

This book, then, is built on fundamental assumptions about the structure of the reading program, the nature of the reading process, the importance of individualization, and the nature of instruction. Because no single view of reading is broad enough to meet the needs of all children, elements of various definitions and approaches are incorporated around a core in which reading is viewed primarily as a learned process. Further, for the child who has difficulty learning to read, the book suggests procedures which emphasize systematic diagnosis, specific instruction, and a comprehensive view of both the reading process and the skills which comprise it.

IMPLICATIONS FOR CLASSROOM TEACHING

This view of reading can be translated into teacher behavior in terms of what the teacher is, what the teacher knows and what the teacher does.

The teacher is a sensitive, empathetic person who cares about each child and that child's self-image.

The teacher knows how children differ in relation to reading, how the process of reading is structured, how to diagnose and instruct, and how to manage individual differences.

The teacher does build a reading program in which each child moves at his or her optimum rate in learning and applying the skills associated with literacy.

SUMMARY OF THE CHILD AND READING

The remainder of the book is an exploration and explanation of the fundamental assumptions and implications described above. Section Two deals in detail with the process of reading—with the skills which comprise the means of reading. Section Three develops the idea of individualization, particularly in relation to how children will differ in terms of reading and how to diagnose these differences. Section Four focuses on the second major aspect of individualization—how to make it work in a classroom. Section Five develops the instructional technique for teaching each of the major kinds of skills, and Section Six provides aids and suggestions for insuring that these learned skills are applied in the act of reading. Section Seven provides assistance in teaching reading to the child who has already achieved functional literacy, and Section Eight provides suggestions to help you continue your professional growth once you become a teacher.

TEST YOUR KNOWLEDGE

1. The ultimate goal of reading instruction is _____.
2. To achieve this goal, the reader must possess certain _____.
3. The reading process should equally reflect both word identification and _____.
4. Two foundations in individualizing are _____ and _____.
5. To individualize, the teacher must be _____ to each child.
6. For the child who learns slowly, reading instruction should be _____.
7. Systematic instruction means, first of all, that the child should learn each skill in _____.
8. Once a skill is learned, the child should be helped to _____ that skill in actual reading.
9. A good reading program will include activities which reflect a balance between the means and the _____ of reading.
10. A good skills hierarchy will include elements of a variety of _____ to reading instruction.

SIMULATION ACTIVITIES

This chapter describes an approach to reading which emphasizes a balanced view of the reading program, an eclectic view of the reading process, a concern for the individual, and a belief in providing the slower child with systematic assistance in learning. Within this framework, various approaches and views could be incorporated and emphasized. Where would personalized reading be incorporated into this model? Psycholinguistics? The phonetic approach? The basal text? Programmed instruction?

SUGGESTED FIELD EXPERIENCES

Observation. When observing in schools, note the extent to which teachers reflect the four assumptions described in this chapter.

Teaching activities. When working with children in a school setting, you should provide instruction which reflects both the means and ends of reading, which incorporates a broad view of the elements of the process, which values the individual child, and which systematically assists those children who do not learn to read easily.

Client impact. Providing a balanced reading program will insure that your pupils receive the broad base necessary to be effective readers.

FOR CLASS DISCUSSION

Examine various journal articles in which various positions on reading instruction are promoted. Describe where these views would fit in the model described in this chapter.

ANSWER KEY
 1. reading for enjoyment and functional purposes
 2. skills
 3. comprehension
 4. individual diagnosis, accommodation of these differences
 5. sensitive
 6. systematic
 7. sequence
 8. apply
 9. ends
10. approaches

SUGGESTED ADDITIONAL READINGS FOR SECTION ONE– AN INTRODUCTION TO READING INSTRUCTION

AUKERMAN, ROBERT C. *Approaches to Beginning Reading.* New York: Wiley, 1971.

BEREITER, CARL, AND ENGLEMANN, SIGFRIED. *Teaching the Disadvantaged in the Pre-School.* Englewood Cliffs, N.J.: Prentice-Hall, 1967.

BLOOMFIELD, LEONARD, AND BARNHART, CLARENCE. *Let's Read: A Linguistic Approach.* Detroit, Mich.: Wayne State University Press, 1961.

CLYMER, T. "What Is Reading?" *Innovation and Change in Reading Instruction.* Sixty-seventh Yearbook for the National Society for the Study of Education. Chicago: University of Chicago Press, 1968.

DUFFY, GERALD G., AND SHERMAN, GEORGE B. *Systematic Reading Instruction.* 2d. ed. New York: Harper and Row, 1977.

ENGLEMANN, SIGFRIED. *Preventing Failure in the Elementary Grades.* Chicago, Ill.: Science Research Associates, 1969.

GOODMAN, KENNETH. "Reading: The Key Is in the Children's Language." *The Reading Teacher,* March 1972, pp. 505–508.

HALL, MARYANNE. *Teaching Reading as a Language Experience.* Columbus, Ohio: Merrill, 1970.

HARRIS, LARRY, AND SMITH, CARL. *Individualizing Reading Instruction: A Reader.* Part I. New York: Holt, Rinehart & Winston, 1972.

LEE, CORRIS, AND ALLEN, R. V. *Learning to Read Through Experience.* 2d ed. Englewood Cliffs, N.J.: Prentice-Hall, 1963.

SMITH, FRANK. *Understanding Reading: A Psycholinguistic Analysis of Reading and Learning to Read.* New York: Holt, Rinehart & Winston, 1969.

VEATCH, JEANETTE. *Individualizing Your Reading Program.* New York: Putnam, 1959. Describes the advantages and implementation of a program of self-selection of trade books as an approach to teaching reading.

WINKELJOHARM, SISTER ROSEMARY (ED.). *The Politics of Reading: Point-Counterpoint.* Newark, Del.: International Reading Association, Inc., 1973.

TWO

THE NATURE OF THE READING PROCESS

THE
READING
PROCESS

OVERVIEW

To teach reading systematically, teachers must know why certain skills are taught as well as what to teach and how. Understanding the "why" comes with an understanding of the nature of the reading process itself. Consequently, this is the first of three chapters designed to acquaint you with the component parts of the reading process and the way each of these parts contributes to successful reading ability. The ultimate objective is:

> Given a description of the three major elements of the reading process, you will state ways in which these elements interact to contribute to effective reading.

KNOWLEDGE BACKGROUND

Reading is an act of communication. Someone—a writer or author—has something to say and wants to be heard. Unfortunately, there is no one present to listen. The audience is absent either through time or distance. The author, therefore, must resort to writing the message on paper and sending the paper to the audience. This system works extremely well *if* the audience can make the scribbles on the paper speak the same message that the author intended when he wrote it.

This act of resurrection—of making the inscrutably silent scribbles talk—is the primary difference between reading and listening. The goal of each is to receive a message, but the reader must first translate or decode the written page into talk before "listening" to what the message is saying. When this first stage is accomplished successfully, the reader then tries to understand the communication. We will now discuss *what* and *how* to teach in the reading process.

WHAT TO TEACH

For the purposes of most of this book, the reading process has been limited to the achievement of functional literacy—the level of reading achievement (frequently defined as a fifth grade reading level) that a person needs to function at a bare minimum in society. Functional literacy, in turn, depends upon the acquisition of three coding systems that make up the twin goals of word recognition and comprehension.

GOALS OF FUNCTIONAL LITERACY

Traditional reading methodology has categorized the two previously mentioned elements of the reading process as *word recognition* and *comprehension*. While these labels do accurately represent the goals of functional literacy (first, making the message talk, and second, understanding it), they tend to isolate the two elements from each other and obscure the interactions that exist between them.

These interactions are crucial and can be more readily understood by defining the beginning reading process as "a psycholinguistic guessing game" or, more accurately, as three such games which are played simultaneously by the reader. Each game consists of signals which help the reader guess or predict the written message and which help in both the word recognition and comprehension acts. These signals—the *graphemic*, the *syntactic*, and the *semantic*—can be described as the rules or skills of each game and, thus, the rules or skills of reading. A good reader has these three sets of signals under control and uses each with appropriate speed and precision. The poor reader either lacks basic skill in one or more of the sets of signals or emphasizes and/or exaggerates one set to the exclusion of the other two. In either case, reading growth suffers. To help children become functionally literate, the teacher must help them learn to use the three sets of signals well and to develop a proper balance among the signals in the total act of reading.

The graphemic signals. The first of the three very distinct but interrelated sets of signals comes from the printed letters and words. A child looks at these and recognizes or remembers words from the way they are spelled. The child is cued to this identification through a series of signals embedded in the English spelling system. Knowledge of and skill with this system allow the child either to know or to predict a word identification. In this system, letters represent to some extent speech sounds, and the child reads by associating these sounds with their visual representations. The rules of this game are fairly simple. The child learns how to look and what to look for; learns how to listen and what to listen for; makes an association between what is seen and what is heard; then is able to identify words. This area of skill is often called the graphemic or spelling process. Its application moves the words from the page into the child's head.

The syntactic signals. The second set of reading signals comes from the syntactic or grammatical structure of the English language. When words are grouped into phrases, sentences, or paragraphs, they are automatically arranged in accordance with the conventions and constraints of grammar. As a child translates the words from the page, the mind processes them into English syntax and guesses or predicts where the message is going and what it will contain. The message leaps from the page in grammatical chunks rather than just limping along from word identification to word identification. Accurate word recognition plus the push of grammatical convention produce a continuous cycle of meaning. A recognized word triggers a grammatical guess, which produces another recognized word, which produces further grammatical predictions, and so on through the message. The good reader guesses the way through the message using spelling and syntactic codes, each of which helps to make the next guess more precise.

The semantic signals. The third guessing game is played at the meaning or semantic level. Words grouped in phrases, sentences, or paragraphs share not only grammatical structure but also a unity of content or idea. Each contributes to the message meaning, and in reading the child is actively predicting what that meaning is. Constant feedback from the graphemic and syntactic systems allow the child to verify or reject these predictions, and the basic context of the message gives further insight. The better the understanding of the content of the message, the better will be the predictions of future word identifications and grammatical forms. The better the predictions of future word identifications and grammatical structures, the better will be the predictions of the message content they are carrying. Again, the interrelationship of word identification, syntactic constraints, and semantic prediction is apparent. The total process contains elements of both word recognition and comprehension, but these elements are never mutually exclusive in the *good* reader. Instead, they become three distinct but interrelated operations, each of which feeds and is fed by the other two. The good reader guesses or predicts the way through the message using graphemic, syntactic, and semantic signals. The better the child's ability to apply each of these codes simultaneously, the better the total reading development will be.

SUMMARY

The following model should help clarify the relationships of the operations just described:

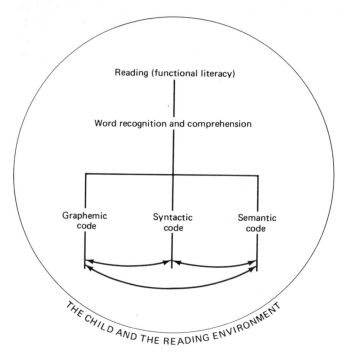

As the model shows, developing reading to the level of functional literacy involves the dual goals of word identification and comprehension which depend on the three coding systems: graphemic, syntactic, and semantic. While these can be arbitrarily separated for discussion and instruction purposes, their interconnection and interrelation are illustrated by the arrows at the bottom. Skills learned in each system blend not only into that system but also into the other two, creating a gradual but steady progression from nonreading to reading behavior. Finally, all considerations of the reading process must be viewed from the context of the individual child (hence, the encompassing circle) since the degree of emphasis on one operation or another varies from child to child depending upon the background brought to the task of reading.

THE ROLE OF LANGUAGE DEVELOPMENT

The above three coding systems are all part of a larger system called "language." The ease with which a child learns to use the three coding systems in the act of reading will depend directly upon the child's facility in using the language orally and the degree to which the home language matches the language of instruction.

Oral language facility. Language develops through a child's experiences with the environment. As the child has experiences, he or she interacts with individuals, both listening and responding. At first, responses are only sounds, but this changes as the child matures, develops, and has an increasing number of experiences with the environment.

By the time a child enters school at age five or six, he or she has mastered the oral language of the home. If the child comes from a verbal home where there is a high degree of communication, the level of verbal facility is higher. Some children listen to their parents read books or tell stories from infancy, have parents who explain reasons for their behavior and who answer their questions, and have varieties of experiences which lead to the acquisition of many concepts. To children who have such a rich oral language base, reading is likely to be a natural continuation of the communication process. The teacher then uses this base to systematically guide those children into reading.

For children who enter school *without* a mastery of the oral language, however, reading is not natural. This lack of language experience may be caused by health, motivation, and limited experiences and interactions. For example, a child with a temporary hearing loss at an early age may exhibit immature speech, weaknesses in auditory discrimination, and ultimate reading problems. Similarly, children who come from homes where there is no interest in reading, few interactions with adults, or limited experiences tend to have a difficult time learning to read.

Home language and school language. Two other language problems which may cause difficulty for the learner in beginning reading instruction are bilingualism and the use of a dialect other than that of the mainstream culture of the community. In each of these cases, the oral language style the child masters prior to entering school is different from the language used at school.

Bilingualism refers to that situation in which children come from a home where English is not the primary language for oral communication. This is frequently the case in neighborhoods with a large ethnic population. Children from such homes often speak the parents' native tongue in the home and neighborhood and must then learn to use English in the school. Because English is learned as a second language, these children have a weak oral language base in the language they are expected to read. Such weaknesses impede the mastery of the coding systems needed for reading.

Dialect differences often reflect both geographical and cultural differences. For instance, the oral language of various urban blacks varies significantly from standard English, and both these types of oral language are different from that found among the hill or mountain populations in the South. Learning to read is impeded to the extent that the dialect is different from the language the child is expected to read.

SUMMARY

The message here is that children cannot be expected to read what they don't say. If they suffer from either a general language deficiency due to deprivation in health or home or if their oral language does not match the language of instruction, you can expect that they will encounter some difficulty in learning to read. Consequently, learning the three coding systems which comprise the reading act depends upon a firm foundation of oral language.

BEYOND FUNCTIONAL LITERACY

Reading is not, however, limited only to word recognition and comprehension. Reading begins with the first acquisition of oral language and continues throughout life. At the early stages of instruction, the skills consist of comprehending oral language and discriminating among printed letters and sounds. As the learner progresses, the emphasis shifts to comprehending written language and identifying words in print. Once these basic skills are mastered, however, skills of efficient study are introduced and the child is taught study techniques, various rates of reading, and other skills associated with reading efficiency. Finally, the instructional emphasis is placed on skills of literary understanding, in which the learner is taught to interpret literary devices and to do higher level thinking. As one proceeds through life, one continues to refine reading skills according to one's particular needs.

While this book focuses primarily on the word recognition and comprehension skills needed to achieve functional literacy, you should be aware that any effective reading program must provide systematic skill instruction appropriate for the students served. At the beginning stages, the emphasis would be on word identification and comprehension, while students reading at the higher levels would normally receive instruction in the areas of efficient study and literary skills.

HOW TO TEACH

If a reader is functionally literate when knowing how to guess the way through a written message by appropriately using the spelling, grammar, and meaning cues imbedded in it, a most logical and important question then becomes: How do I, as a teacher, help a child use these cues? While there is some dispute over how this question should be answered, the overwhelming consensus is that the teacher must instruct the child in the various skills that characterize or constitute these three coding systems. Hence, the teacher uses a skills hierarchy which provides both a listing of the skills which comprise the three coding systems and suggestions on how to teach these skills. This converts the elements of the reading process from a theoretical consideration into a teachable operation.

To help you understand how the process theory is translated into operational teaching objectives, Chapters 5 and 6 describe in some detail the skills associated with each coding system. Consistent with the dual goals of reading instruction, the first focuses on word recognition and the second on comprehension. While the graphemic code is emphasized in the word recognition area and the syntactic and semantic codes are emphasized in comprehension, you are cautioned once again to remain aware of how these three signaling systems work together in creating efficient readers. Similarly, you should particularly note Chapter 6 and the way the comprehension skills, when taught as listening rather than reading comprehension, can be used to develop the oral language base which is so essential for early success in reading. Finally, you should be aware that Chapters 25 and 26 provide an outline of what should be taught to the child who is beyond the level of functional literacy.

TEST YOUR KNOWLEDGE

1. Functional literacy is thought of here as _____ grade reading level.
2. The twin reading goals of functional literacy are _____ and _____.
3. The three coding systems which interact in word recognition and comprehension are the _____, _____, and _____.
4. The graphemic code refers to _____.
5. The syntactic code refers to _____.
6. The semantic code refers to _____.
7. The model of the reading process is circled by "the child and the reading environment" because the _____ of the learners vary.
8. Oral language facility is a crucial prerequisite to reading because it provides the _____.
9. Once a child achieves functional literacy, the focus of instruction shifts to _____ and _____.
10. The coding systems which make up the reading process are made instructionally operational by translating these systems into lists of teachable _____.

SIMULATION ACTIVITIES

Examine the following short paragraph and explain how the reader might use the graphemic, syntactic, and semantic codes in an interacting fashion to identify the words and comprehend the message.

The boy chopped a lot of wood. Then he carried the wood into the kitchen and made a fire.

SUGGESTED FIELD EXPERIENCES

Observation. When observing in schools, note how children use the graphemic, syntactic, and semantic codes in reading.

Teaching activities. As you begin teaching reading, consciously be aware of the graphemic, syntactic, and semantic elements you are asking the child to manipulate.

Client impact. The object of reading instruction is to create well-balanced readers. Attending to all three coding systems insures such balance.

FOR CLASS DISCUSSION

Compare the description of the reading process provided in this chapter with the views of the reading process embodied in the phonetic approach, the linguistic approach, the basal approach, the personalized reading approach, the language experience approach, and the psycholinguistic approach. In what ways are they similar? Different?

ANSWER KEY
1. fifth
2. word identification, comprehension
3. graphemic, syntactic, semantic
4. printed letters and words
5. grammatical structure
6. meaning
7. background experiences
8. base for reading instruction
9. study skills, literary skills
10. skills

THE WORD
RECOGNITION
SKILLS

OVERVIEW

We have seen that beginning reading instruction focuses on word recognition and comprehension and that these twin goals depend upon the child's use of the graphemic, syntactic, and semantic codes. While studying these goals and codes separately is artificial in that it tends to ignore their interconnectedness, it is necessary to do so in order to determine the component skills to be taught in each area. The area analyzed in this chapter is word recognition. The ultimate objective is:

> Given a description of the word recognition process, you will state the role and function of each skill taught in the area of word recognition.

KNOWLEDGE BACKGROUND

The skills in the graphemic system make a major contribution toward the generalized reading behavior we call word recognition. This is one of the major goals of reading skills instruction. Even a cursory comparison of good readers with poor ones yields very dramatic evidence of this. Good readers can identify and name many words, while poor ones show a diminished recognition vocabulary, usually in proportion to their degree of disability. This difference is also reflected in the books children read and the groups in which they are taught. The greater the number of words a child recognizes, the higher the reading level and the more positive the group identification; we label the good readers "rabbits" or "bluebirds," the poor ones "turtles" or "sparrows." It is an absolute necessity that all teachers in all grades recognize the importance of developing a child's word identification skills and that they support this commitment with a sophisticated understanding of the learning tasks and multiple instructional techniques that influence the acquisition of effective word identification skills.

The single most important aspect to remember about word recognition is that it is a *dual,* not a unitary, skill. Two very separate and distinct learning tasks are involved. An example should help to make this clear. One of your students, Johnny, is reading a page of his basal primer. The page has 34 separate words on it, and Johnny has learned to recognize 27 of them with no hesitation. They are familiar "friends" from preceding pages and preceding books. These 27 words represent one kind of word recognition which can be very descriptively called *instant identification.* We could also say that Johnny recognizes these words at sight, that they are part of his *sight vocabulary.*

But what of the seven words that he does not recognize? As Johnny reads, he comes to the first of these, **funny.** He doesn't recognize the word because he has never seen it before. He stops and looks, but nothing happens. There is no memory for a spoken word that connects to that set of squiggled letters. But, as Johnny looks at the word again and puzzles on it, he guesses that it must be **funny** because it begins with the word **fun** (a word he can instantly recognize), and **funny** makes sense in the story he is reading. Johnny has just performed the second and more difficult word identification task; he has figured out or analyzed a word that was not instantly recognized. This can be very accurately called a *mediated identification.* Something, or a series of things, have helped him solve the problem of that unknown word.

The dual tasks of instant recognition and mediated recognition, while two separate and distinct learning tasks, share the common goal of developing fluency in word identification. Mediated strategies serve as a bridge between not knowing words at all and recognizing them instantly. For instance, when a child mediates an unknown word, the child has identified it for the moment and is then able to continue reading. If the child meets it again on the same page, it is seldom that he or she will recognize it instantly this second time. It is much more likely that the child will again be forced to stop and analyze—mediate—the recognition of this word, although the time spent on figuring it out will probably be less than with the earlier recognition and the mediating strategies may be different. The child will continue to use mediating strategies to identify the word each time until, through the increased familiarity that comes from repetition, the word will be recognized instantly. In this way, the dual skills, although distinctly different acts, work together to create fluent recognizers of words.

This description of Johnny's word recognition should serve as an introduction to both instant and mediated recognition and their learning tasks.

INSTANT RECOGNITION

One of the primary goals of word recognition instruction is the development of an ever-expanding sight vocabulary. In order to help a child in this task, a teacher must have both a clear and basic understanding of the nature of the learning involved and a store of appropriate instructional techniques. The first provides a theoretical framework on which to make instructional decisions, and the second enables the teacher to apply these decisions in the actual teaching situation. The following provides an understanding of the task of instant recognition.

VISUAL PREREQUISITES

Instant recognition is a visually based task. Children who learn sight-words quickly and seemingly without effort are children who know how to use their eyes—they know how to look and what to look for. While some children come to school already knowing these things, such children probably constitute, at best, a small majority of the total population of beginners. The remainder of a class must be very carefully taught those specific visual readiness skills which are prerequisite to future success in instantly recognizing words.

These visual prerequisites reflect an arbitrary set of conventions in the English spelling code which must be understood and applied if sight-words are to be learned effectively. These conventions include: (1) the left-to-right progression of letters, (2) the visual representation (letters) of speech sounds, and (3) the left-to-right and top-to-bottom progression of words and sentences. Learning to operate within the framework of these conventions is probably more a conditioned activity than a cognitive one; that is, the child must develop the habit of taking in the visual signals from the page in accordance with these three conventions of English writing. To this end, a teacher must help the child develop this restricted set of prerequisite visual behaviors. Only then will the child be able to efficiently and accurately apply the visual cues necessary for speedy and accurate reading.

Visual discrimination. By far the major learning task involved in these visual activities can be categorized as a *discrimination* learning. Children must learn to see (discriminate) the often subtle differences between letters and between similarly spelled words. Problems involving incomplete closure (**O, C** and **G** have very similar configurations), rotations (**p, d, b, g; m, w, n, u,** etc.), and common elements (**j, i; t, f; R, B**) all must be solved before sophisticated discrimination can be made. Similarly, children are often confused by the constant juggling of comparative and contrastive visual elements in whole words; they need to learn that words share common letters—**run** and **ran**—and that this commonality is a desirable and necessary part of an alphabet writing system, but that seeing only common letters will lead to confusion and inaccuracy. They must know that each word will have one or more distinctive letters that contrast it from all other words and know how to discriminate and use both the common and the unique letters in making a word identification.

Visual sequence. The second visual prerequisite necessary for successful reading achievement is the habituated response of seeing words from a left-to-right, beginning-to-end orientation. While this is really a type of discrimination learning, the unwarranted confusions some children exhibit with "backward reading," "perceptual confusions," and "visual-motor disorientations" suggest that careful programming and instruction beyond the simple discrimination of letter and word differences is a necessity. The goal of this instruction is to train the child to look at words in the same spatial directions in which they are written.

Visual memory. The third prerequisite—visual memory—will normally accrue as an adjunct to the visual discrimination and visual sequencing activities. However, in those few cases where this aptitude for remembering what the eyes have seen is not transferred as a result of discrimination and sequencing instruction, objectives which teach this skill are advisable. The goal of this instruction is once again to teach children how to use their eyes effectively and, specifically, to learn to *remember* what they have seen.

LEARNING SIGHT-WORDS

When a child looks at a word and instantly recognizes it, that child is performing a type of learning called *paired association.* As this name suggests, this learning has two elements which in some fashion become associated with each other. In the case of learning sight-words, the visual spelling of the word is one element and its spoken form, the other. The child learns to pair what is seen with what is said. In other words, the child develops an association between a visual stimulus (a written word) and a spoken response (the name of that word).

All of this seems simple enough, but, in reality, the child who makes a correct identification has used skill with the above visual prerequisites to perform three very difficult and specific activities. First, the child *discriminates* the stimulus (the spelled word) as different from any other spelled word. If the child uses insufficient cues to make this discrimination—that is, sees only the first and second letter or finds some other partial component of the spelled words as the visual discrimination in this particular paired association—then he or she will be continually seeing and saying the first word when coming across other words that share this partial discriminator. For example, if a child looks at the word **run** but sees only the **r** and learns to say **run** each time the **r** appears, then any other word beginning with **r** will also be identified as **run.** A paired association must begin with a discriminated stimulus.

Second, the child makes the connection or association between the discriminated stimulus and the spoken word. The key condition here is the contiguity in time between what the eyes are seeing and what the mouth or mind is saying. If, for example, the child looks at the word **run,** discriminates it in total, but then glances to the teacher's face or to a picture at the top of the page before saying or thinking **run,** there is little chance that the association between the written and spoken forms of this word will be paired. When learning an association, the child must look and say (or think) simultaneously.

Finally, the child *remembers* this association. The fact that the child accurately discriminates the written word and responds on time with the spoken word is all for naught unless the association is remembered the next time the word appears.

So, the child who can read all the words in the preprimer has really learned a very complex task—the child has learned to make a series of paired associations by: (1) discriminating a precise visual array of letters that spell each word, (2) correctly associating the spoken form of each word with its visual form, and (3) creating a memory for this association.

SUMMARY

Instant recognition is a crucial reading skill. With the mastery of a large stock of sight-words, decoding becomes an automatic process, thereby freeing the reader to concentrate on syntactic and semantic considerations. However, instant recognition is not a natural phenomenon for most children. It requires both the mastery of certain prerequisite subskills which orient the child to the visual conventions of the graphemic system and the utilization of paired association learning in building a large stock of sight-words.

MEDIATED RECOGNITION

The second category of skills in the graphemic system produces a child who, when faced with a word which is not in his or her sight vocabulary, attacks and identifies this word through a system of mediating strategies. It is the child's ability to use these strategies that allows the child to figure out new and unknown words.

There are many things a child can do when coming to the unknown word—stop reading; skip the word and pretend it doesn't exist; ask someone else to identify it; sound it out; use the sense of the sentence in which it appears to guess its identity; examine it to see if it contains other known words or word parts on which a guess can be based; or struggle with a dictionary and its pronunciation key. Because all these operations are possible does not mean that they are all equally valued as mediating strategies. Some are more appropriate than others, and, to help a teacher determine the effective from the ineffective, each must be measured by four criteria:

First, is the mediating strategy *independent;* that is, can the child use it without outside help?

Second, is it *accurate?* It does little good to apply a mediating technique that produces a misidentification.

Third, is it *speedy?* It seems obvious that if it takes an inordinate amount of time to figure out a strange word, then the usefulness of the technique should be questioned.

Fourth, does the strategy *generalize* to other unknown words? This criteria suggests that the mediating strategy must be as useful on page 3 of the preprimer as it is on page 67 of the sixth grade reader.

A very quick application of these criteria to the seven mediating strategies identified at the beginning of this section should help us determine which of the above techniques is appropriate. Let's look first at those which fail to meet the criteria. For instance, the child who stops reading entirely when coming to an unknown word is not using *any* analysis strategy. This behavior should be eliminated, not encouraged. In the second example, the child who skips an unknown word is ignoring the need for accurately reproducing the written message and its information. Third, the child who reads only when someone else is there to help with the new words lacks independence; while such a technique is certainly accurate, speedy, and useful at any time that help is at hand, it is not independent. Finally comes the dictionary. Searching for a word pronunciation in this fashion can be done independently, it is accurate if the child knows how to use the pronunciation keys, but speedy it isn't. In fact, it will be the rare child who can sustain interest and understanding in a story that is constantly interrupted because of a need to look up the word in the dictionary. For this reason, use of a dictionary as a mediating strategy in word recognition is useless. This does not mean that a dictionary can't or shouldn't be used for many other school or reading purposes; only that it is too slow and cumbersome to be useful in figuring out a word that is not instantly recognized by a child.

Some mediating strategies *do* meet the criteria. For instance, the technique of sounding out a word—that is, applying the sound–symbol code—can be independent, speedy, and accurate on most words that a child reads. Not all words can be sounded to their correct identification, but this technique is a reflection of one of the codes or guessing games in the reading process and does generalize to most words in most sentences. Similarly, guessing a word identification by using the grammar and meaning in the sentence is also independent, speedy, and generalizes to other sentences on other pages. While its accuracy sometimes suffers, this can be improved by combining it with the sounding process. Because English words can be compounded, inflected, derived, and so on, teaching a child to search out known structural elements is also a useful mediating strategy. It is fast, independent, can be generalized to other words, and is reasonably accurate, especially when combined with either or both the sounding and contextual skills.

In summary, we find that only three strategies meet our criterion needs. Phonic or *letter–sound mediators,* structural or *morphemic mediators,* and contextual or *semantic–syntactic mediators* all offer a reasonable and realistic fit to our selection criteria. These are the mediating skills which, when applied singly or in tandem, produce readers who can accurately and effectively analyze and identify a word that is not instantly recognized. Also, while the mediating strategies are categorized with the graphemic system, it is important to note that both the structural and contextual mediators contain elements of the syntactic and semantic systems, illustrating once again that the three major sets of signals interconnect and interrelate.

Before examining each of the mediating strategies in greater detail, you should consider two other important concerns. The first relates to the fact that mediating strategies frequently result only in approximations of the unknown word. Consider the task of figuring out an unrecognized word. It is difficult because it is a type of learning that is almost problem solving in nature. This suggests a much higher level of cognitive behavior than merely associating a written word with a spoken word. However, not only is the learning task more difficult, but not one of the mediating strategies of phonics, structure, or context has a set of rules that can always be relied on to provide an accurate recognition of a strange word. To the contrary, any prediction that a child makes using these basic strategies has an element of error because the code system is only representative of the message and, as such, can only *approximate* that message.

For example, the three letters **d-o-g** represent the three phonemes we hear in the spoken word **dog.** But, because the correspondence between the way these three letters can sound and the way they do sound when a child simply speaks the word **dog** can be very different, the learner must be made aware that turning letters into sounds and sounds into words will not always produce the word as it should be spoken. The letter sounds will give an approximation of the word as the child usually speaks it, but many times that child will need to say "**D-o-g** as in hot-**dog** says *dog,*" but the word could be pronounced differently in different dialects or different contexts. The point is, written letters are approximations of the sound made in normally spoken words, and, although the child may do a good job of generalizing a sound value and using that generalization to sound out a new word, the resultant pronunciation must always be measured against the child's own spoken language, and the child must be prepared to adjust the approximated sound value to that reality. The child who sounds the word **come** as "com" and then says, "Oh, that's come," is telling you that he or she realizes the need for this adjustment of the spelling–sounding system to fit spoken words. This same need to mediate a fit between the way a word is spelled and sounded and the way it is normally spoken becomes even more apparent as the child sounds out polysyllabic words which reflect both letter–sound and *accent* problems. Here, the need to test what is sounded "against your ear" is an absolute necessity.

In similar fashion, a word identification based on either semantic or syntactic context reflects a child's guess that the person who wrote the sentence was aiming it toward thus-and-such an idea using thus-and-so grammatical structure. The child makes the identification of an unknown word by again approximating what he or she feels the sentence meaning and grammar should end up being. In contextual behavior, this approximation characteristic results from the almost infinite number of grammatical choices plus the almost infinite number of permutations of meaning possible in the experience of an idea. A single example should suffice to illustrate this.

A child is reading the sentence, "Tom gave his dog a ＿＿＿＿＿＿." The blank represents a new and unrecognized word. Grammatically, any noun will produce a closure, that is, any noun will approximate a sentence sense. This fact eliminates the need for a child to predict any other part of speech for this identification. Semantically, the child again faces multiple choices. There are hundreds of things one can give a dog, from a kick to a crust of bread. Thus, the sentence meaning and context do give hints of what the word identification might be, but these hints are only approximations, and the child must be ready to juggle numerous word possibilities in the search for the correct identification. The sentence and its grammatical hints only approximate what the writer is really saying. Is it any wonder that some children never do seem to catch on to what is happening when they try to read?

In addition to the approximation reality of the mediating signals, you should also be aware of the need for balanced skill development in all three of the mediation strategies. The child who is taught to rely only on phonic mediators can develop into a laboriously slow and painstaking reader because, for such a reader, reading is predominantly a visual–sounding activity. Likewise, the child who uses only minimal word identification and lots of contextual guessing can quickly lose sight of the need for getting the writer's message and instead wallow through the page spinning fantasies of what is happening. Instructional balance is imperative in the development of competent, mature readers.

In early stages of reading growth, the child usually needs more attention paid to the graphemic code signals of the reading act since this is really the basic difference between reading and any other communication medium. As skill in and understanding for this visual–aural process occur, there should be a slow but steady shifting toward the meaning or contextual element. A good third grade reader will be using the message sense to a greater degree than the spelling code. As the eyes move across the page, the mind is both receiving and predicting the message. This in turn allows the reader to spend less and less time in examining single words or letters. It is only when the contextual prediction is unavailable—that is, the mental signal does not mesh with the visual one—that the reader resorts to careful looking and sounding in order to establish a word identification, which in turn starts a new set of contextual predictions. In order to reach this point, the reader must have learned the coding skills of phonics and structural and contextual prediction, and their balanced application to deciphering the message found on the pages of a book.

PHONETIC ANALYSIS AS A MEDIATING STRATEGY

The letter-to-sound application of the English-speaking system is the foundation skill for figuring out a word that is strange in print. It is a skill that should be learned and applied early in the child's reading instruction since one of the striking characteristics of good readers is their basic grasp of the letter–sound characteristics of the language. While the way a word is spelled does not always reflect the way it is pronounced, the fact remains that our alphabet is a visual code based on a correspondence between speech sounds and printed letters, and an understanding and application of this phemonenon are necessary for even a modicum of success in learning to read. While this understanding is sometimes generalized by the child without apparent overt instruction, the vast majority of children must be taught this coding property of English writing.

Auditory prerequisites. While instant recognition is primarily a visually based skill, phonetic analysis relies heavily on auditory cues. Children who use phonetic mediators well are children who know how to use both their eyes and their ears; they know how to listen, what to listen for, and how to associate the letters they see with the auditory cues of the graphemic system. Learning to do this requires mastery of specific auditorily based readiness skills which are prerequisite to future success in analyzing words phonetically. These prerequisites include beginning and ending sound discrimination, and sound blending as it is taught in both fusion and closure activities. With these skills, the child begins to generalize the concept of writing and reading as a phonemic–graphemic system rather than a visual–ideographic or pictographic process. With these skills under control, the child can examine written words that have never been seen before and, through letter–sound competence, predict their identification.

Auditory discrimination (beginning, medial and ending sound). In many respects, auditory discrimination is similar to visual discrimination.

Both involve the manipulation of comparative and contrastive elements, and both require instructional skill in determining what these elements are and how to cue or highlight them to the child. The basic difference between discrimination of visual and auditory stimuli is that a visual array is created of spatial dimensions—height, length, depth—and can be referred to with two senses; it can be seen and felt. It remains constant for prolonged examination by these senses. Thus, it can be more easily highlighted for the learner. In contrast, an auditory stimulus is temporal, that is, it exists and then, in a flick of an eyelash, disappears. Further, it can normally be examined only with the ear. These time and single-sense qualities make it considerably more difficult to highlight and are the genesis of much of the spelling code confusions that many children exhibit.

Despite its difficulty, however, auditory discrimination is an essential prerequisite skill for phonetic analysis. Before a child can associate a sound with a letter or otherwise use the phonemic–graphemic relationships of the system, that child must first be able to distinguish one sound from another. As such, auditory discrimination is the foundation of success in phonetic analysis.

Sound blending (fusion and closure). The purpose for teaching the auditory skills is to help the reader use the graphemic system for analyzing written words. This is a two-stage process. First, the child learns to make individual letters or groups of letters talk, and, second, the child guesses the total word. Sound blending skills are designed to help in this second effort. As the name suggests, they help the reader blend isolated letter sounds into familiar spoken words. Sounding out a word normally produces a string of sounds that barely approximate the word as it is really spoken. The reader must be able to compress these sounds into a closer approximation of the real word before it can be recognized. To help in this, sound blending skills called *fusion* and *closure* are taught.

Fusion skills give the child practice in joining isolated strings of sound into spoken words. This is a prereading skill, and in its simplest form, the teacher is modeling the process through which it is done. She might say, "Listen to what I can do. I can say r . . . u . . . n. I can say it fast—**run.** Who else can do this?" A variation might be to pronounce the whole word first, then produce its isolated letter sounds, and *then* say it fast. The point is that *all* sounds are first produced and then compressed into normal spoken cadence.

Closure skills have the same general purpose and format as fusion skills. They too give the reader practice in blending isolated sounds into recognizable spoken words. They differ in one respect only. In closure skills, one or more sounds are *left out* of the string of isolated sounds. This makes a gap that must be filled or clozed in order to produce the spoken word. For example, a teacher might say, "Listen to me, I am going to say a word with some parts left out. See if you can hear what word I am saying and say it the way I really want to say it. Here is the word: –eanutbutter. What is the word I want to say?" Now the teacher waits to see if these *sounds* will be auditorially clozed into **peanut butter.** This skill recognizes that future sounding skills will not always produce an accurate pronunciation of a strange word. The child will make both sound distortions and/or omissions. Closure tasks are designed to prepare the child for this and to give both a confidence and a technique to ignore those gaps and arrive at an accurate spoken word from its sounded approximation.

Letter–sound association. The above auditory skills and the visual prerequisites described under instant recognition converge to create a series of skills of letter–sound association or sound–symbol connection. What the child has previously been taught to see and hear are now connected or associated with each other. "What you see is what you say," or "What you say is what you visualize," might be the general direction of this learning.

The instructional key to teaching letter sounds is to realize the compound nature of the skill. It is simultaneously a discrimination skill (a letter must be seen and a sound heard), an association skill (what the ears hear or the mouth speaks must be paired with what the eyes are looking at), and a memory skill (the association or pairing between visual and auditory components must be remembered). This compounding of tasks demands an equal compounding of the attenders necessary for the learning. For instance, if you wish to teach a child that **m** says the sound **m–m–m** the child must first know that **m** is not **w** or **n**; that it looks to him as it does to people who can read. Next, the child must hear the sound of **m** as /m/, not /ng/ or /n/. If these two conditions are met, the teacher's next job is to ensure that the teaching tactics used force the child to look at the visual letter as he or she hears or says its sound value. The child can't be looking at the teacher's mouth or the student in the next seat. The eyes and ears must be tuned to the same letter in order for association to take place. Finally, the instructional tactic should also contain built-in memory strategies that will cue a recall of the desired letter sound. And this is only half the battle.

The letter–sound skills should *not* be taught in isolation. That is, each time these skills are taught, they are taught *as they occur in spoken or written words.* While this adds another burden to the instructional problem, in the long run this forced application of what letter sounds are for and where they occur will pay immeasurable dividends in the acquisition of more sophisticated word recognition and word analysis skills. A teacher who constantly teaches the sound properties of English spelling *in the context of the words in which they occur* will *not* produce children in third or fourth grade who know a myriad of generalizations about the spelling code but have no appreciation or use for this information in reading words. Thus, the need is to teach letter sounds in application, not isolation.

The sounding skills. The child who begins mastering the prerequisites should then be taught the more sophisticated phonetic analysis skills. These include consonant sound skills, vowel sound skills, substitution skills, and syllabication skills.

Consonant sound skills. The first letter–sound association skills in the phonics hierarchy teach the child to associate regular consonant sounds with their appropriate letters. These include single consonants, consonant clusters in which each letter retains its single letter sound (**br, sl, str,** etc.), and consonant clusters in which new sounds are associated with familiar letters (**th, ch,** etc.). These skills are like miniature sight-word skills in that they contain the same three task elements of discrimination, association, and memory. The child who has accumulated a stock of consonant associations has developed a valuable first tool for sounding out new words that are strange in print. The predictable regularity of consonant sound values also helps to build a confidence in the code properties of English spelling.

The only real difficulty in this learning activity is the confusion many children have between a letter name and a letter sound. These are two distinct concepts and must be so understood if the child is to make normal progress in letter–sound acquisition and application. The *sound* value is the critical element. A letter name is interesting but it does *not* help the child assimilate and apply the graphemic code as a reading tool.

Vowel sound skills. While consonants usually have a consistent sound, vowels do not act in this way. A vowel standing by itself can have a variety of sounds; an accurate sound value can only be predicted when it is seen in relation to the letters that surround it. Therefore, vowel instruction should focus on vowel families or phonograms that have both a high frequency and high predictability in English spelling.

The vowel skill objectives and their instructional techniques should be designed to focus the child on the operation of using known sight-words having standard vowel characteristics and spelling patterns to predict unknown words having the same vowel characteristics but different surrounding consonants. The purpose of this instruction is twofold. First, it helps the child learn to associate vowel sounds with the letter patterns that produce them, and, second, it habituates the realization that known words can be used to learn unknown ones. It highlights the fact that there is a system operating in the way a word is spelled. The child is led to see that the spelling of a word is not arbitrary but, instead, reflects the graphemic code properties of English writing.

Substitution skills. This is the name given to the process of using known words to read unknown words. This might be called a transfer skill. As quickly as a child learns a sight-word that contains a regular vowel phonogram, the child then learns to substitute other consonants, first at the beginning and then at the end, to create new words that can be recognized. For example, if a boy's name is **Sam,** the substitution skills should show him how to read **ham, jam, cram** and even **ran.** The steps in this learning are: (1) the recognition of –am as a vowel sound unit and (2) the substitution of the consonants **h, j,** and **r** and the cluster **cr,** in place of the **s** in Sam and the substitution of **n** for **m** at the end to make the word **ran.** This activity teaches the child to associate vowel sounds with the actual spelling units that produce them. Initially substitutions are done with the beginning letters, but as the child becomes more skillful we can expect the child to see and say a substitution of ending letters (**Sam** to **sat**) and even the vowel itself (**sat** to **sit**).

Syllabication skills. Descriptively, a word that has three syllables is a word that also has three vowel phonograms. Identifying such a word through sounding must, of necessity, begin with recognizing the three vowel phonograms that comprise its syllabic structure. It is as simple as that. The child who has a firm grasp of the vowel units described in the preceding section will have a relatively easy time grasping syllabication strategies and using them to sound out longer words.

To facilitate this behavior, the skills program should include a sequence of syllabication objectives. These objectives should help the child see vowel patterns that are already familiar from previous vowel instruction. Once seen, these patterns (syllables) are easily sounded. The only difficulty comes in helping the child visually group the vowel units that comprise each syllable. The key is to help the child see syllabic divisions (vowel phonograms) that can then be sounded, as explained below.

Traditionally, syllabication is taught as rules that a child learns to help make syllabic divisions. While rules can be written that do reflect the varieties and vagaries of spelled syllables, it's a fact that few good readers can explain these very rules they so easily apply. It's also a fact that children who are taught such a list of rules seldom succeed in applying them as an analysis strategy. Such instruction seems more to clutter than to facilitate a child's attempt at sounding out words of more than one syllable.

Syllabication instruction should teach a child two simple but reliable manipulations when facing a long word that isn't instantly recognizable. The first of these helps the learner to visually isolate probable syllabic units by first identifying vowels and then by arbitrarily assigning consonants to each. As an example of this, examine the word **chocolate.** Step 1 would visually highlight each of the vowels, perhaps as follows: **Ch<u>o</u>c<u>o</u>l<u>a</u>te.** Then, with simple slash marks, the syllables are isolated: **cho/co/la/te.** Previous phonogram instruction has eliminated the final **e** configuration as a vowel unit, and the child is left with three phonograms (syllables, if you prefer) to be sounded **cho–co–late.** These are then pronounced following the generalized patterns learned during vowel phonogram instruction, with this probable result: **chō–cō–lāte.** This division causes all vowels to be seen in their "long" environments.

Then comes Step 2, turning the syllables thus sounded into a recognizable word. This second step is another reflection of the *approximation* characteristic of English spelling. The child is taught to "play with" the long vowel syllabications in an attempt to discover the spoken word that the identification approximates. Both the ear and syntactic–semantic contextual clues from the material being read should help with this. Should the child fail to identify the syllabicated word as **chocolate**, then he or she is taught to simply move the syllabic divisions one place to the right. This, in effect, makes the first two vowels "short" by putting them into a short vowel configuration. Now the word would look like **choc/ol/ate** and would be sounded **chŏc–ŏl–āte**. Again, the child is told to pronounce the syllables and to see if they now approximate a known word. If the word identification remains a mystery, that is, if neither syllabic division gives the necessary clues to the word's real spoken character, then one of two things is wrong. Either the spelling does not give a reasonable approximation of the spoken word, in which case *no* sounding tactics will mediate an identification, or the word is not in the child's speaking or listening vocabulary. In the latter case, the child should have been *familiarized* with the new words to be read prior to the lesson or should have been encouraged to *ask for help*. There is simply no way to independently analyze a word that is strange both in print and to the ear.

To summarize, the analysis and mediated recognition of longer words can be approached through the application of previously learned vowel phonograms. The child is taught to visually separate vowels from one another and then to sound the resulting divisions as vowel phonograms, using the resulting approximation as a basis for guessing the identity of the unknown word.

STRUCTURAL ANALYSIS AS A MEDIATING STRATEGY

The English language contains both a tendency towards compounding and an inflected and derived grammatical system. These factors have produced a very repetitive and rather high frequency set of spelling structures which can be useful in mediating an unrecognized word.

Reading teachers usually refer to these skills as *structural attack* or *structural analysis* techniques. In many ways, they combine elements of phonetic analysis with instant sight-word recognition. They look like units that should be sounded, but they are learned through instant identification.

The multitude of skill objectives taught as structural mediators are designed to show a child how to recognize and manipulate only four basic systems: prefixes, suffixes, contractions, and compound words. As the child gains familiarity with and high-speed recognition of these structural properties, unknown words which contain them will be more accurately and speedily identified. Take, for example, the word **unrecognized.** If a child has learned to spot the common **un-** and **-ed** affixes, then identification of the word is reduced to the sounding of the internal root **recognize.** The number of problem-solving operations has been reduced by two, and ultimate identification is normally achieved that much more quickly. What structural analysis does is cut down on the number and complexity of sounding operations. This, in turn, produces a faster mediation of an unrecognized word.

This results because the child has learned to isolate the structural units, their sounds, and their visual positions for instant identification, leaving fewer unknowns to be syllabicated, sounded, or whatever. These structural units can be isolated because their spelling and position are constant, that is, they transfer from word to word with a predictable regularity. It is this regularity that allows the child to use them like sight-words. They are constants that can be relied on.

To summarize, many words in English contain regularly spelled and positioned units called prefixes and suffixes. When memorized as to sound and position, these units can greatly diminish the unknowns in a word that is being analyzed.

Similarly, compounds can be more easily analyzed when they are recognized as compounds. The child who can instantly recognize **when** and **ever** but who goes through some isolated sounding behavior when meeting the word **whenever** is giving a very strong signal of not being aware of the compounding process. By practicing the analysis of compound words, this habit can be established. In many cases, it will produce faster and more efficient word identification.

CONTEXTUAL ANALYSIS AS A MEDIATING STRATEGY

The final mediating skill involves combining letter sounds with the syntax–semantics of spoken English. This mediation device might be labeled *contextual and letter-sound analysis* since it involves the anticipation of an unrecognized word through the simultaneous pressures created by the meaning of the sentence in which it occurs, the grammar of the sentence in which it occurs, and its recognized letter–sound properties.

Words in context offer an exceedingly powerful tool for mediating the identification of an unrecognized word. This results from the grammatical and semantic pressure to cloze or complete a structure or idea that is being experienced. As a sentence is read, the child allows the recognized words to direct thinking into the same paths and modes as the author intended when placing these thoughts on paper. The child who does such thinking while reading allows the message clues of syntax and meaning to cloze, thereby predicting the identification of any strange word. By combining this syntactical–semantic technique with an examination of the initial letter–sound properties of the unknown word, the child has an exceedingly powerful mediating strategy.

At the prerequisite or readiness level, a teacher's job is to get children in the habit of clozing or finishing phrase and sentence structures by applying what they know about English grammar and the sense of the sentence meaning. The child who habitually uses this contextual–meaning sense becomes the child who moves rapidly from the spelling (word–calling) components of reading into the more mature behaviors we often define as "thought gathering" or "reading for meaning."

While the prerequisite emphasis is on oral closure using syntactical and semantic clues almost exclusively, the child should be directed to use context in combination with known phonetic elements as a sight-word vocabulary develops. In this manner, the child gradually develops skill in using elements of the graphemic, syntactic, and semantic systems to mediate the identification of unknown words.

SUMMARY OF THE WORD RECOGNITION SKILLS

In a very real sense, a good part of learning to read involves learning to decipher the graphemic code of English spelling. Mastery of this code gives the reader the skills of word recognition, both instant and mediated. These skills, in turn, produce a sight vocabulary which becomes the basis for making both syntactic and semantic predictions.

The skills of the graphemic system include visual and auditory tasks, association tasks, and problem-solving tasks. An understanding of each of these skills and their place in the graphemic code is an absolute necessity if a teacher is to help a child master the word identification element of reading.

This view of word recognition creates some new elements for our process chart, as seen on the facing page.

As can be seen, most of the skills in the area of word recognition reflect the graphemic code. Within the graphemic system, however, we find two "streams" of skills; one leads to instant recognition, and the other leads to analyzing or mediating those words which are not immediately known. Within each stream are specific kinds of skills which contribute to the ultimate goals of either instant or mediated word recognition. The arrow going from the mediated stream to the instant stream reflects the fact that after an unknown word has been mediated several times, it ought to become a sight-word. The other arrow with points at either end going between the word recognition and comprehension areas reflects the interconnectedness and interrelatedness of the graphemic, syntactic, and semantic codes. Finally, the whole process continues to be encircled by the child and the reading environment because whether a child will need more emphasis on instant or mediated strategies or on any particular skill within either of those streams will depend upon the background brought to the task.

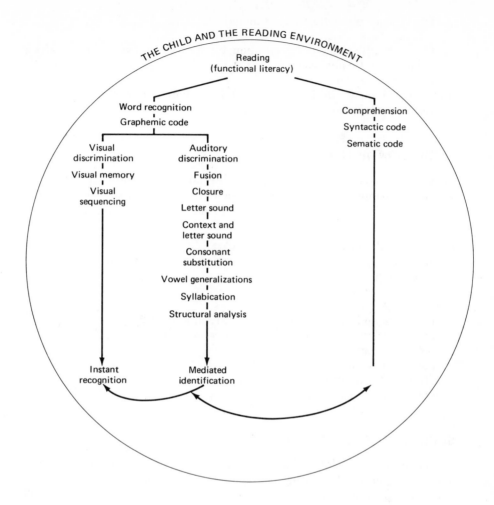

THE CHILD AND THE READING ENVIRONMENT

Reading
(functional literacy)

Word recognition
Graphemic code

Visual
discrimination
Visual memory
Visual
sequencing

Auditory
discrimination
Fusion
Closure
Letter sound
Context and
letter sound
Consonant
substitution
Vowel generalizations
Syllabication
Structural analysis

Comprehension
Syntactic code
Sematic code

Instant
recognition

Mediated
identification

TEST YOUR KNOWLEDGE

1. The two distinct learning tasks in word recognition are
   _____ and _____.
2. Instant recognition uses primarily the sense of _____.
3. The prerequisites to instant recognition are _____,
   _____, and _____.
4. Learning a sight-word requires a type of learning called
   _____.
5. The three strategies for mediated word identification are
   _____, _____, and _____.
6. While most word recognition strategies rely primarily on the graphemic code, a mediating technique which heavily reflects the syntactic
   and semantic code is _____.
7. The prerequisites to phonetic analysis are _____,
   _____, and _____.

8. The skills of phonetic analysis include _____,
   _____, _____, and _____.
9. The main difference between phonetic analysis and structural analysis is that phonetic analysis focuses on _____ while structural analysis focuses on _____.
10. Words which are initially identified by mediated analysis ought to ultimately be recognized at _____.

SIMULATION ACTIVITIES

Imagine that you are teaching a child how to visually discriminate among graphemic symbols and the ancient question arises, "What good is this to me? How is this going to help me be a better reader?"

1. How would you answer the question?
2. How would you answer the same question in terms of visual sequencing?
   in terms of visual memory?
   in terms of instant word recognition?
   in terms of auditory discrimination and sound blending?
   in terms of letter–sound association of consonants and vowels?
   in terms of consonant substitution?
   in terms of syllabication?
   in terms of structural analysis?
   in terms of contextual analysis?

SUGGESTED FIELD EXPERIENCES

Observation. When observing in schools, note how many of the word recognition skills you see being taught. What skills seem to be neglected and/or emphasized? What does such neglect or emphasis tell you about the teacher's view of the word recognition process?

Teaching activities. As you begin teaching reading, select a hierarchy of skills or an instructional guide which reflects both the tasks of instant recognition and of mediated identification.

Client impact. When your students receive instruction in both the skills of instant recognition and of mediated identification, their chances are great of being able to handle all word recognition tasks in reading.

FOR CLASS DISCUSSION

For years, various educators and lay people have argued whether the look–say method (instant word recognition) or the phonic method should be emphasized in elementary school reading instruction. What is your position relative to this argument? Be ready to support your position.

ANSWER KEY
1. instant recognition, mediated recognition
2. sight
3. visual memory, visual discrimination, visual sequence
4. paired association
5. phonic or letter–sound mediators; structural or morphemic mediators, contextual or semantic–syntactic mediators
6. contextual analysis
7. auditory discrimination, sound blending, letter–sound association
8. consonant sound skills, vowel sound skills, substitution skills, syllabication skills
9. sound units, meaning units
10. sight

THE COMPREHEN-SION SKILLS

OVERVIEW

While word recognition is certainly a crucial part of reading ability, the end goal and ultimate focus of reading is meaning-getting. The act of comprehension—like that of word recognition—can be analyzed and broken down into component skills. This chapter provides such a break-down. The ultimate objective is:

Given a description of the comprehension process, you will state the role and function of each skill taught in the area of comprehension.

KNOWLEDGE BACKGROUND

Learning to read is more than recognizing words and assimilating the coding system with which they are written. In its largest sense, reading is a thought-gathering process; learning to recognize and remember the written word is only the first, albeit a critical, step. Once the words are identified, there remains that large and often nebulous task of under-standing or comprehending what they say.

Comprehension appears to happen in two stages. The first stage occurs during the actual reading activity. The child examines the message and simultaneously recognizes words and meaning through skill with the graphemic, syntactic, and semantic systems. Understanding is *instantaneous* at this stage.

Stage 2 can occur anytime during or following Stage 1. This comprehension might best be described as a *reflective* activity. The written message has been translated or received and now can be subjected to a more thoughtful scrutiny or analysis. Surface understandings that were created at the instantaneous level can be examined as to their original accuracy or subjected to more complex mental operations.

Theoretically, there is an infinite number of mental operations which a reader will make in order to comprehend instantaneously and reflectively. It would seem to follow, then, that the reader needs to be taught an infinite number of comprehension skills in order to successfully gather all the thoughts. Fortunately, this is not the case. Through factor analysis, long lists of supposedly distinct comprehension skills have been found to be a limited number of skills which are used for varying purposes; a very small number of *operational skills* are used to understand an infinite variety of written messages. While each message a child reads, be it an arithmetic story problem or a social studies lesson in American history, may be unique in its content, comprehension is realized through the application of a very few operational skills. The teacher's job becomes twofold: first, to show children how to do these basic comprehension operations and then to insure that these operations are transferred to the daily reading activities, whatever they might be.

The operational skills can be classified into the following three subgroups, each defining a comprehension purpose or process. These subgroups are:

1. Comprehension as an informational process
2. Comprehension as a thinking or manipulative process
3. Comprehension as an evaluative or judgmental process

Comprehension as an informational process suggests that the reader is trying to learn the *factual content* of the message. The reader wants to know what the message says literally. To accomplish this, he or she must have meaning for all the words read and a recognition of and memory for the facts they convey.

Comprehension as a thinking or manipulative process suggests that once the informational process is secure, the reader can be expected to "think about" this information, exploring its deeper implications and inferences. To do this, the reader must be able to grasp the significance of various relationships based on past experiences and on understanding of the more complex structures of English grammar.

Comprehension as an evaluative process suggests that after a message has been understood at both its informational and manipulative levels, it can then be acted upon. This action might consist of accepting the message and committing it to memory, rejecting the message, or searching out more information to clarify or understand a position.

Under each of the three subgroups are the operational skills which are used to understand written messages. They include:

1. Informational processes
   Word meaning skills
   Signalers of relationships
   Contextual prediction
   Recognition and memory for factual content
2. Manipulative processes
   Classification and main idea thinking
   Inferential thinking
3. Evaluative processes
   Judgment of content validity
   Judgment of the author's language for purpose or point of view

These skills of comprehension are hierarchical; that is, evaluative operations cannot be done without the preceding manipulative thinking activities, and manipulative thinking can't be done unless there is something to think with and about (information). This means that a teacher *must* originate all comprehension activities at the informational or literal level. When certain that the basic information is understood, the teacher can then instruct for manipulative thinking. With these two processes as a base, the possibility of evaluative–judgmental levels of understanding comes into play and can be examined. An illustration might help make this developmental sequence clear. A third grade social studies class is reading a selection in their text about the Boston Tea Party. The teacher is interested in using the selection to teach all three levels of comprehension. The first goal is to assure that each child has a basic understanding of the facts and details of the Boston Tea Party, which can be tested by asking factual questions about word meanings, relationships, and factual content after the reading is completed. Satisfied that the basic information is understood by the class, the teacher proceeds to help them discover a relationship that is implicit but buried in the information. Finally, when satisfied that each child has made the desired inferences from the material, the teacher asks them to make judgments about alternative actions the colonists could have taken and how this historical event applies to today's society. Hence, the cycle of comprehension goes from information to manipulation to evaluation.

READING COMPREHENSION AS AN INFORMATIONAL PROCESS

By mastering four operational skills, a child can get the basic information from the printed page: word meaning skills, understanding relationships, contextual prediction, and factual recognition and recall.

WORD MEANING SKILLS

Comprehension instruction begins at the word meaning level. A written message is made up of strings of words, all of which contain meanings.

If these meanings are not within the experience of the reader, both minimal understanding and certainly the higher levels of comprehension will be thwarted.

In a larger sense, word meaning is a problem of concept development. Words are the labels we give to concepts. The word **snow,** for example, names the concept of the cold, wet, white stuff we spin our wheels in all winter long. This concept is different from the cold, wet stuff we label **rain.** Each is a separate concept with a separate label. Concepts and the words which we use to label them are the core elements in comprehension. We comprehend as a response to the meanings words carry. The meanings they carry are those which our language assigns to them. Thus, if a learner does not have the assigned meanings for words, both written and oral communication become impossible, and comprehension remains confined to the very limited and personal language of each learner. An understanding of this duality (the concept and the name or label for it) is critically important in expanding the word meaning capabilities of children.

The message in an English sentence comes from two kinds of words. Some can be thought of as carrying the meaning of the sentence. These words are usually called *content words.* Other words act as glue to connect the content words together into English grammatical structure and are called *function words.* For example, in the sentence "We see the goblins on Halloween," the content words are **we, goblins,** and **Halloween.** If a reader does not know what these words mean—that is, the concepts they stand for—that reader will not grasp the content of the sentence. The words **see, the,** and **on,** however, are function words; they signal the grammatical relationships that put **we, goblins,** and **Halloween** into a meaningful context. The functional relationships expressed by these three little words are as important to an understanding of the message as the content itself.

The teacher must insure that the learner has accurate concepts for both the words that carry the content of a message and the grammatical subtleties expressed by function words. This can be illustrated by the following true story: A teacher had a boy named Art in her second grade class who went for weeks without giving any answers on his classwork. Daily she would duplicate problem sheets so that the children could practice their addition and subtraction, but Art's paper never had any answers on it. When she finally questioned him about this, she found that he knew how to add and subtract but was confused by her directions: "Do your own paper and mark the answer under each problem." Art finally screwed up enough courage to ask, "What is an answer?" His was a content meaning problem. He did not have a concept for the word **answer.** (If Art had failed to do his work because he didn't understand where to write his answer, that is, had no concept or meaning for the word **under,** his problem would have been one of function word meaning.)

There are literally thousands of content words that a learner will need meaning for. Each subject you teach—health, language, science, math, social studies, etc.—has its own content vocabulary of concepts related to that subject. You are responsible for directing learners to find both the concepts and the labels for them since the content words carry an essential portion of the information in a message.

Function words, which are as important to comprehension as content words, cannot really be discussed in isolation from the relationships they signal. These are, therefore, placed under the next heading.

UNDERSTANDING RELATIONSHIPS

The learner's function word vocabulary is of crucial concern. It is important to grasp the concepts signaled by such seemingly insignificant words as **on, or, if, while, any,** and **because** since these words signal the syntactical relationships among the content words. For instance, to obtain the basic information from a passage, the child must know the meaning of prepositions, which signal both positional and time relationships; of pronouns, which signal a relationship to an antecedent; and of words which signal chronological, cause–effect, and compare–contrast relationships.

The meaning in an English sentence results from a partnership between content words and function words. In any sentence, the learner must not only know the concepts associated with the content words but must also know the relationships between those content words as they are signaled by function words. Though the function words tend to be short, they are as important as and more subtle than the content words.

CONTEXTUAL PREDICTION

This third information-gathering skill involves the child's fluency with English grammar and the predictive impulse it generates. As a child listens to a communication, a portion of understanding comes from "sentence sense" which allows the child to simultaneously know the idea of the message (its content) and to predict from both this knowledge and the grasp of grammatical relationships what word will follow what word and what idea will follow what idea. When the reader's grasp of the content and fluency of the grammar are equal to the message being read, the child is not simply a passive receiver of the message but is actively anticipating what will be said and how. This, then, is a description of a fluent reader; as the eyes slide across the page identifying those squiggles that spell out words, the mind is racing along with those ideas, unconsciously predicting where they are going (the semantics of the message) and how they will get there (the syntax of the message). Influences on a child's acquisition of this critical language skill are many. Social, cultural, and economic factors all play a part. Dialect differences can stifle its development. Even an overemphasis on word recognition in early reading instruction without parallel commitment to an understanding of the message can cause it to wither or be stunted. Therefore, a teacher faces the responsibility of influencing, as skillfully as he or she can, the breadth of a child's language. This is difficult. Peer pressures and habits that have been developed over years of preschool language activity are not easily modified. Traditional English classes which involve such rote activities as learning the parts of speech, classes of words, types of sentences, and so on are pathetically inadequate to the task. The "let the child talk" program is usually too little and too late. Instead, the skills development emphasized in this book contains frequent *contextual* practice, oral at the beginning level and shifting to reading as quickly as a sight vocabulary is accumulated. With this emphasis, two benefits accrue. First, the child is helped to develop language patterns to fit those needed in order to read or listen with understanding to "standard English usage." Second, the child will habituate the idea of "thinking" with the message and predicting what will be said and how. The simplicity of this instructional device should not be underestimated. It has the potential for alleviating many of the comprehension woes found in later reading instruction.

RECOGNIZING AND RECALLING FACTUAL CONTENT

The ability to understand and retain the factual content of a message is built upon the skills of word meaning, understanding relationships, and contextual prediction. As a child develops an expanded vocabulary of both content and function words and the ability to predict closure from the grammatical form and ideational content of a message, these skills are used to arrange and retain the factual information found in longer stories. This ability to see and remember the facts is of obvious importance in the informational part of comprehension.

The major emphasis in this skill is twofold. First, the learner must be able to identify the important or relevant facts from among the mass of word meanings and relationships contained in the message. Second, the reader must be able to remember the facts. Hence, the twin thrusts of this area are identification and memory.

SUMMARY

Children can be expected to know what is in a message only if they have the concepts for the function and content words, the set to think along with them in a contextual sense, and practice in "sifting and seeing" what facts they contain. While only minimal thinking is involved, the basic information needed to perform higher level manipulative operations is obtained. One cannot think if there is nothing to think about. Word meanings, sentence sense, and the awareness of the informational value that these two give to a communication are the gist of thought and represent the basic informational content of a message.

READING COMPREHENSION AS A MANIPULATIVE PROCESS

Once the child has a firm control over the vocabulary, grammatical, and factual content of a selection, he or she then has the option to think about the information it contains. The problems involved in teaching a child to think while reading are formidable, both for the child and for you. There are at least two major reasons for this. First, a child responds to the words read or heard from a very egocentric position. What the child thinks about when reading or listening is the sum total of a unique involvement with the ideas that come from the page or through the air. That child may or may not have had experiences that match or parallel those the author is reconstructing. The realities that the author speaks from may not be the realities the child listens from. You can well appreciate the possibilities of error. They stagger the imagination.

The second difficulty, equally as confounding as the first, relates to the child's ability to process the input of thoughts and ideas. We know that thinking takes place in the reader who understands what is being read but *how* it takes place is open to conjecture. There are no certified road maps that guarantee readers who can and will think. By now, you are probably ready to throw up your hands in despair. Don't! Even though knowledge of the thinking process is theoretical and full of unknowns, experience does suggest operational skills that produce thinking, even when we are not certain why.

These operational skills are manipulative in the sense that a message or communication contains multiple concepts or ideas which can be structured and restructured, categorized and recategorized, or, in short, manipulated. As a child manipulates the ideas or concepts of a message, the comprehension of that message is made broader and deeper. The child moves from a literal to an inferential understanding. Memory is augmented by thought.

Two types of skills are manipulative: classification–main idea thinking and inferential reasoning.

CLASSIFICATION–MAIN IDEA THINKING

This skill allows children to classify ideas by discovering their relationship and then grouping them into sets on the basis of their shared properties. First, the child is taught to discover how concepts can be related to other concepts, words to other words. These relationships can be causal, chronological, or logically based on use, size, shape, position, or similar and dissimilar features and can exist between single words or in longer structures such as phrases, sentences, paragraphs, and chapters.

This type of manipulation is the first step in finding the focus or point of a mass of information. At its highest level in reading comprehension, the child will be able to extract, through classification thinking, the main ideas of a sentence, paragraph, or larger selection. Having been taught to automatically group and classify ideas, the child will be able to read hundreds of words and not lose sight of their point or focus or main idea—to see both the forest and the trees and know which is which.

INFERENTIAL REASONING

In addition to classification thinking, the child is taught to think beyond the information level of a written communication by "reading between the lines." This involves the manipulation of factual information in order to discover implications which are not stated.

This skill is based on logic and prediction. The child who can do such thinking can use the facts of a selection and background experience to grasp what the facts imply and then infer conclusions based on these implications.

Inferential reasoning is an important comprehension skill since all information worth obtaining is not necessarily stated literally; much valuable data are found between the lines. Such reasoning involves sophistication, however, since the learner must simultaneously examine the factual information in a passage and compare it with personal experiences related to the topic. Such thought is truly manipulative.

SUMMARY

The manipulative level of comprehension contains two separate but related skills. First is the skill of seeing relationships or connections between facts that otherwise might be viewed as distinct and of classifying these relationships into sets which share common properties. Second is the skill of projected or logical implication or inference. With these types of mental operations, a child can take the words and facts of a selection and reach understandings that are far beyond the literal meaning of the message.

READING COMPREHENSION AS AN EVALUATIVE PROCESS

The third stream of comprehension skills involves drawing conclusions and making evaluative judgments. In the first stream, comprehension is limited to information gathering. From this basic or literal understanding, comprehension moves to the second or manipulative stream in which the child is asked to think with and about these elements found in the first level. Now the child is ready to act on this thought. This third or *action* stage focuses on helping a child make judgments about what is being read.

Notice that this comprehension activity can only be valid if it follows both informational and manipulative thinking. It is a comprehension absurdity to ask a child to do evaluative thinking without the necessary prerequisites from the factual and manipulative levels. The teacher's task is to help a child develop the ability to move logically from informational to manipulative to judgmental activities. In this way, the reader learns to make judgments based on facts and thinking. Emotional or stereotyped conclusions are minimized or at least identified for what they are when they do occur. By following this progression at each level, comprehension achieves a precision missing in any slapdash instructional approach.

Two types of operational skills can be taught to help a child make evaluative judgments. The first focuses on judging the content itself, and the second examines the author's choice of language.

JUDGING CONTENT OF MATERIAL

Occasionally, you may read material which just does not make sense in terms of your personal experience, knowledge, or beliefs. In such cases, you judge the material to be invalid.

Children, however, do not always possess this ability. Indeed, they sometimes exhibit a tendency to believe everything they read. This skill, then, is designed to teach them that they should use their experience, knowledge, and values to judge materials, that something is not necessarily true just because it appears in a book.

AUTHOR'S CHOICE OF LANGUAGE

This skill teaches a learner to assess word choice for clues about an author's position on a topic. Careful examination of word choice is an important evaluative skill since it is a major way in which learners make judgments about what they read.

Good readers can detect bias through the author's use of emotion-laden words, words that create bias or stereotype, mood words, propaganda devices, and other elements of word choice. Once the words cue the reader to author bias, he or she is able to make a judgment about the topic and is comprehending critically.

SUMMARY

Comprehension in the informational and manipulative areas is passive in the sense that readers interpret what the author meant. At the evaluative level, however, readers assert themselves—strike out on their own—and make judgments that may or may not be what the author wanted to communicate. In this sense, evaluative comprehension may be the most important kind of thinking to be taught in a democratic society.

SUMMARY OF THE COMPREHENSION SKILLS

While learning to read does demand emphasis on identifying words, it is essentially a communication process in which obtaining meaning is of primary importance. In this book, the meaning-getting process is divided into three streams: informational, manipulative, and evaluative. Graphically, we can fit comprehension into our process chart:

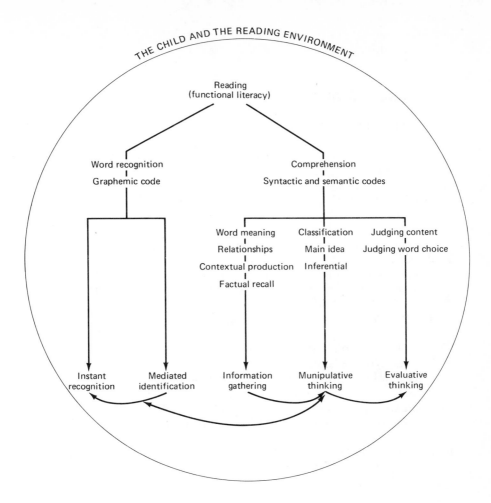

As can be seen, the skills of comprehension reflect the syntactic and semantic codes described in Chapter 4. Within the syntactic–semantic area, however, we find three streams of skills; one leads to obtaining the basic information of a passage, one leads to manipulating and thinking about that information, and the third leads to making evaluations about what is read. Within each stream are specific kinds of operational skills which contribute to the ultimate goals of that stream. The arrows that go from the informational to the manipulative streams and from the manipulative to the evaluative streams indicate that manipulative thinking cannot be done without information and that evaluative thinking cannot be done without previous manipulation of the facts. Similarly, the arrow with points at either end goes between word recognition and comprehension to indicate the continuing interconnectedness and interrelatedness of the graphemic and syntactic–semantic codes. Finally, the whole process description is circled to represent the fact that a particular child from a particular environment will react differently from another child from another environment and that, therefore, it may be necessary to emphasize different elements of the process with different children.

TEST YOUR KNOWLEDGE

1. The three types of comprehension are _____, _____, and _____.
2. Information gathering is primarily a factual thinking task which uses the skills of _____, _____, _____, and _____.
3. Manipulative thinking requires the reader to grasp various relationships and implications and uses the skills of _____ and _____.
4. Evaluative thinking requires the reader to make a judgment and uses the skills of _____ and _____.
5. A reader cannot do evaluative thinking with a piece of written material unless the prerequisite thinking has been done in the areas of _____ and _____.
6. The two kinds of words used in English are _____ words and _____ words.
7. Classification thinking first requires the child to _____ the ideas and/or concepts.
8. Inferential thinking occurs only if the child has background _____ regarding the topic.
9. Contextual prediction, which is taught as an information gathering skill in comprehension, is highly related to the word recognition skill of _____.
10. Main idea thinking is enhanced if the child can do _____ thinking in the manipulative stream.

SIMULATION ACTIVITIES

Imagine that you are teaching a child content word meanings and the child wants to know how your instruction is going to be of any value.

1. How would you explain the role and function of content word meanings to this child?
2. Answer the same question in terms of function word meanings.
   in terms of relationships
   in terms of contextual prediction
   in terms of factual recall
   in terms of classifying and main idea
   in terms of inferential reasoning
   in terms of manipulative thinking generally
   in terms of judging content validity
   in terms of judging an author's choice of words

SUGGESTED FIELD EXPERIENCES

Observation. When observing in the schools, note how many of the comprehension skills you see being taught. What skills seem to be neglected and/or emphasized? What does such neglect or emphasis tell you about the teacher's view of the comprehension process?

Teaching activities. As you begin teaching reading, select a hierarchy of skills or an instructional guide which reflects the three tasks of information gathering, manipulative thinking, and evaluative thinking.

Client impact. When your students receive instruction in all three streams of comprehension skills, they are being helped to think as well as perform factual recall.

FOR CLASS DISCUSSION

Think back to Chapter 4 and the discussion of oral language base. How do the comprehension skills relate to language development? Can thinking be taught in a listening situation as well as in a reading situation? What kinds of comprehension do you teach if the child cannot read yet? What skills would you teach to a child who does not yet have a strong oral language base?

ANSWER KEY
1. information gathering, manipulative thinking, evaluative thinking
2. word meaning, signalers of relationships, contextual prediction, recognition and memory for factual content
3. classification and main idea thinking, inferential thinking
4. judging validity of material, judging author's purpose or point of view
5. information gathering, manipulative thinking
6. content, function
7. relate by a common denominator or classify
8. experience
9. context or semantic–syntactic mediation
10. classification

SUGGESTED ADDITIONAL READINGS FOR SECTION TWO— THE NATURE OF THE READING PROCESS

CHALL, JEAN. *Learning To Read: The Great Debate*. New York: McGraw-Hill, 1967.

GOODMAN, KENNETH. "Reading: A Psycholinguistic Guessing Game." *Journal of the Reading Specialist* 4, May 1967, pp. 126–135.

HILGARD, E. (ED.). "The Analysis of Reading Instruction: Perspectives from Psychology and Linguistics, in *Theories of Learning and Instruction*, N.S.S.E. Yearbook. Chicago: University of Chicago Press, 1964.

Reading Research Quarterly, Volume VII, Number 1, Fall 1971. Newark, Del.: International Reading Association, Inc. This issue is devoted entirely to current research and developments in the area of language development and reading.

SMITH, HENRY P., AND DECHANT, EMERALD K. *Psychology in Teaching Reading*. Englewood Cliffs, N.J.: Prentice-Hall, 1961.

STAUFFER, RUSSEL. *Directing Reading Maturity as a Cognitive Process*. New York: Harper & Row, 1969.

TABA, HILDA. "The Teaching of Thinking." *Elementary English Review* 42, 1965.

THREE

THE CHILD AND READING

TEACHER
ATTITUDE AND
THE CHILD'S
READING

OVERVIEW

Teacher traits and attitudes are always a major factor in effective teaching. Consequently, this chapter discusses the teacher as a personality, giving both information and insight into those qualities that describe the humanistic and affective dimensions of teacher behavior. Without these qualities, the techniques described in the following chapters cannot be implemented effectively. The ultimate objective of this chapter is:

> Given pupils who are hard to love and difficult to teach and who
> have low self-concepts and negative attitudes toward themselves and
> school, you will build bridges of respect between yourself and these
> pupils based on your own humanness and some innate belief in the
> dignity and worth of all children.

KNOWLEDGE BACKGROUND

Have you ever been asked to recall your "best" or "favorite" teacher? Can you do it now? Just pause for a moment and try to remember his or her name. Now, explain *why* that teacher stands out above all the others you have had in your school career. Is it because:

> She always made me feel good, even when I wasn't too smart.

She was fair to everybody.

He made me want to learn. He was hard, but he was fair. He never made you feel dumb.

She made me feel important in her class.

He smiled a lot and had a good sense of humor. He made you work hard, but he could always laugh, even at himself.

He never ridiculed you or made you feel stupid.

She would always help me when I got confused with my math.

In an indirect way, each of these quotes describes a teacher quality that goes far beyond knowledge of content or instructional techniques. Instead, it focuses on personality or character traits that seem to say "I care, I like, I respect, I understand."

As you might expect, many people have tried to research and codify these personal qualities that seem so important to successful teaching. And as you might also guess, clear-cut and definitive information from such research is difficult to find. Teacher characteristics—like learner characteristics—reflect so many different dimensions of humanness and experience that clear insight into what a teacher *ought to be* seems as varied as what he or she might look like. While these individual differences do exist and while teachers who care, who like, who respect, and who understand can come in all sizes and shapes and can *show* that they care, like, respect, and understand in a bewildering variety of ways, there is one core quality that seems to be a part of each teacher who is blessed with this humanism. In a word, teachers who are remembered as "best" have the very rare and valuable quality which, for lack of a better term, we can call *empathy.*

Empathy has a variety of definitions. When used to describe teaching behavior, it can best be limited to the ability *to feel what another feels.* Notice that this concept is totally different from sympathy. Sympathy usually means to feel sorry for. Empathy, however, says: I will not feel sorry for you (a position that often leaves me helpless to help) but, rather, I will know what you are feeling. I will care and respect because I know and understand your condition. Just as I will not hurt myself, I will not hurt you. Just as I will build healthy images of myself, so I will help you build healthy images of yourself. Just as I recognize that I am the most important thing in my world (for without me, it would cease), so I recognize that you are the most important thing in your world, and I will work hard to help you create and maintain the respect that so important a person deserves.

All this sounds well and good. It is very easy to say in the abstract, "Yes, that is the kind of person I am," or "That is the kind of teacher I will be," but the slip comes between recognizing the dimensions of humanism and actually implementing them with the children in your care. Knowing is one thing, doing another.

To help you in this transition between thought and action, we have collected three statements of teacher personality that seem to more clearly define and limit the concept of empathy. If empathy is the goal of humanistic behavior, then these three qualities reflect at least some of the means available for reaching that goal.

CONDITION 1

A teacher's expectations concerning a child's ability to learn appear to influence the child's school achievement.

The concept of *expectancy* is a powerful one. In some mysterious fashion, what parents, teachers, or peers feel a child can or can't accomplish is transmitted to the learner and often expands or limits achievement. Our major concern is the teacher. In this respect, a teacher is a mirror. If the child sees him- or herself reflected as a potent and capable learner, that child becomes a potent and capable learner. If, on the other hand, the teacher reflects an image that says to the child, "You can't learn. You are slow, clumsy, lazy, indifferent, careless, or hostile," then that child becomes a slow, clumsy, lazy, indifferent, careless, or hostile learner.

It should be obvious that a teacher never purposely sets out to develop negative expectancies for the students, and this is the insidious part of this whole concept. It is more an unconscious than a conscious behavior. But a teacher often does develop negative expectancies about a child and his or her ability to achieve, and the question is: Where do these expectancies come from?

Probably the best answer to this question is that teachers too often set negative *stereotypes* rather than positive expectancies. The teacher who interferes with a child's intellectual and educational growth because of low expectancy is saying, "Other children like you that I have known or been told about did not learn or achieve; therefore, you won't either!" It isn't that the teacher doesn't wish the child would learn, but the stereotype takes precedence, and the negative expectancy is formed.

In education, stereotyping and the negative expectancies it creates seem to result from a combination of experience and labels. Some children are difficult to teach, and when the failures accumulate, it's a very human thing for a teacher to protect him- or herself and his or her professional competence by placing the onus of failure on the child. It is then only a small step to sensing similarities between the children who didn't learn last year and those that are new in September. This stereotype creates the negative expectancy that becomes self-fulfilling. Sure enough, by the end of the year, those children haven't learned.

The characteristics that create negative expectancies can assume various and sometimes bizarre forms. For example, a researcher in California observed that in kindergarten and first grade the most obvious criteria for grouping children was whether or not they smelled of urine. Those kids who came to school with soiled underwear were always placed together for group work. Even desks were arranged with a very definite space between their group and the rest of the class. Similarly, an education professor in a major midwestern university attributes his graduation from a rural high school, as well as that of four brothers, to the fact that his mother made certain that each boy had two sets of clothes, one for the barn and one for school. He and his brothers went to school looking and smelling like city kids. The neighbor children were not so lucky; thirteen of them failed to find school a successful, supportive experience and dropped out when the law allowed. Again, let's remember that there is seldom any conscious effort by a teacher to equate how a child smells with a minimal academic expectancy. Instead, it is a subconscious stereotyping behavior.

A more familiar stereotype is created from familial background. A teacher who has had a bad experience with one child in a family can easily project the same sort of problems to brothers and sisters who come later. Similarly, it is very common to visit a classroom and have the teacher very quickly point out those children who come from broken homes and those whose mothers are on welfare as an explanation for the fact that they are not as good at their studies as their classmates who have more stable home lives. Here again, we see a full-blown stereotype and its probable offspring, a negative expectancy for learning.

Many expectancies are generated from second-hand evidence. Conversation in a teacher's room after a frustrating day of teaching can pass on to the insecure teacher images and attitudes that quickly grow into powerful and pervasive stereotypes. A harmless anecdote is assimilated, adjusted, and generalized to fit children who are yet to be born, with children being seen not as they are or can be but rather as stereotyped models who can't learn and so don't. Whatever the stereotype or whatever its source, the effects can be disastrous for the child.

The second source of stereotyping behaviors comes from the indiscriminate and inaccurate use of *labels*. A child—complex, infinitely different, superbly unique—is reduced to a label. Someone says, "Joe has an IQ of 82 so he's a slow learner," as if the number 82 has some divine power to prescribe the limits within which the child can grow. From this, a measure called "reading expectancy" has been created in which various formulas involving age, years in school, and IQ have been devised to pinpoint the limits that a teacher can expect a child to reach. So monstrous is this concept that children who are "abnormal" in the sense that their reading growth exceeds the limits predicted by a formula are relabeled as "overachievers," and a whole new stereotype is created.

Today, we have bushels of labels to pin on children. They can be called dyslexic, bilingual or learning disabled; deprived in language, culture, experience, or gross motor skills; and handicapped because of perceptual confusions, lateral instabilities or maturational lags. We can adopt new and esoteric labels from sociology, medicine, psychology, and anthropology, as well as education and other sources, and to what purpose? The poor teacher—the teacher who is devoid of empathy—will find them a comfort and a solace which shield him or her from admitting ineffectiveness with the children. These labels then create expectancies that are signaled to the child, who grows up or down as the teacher expectancy dictates.

A final thought: all teachers, good ones and bad, are constantly pressured to stereotype. The good teacher retains the ability to view each child as an individual who can be taught, while the poor teacher succumbs to the bombardment of labels and systematically goes about fitting each child to a stereotype. Such teachers, devoid of empathy, are unable to see with another's eyes or walk in another's shoes.

CONDITION 2

Effective teachers are perceived as helpful by children.

This condition needs little amplification. It is a simple condition that shows a child how the teacher perceives teaching. At all times and in all ways, the empathetic teacher views the job as one of *helping* children —helping them to read, to laugh, to wonder, to feel good, to adjust, to change, to grow. It seems so obvious! And yet, there are teachers who operate as if their job was to impede rather than to help. Their classes are an unending series of hurdles that each child must maneuver over with little or no aid. Such teachers are perceived not as helpers but as tyrants, and their classrooms are endured, not loved. Examine yourself. Do you really have the need to be helpful? When you get angry, disappointed, discouraged, and frustrated over the problems inherent in teaching, will you still be able to remain helpful to children? It's a necessary component of empathy.

CONDITION 3

Teachers who perceive themselves positively will be perceived positively.

This dimension of empathy reflects an "I'm all right, you're all right" philosophy. It suggests that the teacher with a *positive self-image,* who feels like a worthy person and member of humanity, will not only allow others to develop this same positive self-image but will also tend to be viewed as strong and trustworthy. The confidence, openness and honesty implicit in such a self-concept are powerful assets to a teacher.

The danger here is that the confidence must be real and not a facade that masks an otherwise unstable, petty, power-seeking personality who only wishes to be competent and secure. Children will sense such a person with uncanny speed and devastating directness. As a teacher, you either are secure or you aren't; you have it or you don't. If you have a positive self-image, it is easy to let others have one too. Such teachers draw strength from themselves and their accomplishments and do not gain status by lowering others. Such personalities can be trusted, and so children learn to trust.

Do you as a teacher or prospective teacher view yourself positively? Do you know your strengths as well as your weaknesses? Can you be follower as well as leader, last as well as first? Are you neither falsely humble nor aggressive? Have you confronted your own reality? Are you an unknowing taker? Have you proved you can live with yourself and are, therefore, worthy to live with others? The questions are unending.

A wise man once said that he could tell if another was worth knowing by the way that person shook his hand. The limp and lifeless grasp signaled a limp and lifeless ego; the heavy squeeze that brought pain to bone and tear to eye signaled a personality that could only find assurance by making others less sure. The wisdom of this observation is surely reflected in this third condition of empathy.

If we assume that a positive self-image is a condition of empathy, the final question is, "How can I, as a teacher, develop such a self-concept?" To ask the question is easy, but to find the answer is very difficult. A positive self-concept is the accumulated total of all the experiences and interrelationships developed in a lifetime. A portion of it comes from just being *vitally* alive, another comes from your reaction to this involvement with life, and a third comes from other people's reactions to you. In a nutshell, the teacher who lives an active, independent life, who can honestly examine personal feelings and motives and who dares to relate to others has a better chance of creating a positive self-image.

Such a teacher need never resort to sarcasm or ridicule. Such a teacher can laugh at him- or herself without fear of students' contempt. That teacher is free to make mistakes because he or she is stronger than those mistakes. And most important of all, because he or she is this kind of person, that teacher helps all pupils develop the same positive awareness and self-concept.

SUMMARY OF TEACHER ATTITUDE AND THE CHILD'S READING

In the following chapters of this book, you will become deeply involved with the *techniques* of diagnosing and teaching reading. A heavy emphasis will be placed on procedures, methods, tools, and principles which have their genesis in the behavioral sciences. Such "scientific" elements are crucial to effective instruction. However, you must never lose sight of the fact that teaching is an art, a human endeavor. As such, teacher personality and its impact on children will always be a major factor in the success of any instructional program, and you must prepare yourself by developing your affective dimensions as well as your technical expertise. While the latter may be mastered in a matter of weeks, the humanistic elements may take you a lifetime.

TEST YOUR KNOWLEDGE

1. Empathy is the ability _____.
2. Humanistic behavior in the classroom can be implemented by three conditions. List them.
   a. _____
   b. _____
   c. _____
3. Stereotyping can be based on a combination of such conditions as _____ and _____.
4. Inaccurate and indiscriminate use of labels is dangerous because it leads to _____.
5. Teachers can avoid the misuse of labels by viewing each child as an _____.
6. Teachers can create a positive self-image by:
   a. _____
   b. _____
   c. _____

SIMULATION ACTIVITIES

Teachers who are successful tend to be humanistic. They set positive expectancies, they are helpful, and they perceive themselves in a positive manner. To help you better visualize the differences between a humanistic and a nonhumanistic teacher, examine the following descriptions of two third grade classrooms.

Superficially the classrooms look very much alike. Both have bright, colorful bulletin boards and other decorations. Both have the pupils' desks clustered in groups of two. Both have centers of interest that deal with topics being discussed in social studies, science, and other subject areas. As you look more closely, however, you will notice some subtle but crucial differences:

Both classrooms list rules of acceptable classroom behavior on a bulletin board. In the first classroom, however, this list is entitled "The Way You Will Behave in This Room." The second classroom's list is entitled "What We Have Decided about Getting Along Together."

Both classrooms list the names of several pupils on the blackboard. In the first classroom the list is labeled "Detention List." In the second classroom the list is labeled "Excellent Progress Today."

Both teachers deal with minor discipline problems. In the first classroom the teacher publicly scolds a student for talking too loudly and threatens suspended playground privileges. In the second classroom the teacher ignores the talking student and instead praises a nearby pupil for diligence demonstrated in pursing the task.

Both teachers deal with serious discipline problems. The first teacher sends the student to the principal's office. The second teacher takes the pupil to one side and talks quietly to that pupil.

There is movement in both classrooms. In the first classroom movement comes after the student has raised a hand and asked permission to go somewhere. In the second classroom students move purposefully from place to place without specific instructions from the teacher.

Both teachers make use of facial expressions. The first teacher has mastered and uses the hard-eyed "teacher scowl." The second teacher smiles a lot.

Both teachers make individual comments to pupils. The first teacher say to Tom, "You know, I'll always remember you because you never do what you're told." The second teacher says to Tom, "I like the way you are trying so hard to be considerate of others."

Both classrooms display pupils' work on bulletin boards. In the first classroom the display includes the work of the top six pupils. In the second classroom every student has something on a bulletin board.

In both classrooms there is a student who does not wish to perform the task outlined by the teacher. The first teacher says, "You'll do it whether you want to or not." The second teacher says, "Let's see if we can relate it to what you're interested in."

Both classrooms were in session on the afternoon of the winter's first snowfall. When the pupils in the first classroom noticed and started buzzing about the snow, the teacher immediately told them to return to their assignments. When the pupils in the second class-room exhibited the same behavior, the teacher let them look for a while and talked quietly with them about the snow.

On the basis of these two descriptions can you list characteristics of a humanistic teacher?

SUGGESTED FIELD EXPERIENCES

Observation. When observing in schools, you should note what kind of expectancies the teacher sets and how those expectancies are created. Look for instances where the teacher is helpful with the children. Look for indications that the teacher's self-image is positive. Note how the teacher's attitudes affect the students.

Teaching activities. When teaching children, you should consciously examine your attitudes. Are you empathetic to all children? Are you setting positive expectancies for all children? Do you see your role as that of helper? Do you perceive yourself as adequate?

Client impact. By being empathetic to all students, you are helping them reach their potential in the classroom in general and in reading in particular. You are also developing a positive self-concept in each child, a concept that says "I'm good. I can do."

FOR CLASS DISCUSSION

Using what you know about expectancy, evaluate the following statements:

> The third grade teacher across the hall from you says, "My job as a third grade teacher is to make sure that all my kids get through the third grade reader."
>
> The president of your school PTA group says, "Every child who does not achieve at grade level in reading should be made to repeat the grade."
>
> Your principal says, "All children who are below grade level in reading should receive remedial reading instruction."
>
> A senator in the state legislature says, "We are going to institute a mandatory statewide assessment test in reading so that we can be sure that all our children are able to read at grade level."

ANSWER KEY
1. to feel what another feels
2. a. teacher expectancies influence learning
   b. effective teachers are helpful
   c. teachers who perceive themselves positively are perceived positively by others
3. experience and labels
4. stereotyping
5. individual
6. a. honestly examining their own feelings and motives
   b. living active, independent lives
   c. daring to relate to others

DEVELOP-
MENTAL
STAGES OF
READING
GROWTH

OVERVIEW

As the previous chapters have stated, children differ in terms of their interactions with the reading process. This chapter helps you place your learners in terms of one of these differences—the developmental stages they pass through en route to mastering reading. The ultimate objective is:

> Given data about each child's reading level and skill proficiency, you can establish the stage of developmental growth for each.

KNOWLEDGE BACKGROUND

Reading is a developmental task. That is, a child learns to read in a series of interrelated stages, each stage being the prerequisite for the next. The four major stages, together with descriptions of the major teaching focus of each, are listed below.

1. READINESS. Focuses on the prereading skills that are prerequisites to learning to read. These include the acquisition of oral language, visual and auditory discrimination, and development of concepts. In other words, the child is *getting ready to learn to read*.
2. INITIAL MASTERY. Focuses on the beginning skills of word identification

and comprehension, such as learning to recognize words instantly, to decipher unknown words by using letter sounds, and to remember what was read. The child is *learning to read.*

3. APPLICATION TO CONTENT AND RECREATION. Focuses on the more specialized reading skills, such as using indexes, footnotes, and other reading aids; reading for various purposes and at various rates; and learning technical terminology. At this stage, the child is *reading to learn.*

4. POWER. Focuses on the most refined reading skills, such as speed reading, higher level critical and creative reading, advanced study skills, the reading of specialized materials, and literary interpretation. Now the child is *becoming an expert reader.*

A learner's stage of developmental reading growth reflects reading level and skill proficiency. For instance, a child who is reading at first grade level and mastering skills such as visual and auditory discrimination will not be at the power stage of developmental reading growth. Similarly, the child who is reading Shakespeare and successfully interpreting the literary devices used will not be at the readiness stage of reading growth. Rather, the first child will be at either the readiness or the initial mastery stage, while the second child is likely to be at the power stage.

The relationship between a child's developmental stage of reading growth and the child's reading ability can be illustrated by looking at the following illustration of the reading skills hierarchy:

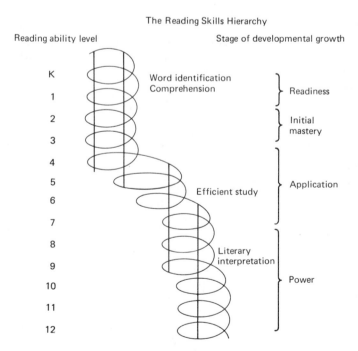

The Reading Skills Hierarchy

On the left-hand side are the reading ability levels from kindergarten through grade twelve. On the right-hand side are brackets indicating each of the four major stages of developmental reading growth. Interpreted, the illustration means that the readiness stage of developmental reading growth usually includes children reading at the prereading and first grade levels, with instruction focusing on the lowest level skills of word recognition and comprehension. Initial mastery normally includes children reading at second, third, and fourth grade levels, with instruction focusing on the remaining skills of word recognition and comprehension as well as the beginning stages of study skills. The application stage includes children reading at levels from fifth to eighth grade, with emphasis on some study skills and the beginning skills of literary understanding, while the power stage includes high school level reading and focuses on the last of the study skills and the skills of literary interpretation.

Judgments can be made, then, regarding a learner's stage of developmental reading growth by noting reading ability level and level of skill proficiency. Two cautions should be noted, however. First, because a child is in a particular grade in school does not necessarily mean that the child will be at a particular stage of developmental reading growth. For instance, a fifth grader *might* be at the application stage if reading at fifth grade level and having mastered the previous skills in the hierarchy. If, however, that student is a fifth grader who reads at the first grade level and is learning skills such as visual discrimination, then the student would be at the readiness stage regardless of chronological age. On the other hand, if a pupil is reading at ninth grade level and is learning skills such as speed reading, that pupil will be at the power stage even if only a third grader. Consequently, the teacher must make the decision regarding a child's stage of developmental reading growth not on the basis of what grade the child is in but, rather, on the basis of the child's reading level and skill proficiency.

The second caution is that the developmental stages are not distinct; that is, no clear line separates one stage from another. It is impossible, therefore, to specify exactly where initial mastery ends and application begins, and, similarly, it is not unusual for a child to receive some incidental instruction in study skills in the early grades or to receive advanced instruction on word identification in the upper grades. The point is that the developmental stages are approximate benchmarks which the teacher can use to "get a feel for" what can be expected from learners operating at various levels.

TEST YOUR KNOWLEDGE

1. The earliest stage of developmental reading growth is the
   _____ stage.
2. The stage at which a child is reading to learn is the _____
   stage.

3. The child receives instruction in the beginning skills of word identification and comprehension at the _____ stage.
4. The highest level of developmental reading growth is the _____ stage.
5. A child who was at the initial mastery stage of developmental reading growth would be receiving skill instruction in the areas of _____ and _____.
6. A child at the initial mastery stage of growth would have a reading level of approximately _____.
7. The power stage of developmental reading growth concentrates on the skills of _____ and _____.
8. To determine a learner's stage of developmental reading growth, the teacher must look at _____ and _____ and not at the child's age or grade.

SIMULATION ACTIVITIES

Imagine that you are a reading specialist who comes in contact with a great variety of different readers throughout a school system on any given day. You meet various students such as those described below. State the stage of reading growth for each.

A 47-year-old illiterate is receiving reading instruction. The tasks performed today were to discriminate visually between the letters **d** and **b** and to pick out like beginning sounds.

A 10-year-old is making a chart of the library books read and categorizing them by subject area or type of literature.

A 16-year-old is taking a nine-week course in speed reading and advanced study skills.

An 8-year-old is using the encyclopedia to obtain supplementary information for a social studies assignment.

Imagine now that you are a classroom teacher assigned to the third grade. Each of your pupils is eight years old. Some of these students are described below. State the stage of developmental reading growth for each.

Denise is reading at the third grade level and is very strong in identifying words. She has some trouble with the basic comprehension skills. She is quiet and shy and prefers to work alone.

Chris has mastered the basic word identification and comprehension skills and is reading at a sixth grade level. He is receiving instruction on using reading aids such as indexes and footnotes. He has had rich experiences in traveling with his parents.

George has an average intelligence but is having great difficulty in learning how to read. He is unable to read any level book without help, and he is receiving instruction in visual and auditory discrimination and in oral comprehension. He does not pay attention in class.

Kathy is reading books which are meant for ninth graders and is understanding them. She enjoys the classics of literature and is receiving instruction in critical and creative reading.

Imagine again that you are a third grade teacher. You have determined the reading ability level of each of your pupils. Now state what you believe would be the developmental stage of reading growth for each and the kind of skill instruction each would be likely to receive from you.

Mike's reading level is third grade. What would his probable developmental stage be? In what areas would he probably need skill instruction?

Tom's reading level is seventh grade. What would his probable developmental stage be? In which areas would he probably need skill instruction?

SUGGESTED FIELD EXPERIENCES

Observation. When observing in schools, you should note the range of developmental reading growth in various classrooms. Do you find any classrooms which have children representing each of the four stages? Does the instruction provided by the teacher reflect each child's developmental stage?

Teaching activities. When working with children in a classroom setting, you should be able to use school records and your own observation of each child's reading level and skill proficiency to determine stages of developmental reading growth. How will your instructional plans vary for children at different stages of growth?

Client impact. By determining stages of developmental reading growth and providing instruction appropriate for each child's stage, you should have a positive effect on your students. This impact will be noted in the child's increased interest and motivation which come from working at tasks appropriate for his or her development at any particular point in time.

FOR CLASS DISCUSSION

Examine the following statements and be prepared to discuss them with your instructor.

When I start teaching my third grade class, I can expect to have many stages of developmental reading growth reflected in the pupils I teach.

Before I can expect Johnnie to read adequately from his social studies text, we will have had to have completed the readiness and initial mastery stages of reading growth.

ANSWER KEY
1. readiness
2. application
3. initial mastery
4. power
5. word identification, comprehension
6. second through fourth grades
7. efficient study, literary understandings
8. reading level, skill proficiency

ESTABLISHING INSTRUCTIONAL READING LEVELS

OVERVIEW

This chapter helps you determine the level at which a pupil is reading. The ultimate objective is:

Given the children you are teaching, you can establish an instructional, independent, and frustration reading level for each.

KNOWLEDGE BACKGROUND

We have learned that children differ in terms of the potential they bring to the classroom and that, consequently, they will learn to read at varying rates. If you have a class of third graders who are all learning to read at different rates of speed, it stands to reason that you will have some children reading at a low level and other children reading at a high level. The purpose of this chapter is to provide you with the tools for determining each child's particular reading level at any given point in time.

Reading achievement is normally described in terms of a child's instructional, independent, and frustration reading levels. The instructional level is that level of reading at which a child can read *with* the teacher's help. For instance, if Susie is a third grader and can read books of fourth grade difficulty with some help from you, we say her instructional level is fourth grade; it is the most difficult level of reading that we can expect her to do. Logically, then, the independent level is that level of reading which the child can do *without* your help, and it will be, of course, easier than instructional level material. Susie's independent level, for instance, will probably be third grade. Frustration level is that level of reading which the child cannot do under *any* circumstances because it is too difficult, and it will consist of material which is harder than the instructional level. Looking at Susie again, her frustration level at this point in time will probably be material of fifth grade difficulty.

A learner's success in learning to read will depend in large part on your accuracy in determining each child's instructional, independent, and frustration reading levels. If a child is given a book to read which is at his or her instructional level, that child will feel comfortable with the material because it is neither too hard nor too easy. In contrast, the learner given frustration level material will become discouraged, frustrated, and upset and will rebel against instruction, while a child given material which is too easy will make little progress because he or she will not have to use any skills other than the ones already thoroughly mastered. Consequently, the success of reading instruction is directly tied to giving learners material to read which is of an appropriate difficulty level. Determining reading levels is a major diagnostic task faced by the teacher. The best way to do so is to use a combination of data collected from both standardized reading achievement tests and from informal diagnostic devices such as graded oral reading paragraph tests and cloze tests.

STANDARDIZED TESTS

A standardized reading achievement test is usually developed by a recognized expert in reading and is produced commercially by a publishing firm. These tests are labeled "standardized" for two reasons. First, such a test is usually administered to a large population of typical pupils before it is released for general use. The results of these trials are used to establish *norms*—that is, to determine the average scores for children of a particular grade. Second, these tests are administered and interpreted in a standard fashion, with the teacher rigidly following the directions prescribed in the test manual. Because of the care taken in developing and administering such tests, they are called *formal* devices.

Two major advantages exist in using a standardized reading achievement test for determining reading levels. First, they yield standard scores or units of comparison by which you can judge how well your students are doing as compared with other students in their grade. Second, they are usually group tests and can be administered and scored for an average-sized class very quickly and accurately.

In spite of these positive characteristics, standardized tests do have a major disadvantage. They tend to overestimate pupils' reading levels. This is especially true of children who are poor readers in upper elementary grades. In these cases, the standardized score more often reflects the pupil's frustration level than the instructional level, and to the unsophisticated teacher this difference is often confusing. To illustrate, a standardized test score for Mike, a fifth grader, might indicate a grade equivalent of 5.3. The test scores seem to indicate that Mike compares favorably with the average fifth grade child. Actually, however, because the score overestimates reading levels, Mike's instructional level might be closer to fourth grade.

INFORMAL DIAGNOSTIC TESTS

In contrast to the standardization and formality of the standardized reading achievement test, informal devices for determining reading levels depend much more heavily on teacher judgment, particularly in the interpretation of the results.

GRADED ORAL READING PARAGRAPH TESTS

A typical informal device for determining reading levels is the graded oral reading paragraph test. In such a test, a series of paragraphs of increasing difficulty is used, with the first paragraph of first grade difficulty, the second paragraph of second grade difficulty, and so on. Comprehension questions for each grade level are provided. The teacher prepares a copy of the paragraph (minus the comprehension questions) for the student, keeping a second copy of the paragraph and the related comprehension questions. Each paragraph is given to the student with directions to read it orally and to try to remember what the paragraph said. The teacher then notes any errors of pronunciation as the child reads. When the child finishes the paragraph, the teacher takes the paragraph away, asks the comprehension questions, and notes any errors. If the child makes many errors, thereby reaching the frustration level, the teacher stops, then examines the pupil's performance on each paragraph and makes a judgment concerning the appropriate instructional level.

The major advantage of an informal device such as the graded oral reading paragraph test is the opportunity it provides for the teacher to directly observe the student's reading performance. Its major disadvantages are the extent to which such a test depends on teacher sensitivity and judgment in interpreting the student's reading performance and the fact that its individual administration takes a good deal of teacher time.

Although determining reading levels with a graded oral reading paragraph test depends a great deal on teacher judgment, a set of criteria is available to help you determine when a student has reached frustration. These criteria require that you count both the number of word identification errors and the number of comprehension errors made by the child at each level. The student who makes no more than one pronunciation error in every 100 running words and can comprehend the material with 90 percent accuracy can handle material of that level of difficulty independently. If the student makes two to five pronunciation errors in every 100 running words and/or comprehends the material with 75–89 percent accuracy, material at that level of difficulty is instructional for the student. If more than five pronunciation errors in every 100 words are made and/or if comprehension of the material is less than 75 percent, the material is too difficult for the student. The following chart illustrates these criteria for you.

Word recognition

100%	99%	95%	
Independent	Instructional	Frustration	

Comprehension

100%	90%	75%	
Independent	Instructional	Frustration	

When reading, the pupil might make many kinds of word identification errors. Consequently, for recording you should use a notation system which distinguishes one type of error from another because your analysis of strengths and weaknesses depends on the patterns of errors the child makes. A suggested notation system follows:

/ = The pupil hesitates before pronouncing words. Although infrequent or very brief hesitations may not be significant, frequent and lengthy hesitations indicate that the reader is not sure of the next word or is sounding out the word silently. Such hesitations indicate that the reader does not know the word well; this is a pronunciation error.[1]

took = The pupil does not know the word, and it has to be pronounced by the teacher.

took = The pupil substitutes an incorrect word for the printed word.

little = The pupil repeats the word twice. This is an error, because the pupil is unsure of the next word and repeats the preceding word or words while trying to analyze the unknown word.

and
∧ = The pupil inserts a word that does not belong.

wh c = The pupil starts to pronounce the word incorrectly but corrects there him- or herself. This is an error despite the fact of self-correction

---

[1] *Note:* When a pupil hesitates before a word and then fails to correctly pronounce that word, count only the word as an error, not both the hesitation and the word.

because it indicates that the initial perception of the word was inaccurate.

(was) = The pupil omits a word.

(X) = The pupil ignores punctuation.

CLOZE TEST

Another informal technique for diagnosing reading levels is the cloze procedure. This procedure, based on the Gestalt theory of clozure, relies on the *impulse to supply the missing element*. Therefore, in reading, the student supplies the missing words in a written selection. The number of correctly supplied words is converted to a percentage score, and the instructional level is determined from that score. Its most important feature to a teacher is that, in contrast to graded oral paragraphs, it can be administered as a group test and will quickly give an approximate level of placement for each student in your class.

1. Take three passages of approximately 100 words each from the beginning, middle, and end of graded reading materials (the basal reader is usually most convenient).
2. Duplicate each passage and, after the first sentence, delete every seventh word. Replace each deleted word with a line.
3. Make all the lines of equal length so the word choice will not be influenced.
4. Give the passage only to students who have not yet read the selection.
5. Have the students supply, with no set time limit, the words that were deleted.
6. Score responses as correct when they match or are synonymous with the deleted words. There is presently much controversy about counting synonyms as correct. Because no solid research indicates whether or not to count them, we recommend that you count them when deciding the correctness of a response. Spelling errors should be disregarded.
7. Change the point score to a percentage score by dividing the total number of correct answers by the total number of deleted words. If the number of correct words is between 45 and 55 percent of the possible total, the material is at the instructional level of the student. If it is higher, the material is too easy; if it is lower, the material is too difficult.

Like any diagnostic tool, this technique has advantages and disadvantages. The advantages of the cloze procedure are:

1. It can be given to an entire class simultaneously.
2. Any written material can be used.
3. It is extremely useful in conjunction with other diagnostic tools.
4. With directions, any person can prepare cloze tests.

The disadvantages of the cloze procedure are:

1. This test procedure is based on filling in words that make sense in the sentence. The child who is in the primary grades or has not had experience in using context will be unable to do this task effectively. Therefore, its usefulness is limited to upper grade children.
2. If the test includes only one passage, the difficulty of the selection will depend on the words that happen to be deleted.
3. Research has given us little information on how various features of a passage influence the reader's word choice. Therefore, results can sometimes be misleading. Although this procedure can give a quick and relatively accurate estimate of a student's ability to read a story or a book, it can also sometimes give poor information that will lead to an incorrect judgment on reading level. If your students know how to use context and if they have the word recognition and comprehension skills necessary for reading the selected passage, you will get a useful placement score.

SUMMARY OF ESTABLISHING INSTRUCTIONAL READING LEVELS

An appropriate reading level can be determined for a student by using either a formal device such as a standardized reading achievement test, or an informal device such as a cloze test or a graded oral reading paragraph test. However, it is always a good practice to collect as much data as possible before making instructional decisions. Consequently, in establishing reading levels it is best to use both formal and informal devices *in combination;* you then are in less danger of placing the student incorrectly. A second sound principle states that if you have two seemingly contradictory pieces of diagnostic data and are in doubt about the level in which to place a student, always go lower, because it is easier on a child's self-concept to be *promoted* to a harder book than *demoted* to an easier book.

TEST YOUR KNOWLEDGE

1. The level at which a child can read with the teacher's help is called the _____ level.
2. If a child selects a library book to be read without any assistance, it should be written at the child's _____ level.
3. The teacher should avoid giving the child material which is written at the _____ level.
4. A diagnostic device which has norms and which requires the teacher to follow strict directions in its administration is called a _____ test.
5. A major disadvantage to a standardized test is that it tends to _____-estimate a child's reading ability.
6. The graded oral reading paragraph test requires that the teacher note errors of _____ and _____.

7. If, at the third grade level on a graded oral reading paragraph test, a child scores 100 percent in comprehension but makes more than five errors in identifying words, the material would be at the _____ level.
8. If the teacher notes a *p* over a word in a graded oral reading paragraph test, he/she is indicating that the word was pronounced by the _____.
9. A major advantage of the cloze test is that it can be administered to _____ rather than being administered individually like the graded oral reading paragraph test.
10. When you are in doubt regarding a child's instructional reading level, you should place that child at a _____ level.

SIMULATION ACTIVITIES

Tom is a fifth grader. He scored 4.1 on a standardized reaching achievement test.

1. What would you estimate his instructional reading level to be?

Examine the data provided for each of the following students and list instructional, independent, and frustration reading levels.

BURT

Grade level of test material	Word recognition	Comprehension
First	99%	100%
Second	96%	85%
Third	93%	70%
Fourth	85%	60%

2. Burt's independent level is _____.
3. His instructional level is _____.
4. His frustration level is _____.

RHONDA

Grade level of test material	Word recognition	Comprehension
First	100%	95%
Second	100%	90%
Third	99%	80%
Fourth	95%	65%
Fifth	90%	40%

5. Rhonda's independent level is _____.
6. Her instructional level is _____.
7. Her frustration level is _____.

ANNIE

Grade level of test material	Word recognition	Comprehension
First	100%	100%
Second	99%	95%
Third	99%	95%
Fourth	97%	90%
Fifth	92%	85%
Sixth	83%	74%

8. Annie's independent level is _____.
9. Her instructional level is _____.
10. Her frustration level is _____.

Now examine the notations of Oscar's word identification errors in the following paragraph of second-grade difficulty.[2]

A (little) black dog ran away ~~from~~ *for* home. He | pl*ƀ*yed with two big

dogs. They <u>ran away</u> | from him. It | b*é*gan *begun c* | to rain. He | went

under a big tree. He wanted to go | h*ƀ*me, but <u>he did not</u> | kn*ƀ*ow

the way. He | saw a boy he knew. *and* The boy took him home.

11. By examining the word identification errors, we can say that this second grade material is Oscar's _____ level.

The following is Andy's performance on the graded oral reading paragraphs. Note his errors and establish independent, instructional, and frustration reading levels for him.

Muff is a little yellow kitten.
She drinks milk.
She sleeps on a | chair.
She does not like to get wet.

___+___	1. What color was the kitten?
___+___	2. What does she drink?
___+___	3. Where does she sleep?
___+___	4. Why doesn't Muff like to go out on rainy days?

A l*big*ittle black dog ran away from home. He played with two big

dogs. They ran away from him. It began to rain. He | went under a

[2] Reading paragraphs here and on pages 98, 103–107, 114–116 are taken from the *Durrell Analysis Reading Difficulty Test*, copyright © 1937, 1955 by Harcourt Brace Jovanovich, Inc. Reprinted by special permission of the publisher.

tree. He wanted to go home, but he did not | know the way. He saw

a boy he knew. The boy took him home.

big, black dog 1. Who ran away from home?
____+____ 2. How many other dogs did he play with?
____+____ 3. Why did the dog go under the tree?
____+____ 4. What did the dog want then?
____+____ 5. Whom did he see?
____+____ 6. How did he get home?

Six boys put up a | *p* tent by the side of the river. They took | things

to eat with them. When the sun went down, | they went into the

| tent to sleep. In the night, a cow came and began to eat | grass |

around the tent. The boys were | *p* afraid. They | *think c* thought it was a

bear.

____+____ 1. How many boys went camping?
near the river 2. Where did they put up their tent?
____+____ 3. What did they take with them besides their tent?
____+____ 4. What did the boys do when the sun went down?
____+____ 5. What came around their tent in the night?
____+____ 6. What was the cow doing?
____+____ 7. What did the boys think the cow was?

Henry goes to a | large lake in | summer. Last | summer, a | motor|

boat sank near his | *p* house. The | boat had ten men in it. The man

who was | running the | boat brought it very close to the shore when
cloz   in c

the | water was low. He hit a big | rock | under | water. It made a
p   the c   9 to c

hole in the | bottom of the boat. The | water came in very fast. All
p   on

of the | men swam to shore.
on

to the lake 1. Where does Henry go in summer?
____+____ 2. What happened near his house?
____+____ 3. What kind of boat was it?
____+____ 4. What did the boat hit?
____−____ 5. How fast did the water come in?
____−____ 6. How many men were in the boat?
were rescued 7. What happened to the men on the boat?

12. Andy's independent reading level is _____.
13. His instructional reading level is _____.
14. His frustration reading level is _____.

Byrch was given the cloze test using basal readers. The results follow:

first grade   80%
second grade   70%
third grade   50%
fourth grade   35%

15. In what level text should Byrch be placed for reading instruction?

The following passage has been prepared for the cloze procedure and includes Kathy's responses.

Ever since last week when Ken saw the circus, in his mind's eye he

had been controlling wild tigers and lions or balancing on a tight

wire. He dreamed he was cracking the ___*whip*___ to make the

lions and tigers ___*roar*___ while everyone cheered. He saw

himself ___*high*___ above the tent floor crossing the

___*tight*___ wire while everyone below him held

___*his*___ breath. He finally made up his ___*bed*___ to

be a circus performer. All ___—___ week he practiced and

practiced walking ___*up*___ a tight rope and cracking a

___*whip*___. One night, after he fell asleep, ___*Ken*___

dreamed he was in a real ___*circus*___. He walked into the cage

of ___*the*___ animals and started to make ___—___ do

their act. Suddenly a lion ___*jumped*___ and leaped at him. Just

● 99

as ___*the*___ lion closed his big mouth over ___*his*___

head, Ken found himself lying on ___*his*___ bedroom floor.

He was trying to ___*open*___ a pillow case off his head.

___—___ crawling back in bed, Ken decided ___—___

maybe he should be a jet ___*pilot*___.

Correct answers reading across: whip, perform, far, tight, his, mind, that, on, whip, he, circus, wild, them, roared, the, his, the, get, After, that, pilot.

16. Is this material at Kathy's instructional level?

The following two pieces of diagnostic data have been gathered for John, a pupil in your fourth grade.

Standardized reading test: total score, 4.1
Graded oral reading paragraph test: independent level, 2; instructional level, 3; frustration level, 4
Cloze: scored 47 percent on a 3^2 reader

17. With what level book would you begin to teach John?

SUGGESTED FIELD EXPERIENCES

Observation. When observing in schools, you should note the range of instructional reading levels. Do you find many different reading levels in a single classroom? Do you find any pupils who have been given frustration level materials? Do the pupils select library books and other independent reading according to their independent reading levels?

Teaching activities. When working with children in a classroom, you should administer graded oral reading tests and cloze tests, as well as using the results of standardized reading achievement tests, to determine the instructional, independent, and frustration reading levels for each pupil.

Client impact. Because you determine each child's instructional reading level, you should not have pupils in your classroom who are frustrated by material that is too difficult or who are bored by material that is too easy.

FOR CLASS DISCUSSION

1. Listen to a tape of two students reading graded oral paragraphs and establish the independent, instructional, and frustration reading level for each pupil.
2. Examine the results of standardized tests and cloze tests, and determine reading levels.
3. Discuss with your instructor how success and failure affect self-concept and, ultimately, various kinds of achievement. For instance, how do you feel when you play tennis against someone who is clearly superior to you, as opposed to an opponent who is just slightly weaker? How does your attitude toward swimming change when you are placed in a swimming class that is two levels above your proficiency level? What is the implication for reading instruction?

ANSWER KEY
1. instructional
2. independent
3. frustration
4. standardized
5. over
6. word recognition, comprehension
7. frustration
8. teacher
9. the whole class
10. lower

DIAGNOSING SKILL STRENGTHS AND NEEDS

OVERVIEW

This chapter provides you with a strategy for determining each child's specific strengths and weaknesses in word identification and comprehension. The ultimate objective is:

> Given a group of elementary school children, you can determine what skills of word identification and comprehension each child needs to learn.

KNOWLEDGE BACKGROUND

As a result of your work in previous chapters, you know that children can differ widely in at least two characteristics important to reading. First, some can be expected to achieve at a more rapid rate than others. Second, some will read at a low instructional reading level, while others will read at a higher level.

While these data are important, they are not all that a teacher needs to know prior to beginning instruction. In addition to knowing what book to give a child and how fast we can expect the child to progress, we must also know what we must teach; which skills of reading does the child already possess and which ones are yet to be learned?

In the final analysis, it is the data regarding a child's specific skill needs which are most crucial to the reading teacher, for if we do not determine precisely what is known and what must be taught we may end up teaching nothing. To illustrate, let's look at an instructional area such as swimming. If you took your child to a swimming instructor, you would expect that the instructor would do more than simply put the child in the water and let him or her swim. Rather, you would expect the instructor to determine what skills of swimming your child needed and to provide specific instruction designed to create those skills. By the same token, if you hire someone to teach your child to read, you would expect that person to do more than simply give your child a book and let him or her read. You would, instead, expect the instructor to determine what reading skills your child needed and to provide specific instruction designed to create these skills. In short, you expect that a good teacher will know precisely what to teach each child to make him or her a better reader. How to determine this is the focus of this chapter.

We will look at three ways to determine skill strengths and needs. The first is a generalized technique to determine whether a child needs help in word identification or comprehension. The second is a means for determining, in a rough manner, what kind of word identification and/or comprehension skills a child relies upon. The third is a very precise strategy for determining specifically what skills of word identification and comprehension a child has already learned and which ones are yet to be learned.

DETERMINING A GENERAL AREA OF DIFFICULTY

In the previous chapter, we learned that graded oral reading paragraphs can be used to determine a child's instructional reading level. In addition, however, they can be used to determine generally whether a child has difficulty in either word identification or comprehension. For instance, if a student reads several graded oral reading paragraphs and makes errors of word identification while making no errors of comprehension, we can assume that the area of difficulty is word identification. Conversely, if the student reads several graded oral reading paragraphs and makes errors of comprehension while making few errors of word identification, we can assume that the area of difficulty is comprehension.

This can be illustrated by examining the results of Andrea's graded oral reading paragraphs, as follows:

FIRST GRADE PARAGRAPH

Muff | is a little | yellow | kitten.
She drinks milk.X
She sleeps | on a chair.
She | does not | like | to get wet.

+	1. What color was the kitten?
+	2. What does she drink?
+	3. Where does she sleep?
+	4. Why doesn't Muff like to go out on rainy days?

SECOND GRADE PARAGRAPH

A little black dog ran away from ~~home.~~ *him* He ~~played~~ *pro c* with two big

dogs. They ran away | from him. It began to rain. He | went | under *then* *They*

| a tree. He wanted | to go home, (but) he did not know the way. He

saw a boy he | knew. The boy ~~took~~ *take c* him home.

+	1. Who ran away from home?
+	2. How many other dogs did he play with?
+	3. Why did the dog go under the tree?
+	4. What did the dog want then?
+	5. Whom did he see?
+	6. How did he get home?

THIRD GRADE PARAGRAPH

Six boys | put up a tent | by the side | of the river. They took ~~things~~ *them*

to eat ~~with~~ them When | the | sun | went | down, they went into *when*

the tent to | ~~sleep.~~ *eat* In the night, a cow came and | began to eat *cat* *b-b-b p*

| ~~grass~~ | around the tent. The boys were | ~~afraid.~~ They (thought) it *garbage* *after c*

~~was~~ a bear. *saw c*

+	1. How many boys went camping?
+	2. Where did they put up their tent?
+	3. What did they take with them besides their tent?
+	4. What did the boys do when the sun went down?
+	5. What came around their tent in the night?
+	6. What was the cow doing?
+	7. What did the boys think the cow was?

FOURTH GRADE PARAGRAPH

Henry goes | to a large | lake in summer. Last | summer a | motor- *the* ^

boat sank near his ~~house.~~ The boat had | ten | men in it. The | man | *home* *on*

who ~~was~~ | running the boat brought it (very) close | to the shore ~~when~~ *saw* *p* *went* the water was low ~~X~~ He hit a big | rock | under water. It made a |

boat

hole in the ~~bottom~~ of the boat. The water came in | very | fast.

All (of) the men swam to shore.

+	1. Where does Henry go in summer?
+	2. What happened near his house?
+	3. What kind of boat was it?
+	4. What did the boat hit?
+	5. How fast did the water come in?
+	6. How many men were in the boat?
+	7. What happened to the men in the boat?

In examining these paragraphs, we can see that Andrea does not make comprehension errors at any level. However, her skill in identifying words deteriorates steadily from the first grade paragraph to the fourth grade paragraph. Consequently, we can say that Andrea's general area of reading difficulty is in word identification rather than comprehension. If the phenomenon were reversed, with Andrea making few word identification errors but may comprehension errors, we would conclude that her area of difficulty was comprehension rather than word identification.

DETERMINING TYPES OF WORD IDENTIFICATION AND COMPREHENSION DIFFICULTIES

While it is helpful to determine general areas of difficulty as illustrated above, we can obtain even more specific information by examining graded oral reading paragraph data more carefully. In word identification, for instance, we can examine the types and pattern of errors and determine whether a child is overrelying on one or another of the various types of word identification skills. For instance, a child who makes little or no attempt to analyze and pronounce unknown words is probably relying on sight-word recognition, and, by inference, we can assume that the child needs instruction in using phonetic and contextual analysis. On the other hand, a child who reads in a nonfluent and irregular fashion and who tries to pronounce every word according to phonetic principles is probably overrelying on phonetic analysis, and, by inference, we can assume that the child needs instruction in sight-word recognition or context.

This phenomena can be illustrated by looking at the patterns of errors made by Greg, Jerry and Bob. Each makes significantly different kinds of errors on the same paragraph, and so, different conclusions can be drawn about the word identification skills they possess and those they need to learn. Let's look first at Greg's performance:

Harry *long* *the* *lake* *p*

~~Henry~~ goes to a | large lake in summer. Last | summer, a motor-

p next to · *motor* · *men*

boat | sank near his house. The boat had ten men on it. The man

motor · *p* · *every* · *p* · *p went*

who was running the boat | brought it very close to the | shore when

the · *p*

the water was | low. He hit a big rock under water. It made a | hole

boat c · *come* c · *And*

in the bottom of the | boat. The water came in very fast. All of the

p

men swam to | shore.

Aside from the hesitations, Greg consistently makes two kinds of errors. First, he has to have many of the words he does not know pronounced for him. In fact, he apparently does not even attempt to analyze those words and just waits for his teacher to pronounce them for him. Second, he substitutes one word for another. On examining these substitutions, note that they appear to be errors of visual discrimination; the word he substitutes is almost always similar in visual form and shape to the actual word. If this is the case, we can say that Greg has few analysis techniques and is relying on visual form to help him; he is over-relying on sight-word recognition, and he will need instruction in analysis techniques (phonetic analysis, structural analysis, and context).

In contrast, examine Jerry's performance on the same paragraph and compare what he does with what Greg did.

lar-gee · *La....st sue...mer*

Henry | goes | to a | large | lake in | summer. | Last | summer, a |

motor—bo·at n-n-near ho...hove bo-at

motorboat | sank near his | house. The | boat had | ten | men on it X

bro...c · *sloze*

The | man who was | running the | boat | brought it | very | close to

p · *water* · *p*

the | shore | when the | water was | low. He | hit a big | rock | under

b-b-b c · *wā—ter*

| water. It | made a | hole in the | bottom of the | boat. The | water |

sh-sh- shore

came in | very | fast. All of | the | men swam to | shore.

Clearly, the most prevalent error made by Jerry is his hesitations. He seems to pause significantly before nearly every word. The question is, of course, why is he pausing? Most readers pause to analyze, because analysis requires time. Jerry, in fact, is probably analyzing too much. Another prevalent error Jerry makes is mispronunciation. When pronouncing words, he almost always breaks them down into sound elements of one kind or another, and he always tries to attach a sound to a letter, even if it is the wrong one. We can say, then, that Jerry is overanalyzing and is relying on phonetic analysis. He needs to learn to use more sight-word skills if he is to identify words efficiently.

Finally, examine how Bob reads the same paragraph:

went · *the* · *time*

Henry goes to a large lake in summer. Last summer, a motorboat

106 •

next to cottage ~~This~~ *people*

sank near his house. The boat had ten ~~men~~ on it. The man who

ran *up* *cottage*

(was) ~~running~~ the boat brought it ~~very~~ close to the shore | when

down *It* *under*

the water was low. He hit a big rock ~~in the~~ water. It made a

big *ran*

hole in the (bottom of the) boat. The water came in (very) fast.

^*after*

~~All of~~ the men swam to shore X *they were saved.*

Compared with Greg and Jerry, Bob does not seem to make the same kinds of errors. He almost never has to have a word pronounced by his teacher, he almost never hesitates before a word, and he gives very little evidence of any reliance on sound elements. He does, however, omit a number of words and insert others without seeming to seriously alter the meaning of the passage. He is over-relying on context and must learn to use visual and analysis skills in combination with context as a means for becoming a more efficient identifier of words.

Note: On a graded oral reading paragraph, students will seldom make errors that are as obvious as the ones above. We have exaggerated the responses of a sight reader, a phonetic reader, and a context reader so that you can easily see the relationship between the type of error and the technique being utilized. Nevertheless, the principle of looking for a pattern of errors in graded oral reading paragraphs is sound and can be used efficiently even in those situations where the errors are not so obvious. One additional caution, however. When determining the type of word recognition errors, you should use the errors made at the pupil's instructional level rather than at the frustration level. Errors made at that level are often exaggerated, reflecting the pupil's frustration rather than the actual word recognition problem. For instance, a pupil who knows all the "small" words in a second grade paragraph will often begin to miss these same words when struggling through a fifth grade paragraph.

Similarly, you can use information from graded oral reading paragraphs to determine types of comprehension errors. This is done by controlling more carefully the kinds of comprehension questions asked in the testing situation. Rather than simply asking a series of factual questions about the content of the paragraphs, you would ask different types of questions to obtain different types of information about the child's comprehension of a passage. For instance, you would structure questions to determine whether the child knows the meaning of words, whether he or she can comprehend the material literally, whether he or she can do manipulative thinking, and whether he or she can do evaluative thinking. If the child answers each of the questions well, you can assume the ability to do that kind of thinking at that level. If the child answers one or more of the questions incorrectly, however, you can assume the need for instruction in the type of thinking being tested in that question.

To illustrate, let's look at the following paragraph: [1]

> A boy named Fred visited his Uncle Bill, a sheepherder who lived in a covered wagon in the foothills. Two horses were eating grass beside the wagon. During the first few days of his visit, Fred was concerned with his uncle's shepherd dogs, who stayed out with the sheep at night, even in bad weather. One night Uncle Bill took Fred out to the herd while a storm was raging. He called the dogs. They appeared from the midst of the herd of sheep, but they did not want to leave their woolly hiding place. Fred said, "All right, I won't worry about them anymore."

To determine a child's comprehension strengths and weaknesses relative to this paragraph, you would ask several different kinds of comprehension questions. For instance, to determine content word meaning skills, you might ask the following questions:

What is the meaning of the word **sheepherder?**
Can you tell me what a **foothill** is?
If a dog appears from the **midst** of something, what does this mean?

To determine whether a child can comprehend relationships signaled by function words in this paragraph, you might ask questions such as the following:

What was the weather like when Uncle Bill took Fred out to see the herd?
Who was Bill talking about when he said he **wouldn't worry about them anymore?**
When Uncle Bill called the dogs, did they want to stay with the sheep?

To determine recognition and memory for factual information, you might ask questions such as:

Who did Fred visit?
What happened on the night they visited the herd?
At what time of day did they visit the herd?

To determine whether a child can do manipulative thinking, you might ask questions such as:

What would be a good title for this story?
Of what use were the two horses eating grass beside the wagon?
In what part of the United States did this story take place?
How did Fred feel about the sheep dogs after his experience?

[1] Source unknown.

To determine whether a child can do critical or evaluative thinking in this story, you might ask questions such as:

Do you think Uncle Bill had a cruel attitude toward the dogs?
What are some of the differences between keeping dogs as pets and keeping dogs as Uncle Bill did?
If you owned a herd of sheep, would you hire a sheepherder?

Thus, the graded oral reading paragraphs can provide more information than simply what the child's instructional reading level is. By noting the particular types of errors made in word identification and comprehension, you can determine more precisely the types of strengths and weaknesses a child possesses.

SYSTEMATIC DIAGNOSIS OF SKILL NEEDS

The above techniques for diagnosing skill needs will provide us with information on whether the child's difficulty is in word identification or comprehension and, more specifically, whether the difficulty is in sight-word recognition or word analysis or in one of the various areas of comprehension.

However, from Chapters 4, 5, and 6 you know that word identification and comprehension consist of various streams of skills which are built in a hierarchy from the simple to the complex. Therefore, while it is helpful to know which stream a child is having difficulty with, this information does not tell us where in that particular hierarchy a child's difficulty lies. If a learner's problem seems to lie with inadequate sight-word recognition skills, how do we know which of the sight-word skills to start with? If the problem lies with inadequate phonetic analysis skills, how do we know which of the phonetic analysis skills to start with? Similarly, if the problem lies with one or another of the skill categories in comprehension, how do we know where to start teaching in a particular category? Obviously, if our instruction is to be precise and efficient, we must be able to connect the child with the specific skill needed; we must be able to place each child in relationship to the specific elements of the reading process. To accomplish this kind of diagnosis, we must proceed from a systematic base.

Systematic skill diagnosis requires, first, that you have a thorough understanding of the nature of the reading process and the various streams of skills of which it is comprised. The fundamentals of this understanding were provided in Chapters 4, 5, and 6, where the skills of word identification and comprehension were described.

Once you have a grasp of the "big picture" of the skills of reading, you must then be able to specify exactly which skills are taught first, second, third, and so on in the various skills hierarchies. Only if you know what the specific skills are can you connect a child to one or another of those skills. However, it is not intended that you should memorize all these skills, since they are very nitty-gritty and number in the hundreds. Rather, you should have a source list of these skills to refer to as your guide in moving children through the skills hierarchy. There are many sources of such lists.[2] They specify each of the skills to be learned in a manner similar to the following:

1. Given three letters that are exactly alike and one that is somewhat similar, the learner marks the one that is different.
2. Given a few seconds to examine a letter that is easily confused with other letters, the learner reproduces the letter from memory, to the satisfaction of the teacher.
3. Given three words that are exactly alike and one word that is somewhat similar, the learner marks the word that is different.
4. Given a few seconds to examine a word that is easily confused with other words, the learner reproduces the word from memory, to the satisfaction of the teacher.
5. Given a few seconds to examine a word, the learner picks out another word having the same initial consonant from among a group of four words.
6. Given a fraction of a second to examine each of ten flashcards with words the learner selected to learn to read printed on them, the learner pronounces each word within one second.

With such a listing available, you can use a system of pre- and post-testing to determine precise strengths and needs in the skill areas. These tests, frequently referred to as *criterion-referenced tests*, would reflect exactly the skill specified in the objective. For instance, the pretest for the first skill objective listed above would require the child to pick out the different letter from among four similar letters, somewhat as follows:

SET I	q	q	g	q
SET II	o	a	a	a
SET III	m	n	m	m
SET IV	v	v	v	u
SET V	b	d	b	b

The pretest for the second objective above would require the child to draw on a piece of paper the letter which had just been flashed by the teacher. For each succeeding objective, the pretest would require the child to do the task described in the objective. The idea is to provide a

[2] Examples include *Systematic Reading Instruction*, 2nd ed., published by Harper & Row, and *The Wisconsin Design*, published by the Wisconsin Research and Development Center for Cognitive Learning, University of Wisconsin, 1970.

short, efficient, and precise means for determining each child's ability to perform each of the separate skills needed to become a good reader. While such pretests are sometimes included as part of commercial reading products purchased for classroom use, they can also be independently produced by the teacher having a source list of skills available to use as a foundation.

Armed with a list of each of the skills in the reading hierarchy and a series of pre- and posttests to determine whether a child can or cannot perform each of these skills, you can implement a four-step sequence of systematic skill diagnosis: (1) pretest, (2) teach, (3) posttest, and (4) apply.

In action, the system works as follows. First, administer the pretest for the lowest level skill in the hierarchy. If the learner satisfactorily completes that pretest, assume the child has already mastered that skill. Go on to the next skill, administer the pretest, and note the learner's performance. If the child once again performs satisfactorily, assume mastery of this skill and move on to the next. Continue until you encounter a skill the learner cannot perform. Thus, the first step in the strategy is that of data gathering, in which the series of simple pretests is used to determine what the learner can and cannot do. Time is not wasted teaching a skill the child has already mastered and effort is not wasted teaching a skill which is too difficult for the child.

Having determined the individual skill needs of the learner, the second step is to provide direct instruction to develop that skill. Here, the skill specified in the objective and tested in the pretest is taught. The lessons are highly intensive and direct. There is no misunderstanding concerning what should be taught, nor is the skill left to develop "naturally" or as a result of generalized reading lessons. The objective for the lesson is clear, the instruction specific.

The third step is the administration of the posttest to determine whether the instruction has been successful. This procedure is similar to the first step. If the learner performs satisfactorily on the posttest, the instruction has been successful, the skill has been mastered, and the learner can be moved to the next skill. If the learner fails, however, you must assume that the instruction has not been successful, and another lesson designed to develop this skill must be planned and taught. Thus, the third step in the system insures that each skill in the sequence is mastered in turn and that no learner is moved on too quickly, preventing the assumption that the skill was learned simply because it was taught.

Finally, in the fourth step, the teacher helps the learner apply this newly learned skill in actual reading. The teacher gives the child a book having a readability level appropriate to the child's instructional reading level and shows the child how to use the skill when actually reading. This step insures learner transfer of the skill to the ultimate act of reading and eliminates the possibility of teaching skills in isolation from reading.

The system can be diagrammed in the following way:

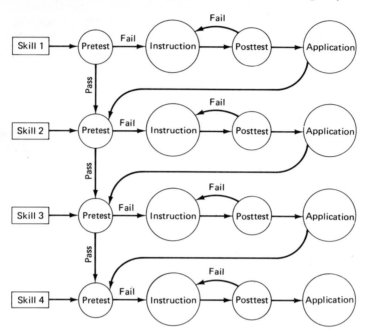

As can be seen, a learner proceeds through the skills hierarchy in a sequential fashion, from the simplest to the most complex. The structure is systematic; the pretest for each skill insures that instructional time is spent only on what needs to be mastered, instruction for each skill is direct and specific, the posttest insures that no student moves from one skill to another until the prerequisite has been mastered, and application activities insure that the skill will be used. Utilization of this pretest–teach–posttest–apply cycle of skill teaching insures that each child receives the basic instruction needed to become functionally literate.

This strategy has a number of advantages. First, and most important, it is precise, telling the teacher exactly where each child's skill instruction should begin. Second, it is systematic, insuring that no child will be moved into higher level skills until demonstrating mastery of previous skills. Finally, it is efficient in that it only requires children to work on those skills for which they have demonstrated a need.

SUMMARY OF DIAGNOSING SKILL STRENGTHS AND NEEDS

This chapter provides you with three techniques for diagnosing skill needs. They range from the general to the specific, and they should be employed in the classroom in that order to help you obtain a complete picture of a child's skills.

The first two techniques utilize data which you obtain by using graded oral reading paragraphs to determine instructional reading levels, as described in Chapter 9. In the process of listening to children read orally, you will note errors of word identification and comprehension. Using these data and by noting where most errors are made, you can determine first whether the child is stronger in word identification or in comprehension. Second, you can determine which type of skill the child seems to rely upon within word identification and comprehension by noting the types and patterns of errors made in oral reading.

With the information you have gleaned from the above two techniques, you already have a pretty good idea of the child's strengths and needs. You then use the pretest–teach–posttest–apply system to determine precisely which skill in the hierarchy must be taught first. You will then be able to plan instruction which is immediately relevant and helpful to that child.

TEST YOUR KNOWLEDGE

1. In terms of reading instruction, pupils are likely to differ in terms of the rates at which they will learn to read, the difficulty levels of the book they will read, and the _____ they will need to learn.
2. If a child reads several graded oral reading paragraphs and makes no errors of word recognition while making several errors of comprehension, we can assume that the area of difficulty is _____.
3. If, when reading graded oral reading paragraphs, a child makes little or no effort to analyze words not known, we can assume that the child is relying upon _____.
4. If a child hesitates significantly before many words and laboriously sounds them out, we can assume that the child is relying primarily on word analysis and should receive instruction in _____ or _____.
5. When examining graded oral reading paragraph data to determine the types and patterns of errors a child is making, you should use the errors made at the child's _____ reading level.
6. Determination of the general type of comprehension skills a child needs requires that the teacher ask different types of _____.
7. Systematic and precise diagnosis of skill needs requires that you first have available a _____ of the skills in the hierarchy.
8. In systematic skill diagnosis, there should be a _____ and a _____ for every skill objective.
9. The steps in a systematic skill diagnosis are (1) pretest, (2) teach, (3) _____, and (4) apply.
10. If a child passes a pretest, the next step would be to _____.

SIMULATION ACTIVITIES

Imagine that you are teaching a third grade. Ralph, one of your students, read the following graded oral reading paragraphs and made the errors noted.

Muff is a | little yellow kitten.

She drinks milk.

ch–ch p
She sleeps on a | chair.

She does not like to get wet.

___+___	1. What color was the kitten?
___+___	2. What does she drink?
no response	3. Where does she sleep?
___+___	4. Why doesn't Muff like to go out on rainy days?

A little black dog ran away from home. He played with two big dogs.

run c   *be–gan*
They ran away from him. It began to rain. He went under a tree.

He wanted to go home, but he did not know the way. He saw a

boy he | knew. The boy took him home.

___+___	1. Who ran away from home?
three	2. How many other dogs did he play with?
___+___	3. Why did the dog go under the tree?
to play	4. What did the dog want then?
a friend	5. Whom did he see?
___+___	6. How did he get home?

tee–nt c si·dē
Six boys put up a tent by the side of the | river. They took things to

eat with them. When the sun went down, they went into the tent to

cam c
sleep. In the | night, a cow came and began to eat grass around the

tent. The boys were | afraid. They thought it was a bear.

three	1. How many boys went camping?
woods	2. Where did they put up their tent?
___+___	3. What did they take with them besides their tent?
___+___	4. What did the boys do when the sun went down?
bear	5. What came around their tent in the night?
no response	6. What was the cow doing?
cow	7. What did the boys think the cow was?

1. What is Ralph's probable area of skill difficulty?

Mary, another student in your third grade, read the following graded oral reading paragraph and made the errors noted.

Six boys put up a | tĕnt by the side of the | rĭver. They took | things to | ĕat with them. When the sun went down, they went into the | tĕnt to | slĕep. In the | nĭght, a cow came and began to eat | grăss around the | tent. The boys were | ăfraid. They | thoŭght it was a bear.

2. In identifying words, is Mary relying primarily on sight-word skills, phonetic analysis, or context?

Sam is also in your third grade. The results of a graded oral reading paragraph test indicate that he is reading well above grade level and that he has no problem in identifying the words on the printed page. However, you had him read the following paragraph: [3]

The richest diamond field in the world is in South Africa. Deep pits yield a hard substance called "blue ground" which contains the diamonds. The blue ground is spread over the drying fields for a year. The weather gradually crumbles it. Then it is taken up and run through washing machines which sort out the stones and the diamonds. The value of the diamonds is determined by color, size, and purity. Blue, yellow, orange, brown and green diamonds have been discovered. The most valuable ones are pure white. The largest diamond ever found weighed almost two pounds.

When he finished, Sam could not answer questions such as:

What does it mean when it says that the deep pits *yield* a hard substance?

If I give you a dirt clod, what would you be doing if you *crumble* it?

3. Sam is probably having a comprehension difficulty. However, what type of comprehension skill is he having difficulty with?

In working with Rodney, another pupil in your third grade, you noted the following errors in word identification on the first grade paragraph, although he made no errors in comprehension.

[3] Durrell, op. cit.

Muff | is a little | yellow | kitten.

d-d-d p
She drinks milk.

ch-ch p
She sleeps | on a | chair.

She | does not | like | to get wet.

4. What skill of word identification is Rodney probably relying upon?

5. When you begin your systematic skill diagnosis, do you expect that Rodney will first encounter difficulty with the pretests in word identification or the pretests in comprehension?

6. If he has difficulty with the pretests in word identification, do you suppose his earliest difficulty will be in the skills of visual training and sight-words or the skills of word analysis?

The following is a series of three pretests which you administered to Rodney. The items he did incorrectly are checked.

A. THE PERFORMANCE OBJECTIVE   Given three letters that are exactly alike and one that is somewhat similar, the learner marks the one that is different.

THE PRE-TEST   Direct the learners to indicate (mark or point to as appropriate) which letter in each of the following sets is different. Criterion for mastery is 80 percent.

SET I	l	l	i	l	SET VI	t	l	t	t
SET II	o	o	o	c	SET VII	e	e	e	a
SET III	y	y	g	y	SET VIII	q	p	q	q
SET IV	d	b	d	d	✓SET IX	n	m	n	n
SET V	u	u	u	v	SET X	w	w	m	w

B. THE PERFORMANCE OBJECTIVE   Given a few seconds to examine a letter that is easily confused with other letters, the learner reproduces the letter from memory, to the satisfaction of the teacher.

THE PRETEST   Prepare ten flashcards, each card having one of the following letters printed on it.

g   a   m   v   b   o   p   h   w̌   i

Flash each for the count of three. Then direct the learner to reproduce it. Criterion for mastery is teacher judgment.

C. THE PERFORMANCE OBJECTIVE   Given three words that are exactly alike and one word that is somewhat similar, the learner marks the word that is different.

THE PRE-TEST   Direct the learner to indicate (mark or point to as appropriate) which word in each of the following sets is different. Criterion for mastery is 80 percent.

SET I	dog/dog/cat/dog	✓SET VI	look/book/look/look
SET II	girl/boy/girl/girl	SET VII	like/lake/lake/lake
SET III	to/to/to/on	✓SET VIII	box/dox/box/box
✓SET IV	ten/ten/net/ten	✓SET IX	chair/chair/chain/chair
SET V	fox/box/box/box	SET X	saw/was/was/was

7. On the basis of these pretest data, where should Rodney's skill instruction begin?

8. On the basis of these data, what would be your next step in working with Rodney?

9. After completing your instruction, you will want to give Rodney a posttest to insure that your instruction was successful, that he can now perform the task satisfactorily. Because he might remember specific items from having completed them before, you would not want to use the pretest for this purpose. Create some new items which could be used as a posttest for this skill.

SUGGESTED FIELD EXPERIENCES

Observation. When observing in schools you should note differences in reading skills among the pupils and you should note the degree to which the teacher employs one or more of the three techniques described in this chapter to precisely determine each child's skill strengths and needs.

Teaching activities. When working with children in classroom settings, you should be able to use graded oral reading paragraphs to determine the general area of skill deficiency and the type and pattern of error, and you should be able to use a list of reading skills with accompanying pretests to determine precisely where each child's instruction in reading skills should begin.

Client impact. By systematically diagnosing each child's skill needs and strengths, you are insuring that your pupils will receive instruction which is relevant to their stage of reading growth, which gives them a fair chance of achieving success, and which will have an immediate payoff for them as beginning readers.

FOR CLASS DISCUSSION

Skills alone are not enough. If students learn the skills in isolation, without applying them to real reading situations, we have gained nothing. Some students may pass a pretest for a skill and yet not be able to read efficiently because they do not apply the skill to the ultimate task of reading. Discuss how you can avoid "isolated" skill instruction.

ANSWER KEY
1. skills
2. comprehension
3. sight-word recognition
4. sight word recognition, context
5. instructional
6. questions
7. list
8. pretest, posttest
9. posttest
10. pretest the next skill

BUILDING INTEREST AND MOTIVATION

OVERVIEW

This chapter helps you assess your pupils' interest in reading and provides you with strategies for motivating reading instruction. The ultimate objective is:

Given a group of elementary school children, you can assess their interests and use this information to create a motivation for reading.

KNOWLEDGE BACKGROUND

There are many aspects to reading assessment. Most of these are process oriented in the sense that they reflect the reading act itself. For instance, in previous chapters you have learned how to assess pupils in terms of their rates of reading growth, their instructional reading levels, and their reading skill needs.

While such diagnosis is crucial, it is not all there is. Assessment must also reflect the affective dimension of reading. This dimension—usually described in terms of the pupil's interest and motivation toward reading—can often mean the difference between a child who reads and a child who does not. It is not unusual, for instance, to encounter a child who *knows* how to read but who just doesn't want to. Such pupils need teachers who understand the affective dimension of teaching reading—

teachers who can assess interests and who can build in children a motivation to read.

HOW DO YOU DETERMINE INTERESTS AND MOTIVATION?

Assessment data regarding a child's current interests and his or her attitude toward reading can be collected in two ways: by direct observation and through the use of questionnaires.

DIRECT OBSERVATION

Much can be determined about your learners simply by observing their behaviors. What kinds of things do they talk about with you? With their friends? What do they do when they are given free time in class? What do they do on the playground? What do they say they want to do when they get home from school? The data from all such observations can provide you with valuable clues about your children's interests.

Similarly, direct observation can help you determine the children's attitudes toward school generally and toward reading in particular. Certainly, the child who responds happily to suggestions and directions from the teacher is more interested than the child who constantly disrupts classroom activities, who frequently ends up being disciplined, and who generally causes the teacher difficulty. This assessment technique, while being obvious, is nevertheless a primary source of data regarding attitudes.

Similarly, such daily observation can help you assess the children's feelings about reading. How do they act when you say it is time for reading? How often do you see each of them reading a book? When they are given time to read a book of their choice, how absorbed do they become? Do they look for opportunities to read on their own? Do they ever make positive comments about their recreational reading? Whether a child is content or bored when reading is easily observed and provides valid information about his or her feelings toward reading.

The only difficulty with the direct observation technique for determining interests is its lack of efficiency. Teachers who have twenty-five pupils often find that "mental notes" regarding a child's interests are forgotten or confused with observations of another child. Consequently, it is often helpful to employ a systematic, rather than a haphazard, means for observing pupils. An example of such a technique would be a tally sheet such as that on the following page.

As can be seen, the teacher lists across the top the typical behaviors which provide insight into interest toward reading and simply puts a tally mark in the appropriate space whenever a positive or negative feeling about reading is observed. While no attempt is made to tally *every* positive and negative behavior, such a device does help the teacher systematize observations.

	Does read books	Does not read when told he/she can	Responds *positively* when told he/she can read	Responds negatively when told he/she can read	Finds a book and settles down with it during library period	Needs direct help in settling down during library period
Mary	|||		卌		|||	
Sue			|||		卌		||
John	||	||||		||	||	
Tony	卌 |||		||		||||	
Frank	||||		||||			
Jessie	|||	|||		卌 ||	||	|||
Jeff	卌 ||		|||		卌 |||	
Oscar	||	||			|||	||	||

Similarly, many good teachers make anecdotal notations during the school day regarding various pupils. These notations describe, as objectively as possible, the teacher's observation of a child's behavior. Because the notations take time, you would normally use this technique only with a few pupils at a time. For instance, if you had a pupil who frequently seemed to be "down" on him- or herself, you might write an anecdote describing the behavior and the circumstances each time it is noted. In this way, you might detect a pattern in the specific activities which seem to trigger the feelings of inadequacy and, therefore, be in a better position to help.

In any case, whether you do it informally or attempt to systematize it, direct observation of a child's behavior can provide valuable insights into that child's interest in reading.

QUESTIONNAIRES

The direct observation techniques described above provide interest and attitude data from the viewpoint of the teacher. Questionnaires, however, solicit the pupil's feelings as *he or she* sees them and are, therefore, particularly relevant data sources.

Several kinds of questionnaires can be used, but they all should have one characteristic in common: they should be easy and quick to complete. Complicated questionnaires frequently confuse and/or discourage the pupil and result in inaccurate information.

A typical type of questionnaire involves sentence completion. The children are given a sheet of paper containing sentence fragments such as the following and either write the answers themselves or dictate the answers to the teacher if they are not yet able to write fluently.

1. My idea of a good time is _____.
2. When I have to read, I _____.
3. I hope I'll _____.
4. I like to read when _____.
5. In reading, I wish someone would help me to _____.
6. I'd rather read than _____.

A similar device is the questionnaire which makes a statement and asks pupils to indicate whether they feel the statement is true or false about themselves. Examples might include:

_____ I get nervous whenever reading class begins.
_____ The teacher knows what I need to learn about reading.
_____ If I didn't have to, I would never read.
_____ The things we read about in school are important.
_____ I wish I had more time to read what I want to in school.
_____ I feel successful during reading class.

Questionnaires such as these provide valuable insights about the child's self-concept as it relates to reading. When combined with data gathered from direct teacher observation, a valid picture emerges and you can make judgments regarding the child's interests in and attitude toward reading.

HOW DO YOU BUILD INTEREST AND MOTIVATION?

Assessment of interests and attitudes is just the beginning. The teacher's true test begins after the data have been gathered. What do you do when your assessment indicates that the child hates reading? What do you do if the child dislikes school generally? What do you do if the child knows how to read but just doesn't want to? In other words, how does a teacher *create* a positive attitude toward reading when none exists? How does a teacher build motivation toward reading? How does a positive motivation toward reading build interest?

The time-honored technique is to explain how crucial reading is for success in society—that one cannot get a good job, obtain a driver's license, or even pay taxes without being able to read. All this is true, but, unfortunately, it has little impact on the elementary-school child. It is an unusual pupil who is "turned on" by the teacher's stern admonition that "it will help you when you grow up." "Growing up" is both too abstract a concept and too far in the future to seriously influence a child's current attitude, and this is, consequently, almost useless as a technique for creating motivation which should lead to an interest in reading.

There are, however, three techniques which, when applied together, consistently result in increased motivation and interest. These include the concepts of success as a motivator, materials selection, and immediate usefulness of the activity.

SUCCESS AS A MOTIVATOR

As a rule, human beings want to do those things they can do well and don't want to do those things they have persistent difficulty with. Look at yourself. List the things you like to do and the things you don't like to do. The chances are that you're pretty good at doing all the things you like to do, that you've had success doing these things. Similarly, you're probably not as good at the things you don't like to do; you've probably experienced failure in doing these things. In other words, we're motivated to do what we do well but we evidence a "bad" attitude toward those things we do less well. This is natural since no one enjoys failure.

Just as it is natural in our lives, it is also natural for our pupils. Children will want to do those school activities they do well and will resist those where they fail. Look at reading as an example. Children who say they like reading are always the ones who are good readers, just as those who like math are good mathematicians and those who like gym class are good athletes. Similarly, look at the children who consistently get into trouble in reading class. Almost always they are the children who cannot read and who, in attempting to escape the failure they are encountering, resort to disruptive behavior in the hope that they will be sent from the room (and away from reading class). In the meantime, while the poor readers are making trouble, the good readers are reading and acting thoroughly motivated.

How does a teacher use the concept of success to motivate? It cannot be done by making all pupils successful to the same degree since we have already seen that such regimentation is impossible. Rather, the answer lies in assigning each child reading tasks which are consistent with ability, while constantly showing the child the progress he or she is making. This dual strategy works because (1) the child is able to do the task and the frustration which accompanies failure is eliminated, and (2) the child sees that, while perhaps behind, he or she is making consistent progress and will not be at a low level forever. In brief, this strategy gives the child dignity and hope, the dignity which comes from being able to perform a task capably rather than looking like a fool and the hope that comes from knowing that the goal is achievable.

Slow readers will always be with us and they will always be the hardest pupils to motivate. However, they can be kept from becoming severe behavior problems. They only need to see that they are able to do the task and that they are making steady progress. With such success as a basis, the pupil has a foundation for building positive motivations and therefore a positive attitude toward reading. When this success is denied, however, the same pupil will exhibit avoidance behaviors and resist attempts to motivate.

MATERIALS SELECTION

The success principle creates a positive self-concept for the child—he or she feels able to learn. The next step in motivating is to have the student read materials that are of interest.

Traditionally, children are required to read material selected by the teacher. This material may or may not be to the child's liking and, consequently, may or may not motivate. In fact, all too often, the material selected by the teacher is irrelevant for certain children and creates a negative, rather than a positive, attitude toward reading.

The heart of this principle lies in the concept of content validity. Some books have content which is valid for Mary, while other books have content which is not valid because they do not capitalize on Mary's experiences and inclinations. Further, a book valid for Mary may *not* be valid for Johnny, who has different experiences and different inclinations.

The teacher can use this principle in two ways: first, to assess the preferences of the pupils and, whenever possible, assign reading material that matches preferences, and second, to allow a high degree of pupil self-selection of reading material. Obviously, when children pick out reading material that they enjoy, they will be more motivated than when forced to read something they don't care about.

This principle is operationalized in several ways. First, recreational reading should be an integral part of a good reading program, and the materials read should be self-selected to capitalize on individual preferences (see Chapter 24). Second, children can be allowed to choose the stories they will read in their basic reading books, thereby insuring that the stories read will be of personal interest (see Chapter 23). Finally, subject areas such as social studies can be organized so that each unit of study is broken down into subtopics, with children reading material related to the subtopic which most interests them and sharing their findings with the rest of the class (see Chapters 26 and 27). In each case, the teacher attempts to create motivation by matching the material to be read with the preferences of the child.

While materials selection is a powerful motivating strategy, two cautions must be observed. First, while it would be ideal to read only that which is of interest, reality requires that this principle be applied flexibly in those situations where it is practical. You must remember that sometimes it is necessary to assign uninteresting reading material but that this should be done *only* when necessary, matching each child to a piece of interesting material whenever possible.

The second caution is a reminder to use the principle of materials selection together with the success principle. Often teachers say, "If only I could get Sam a book that interests him, he'd learn how to read." Such a statement is naive unless the principle of success is also considered. For instance, if you have a 10-year-old boy who is interested in sports and is reading at a first grade level, you cannot expect him to automatically achieve success simply because you give him a book about Henry Aaron. If the book is written at a first grade level or even at a second grade level, your strategy will probably be effective—he will be able to read the book and will be motivated. If the book is written at fourth or fifth grade level, however, all the interest in the world is not going to help him—he will be unable to read the book, will be frustrated because he can't and will exhibit definite signs of being unmotivated.

IMMEDIATE USEFULNESS

The third strategy for building motivation for reading calls for giving the child reading tasks that result in an immediate payoff—by doing the reading, the child should be able to do something of importance which he or she previously was unable to do. This is the principle of making the reading rewarding and should be used in conjunction with the previous two: The reading task should be useful, it should also be something the student is capable of achieving successfully, and the material should, wherever possible, be something which matches personal preferences.

This principle of usefulness can be operationalized on two levels— the extrinsic and the intrinsic. If the reading is of use because the teacher offers a tangible reward when the task is completed, such as an apple or a token that buys a toy at the end of the week, it is extrinsic. If the reading is of use because it helps the child solve a problem which is important to that child, such as reading the directions for building a model airplane, it is intrinsic.

While both can be used effectively to motivate reading, the intrinsic devices are preferred; extrinsic motivation is reserved for use in special situations. For instance, if you have a pupil who has been frustrated in school for several years and who has developed elaborate defense mechanisms to avoid the reading instruction which is the cause of this frustration, you have a pupil who will not normally be immediately receptive to intrinsic motivation. Instead, you may have to use tangible rewards to create a reward system for that pupil; you make reading rewarding not through the reading itself but because the completion of the reading task can "buy" a desired reward such as candy or money. You then proceed to gradually modify this behavior in reading, steadily replacing the extrinsic rewards with intrinsic ones.

While extrinsic reward systems do work with children who exhibit a severe lack of motivation, intrinsic rewards are better for general use because they are more closely associated with reading itself. When a child does a reading task for an extrinsic reward, the reading is simply something to be gotten through in order to reap the reward; the child does not really see reading itself in a more favorable light and is not motivated to read as much as to get the reward. Intrinsic rewards, however, reflect the reading act itself, and, as a result, the child sees reading as an enjoyable or useful activity in itself.

There are many ways to create situations which motivate intrinsically. A particularly fruitful strategy, however, is to create problems which children see as viable and which can be solved only through reading. For instance, having children bake cookies or build a generator or play a board game or keep classroom animals alive are all viable problems and require that children be able to read directions to solve the problem. Reading becomes an act to be valued because it helps solve real problems, and motivation results.

Another strategy is to make reading useful by associating it with acts which give the child status or credibility in the child's world. For instance, having a third grade child read a story in preparation for presenting it to the kindergarten class is a real-life situation of this kind. A similar example would be situations in which the teacher invites local celebrities or dignitaries to visit the classroom and has the pupils read about the visitor's field before the visit as a means for asking appropriate questions. Various classroom projects involving the pupils, such as field trips, outdoor educational outings, and classroom exchanges can all be structured to include prior reading which the child can then use fruitfully in the culminating project.

The basic concept of the reward principle of motivation is that the individual child view reading as having some use which is relevant to that child and his or her needs. Few children enjoy reading simply because the teacher wants them to, and motivation does not result from the artificial attempts at relevancy commonly found in the teachers' guides of textbooks. Rather, the need must be appropriate to the particular child and the particular situation.

SUMMARY OF BUILDING INTEREST AND MOTIVATION

Learning to read, like all other learning, is closely tied to the learner's interest and motivation for reading. If the child is interested and motivated, he or she will learn more and learn it faster than if uninterested and unmotivated. The key to creating motivation is accurate assessment of interests and the use of strategies appropriate for motivating children. There are many good "adult" reasons for learning to read, but these are of little relevance to children. Consequently, you must use the three motivating strategies children respond to. First, children want to view themselves as successful and will tend to do those things in which they are making tangible progress, so use success as a motivator. Second, children have some things that they enjoy more than others and prefer to do those things, so match a child's reading material to the child's personal preferences. Finally, children prefer to do things which have tangible use in their lives, either because those things are enjoyable or because they help the children do something relevant to their needs and their lives, so make reading a useful activity rather than a teacher-dominated "assignment." Implementation of these three strategies will result in creating positive motivation and increased interest.

TEST YOUR KNOWLEDGE

1. Assessment data for children's interest can be collected by
   _____ and _____.
2. A systematic way to record children's interest is by using a
   _____.
3. Anecdotal records should be used with _____ children at one time.
4. Questionnaires solicit data according to how the _____ feels.
5. The three techniques to increase motivation are:
   a. _____
   b. _____
   c. _____
6. Children will choose activities where they are _____ and avoid those where they _____.
7. The dual strategy of assigning reading tasks that are consistent with ability and of keeping records of progress are successful with learners because it gives them _____ and _____.
8. Children should be allowed a high degree of _____ of reading materials.
9. Two types of rewards are _____ and _____.
10. Reading to younger children is useful because it builds a child's
    _____.

SIMULATION ACTIVITIES

Fred and Dana are both fifth graders in a suburban school. Fred is reading at an instructional level of beginning third grade, while Dana is reading at an instructional level of beginning fourth grade.

The following behaviors have been noticed about Fred: He rarely initiates conversation with teachers. To his friends, he talks about hockey and how good he is. In his free time he has a tendency to wander and talk but will settle down when told to work with any activity related to sports. At home he is very much involved in street hockey, ice hockey, and most other sports. The only positive comment that he has made about reading was when he was given a book on Bobby Hull that had lots of pictures. He said, "I can read about Bobby Hull."

The following behaviors have been noticed about Dana: He constantly wants to talk to the teacher about almost anything. He loves animals, goes many places with his family, and wants to tell everyone about it, especially the teacher. In his free time he reads, plays games, and helps the teacher. He participates in most activities on the playground and runs an animal hospital at home for neighborhood injuries. Dana has a tendency to respond positively to any book the teacher offers him.

The following chart contains information that was recorded during school time:

	Does read books	Does not read when told he can	Responds positively when told he can read	Responds negatively when told he can read	Finds a book and settles down with it during library period	Needs direct help in settling down during library period
Fred	‖	卌 ‖		卌	‖	卌
Dana	卌 卌	‖	卌 ‖	‖	卌 ‖	

The following questionnaire was given to Dana and Fred:

INTEREST QUESTIONNAIRE FOR DANA

DIRECTIONS "I'm going to begin some sentences for you. I want you to finish each sentence with the first idea that comes to your mind."

1. My idea of a good time is ___riding a horse___.

2. When I have to read, ___I love it___.

3. I wish my parents knew ___I wanted my own dog___.

4. I can't understand why ___we have contracts___.

5. I feel bad when ___the teacher yells at me___.

6. I wish teachers *would keep their mouths shut*.

7. I wish my mother *is never a grouch*.

8. Going to college *is fun*.

9. People think I *am guilty and dog crazy*.

10. I like to read about *dogs and horses*.

11. To me, homework *is terrible*.

12. I hope I'll never *die*.

13. I wish people wouldn't *blame me for everything*.

14. When I finish high school I'll *go to college*.

15. When I take my report card home *I burn it*.

16. Most brothers and sisters *make me sick*.

17. I'd rather read than *do math*.

18. I feel proud when *my dog behaves*.

19. When I read arithmetic problems I *get a headache*.

20. I wish my father *would give me twenty dollars*.

21. I like to read when *I can sit in a bean bag chair*.

22. I would like to be *a doctor or a dog trainer*.

23. I often worry about *math*.

24. Reading science *is learning*.

25. I wish someone would help me *being a dog trainer*.

● 129

INTEREST QUESTIONNAIRE FOR FRED

DIRECTIONS   "I am going to begin some sentences for you. I want you to finish each sentence with the first idea that comes to your mind."

1. My idea of a good time is ___*hockey*___ .

2. When I have to read, I ___*hate it*___ .

3. I wish my parents knew ___*had*___ .

4. I can't understand why ___*I'm so stupid*___ .

5. I feel bad when ___*I'm caught*___ .

6. I wish teachers ___*were dead*___ .

7. I wish my mother ___*was rich*___ .

8. Going to college ___*is fun*___ .

9. People think I ___*am good*___ .

10. I like to read about ___*fun stories*___ .

11. To me, homework ___*is dumb*___ .

12. I hope I'll never ___*die*___ .

13. I wish people wouldn't ___*bother me*___ .

14. When I finish high school ___*I'll go to college*___ .

15. When I take my report card home ___*I go to the barn*___ .

16. Most brothers and sisters ___*bug me*___ .

17. I'd rather read than ___*kill*___ .

18. I feel proud when ___*I win my hockey game*___ .

130 ●

19. When I read arithmetic problems I *need Alka Seltzer*.

20. I wish my father _____ *would ski* _____.

21. I like to read when _____ *I'm dead* _____.

22. I would like to be _____ *a hockey player* _____.

23. I often worry about _____ *myself* _____.

24. Reading science _____ *is dumb* _____.

25. I wish someone would help me _____ *read* _____.

Based on all this information about Fred and Dana, decide how you would use their interests to build motivation for each of them by (1) using success, (2) by selecting reading materials, and (3) by assigning reading tasks that provide immediate payoff.

SUGGESTED FIELD EXPERIENCES

Observation. When observing in schools, you should note the different ways a teacher collects data on interests. What principles do you see in effect for motivation? Is success used as a motivator? Are materials geared for each student's ability and interests? Does the teacher show usefulness of reading tasks for application?

Teaching activities. When working with children in classroom settings, you should be able to gather data on interests and then motivate children using strategies based on that assessment.

Client impact. By assessing each child's interests and creating strategies that motivate, you are insuring that the affective domain of reading instruction is being accounted for.

FOR CLASS DISCUSSION

There is an element of American society that takes a "hard-nosed" position about children and their schooling. This element tends to view motivation strategies such as success, interest, and usefulness as "being soft on kids." They take the view that children should do their schoolwork out of respect for the teacher and that forcing the child to do work that is too difficult is "good discipline." What is your position on this view of motivation?

ANSWER KEY
1. direct observation, questionnaires
2. tally sheet
3. only a few
4. student
5. a. success as a motivator
   b. materials selection
   c. immediate usefulness of activity
6. successful, fail
7. hope, dignity
8. self-selection
9. intrinsic, extrinsic
10. credibility or status

SUGGESTED ADDITIONAL READINGS FOR SECTION THREE– THE CHILD AND READING

BEREITER, CARL. "The Future of Individual Differences." *Environment, Heredity and Intelligence.* Cambridge, Mass.: Harvard Education Review, Reprint Series 2, 1969.

DINKMEYER, DON, AND DREIKURS, RUDOLPH. *Encouraging Children to Learn: The Encouragement Process.* Englewood Cliffs, N.J.: Prentice-Hall, 1963.

DURKIN, DELORES. "When Should Chlidren Begin to Read?" *Innovation and Change in Reading Instruction,* Sixty-seventh Yearbook of the National Society for the Study of Education. Chicago: University of Chicago Press, 1968.

EKWALL, ELDON E., (ED.). *Psychological Factors in the Teaching of Reading.* Columbus, Ohio: Merrill, 1973.

FARR, ROGER. *Reading: What Can Be Measured?* International Reading Association Research Fund, 1969.

KIRK, SAMUEL A., AND BATEMAN, BARBARA. "Diagnosis and Remediation of Learning Disabilities." *Exceptional Children* 29, October 1962, pp. 73–78.

LINDVALL, C. M., AND COX, R. C. "The Role of Evaluation in Programs for Individualized Instruction." *Educational Evaluation: New Roles, New Means.* Sixty-eighth Yearbook of the National Society for the Study of Education. Chicago: University of Chicago Press, 1969.

ROSENTHAL, R., AND JACOBSEN, L. *Pygmalion in the Classroom.* New York: Holt, Rinehart & Winston, 1968.

———. "Teacher Expectations for the Disadvantaged." *Scientific American* 218.3, April 1968.

FOUR
MANAGING INSTRUCTION

ORGANIZING
FOR
INDIVIDUALIZED
INSTRUCTION

OVERVIEW

This chapter provides you with the basic principles for managing individualized instruction in reading. The ultimate objective is:

Given the responsibility for reading instruction in an elementary classroom, you will organize your classroom to insure efficient management of individualized instruction.

KNOWLEDGE BACKGROUND

Individualization is an integral part of effective reading instruction since no group of children will all need simultaneous instruction at a particular instructional level or in a particular skill. On any pretest, for instance, some children will fail and some will pass, and you will, consequently, be teaching some children at the very low levels and others at higher levels. How to organize and manage instruction in which different children receive different instruction on different skills is a major problem.

The need for specific, sophisticated, and workable skills in classroom organization and management is based on several teaching realities. First, the most common school structure is the self-contained classroom. This means that the typical teacher is totally responsible for the reading instruction that the students receive. Second, the spread of achievement differences at any given grade level forces the teacher into multilevel and multiskill grouping. This in turn suggests that, during the formal reading period, the instructor will be in direct contact with and have instructional control over only a small number of the class members at any one time. Third, instructional success will depend in large measure on the teacher's ability to concentrate on those children who are receiving direct instruction. This means that, at any given moment, the majority of the class must be working successfully without instructional intervention or attention, thus the need for a workable management and organization system.

Teaching is as much an art as a science, but management is one area that requires a particularly high degree of artfulness. There is no sure-fire formula for ensuring successful management; much depends upon the teacher's sensitivity, common sense, and diligence. However, the following six principles can be identified as guidelines in establishing a system of grouping.

INDEPENDENT ACTIVITIES

The solution to the problem of what to do with the children who are not in the group you are currently teaching lies in providing independent activities. While you are teaching the group, the rest of the children can be actively involved in work which they complete by themselves. Such independent work usually relates to ongoing projects in the classroom and can include recreational reading, independent reading of basal textbooks, pursuit of social studies assignments, completion of science experiments, practice on previously taught reading and math skills, work on art projects, handwriting practice, creative writing, and any other class-related activity which learners can complete on their own.

To make independent activities work, however, the teacher must meet four conditions: planning, gearing to ability level, giving directions, and achieving relevancy.

Individualized instruction is difficult because the planning load is doubled. Not only must the group lessons be planned but so must the independent activities. Suppose, for example, you have three skill groups and wish to give each group 20 minutes of direct instruction. Your planning grid would look like this:

Time:	9:00	9:20	9:40	10:00
Group A	X			
B		X		
C			X	

Each X indicates your presence with that group. Your teaching plans for this hour would include a minimum of three or a maximum of nine subplans. Each plan would include specific objectives, materials and evaluation procedures. Despite the added work, however, such planning is an essential ingredient of success. With careful planning, the children not receiving group instruction will be meaningfully occupied for the duration, but careless planning results in frequent interruptions of group lessons by learners who are confused about their independent work.

The second condition requires that the independent activities be geared to each child's ability level. Assigning independent reading of a fourth grade social studies book would be inappropriate for the child with a second grade reading level; if the student is unable to complete the work alone, the purpose will be defeated. Independent work must be individualized just as skill work is individualized since there are few tasks which all the children will be equipped to handle.

When planning is complete, you must give children directions on their independent activities. Directions may be given in writing or orally, but however they are given, they must be totally understood by the class; each learner must know what is expected and must be able to determine when the task has been accomplished. Given inadequate directions, some learners will decide that they have finished after only a few minutes, and, with time on their hands, they will disrupt the class—particularly the group which is working with you. Consequently, successful management requires thorough direction giving.

The final condition—relevancy—describes that condition which is the opposite of "busy work." When you plan, you must create independent work that is not just "so many problems" or "fill in the blanks." Such busy work invariably *creates* disruptive behaviors in children. Whatever the independent work, it must have a motivating relevancy for the child. If it does not, it will not hold attention and will create a double failure; the child will not only leave the meaningless work undone but will disrupt you as you work with the skill group. Independent work is relevant when the learner knows why it is important or that it will be used in some important way. For instance, some teachers achieve relevancy by sending independent material home regularly for parental inspection. In any case, successful management depends upon each learner's having independent work which he or she considers worthwhile.

SAFETY VALVES

The first step in individualizing is creating independent activities for learners to pursue while you are teaching small groups. However, children being children, we know that they will not all finish their independent work at the same time. Some will get done before you have finished teaching your groups, and, if you have not anticipated this, disruptive activities may result. Consequently, you should plan safety valve activities which children can fall back on when they finish their independent work.

Such safety valves usually take the form of learnii
activities which children can participate in at any time. 'i
ferent from independent activities because they do not c.

they are not always associated with the ongoing academic work in the classroom, and they tend to be viewed as fun. For instance, appropriate safety valves would include a recreational reading corner, listening centers, vocabulary and math games, purely recreational games such as checkers and chess, art centers, a sandbox, a play house, or anything else learner could fall back on with little direction from the teacher.

An important criteria for safety valves is that the learner consider them rewarding. As such, two conditions should be present. First, there should be a variety of safety valves to insure that there will be something to interest everybody. Second, children should help create safety valves to insure that these activities reflect the group's particular interests. When these conditions are met, safety valves become an extremely effective management device. Without them, those slack times which occur in every classroom will be filled with disruption, and you will find yourself yelling and playing the dual role of traffic cop and disciplinarian, with all thoughts of your instructional plan lost in the noise.

PHYSICAL SETTING

The physical setting of the classroom is another crucial component. If the classroom is to simultaneously accommodate small-group skills teaching, independent activities, and learning centers containing safety valves, then the traditional arrangement of five rows with five children per row will not be appropriate. There simply will not be enough room because the rows of desks and chairs take up all the floor space.

One way to handle this kind of dilemma is to rearrange the furniture, pushing the children's desks together in clusters of four in the middle of the classroom. By so doing, you still have the desks where children can do independent activities, and you have also created new space around the edges of the classroom for a skills teaching corner and safety valve activities. Such a floor plan might look like this:

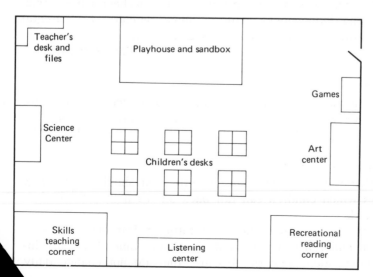

There are, of course, many ways to physically arrange the classroom. The only limitations are the particular dimensions of your room and the limits of your creativity in arranging within those dimensions. Some teachers, for instance, are very elaborate and use large refrigerator boxes, portable screens, old furniture, large floor pillows, and hanging screens as part of the physical setting. Others accomplish the same thing simply by moving furniture. For the purposes of individualization, either approach is suitable so long as there is room for independent activities, safety valves, and skills teaching.

TRAINING

Individualized instruction requires that children often work by themselves or in small groups on independent activities and safety valves while the teacher is, for all practical purposes, isolated from them in the skills teaching corner. If the children are unprepared for such independence, they will be unable to handle it, and the management system will collapse. Consequently, the teacher must orient the children to the system and train them to work independently.

This orientation and training should begin in September and continue until the children have adjusted. The time needed will vary from group to group; generally, the younger children who have not been exposed to any other kind of classroom organization will adjust very quickly, while older children who may be used to a more traditional system allowing little independent movement or action will sometimes require six weeks or more of training. The time is well spent, however, since it will insure the smooth operation of your reading program for the remainder of the year.

You should initiate the orientation and training with a full explanation of exactly how the reading program will operate. Then involve the class in the development of procedures and rules which will expedite management. You can clarify this process by setting up hypothetical situations, having the learners decide how they could be handled. For instance, you could pose questions such as:

1. What should we do if we have to move chairs around and someone is swinging a chair so carelessly as to hurt someone?
2. What should we do if you have to go to the bathroom or get a drink of water and the teacher is busy in the skills corner?
3. What should we do if two children want to use the listening center and there is only room for one at the moment?

To pose the right questions, you must anticipate what might go wrong, thereby preventing the problem before it occurs. Despite such forethought, however, you can expect additional unanticipated problems to arise during the year. This is natural, and you must resign yourself to resolving them as they occur.

Once anticipated problems have been identified and procedures established, you directly supervise the children as they try out independent activities and safety valves. By so doing, you are immediately available to develop appropriate independent behavior in the initial stages when the routines have not yet been established. As children adjust to the system, you can gradually move into skills teaching, perhaps teaching only a single skill group on the first day and spending the balance of the period supervising, moving to the teaching of two skill groups the next day, and so on, until eventually you spend the entire period teaching skill groups while the learners work entirely independently.

Some teachers insist that their particular students cannot work independently, that this system of organization and management might work for "good" children but it will not work for theirs. Our experience does not support this position. All children can work independently *if* the teacher is sensitive to the children, is committed to making the system work, and spends enough time in training.

While such orienting and training is sometimes frustrating and boring, it is nevertheless crucial to successful management of individualized teaching. Children cannot be expected to work independently just because we want them to. They must receive direct teacher assistance in *how* to work independently and in routinely handling the variety of problems that are likely to occur. Only then can you expect to create an efficient management system.

Additional assistance on orienting children to your classroom system of organization and management are detailed in Chapter 13.

BUFFER

Despite good planning, individualized instruction can fail for lack of a mechanism for handling unanticipated routine matters. Such situations will always develop when learners work independently. Your time, however, must be totally free to work with the small group. Consequently, you may create a buffer between you and the children working independently—a person who handles unanticipated situations while you remain free to teach the group. Minor problems ranging from assignment directions to toilet turns become the buffer's responsibility.

In addition to handling unanticipated situations, the buffer can also supervise practice activities, play learning games with children, listen to children read, insure that learners are applying previously learned skills in their reading, give pretests and posttests, assist with correcting papers and keeping records, and generally provide any needed kind of nonprofessional classroom assistance. The buffer should not teach, however, since this is a highly technical task requiring professional skill and training which most buffers do not possess.

Who is the buffer? It can be almost anyone the teacher can get. At the most desirable level, the buffer would be a trained paraprofessional or teacher's aide. At the next level, buffers could be chosen from among parents who have volunteered their time. The buffer could also be a high school student who is a member of the Future Teachers of America and who can, as such, be released from school to perform such duties. Another source is students from higher grades in the same school, such as a sixth grader who helps the third grade teacher for an hour a day. Finally, at the very lowest level, the buffer can be a student from your own classroom who has been trained to assist you.

No matter who performs the function, however, you must recognize that managing individualized instruction is a very difficult task, and, while it can be done without assistance, the problems are much fewer if you have help. The buffer can provide that help and will, therefore, make it much easier to achieve the goal of individualized instruction.

RECORD-KEEPING

Because of the multitude of skills to be taught and the individual differences in children, monitoring each child's progress is often a monumental task. It is essential, therefore, that you develop an efficient system for keeping records.

There are many ways to keep records efficiently. One that we have used with success consists of using a regular loose-leaf notebook and pages of quarter-inch graph paper. There are pages for each group (or cluster) of word recognition skills and for each group (or cluster) of comprehension skills. Along the left-hand side of the page, each pupil's name is recorded. Every quarter-inch square on the graph paper represents a single skill, notated by name and number at the bottom and top of that column of squares. As you pretest each child, simply put a slash (/) in the square to indicate a failure to pass the test, and color the square if the student passes the test. A sample page might look like the one shown in the illustration on page 144.

Keep the notebook in the skills teaching corner, and, by glancing at it, you will know immediately who must receive what skill instruction. For instance, starting from the first skill in the example, we see that Bert must be taught visual discrimination of geometric figures, that Sam and Mike can be grouped together for instruction in visual memory of geometric figures, that Susie and Andy need instruction in recognizing their names, that Tom and Anne are ready for a sequencing lesson on first and last letters, and that George has mastered all the skills in this particular cluster.

This is a good record-keeping device because it is not bulky or cumbersome; it requires little time or effort to mark test results, and it provides an immediate visual picture of where each child is in the skills sequence and how he or she can be grouped with other children for instruction. It is efficient for the task and is, therefore, a good tool. Further, however, it allows both you and the child to *see progress*. It is terribly debilitating to both teachers and pupils to wonder whether any-

Word Identification

Cluster 1A

	1	2	3	4	5	6	7
Sam							
Susie							
Tom							
George							
Mike							
Andy							
Anne							
Bert							

1– Visual memory—student's name

2– Sequencing—first and last letters

3– Visual discrimination—student's name

4– Naming—student's name

5– Naming—geometric figures

6– Visual memory—geometric figures

7– Visual discrimination—geometric figures

thing is being learned. Graphic records make this apparent and can act as strong motivating devices.

Of course, record-keeping devices need not look like this one. You can make modifications and elaborations to adjust yours to your particular needs, or you can devise a completely different system. Whatever the device, however, it must be manageable in size and easy to use, while providing a good visual picture of the skill instruction needed. With such a record-keeping device, implementation of individualized instruction is eased greatly.

SUMMARY OF ORGANIZING FOR INDIVIDUALIZED INSTRUCTION

To teach reading skills effectively, we must provide each learner with instruction at that child's particular level. As such, instruction must be individualized since it is virtually impossible for a single class, regardless of the level, to be populated by students who all require the same instruction at the same time.

Individualization traditionally fails because of lack of attention to the mundane details of implementation. Any individualized instruction is complex, with many different things going on at once, and it cannot be realized through a casual approach or with minimum effort. To the contrary, it requires a consistent expenditure of teacher effort and time, and, even then, it will not be perfect and will need constant adjusting. However, attention to the principles of independent activities, safety valves, physical setting, training, buffers, and record-keeping significantly eases the difficulty of the task.

TEST YOUR KNOWLEDGE

1. The crux of the classroom management problem is accounting for the students who are not under your direct _____ during individualized instruction.
2. A central feature of individualized instruction is that while you are working with a small skills group, the remaining children in the class are working _____.
3. A crucial aspect of independent activities is that they be geared to each child's _____ level.
4. Well-organized classrooms have _____ activities on which children can fall back when they have completed their independent work.
5. It is difficult to individualize instruction in a classroom where the furniture is arranged in five rows because there is not enough _____.
6. Children cannot be expected to automatically adjust to a classroom utilizing individualized instruction and independent activities. They must first go through a period of _____.
7. In training children to work independently, it is crucial that the daily _____ of the classroom be firmly established.
8. The buffer is a nonprofessional assistant and should not be given responsibility for _____.
9. The major criteria for a good record-keeping device is that it present a visual picture of the skill needs of the class and that it be _____ to use.
10. Efficient management is attained through attention to mundane _____.

SIMULATION ACTIVITIES

This activity is designed to help you use the principles of efficient classroom management described in this chapter. Read each selection and decide what principle of efficient management has been neglected in each and how the problems could have been avoided.

Assume that you are teaching a third grade class and have planned a reading lesson for Wednesday morning. According to your diagnosis, you need to teach Mary and Andy the sight words **just, off,** and **first;** you need to teach the **it, ot, et** phonogram skills to Bert, Sam, June, Mark, Alex, Sandy, and Ann; you need to teach the silent **e** vowel principle to Greg, Mike, John, and Patti. In addition, you want to work briefly and separately with Breck, Marty, and Sue on particular sight-words with which they are having difficulty. You estimate that this will require 65 minutes. You have planned your morning accordingly, and you begin your lesson. During the course of the reading period, you encounter the following situations:

You tell the class that you will be teaching skills to small groups back in the corner and that you want the children not involved in skill instruction to read pages 53–66 in the third grade social studies textbook and to answer the questions at the end of the chapter. You also tell the class that they may pursue the safety valves when they finish the social studies work. Then you take your first skills group back to the corner and begin teaching. After five minutes, you begin to notice that some children are becoming restless, are talking, fooling around, and generally creating a distraction. It finally gets so bad that you have to stop your skills teaching and discipline the class.

You return to teaching your skills group. All goes well for about eight minutes. Then, all of a sudden, there is a noisy disruption over by one of the safety valve activities. Again, you have to leave your skills group to quell the disturbance. Your investigation reveals that four children arrived simultaneously at a safety valve which could accommodate only two children at a time, and they were arguing over which two should use the activity.

You again return to your teaching. You are just getting started when George comes up to you and asks permission to go to the bathroom. You say yes and go back to teaching. Then Kathy comes up, says she forgot to give you her milk money, and wants to know what to do. You take care of this problem, resume teaching, and Candy comes up to you for a Band-Aid for a small paper cut. You minister to her, resume teaching, and Andrea comes to you with tears in her eyes, saying that Sam has been calling her bad names.

You finally finish with the first skills group. Miraculously (considering all the interruptions), both children seemed to do well, and you give them practice exercises to do at their seats. At 9:35 you go to your desk, rummage through the second drawer, and find the file folders in which you keep the children's record of progress. Then you locate Mary's folder, look through it until you find the appropriate page, and note that she has mastered the skill. You repeat the same procedure for Andy. Putting the folders back in the drawer, you look at your watch and note that it is 9:42. You say, "Where does all the time go?"

After getting the next skills group started (the seven children working with phonogram skills), you make a quick trip around the classroom. You note that Chris is sitting at his desk with the social studies book open but is doing nothing. You ask him what the trouble is, and he says, "I can't do the social studies because I don't know where the questions are that we're suppose to answer."

You return to the skills group and continue teaching. When you finish the lesson, you take a quick look around the classroom. You note that Bill is sulking in his chair. You go over to him and ask if he finished his social studies. He says yes. You ask him why he isn't doing a safety valve. He replies. "Aw, there's nothing I want to do there; it's just more work to do."

SUGGESTED FIELD EXPERIENCES

Observation. When observing in schools, you should note whether teachers individualize instruction. If they do, how do they account for the children that are not under their direct supervision at any one time? Do they use some variation of the principles of independent activities, Safety valves? Physical setting? Training? Buffers? Record-keeping?

Teaching activities. When working with groups of children in a classroom setting, you should make use of the principles described in this chapter to efficiently manage individualized instruction.

Client impact. By carefully managing and organizing your classroom, you will insure that each child receives the particular help needed to grow in reading and to develop a healthy view of him- or herself as a learner.

FOR CLASS DISCUSSION

Read the following statement and be prepared to discuss it with your instructor.

Many leaders in elementary education have voiced concern for the rigid and authoritarian manner in which many classrooms are operated. In contrast to such "closed" learning situations, these leaders promote "openness" in classrooms. As opposed to traditional classrooms, an "open" classroom would display freedom of movement, encouragement to speak honestly, choices regarding what is to be learned and flexibility in routes available for achieving educational objectives.

Could the classroom described in this chapter be categorized as "open"? Why or why not? In your opinion, does systematic instruction in the basic skills preclude any possible utilization of open classroom principles? Can you see any way in which both systematic instruction and open classroom principles can be put to use in a single classroom?

ANSWER KEY
1. supervision
2. independently
3. ability
4. safety valve

5. room
6. training
7. routines
8. instruction
9. easy
10. details

ESTABLISHING MANAGEMENT ROUTINES IN THE CLASSROOM

OVERVIEW

This chapter builds on Chapter 12 and details some of the time-consuming tasks of organization and management. The ultimate objective is:

> Given responsibility for reading instruction in an elementary classroom, you will do the preclass preparation and will implement and maintain patterns necessary for efficient management.

KNOWLEDGE BACKGROUND

In Chapter 12, you were given background information on organization and management. This chapter takes that background information one step further by exploring more fully how one develops a management system for efficient individualization.

The means–ends components of the elementary reading program—the development of the skills of reading and the development of a life-long reading habit—must both be reflected in your classroom. First, you must create a classroom environment where students are surrounded by books and printed materials, where a multitude of needs can be satisfied by reading, and where ample time is given to reading for informative and enjoyable purposes. Second, you must decide what skills the students need, teach those skills, evaluate attainment of the skills, and then put students in situations where they apply the skills. During the application stage, the means–ends components overlap since application of skills is tailor-made for developing the reading habit.

The development of such a comprehensive reading program is time consuming and tedious. However, the benefits make the effort worthwhile since such a program provides you with a method for fully using the reading time in your class day. To achieve these benefits, you must be able to answer six crucial questions:

1. What can I reasonably expect from myself?
2. How do I establish the patterns I want?
3. How do I implement and maintain the reading program in the classroom?
4. What must I do to create a lifelong reading habit?
5. What must I do to create the skills component in my reading program?
6. Where do I begin?

WHAT CAN I REASONABLY EXPECT FROM MYSELF?

The first step is to set a reasonable expectancy for yourself. An honest assessment will allow you to set attainable goals for the development of your reading program, while an unrealistic expectancy will create failure not because you weren't able but because you didn't look clearly at your situation. Such an expectancy should be based on the materials you have available and the experience you bring to the task.

An inventory of available materials might include basal texts, workbooks, practice materials and games filed by specific skill, books for recreational and informational reading, other printed materials for reading, additional commercial materials, teacher-made materials, supplies, files, and ideas. These should be classified as supporting either the component for developing the lifelong reading habit or the component of skills instruction. Material which fits both components should be so noted. The more materials you have, the easier your task will be.

Once you have some idea of what you have to work with, you can set a timetable for implementation based on both your experience and what materials are available. Experienced teachers may be able to implement with a summer and one school year of effort; inexperienced teachers may require two years or more.

The crucial factor is to set a realistic expectancy of your capabilities. With this as a framework, you can begin developing what needs to be done before the reading period begins and what you do during the reading period. If you are inexperienced and have few resources to work with, you may have to work very gradually toward this goal, but if you are willing to persist, the content of this chapter will assist you.

HOW DO I ESTABLISH THE PATTERNS I WANT?

Because children spend so much time working independently, patterns or routines are crucial to the success of any individualized reading programs. The teacher and the pupils must have a common agreement regarding the patterns that structure the reading period. For instance, if you want the pupils to use an independent activity during the reading period, they need a pattern to follow which signals the sequence of steps. It is vital that not only are patterns developed but also that these patterns are understood and used enough to become routines of behavior that operate independently of direct teacher supervision. These patterns include independent activities and safety valve patterns, procedural patterns, and interaction patterns.

INDEPENDENT ACTIVITIES AND SAFETY VALVE PATTERNS

Independent activities and safety valves were discussed extensively in Chapter 12. Now you must decide what has to be done prior to the reading period and during the regular school day to make these activities operate smoothly.

As an example, let's assume you decide to develop a creative writing center as an independent activity. Prior to the reading class, decisions have to be made about where to put the center, what to include in it, and the patterns for its use. You could bring in a refrigerator carton to house the center and initially place it in the work area of the room where students decorate the inside and/or outside of the carton. You could then place it in a quiet area of the room. It would probably include "starters" for creative writing such as pictures, a file box of suggestions, or the beginning paragraphs of stories. The completed stories, whether dictated on tapes or written, would be turned in to a designated spot. So, once you decide to have the center, you must find a carton, develop the center, and create the materials and routines for it. Attention to such detail, while mundane, is crucial to the success of independent activities.

Patterns will vary greatly from teacher to teacher depending upon each particular classroom style. For instance, assume that one of your safety valves is a "celebration corner" where students go to celebrate after completing their work. Such a corner might include three yo-yos, two Battleship games, some pick-up-sticks, two chess games, and a small pinball game where the objective is to roll the ball across the United States without dropping it through one of the holes. The corner is large enough to hold six students comfortably so, in terms of management, no more than six students can be there at one time. While the yo-yos, pinball game, and pick-up-sticks are distracting games and cannot be taken from the corner, the Battleship and chess games are quiet and can be played anywhere. You expect this to be a frequently used safety valve, so the length of time in the corner should be regulated because of the six-student limitation. While there is no "best" set of patterns regulating the use of a safety valve, cooperative teacher–pupil planning of the patterns of behavior might result in the following: when work is completed, a student may choose to use the celebration corner; however, when six students are in the corner, no more may enter. The Battleship and chess games can be taken to other parts of the room, making it possible for more than six students to use the safety valve at any one time. If another student wishes to enter the celebration corner when it is full, the student places a "waiting token" on a peg-board. When there are students waiting, anyone completing a game must choose something else outside the celebration corner, and anyone using a yo-yo or the pinball game has three remaining minutes before moving to another option outside the corner. A timer may be used to mark the remaining three minutes. If there are no waiting tokens, students may stay in the celebration corner.

PROCEDURAL PATTERNS

Procedural patterns include routines on how-to-start, how-to-change, how-to-keep-track-of-progress, and how-to-stop. Each of these patterns should be carefully analyzed and decisions made on how to implement and maintain these patterns prior to class use.

How-to-start patterns. How-to-start patterns are the methods used to get initial information to the students, such as directions and opening procedures. One way to handle these would be to provide mailboxes for each student, with each mailbox containing the directions for the period and other needed information. Some of these directions can be on mimeographed sheets to minimize preparation time. The direction sheet below, which tells the child what to do fist, second and so on, is one example.

_____	Skill lesson
_____	Practice
_____	Guided application
_____	Independent application
_____	Safety valves
_____	Independent activities

By using such a technique, you need only list the sequence for the day and the specifics of the practice and guided or independent application.

Starting procedures for nonreaders can make use of color. For example, you could use a manila folder that has been stapled to form a pocket like this:

Needed materials are placed in the pocket according to colors which correspond to the different centers. You could also use clip clothespins that are numbered and color-coded according to center.

Once the students have a way of receiving information and directions, they need to know how to behave while working alone. These procedures depend on the preference of the teacher and the abilities of the children. For instance, pupils can go to their mailboxes, pick up their directions and needed materials, return to their designated places (desk, floor, cushion, etc.), look at their directions, and begin; or the teacher may give directions to the entire class and then have pupils proceed independently. In any case, you will first need to decide how you want this done and orient your pupils accordingly.

How-to-change patterns. After the how-to-start patterns are developed, patterns for how to change are required. The options here are as varied as teacher preferences. You may decide to change activity on a signal from the teacher or a buffer, or you may decide to change when the student completes an activity or simply wants a change. If students change activities independently, one of the problems will be unfinished activities. For some activities, such as reading or mimeographed sheets, interruption poses little problem. However, an independent activity involving complicated steps (art projects, science experiments, etc.) may create a problem. You may circumvent this problem by offering, during the reading period only, independent activities that can be interrupted or by dividing the reading period into sections of time. In the latter case, for instance, a reading period of one hour could be divided into four 15-minute segments. One segment could be used for skills (testing, teaching, or practicing), one segment for application, and the two other segments for independent activities. At the end of 15 minutes, the students would change activities on a signal such as the teacher's voice a phrase of music, a bell, or some other device. A major concern with this arrangement is the need for safety valves with each segment. For instance, one segment of independent activities could be a listening center. Assume the activity for the day is listening to a taped discussion of animal tracks, followed by a written activity. Since all the children will finish at different times, a safety valve is needed for those finishing before the 15-minute segment is finished. You must also consider the student who doesn't finish the activity in 15 minutes by providing time later in the day or the next day for completion of the activity. However you decide to change activities, you must have an awareness of the aspects of these changing activities and an establishment of patterns that allow smooth change.

How-to-keep-track-of-progress. Once the reading period has started and activities are changing, you need a way to keep track of the students' activties. As was indicated in Chapter 12, you need a record of progression through the reading skills for each student. In addition, you should have at least a simple listing of materials read for guided application.

The independent application activities, the independent activities, and the safety valve activities may or may not need to be recorded. That decision is left to the teacher's preference.

You can keep a record of the books read for recreational purposes by use of a round chart such as this:

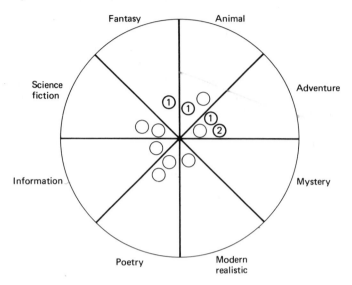

The chart is divided into segments according to type of books preferred. As a student reads his or her first book, the student writes the number 1 in each segment the book fits. If the book *Charlotte's Web* was read as the first book, the number 1 could be placed in the animal section, the fantasy section, and the adventure section. If the book *Little House on the Prairie* was the second book read, the number 2 could be placed in the adventure section. In this way, both the teacher and the student know immediately what type of books are being read. If desired, a list of the titles can be kept on the back of the chart. A teacher may also wish to use this method to keep track of books read for other content areas (science, social studies, math, etc.).

Contracts are also useful for keeping track of reading activities such as application or skill instruction. The students and the teacher set the goals of the contract which may vary in length (a week, several days, etc.) according to needs and desires. The completed contract then becomes a record of what the child has completed and can be placed in each individual student's folder.

Whatever techniques are used, students should keep their own records as much as possible. This eases your time problem and gives each student a continued awareness of his or her progress in reading.

How-to-stop patterns. When the reading period is over, you need to establish patterns for putting away materials, storing incomplete activities, and handing in completed activities. This requires that all students know where various materials belong and what kinds of filing systems and storage arrangements are being used. Prior to fully implementing your reading program, you would need to develop the patterns regarding these procedures.

Summary. The important element to remember in establishing routines is setting patterns. This requires careful planning ahead so you won't unwittingly cause confusion by occasionally switching patterns. It is much more difficult to unlearn a pattern and learn a new one than to learn a new one initially. Once the pattern of the routine is set, it becomes an element of the classroom and does not require your close supervision, thereby allowing you to work individually with students. Because of the many patterns that need to become habituated and the limits of your sanity, the implementation process needs to be gradual. You will need to give much directed assistance initially, with this assistance diminishing as the patterns become established. Once the organization and management of the reading period are running smoothly you can then begin your reading program.

INTERACTION PATTERNS

Interaction patterns include procedures for socialization among students and between the teacher and students. Socialization is an important factor to be considered in any elementary school classroom; it is a major contributor to maturation and occurs with or without teacher forethought. In order to best make socialization work for you, you are wise to develop patterns for its use.

Again, there is no single way to manage interaction in the classroom. The major guidelines are (1) that some sort of patterns be established, and (2) that the teacher adjust these patterns for particular students and situations. For instance, one way to pattern interaction is to divide the classroom into a noisy half and a quiet half. All verbal communication will be done in the noisy half, leaving the quiet half relatively noise-free. Other teachers, because of personal preference or special circumstances, may wish to confine social interaction to either a "rap" center where students can go to talk, or to communication centers, such as listening centers or drama centers, where interaction has a set purpose.

Regardless of the patterns established for verbal interaction, there seems never to be time enough for sufficient verbal interaction for all students. Establishing times for written interaction can help alleviate this difficulty. Each person in the room may have a mailbox where messages can be left. This allows for all members of the classroom to interact via letters or notes. The patterns should specify when mail can be left and when students and teachers can pick up their mail.

There are two keys for understanding social interaction as it relates to classroom management. First, it is a means to maturity and is, therefore, beneficial to child development. Second, it can be enhanced by establishing behavior patterns that best meet the needs of the students, the teacher, and the learning activities.

HOW DO I IMPLEMENT AND MAINTAIN
THE READING PROGRAM IN THE CLASSROOM?

Once the teacher has set reasonable self-expectations and established the various necessary patterns, the next stage is implementing and maintaining the reading activities within the classroom. This involves several steps.

IMPLEMENTING INDEPENDENT ACTIVITIES

First, explain the purpose or reason for the independent activity or activities. Describe what you expect the students to do and explain why. If you are implementing a safety valve activity, such as the celebration corner described earlier in this chapter, give the students all the information they need about it. Tell them that it's a center to be used when work is finished (a place to go and celebrate), that it includes a number of games and activities, and that the number of students is limited to six because of the lack of room.

Second, connect the background experiences and preferences of the students to the procedures and activities being implemented. If the students have had experience with independent movement and decision making, this step is quickly passed through. If the students do not have the background, this step must be implemented after the procedural pattern of how-to-start an activity is running smoothly. You can control the students' interest by including activities that they enjoy.

The third step includes communicating clearly a description of the activities that are in the center. Give time conditions, describe what to do when activities are completed, and explain any further rules for maintenance of the center.

The last step involves a check of the students' understanding of the implementing process. This can be done by having the students relate to you what they're going to do. Once the students clearly understand the steps, have them try out the activity and the proceed with the following maintenance steps.

MAINTAINING INDEPENDENT ACTIVITIES

To maintain the activities during the reading period once an activity or pattern has been implemented, the teacher must take steps to keep that activity or pattern developing smoothly. To do so, the teacher must stay one step ahead of the students by maintaining three variables—student variables, environmental variables, and subject matter variables.

Maintenance of student variables includes such steps as redirecting or assisting students in the activity, using verbal or nonverbal signals when student progress on an activity begins to falter, and reinforcing desired student behaviors. Maintenance of environmental variables includes ignoring or removing minor distractions, teacher movement to maintain proximity to all students, and regrouping students when necessary. The third variable—the content subject—requires that the teacher take steps in shifting activities and/or materials when it becomes apparent that an assigned task is too easy or too difficult, if an assessment procedure indicates a need for change, or if a time problem occurs.

Efficiently implementing and maintaining independent activities is crucial to the success of reading instruction. The specific procedures are left to teacher discretion, but all plans should initially incorporate an explanation of the purpose, a connecting of the students' backgrounds and personal interests to the activity, a clear description of the activity, and an opportunity for students to indicate that they undersand; maintenance of the activity requires ongoing surveillance of the student, environmental, and content variables so that activities continue to progress smoothly.

WHAT MUST I DO TO CREATE A LIFELONG READING HABIT?

In creating a lifelong reading habit in your students, you must be concerned both with the physical environment of the classroom and with the techniques you will use. While these are discussed in greater detail in Chapter 25, the management implications can be examined here.

In terms of physical arrangement of the room, you must provide both space and materials. The space would include recreational reading corners or nooks which are enticing and relaxing and also materials which attract children to recreational reading. This requires that you inventory the equipment and materials available, manipulate it to best meet your needs, and obtain other materials and equipment from whatever sources you can find.

The techniques you use will include book sharing by both the teacher and the students, recreational reading periods, and a variety of interest grabbers. Book sharing requires that you prepare the materials and identify a time for this activity. Recreational reading involves everyone, including the teacher, in reading a book or other printed material of personal choice and requires that you plan ahead so that everyone has something to read. Finally, interest grabbers include audio-visual materials; situations that draw attention to books such as skits, book fairs and art projects; various printed materials and visually appealing materials which focus on books such as posters, pictures, dioramas, advertisements, and bulletin boards. All three techniques could be done as a group or as independent activities or safety valves. However they are used, you must prepare for them prior to the reading period, having the materials ready and making sure that the pupils are clear about the patterns to follow during these activities.

WHAT MUST I DO TO CREATE THE SKILLS COMPONENT
IN MY READING PROGRAM?

A major part of a reading program is developing skills. Since decisions regarding skills instruction are based on assessment and assessment is primarily individual, the classroom organization and management must allow for one-to-one opportunities. Hence, the principles suggested in Chapter 12 and in the earlier parts of this chapter are appropriate for this task. Once an organization and management system has been established, the skills component can be implemented in five steps which make use of these principles.

The first step is the assessment of reading skills and incorporates four tools previously discussed: graded oral reading paragraphs, pretests for word identification and comprehension, informal observation and questionnaires about interest areas in reading, and a procedure for determining rate of learning for each student.

The second step involves examination of the data gathered in assessment and decision making to determine where to begin skill instruction, the goals of instruction based on expected *rate* of learning, the level of books to be used for instructional and independent reading, and the *content validity* of books for various students. This may be done prior to class or during the reading period, but, regardless of when it is done, you need to examine all data and make the best possible decisions.

The third step focuses on instruction and is divided into the four areas of word identification, comprehension, study skills, and literary appreciation skills. While the specific skills taught during a given day will depend on the assessment and goals set for each student, you need to be ready to teach a wide spectrum of skills since your classroom will contain students operating at many different levels.

After skills instruction, the fourth step is evaluation by specific posttests. The posttests need to be prepared prior to class to be ready for handy use.

The fifth step focuses on application. As stated earlier, this is the segment where the skills component and the love-of-reading component overlap since a child can be developing a love for reading as he or she applies learned reading skills. Application is divided into guided application and independent application (see Section Six of this book). Guided application includes the use of basal readers, commercial materials such as SRA kits, Readers Digest Skill Builders, library books, and content area materials. Prior to class, the teacher needs to prepare these materials for student use by creating interest, giving needed background information, and setting purposes for reading. In addition, a device such as contracts must be developed for recording guided application. Independent application includes the independent reading of a variety of printed materials and requires that you find and prepare the material and devise appropriate recording devices.

WHERE DO I BEGIN?

The organization and management of a reading program require the melding of many little pieces. This is a monumental task, but the following guide offers structured assistance. You, as a teacher, can use these steps in developing your own program in your own way.

STEP ONE (prior to the opening of school and prior to knowing assigned students)

a. Develop a source file for oral reading, recreational or independent reading, interest grabbers, independent activities, safety valves, guided application (basals, other commercial materials), and room arrangement.
b. Collect and categorize books and other printed material or recreational or independent reading, guided application materials, and interest-grabbing materials.
c. Develop activity card files for learning centers, independent activities, safety valves, and interest grabbers.
d. Collect and develop assessment and evaluation tools, including graded oral paragraphs, pretests, posttests, and interest inventories.
e. Develop a kit of materials for each skill objective. Include attenders, highlighting, practice, and suggestions for guided or independent application.
f. Develop a general pattern for reinforcement that can be adjusted after you know your students.
g. Develop bibliographies of books according to readability level and interest area.
h. Collect and categorize according to readability and interest all books and other printed material that your students might read.
i. Develop patterns for how-to-start procedures.
j. Develop patterns for how-to-change procedures.
k. Develop patterns for keeping-track-of-students procedures.
l. Develop patterns for the optional activities (independent activities and safety valve activities).
m. Develop patterns for how-to-stop procedures.
n. Develop patterns that allow for interaction among teachers and students.
o. Develop the general role of the buffer and the steps in training the buffer.
p. Develop your philosophy about approaches (basals, language experience, etc.) in reading and how skills instruction fits into that approach. How will you strike a balance between developing skills instruction and developing the lifelong reading habit?
q. Integrate your chosen approach to reading with the skills instruction.

STEP TWO (prior to the opening of school, after you have been assigned a specific classroom)

a. Continue to develop sourcebooks, activity card files, assessment tools, materials for skill instruction, materials for application of skills, lists of recreational books, procedures for patterns, procedures for the buffer, and your philosophy about approaches.
b. Develop a floor plan for the physical arrangement of your classroom.
c. Make an inventory of the materials you have for the coming school year.

STEP THREE   (after the school year begins)
a. Implement the love-of-reading component.
b. Implement patterns for procedures and interaction.
c. Implement independent activities and safety valves.
d. Implement the role of the buffer.
e. Evaluate progress so far, including patterns and procedures.
f. Determine reading preferences of each student.
g. Initiate plans for the students to develop their own expectancies for the lifelong reading habit.
h. Administer the graded oral paragraphs.
i. Administer pretests.
j. Determine expectancies for each pupil's rate of learning.
k. Implement skill instruction, including practice, posttests, and application.
l. Evaluate progress of reading program to date.

STEP FOUR   (continued growth and evaluation)
a. Continue to develop materials, ideas, sources, a reading library, patterns, and teaching style. Be alert for ways you can vary safety valve activities as the year progresses, and be alert for new ideas and materials.
b. Continue to evaluate the ongoing reading program. Are your self-expectancies reasonable? Are patterns developing as expected? Is the lifelong reading habit being established? Is the skills program as successful as you want? Are you implementing and maintaining the reading program?

TEST YOUR KNOWLEDGE

1. An elementary school reading program is divided into the two major components of _____ and _____.
2. These two components overlap each other during _____.
3. Since organization, and management require a great amount of time, the teacher can better handle any problem by deciding what can be done _____ and what can be done during class.
4. The teaching of skills can occur when _____ for independent activities and safety valves are established.
5. The graded oral paragraphs, pretests, and interest inventories are used primarily to _____ the individual differences in readers.
6. The five steps for initiating a skills component are: _____, _____, _____, _____, and _____.
7. Book sharing, recreational reading, and interest grabbers are techniques to build the _____.
8. Procedural patterns include _____, _____, _____, and _____.
9. Patterns should operate _____ of direct teacher supervision.
10. A reasonable expectancy for yourself as a teacher is necessary because unrealistic expectancies create _____.

SIMULATION ACTIVITIES

Consider the following episodes in terms of management and organization. Pinpoint what the difficulties are and then (1) decide what could have been done prior to class to eliminate this problem, and (2) decide what could have been done during the implementation process and maintaining process to eliminate the problem.

EPISODE 1: A first grade teacher had prepared a pasting project for the students. All the children sat on a section of the floor, and each was given materials and a pat of paste on a paper towel. As the students finished, the teacher had them pass their paste over to the side of the room next to the windows. All but three of the paste pats were picked up. Eventually, all the students had finished but five minutes still remained. The students asked if they could look at their individual bean plants growing on the window sill. The teacher picked up each plant and gave it to its owner, carefully stepping over the paste. The children became very excited and interested in showing each other the plants. One boy, while running up to the teacher to show his plant, stepped on a paste pat. He took three more steps, leaving paste spots behind him. The teacher had to stop and clean the paste off the floor. One girl leaned over to show her plant to a friend and ended up with a paste pat on the side of her slacks. When she eventually noticed the paste, she pulled off the paper, leaving the paste which she scraped off with her pencil. She then asked the teacher to take her pencil to the sink and wash it off. The teacher finally picked up the remaining pat of paste.

EPISODE 2: As Mrs. Wilson finished with a skill group, she told the children to line up by her chair. Several students ran to the chair, crashed into it (luckily she wasn't in it), and fought over who had been first. She told them to quiet down. Some did, but they still pushed at each other. She let them go, and they pushed and squabbled back to their seats.

SUGGESTED FIELD EXPERIENCES

Observation. When observing in schools, you should note how teachers organize and manage their classrooms. What is prepared before the class starts? What happens in the classroom in terms of student assistance for managing and organizing? What is evidenced in the classroom that the teacher has organized? Are the transitions smooth? Are the love-of-reading habit and skills learning an integral part?

Teaching activities. When teaching students based on individual needs and differences, you have to develop routines for independent activities and safety valves that then allow skills instruction. You can facilitate preparation for this type of reading program by dividing the work into what is done prior to class and what is done during class. This gives you the information necessary for setting realistic expectancies for developing this type of program.

Client impact. Developing routines for the reading period enables your students to become independent in handling schoolwork. This independence allows individualization of students for instruction. The impact is the independence of students in completing activities and the development of classroom organization that meets individual needs and interests.

FOR CLASS DISCUSSION

The amount of preparation for this type of program is overwhelming. Considering this, what are the advantages of this type of organization and management? What are the disadvantages, and how can these disadvantages be lessened?

ANSWER KEY
1. skills instruction, developing the reading habit
2. application of skills
3. before
4. patterns
5. assess
6. assessment, data gathering and decision making, skills instruction, evaluation, application
7. reading habit
8. how-to-start, how-to-change, how-to-keep-track-of-progress, how-to-stop
9. independently
10. failure

SUGGESTED ADDITIONAL READINGS FOR SECTION FOUR– MANAGING INSTRUCTION

ANDELMAN, FREDERICK. "Open Education: What Does It Mean?" *The Massachusetts Teacher*, November 1972, p. 14.

GIBLIN, MARGARET, *Elementary School Teaching: Problems and Methods*. Pacific Palisades, Calif.: Goodyear, 1972.

Individualizing Instruction. Sixty-first Yearbook of the National Society for the Study of Education. Chicago: University of Chicago Press, 1962.

NEWTON, J. ROY. *Reading in Your School*. New York: McGraw-Hill, 1960.

OLDS, ANITA. "The Classroom Setting." *Learning*, November 1972, p. 36.

O'LEARY, D., AND O'LEARY, S. *Classroom Management*. Elmsford, N.Y.: Pergamon Press, 1972.

PILON, GRACE H. *The Workshop Way*. New Orleans, La.: Xavier University Press, 1970.

THOMAS, JOHN. *Learning Centers: Opening Up the Classroom*. Boston: Holbrook Press, Inc., 1975.

FIVE
TEACHING THE SKILLS

HOW TO TEACH
A SKILL

OVERVIEW

This chapter provides you with the instructional principles needed to teach skills effectively. The ultimate objective is:

> Given a skill to teach, you will instruct using the principles of creating a set for learning, directing attention, highlighting, diminishing the assistance, insuring responses, reinforcing, and practicing.   ◄

KNOWLEDGE BACKGROUND

The basic structure of effective skills instruction, as described in Chapter 11, follows a test–teach–test–apply sequence. The easiest step to implement is testing because specific tests and directions for their administration are provided by many publishers,[1] and because tests can be rapidly and efficiently administered to learners. Basically, it is simply a matter of giving the learner the pretest and saying, "Can you do this?" If the answer is yes, you go on to the next skill; if no, you teach that skill and help the learner apply it.

---

[1] Examples include *Systematic Reading Instruction*, 2nd ed., published by Harper & Row, 1977, and *The Wisconsin Design*, published by the Wisconsin Research and Development Center for Cognitive Learning, University of Wisconsin, 1970.

It is at the teaching and applying steps, however, that the task becomes more difficult. Too many teachers just continue testing and call it teaching. That is, they keep asking the learner to do the skill again, or they supply a commercial workbook which asks the learner to do it again, or they play a game which requires the learner to do it again, all without ever providing any assistance in *how* to do it. There is, however, a great deal of difference between testing, teaching, and applying. *Anybody* can test; *anybody* can pass out workbooks or kits and hope that the material will do the teaching; *anybody* can listen to children read orally from a basal reader; and anybody can get the bright, well-adjusted, and advantaged children to read. It takes a special ability, however, to create a skill competence in a child who formerly was totally unable to perform the task. While testing and diagnosis are crucial, it is your abilities for teaching and applying which ultimately determine whether skills will be mastered. Consequently, this chapter emphasizes techniques for skills teaching, while Chapters 24 and 25 stress strategies for helping children apply learned skills.

THE DIFFERENCE BETWEEN TEACHING AND TESTING

To develop reading skills in children, you must both test and teach effectively. However, because testing and teaching are two distinctly different types of teacher behavior, it is crucial that your work in the classroom reflect this difference.

TESTING

Testing is the diagnostic step—the point at which you determine whether the learner can perform the desired skill. Normally, it will be done twice: prior to teaching (pretesting), to determine if the learner already knows the skill and therefore needs no instruction, and following teaching (posttesting), to determine whether those who failed the pretest have now achieved mastery as a result of your instruction.

Testing requires first that you specify what skill you want to assess. Second, testing requires that you structure a situation in which the learner is forced to respond—that is, to perform the skill in its totality, not broken down or simplified. For example, if you are testing for sight-words, you flash the whole word and require a response to the rapid exposure; if you are testing for sound–symbol connection, you present the student with a sound and require him or her to identify the symbol; if you are testing for ability to analyze words by substituting initial consonants in phonograms, you present the student with a list of unknown words having the same phonogram element but different initial consonants and require the student to pronounce them; and if you are testing for ability to identify the meaning of unknown words through the use of context, you give a sentence using an unknown word and require the student to state its meaning. In any case, testing requires little teacher effort beyond insuring that the test does indeed assess the specified skill.

TEACHING

Teaching is the instructional step—the point at which you provide the learner with the input that allows him or her to perform the task he or she was unable to perform on the pretest. Because of that inability to respond correctly during the test, it stands to reason that teaching requires more than simply asking the student to respond again. You, the teacher, must *directly assist* the learner in mastering the skill. It is the provision for directed assistance which sets teaching apart from testing.

TECHNIQUES FOR TEACHING

To teach, there are six specific ways to directly assist the learner, all of which should be present, in one form or another, in every instructional episode. These steps include creating a set for learning, directing attention, highlighting, diminishing the assistance, insuring responses, and reinforcing. The seventh principle, practice, will be dealt with separately.

CREATING A LEARNING SET

Learning, by definition, requires a change in behavior. The act of teaching, then, is the act of changing behavior in specified ways. One of the greatest impediments to creating such change, however, is the expectation of society generally and of teachers particularly that everyone should succeed at everything the first time and that failure is bad. This expectation produces children who resist learning because of a fear of failing.

A more realistic view of learning, in contrast, accepts the fact that some frustration is associated with all learning and that it is all right to fail sometimes. When this fact is communicated to children, they become less resistant to learning because they know that they will not be viewed as "abnormal" or "dumb" if they do not master the task the first time; they know they can fail without jeopardizing their self-concept as learners. The first directed assistance offered by the teacher should, therefore, be the recognition of the difficulty of learning and the sensitive acknowledgement of the difficulty of the task, thereby allowing the learner to respond confidently without endangering self-image.

Let's illustrate by looking at pie baking. Suppose I bake a pie and invite you to eat it with me. You taste it and exclaim over the deliciousness of the pie and my skill at pie baking. "I wish I could bake a pie like this," you say. Now is when this principle should come into play.

If I am a poor teacher, I will say to you, "Fine. Pie baking isn't hard, so let's learn to make a pie." In my efforts to give you the necessary confidence to try, I may even say, "Anyone can bake a pie." With these two encouragements, I have probably spoiled your opportunity to learn to be a successful pie baker by removing the challenge of learning. Let's see what happens.

You take the recipe and my directions, and you proceed to bake a pie. When it is finished, you take the first taste, and the pie is delicious. You are a successful learner of pie baking. But wait! Is this anything to be proud of? Didn't I explain that pie baking was easy and anyone could do it? Now do you feel like a successful pie baker, when you know that the task is easy and that anyone can perform the skill? The answer is obvious.

Let's back up a minute and see what happens if your first pie baking effort is a failure. You take the first bite, and it tastes terrible. Now, what can you say about yourself? The task, according to me, was easy, but you couldn't do it. What does this make you? "Anyone can bake a pie," I said. Does this make you less than anyone? Do you suppose you will try baking pies again? Probably not, because by failing to acknowledge the difficulty of the learning, I canceled your success as a learner. So, you are in a bind: if you do the task successfully, it really isn't worth doing in the first place because it was so easy, while if you fail the first time, it is because of a defect in you since anyone else could do it. You are damned if you learn and damned if you don't.

In contrast, what does a more sensitive teacher do? When you indicate interest in baking a pie, the good teacher recognizes that the task is not easy or sure-fire. This teacher expresses these reservations to you by saying, "I will give you the recipe and careful directions, but pie baking is not easy. You can do everything right and still not bake a good pie. Not everyone can bake a good pie the first time." The task is now realistic. The difficulty of the task has been acknowledged.

What happens when you bake a pie and it is delicious? You feel much success about yourself as a pie baker. Chances are you will bake other pies and go on to other successful learning performances. The task was a difficult one, but you did it. Your self-concept as a learner receives great reinforcement.

But, suppose the pie is poor. What happens then? Well, you had been forewarned that the task wasn't easy. You had been told that not everyone can bake a good pie the first time. Is this damaging to your self-concept? No. It was not you that was defective, it was the task itself that was difficult. You can try again knowing that failure is no stigma when the task is hard.

So you see that recognizing the difficulty of learning and sensitively acknowledging this difficulty to the learner are important aspects of *any* instruction. It is a wise teacher who recognizes that learning is seldom a "one-shot deal," that failure will probably occur as often as success, and that recognition of the difficulty of the task to be learned is essential if the learner is not to feel personal failure as a learner.

This principle is particularly relevant to teaching reading skills, when, for example, children are too often told that learning to visually discriminate between a **d** and a **b** or learning the sound associated with the **ch** digraph are easy tasks. While they may be easy for the teacher, the child does *not* find them so. After all, he or she may just have failed the pretests for those skills, demonstrating the difficulty rather dramatically. If the child thinks the teacher is saying, "It *ought* to be easy for you and if it's not, you must be dumb," quite naturally that learner will not want to appear dumb and so may not respond at all.

You can counter this behavior and directly assist the child in learning by stating that the task *is* difficult and that many perfectly normal people cannot do it the first time. By creating empathy in this way, you are making it possible for the child to respond in the learning situation without endangering self-concept. With this as the foundation, the lesson is off to a good start.

DIRECTING ATTENTION

When we talk about *attention* in the instructional situation, we do not necessarily mean the sitting-up-straight-in-the-seat-with-arms-folded kind. Rather, we mean that the learner must attend to the salient features of the task at hand. For instance, when learning to read his or her name, the learner must *listen* to the sound of the name and simultaneously *look* at the spelling of the name. If the child is not attending with these two senses simultaneously, a pairing of the name with the written form of the name will only occur by accident. If the child is listening but looking at a fly on the window, the name could conceivably be paired with the fly. This is an exaggerated illustration but should put you on guard that if you do *not* control the input to the learner's senses, both visual and aural, no learning of the desired pair can result.

As teachers, we are always saying, "Now, pay attention." Unfortunately, this is all too often the sum total of our instructional repertoire for creating attending behavior in learners. This is not enough, for it does not tell the learner what specifically must be attended to in order to master the task. Attention needs specific cues, both verbal and physical, which eliminate the necessity for the learner to wonder what to do to learn the task and which remove the guessing-game element of learning.

There are two ways in which you can direct the learner's attention. The first, and the simpler of the two, is to state for the learner what it is that is to be learned. If the child is to learn to read his or her name, you say, "Today, you are going to learn how to read your name." If the learner is to learn to read the word **dinosaur** at sight, you say, "Today, you are going to learn how to instantly recognize the word **dinosaur** when I flash it to you." If the child is to learn the sound–symbol connection for the **ch** digraph, you say, "Today, you are going to learn the sound that the **ch** makes at the beginning of words."

While this technique may seem, at first glance, quite simplistic, it is actually a powerful way to direct attention. When a child knows what he or she is supposed to learn, the purpose of the learning becomes clear, and the child can apply him- or herself more directly to the task. The child who is unsure of what is supposed to be learned is put in the position of trying to "psych out" the teacher's purpose and becomes easily confused and frustrated. Consequently, you can directly assist the child in learning by clearly stating the purpose of the lesson at the outset.

The second and more complex technique for directing attention involves analyzing the skill performance to determine precisely what components of the task the learner must pay attention to in order to master the skill. As such, when teaching the learner to read his name, the teacher directs the learner to look at the printed form of the name while simultaneously listening to the sound of the name. If learning to instantly recognize at sight the easily confused words **was** and **saw**, the learner is directed to the left-to-right sequence of the letters in each word. If learning to identify the meaning of an unknown word through the use of context, the learner is directed to the words in the sentence which provide clues to the meaning of the unknown word.

Failure to direct the learner to the task's salient features will result in the child's not paying attention or paying attention to the wrong thing. That child is again in the position of trying to "pysch out" the situation— of trying to determine for him- or herself what must be attended to in order to be able to do the task. The failure on the pretest indicates that the child is unable to figure this out. If you do not direct the learner to the crucial features, confusion and frustration are likely to continue. Consequently, you should directly assist the child in learning by specifying the salient features of the task.

You should, then, make use of two techniques in directing the learner's attention. You should specify the task that is to be learned, and you should be precise in directing the learner to the important aspects of the task to be mastered. Both techniques, when used well, will directly assist the child in learning the skill.

HIGHLIGHTING

Once you have analyzed the skill and determined the salient features which are crucial for learning, the task becomes one of dramatizing or highlighting these features so that the attending task is simplified for the learner. This highlighting can take the form of auditory emphasis, color coding, underlining, circling, use of the flannelboard, or any other device which helps the learner focus attention on the crucial features of the task.

In highlighting, you are actually providing the learner with a crutch to get over the first few difficult steps in learning the skill. For instance, in teaching learners to analyze words by substituting initial consonants in phonograms, you might highlight by presenting the words as follows:

ⓒ a t
ⓑ a t
ⓡ a t
ⓕ a t
ⓢ a t

In teaching learners to use left-to-right sequence in distinguishing the letters **d** and **b**, you might highlight by presenting the letters as follows:

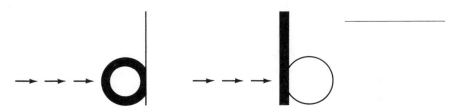

The type of highlighting used is not particularly crucial as long as it *works*—that is, as long as it succeeds in getting the learner to focus on the salient elements of the task. Consequently, there is no particular advantage in using color coding rather than underlining or vice versa. It *is* crucial, however, that some form of highlighting be provided in the early part of the lesson and that this highlighting focus on the correct component of the task. When this is the case, the learner is directly assisted in learning, and you are providing good instruction.

DIMINISHING THE ASSISTANCE

While the learner is provided with highlighting devices early in the lesson to help focus attention and to insure successful responses, the ultimate goal is to elicit responses without the assistance of "crutches." Consequently, with each successful response, the highlighting should be gradually diminished so that the learner has fewer and fewer crutches. Ultimately, the student responds without any highlighting assistance at all and, at this point, has succeeded in performing the task as it was specified in the objective.

For instance, if auditory emphasis was used as a highlighter, the degree of auditory emphasis would be gradually reduced with each successful response until the word or sound would be said normally with no emphasis. If circling and underlining were used, the highlighting might be diminished in the following manner:

ⓒ	a	t
ⓑ	a___	t
ⓡ	a _	t
ⓕ	a .	t
s	a	t

Just as it is crucial that highlighting be provided at the initial stages of instruction, it is equally crucial that this highlighting be gradually diminished. If crutches were provided and never taken away, the learner would be unable to perform the task in a real reading situation without these crutches. If the crutches are removed too quickly, the student will lose sight of what is to be attended to and will become confused. The trick is to gauge, with each individual learner, the amount of highlighting that is needed and how quickly it can be removed. There is no formula for determining this ahead of time; the judgment must be made by the teacher on the basis of the quality of the learner's response each time a crutch is diminished.

INSURING RESPONSES

As implied in the discussions of highlighting and diminished assistance, good instruction calls for frequent responses on the part of the learner. Learning does not take place without an expenditure of energy, and, for the learner, that energy is expended in making responses.

The good teacher calls for frequent responses during a lesson and, since repetition is a necessary part of all learning, finds many ways to elicit responses without making them a boring rote. Responses will be called for in the initial stage when a maximum amount of highlighting is provided, and they will be called for again each time the highlighting is diminished. In fact, the only way for you to know whether to continue diminishing the amount of highlighting is by noting the quality of the learner's responses. If a learner responds correctly with a given amount of highlighting, the crutch can be diminished; if not, the crutch must be maintained and perhaps even strengthened.

There are basically two strategies for eliciting responses from learners. One is by *modeling* and the other is by *discovery*.

In the first technique, you model—or demonstrate—the performance of the task for the learner and then have the child mimic your actions. This technique requires that you "talk through" the steps in performing the task, directing the learner to "do as I did." Hence, through such imitation, the child learns to perform the skill.

The second technique, discovery, requires you to set conditions so that the learner can generalize to the learning by himself. Rather than demonstrating and having the learner mimic, you set up a situation in which the principle to be learned is highlighted and then, through a series of questions, lead the learner to discover the principle.

The two techniques can be contrasted by examining how each would be used to teach a skill such as substituting initial consonants in known short vowel phonograms. In both cases, you would create a learning set, direct attention, use highlighting, and diminish assistance. The dialogue between you and the student would differ, however. When using the modeling strategy, the dialogue might go somewhat as follows:

TEACHER: Today we are going to learn to change the first letter in related words and pronounce the new words. This is not always easy, so I have listed some of the words on the board, circling the first letter of each word and underlining the parts of each word that are related. Watch me while I show you how to do this. I already know the first word is **cat.** Now I look at the second word. It has **at** in it just like the first word. It must sound like the **at** in **cat.** But the second word is not **cat** because it starts with the letter **b.** I'll get my mouth ready to make the **b** sound and say the new word. **B . . . at, bat.** Now, let's look at the next word and do it together.

At this point, you direct the learner to the word **rat** and repeat the procedure but with learner responses. The process continues using other words, with both the amount of teacher modeling and the highlighting being gradually diminished and the learner response being increased until the learner is able to independently substitute initial consonants in known vowel phonograms and pronounce the new words.

In contrast, the discovery strategy would go somewhat as follows:

TEACHER: Today we are going to learn to change the first letter in related words and pronounce the new words. This is not always easy so I have listed some of the words on the board, circling the first letter and underlining the parts of each word that are related. We know the first word in the list because we learned it the other day as a sight-word. What is it?

LEARNER RESPONDS.

TEACHER: Let's look at all the words in the list. In what way do they all look alike?

LEARNER RESPONDS.

TEACHER: In what ways do each of the words look different?

LEARNER RESPONDS.

TEACHER: Let's go back to the first word again. We said we know that word because we learned it the other day. It is **cat.** It is like all the other words on the list because it ends with **at.** It is different because it starts with a different first letter. Let's concentrate on the ending for a minute. I'm going to say **cat** slowly and I want you to listen and tell me what sound you hear at the end of the word. C . . . at, cat.

LEARNER RESPONDS.

TEACHER: If the ending of **cat** says **at**, what sound do you suppose you will hear at the end of the next word? And the word after that?

LEARNER RESPONDS.

TEACHER: OK, we can say that all the words in the list are related because they end with the same letters and the same sounds. They are different, however, because they have different beginnings. We have learned the sounds for these beginning letters though, and if we get our mouths ready to say the beginning sound, say it, and then add the **at** sound of the ending, we can say the word. Can you do that with the first word?

LEARNER RESPONDS.

This process is repeated for other words, with the amount of highlighting being gradually diminished until the learner is able to independently substitute initial consonants in known vowel phonograms and pronounce the new words.

It can be seen, then, that both the modeling and the discovery techniques elicit learner response, and either strategy can be used in teaching. The modeling technique has the advantage of controlling more tightly the learner's response pattern, while the discovery technique involves the learner more actively in the thinking process.

As a teacher, you will constantly have to decide which approach to use. This decision will depend upon a number of factors, for neither technique is useful in all teaching situations. You will need to make a choice minute by minute, skill by skill, child by child. The information that follows should help you do this.

Modeled learning has three very powerful and positive effects. First, there is usually a high initial success factor, that is, a child will usually be able to demonstrate the learning quickly and accurately. Therefore, the child who needs the stimulation that comes from immediate and successful effort and its concomitant rewards should often be taught in this manner. Second, task attenders are generally more easily controlled and highlighted using a modeled instruction. The child is not left to wonder what the eyes, ears, or mind is supposed to be cueing to, and the possibility of confusion is minimized. Third, modeled instruction can be made to fit most any learning task very quickly and easily. It is literally a universal teaching tactic that adapts to all kinds of learning from simple associations to complex problem solving. And it does this while still allowing the actual instructional act to occur in a very short space of time. These factors all favor a modeled cue system.

On the negative side, however, we find that modeled instruction is primarily mimicking and is based on a short-term memory function. As such, what has been learned quickly and concisely today is often forgotten just as quickly and concisely tomorrow. Retention is often a problem with this tactic. Therefore, initial instruction *must* be followed by repetitive practice activities before you can feel secure that what might have been taught so easily and learned so quickly has been remembered. Similarly, a modeled learning, no matter how thoroughly learned, does not generalize or transfer easily to new and similar situations. What has been learned tends to remain isolated and specific. Again, this is not an insurmountable problem because you can teach a child to generalize and transfer specific learnings. The point is that modeled instruction does not have this effect built in.

Discovery cueing has the opposite positive and negative elements. On the plus side are two very significant factors. First, there is a high retention rate; what has been discovered today is usually remembered next week. A corollary of this is the diminished need for practice and drill. This benefit can be very significant in teaching some skills to some children. Similarly, what has been learned through a discovery approach tends to be easily generalized and almost automatically transferred to new learning tasks. The act of discovery produces a broad base of learning behavior that allows the child to see its application and usefulness in other new learnings.

On the negative side is the problem of time. Discovery teaching takes time. The path that leads the child from knowing nothing to knowing something will often be filled with long pauses, ambiguities, and side tracks that lead nowhere. These in turn can make a long and arduous activity out of a task that could more quickly be taught through an efficient modeling activity. Similarly, the attenders highlighted through discovery teaching are oftentimes missed or misinterpreted by the child. Sustained concentration and the ability to both follow and modify vague cues are learner necessities. In other words, thinking behavior is optimized with discovery teaching, but the child who is not prepared for this activity will usually flounder.

Obviously, you will need to make use of both strategies according to the needs and learning styles of the particular learner. In either technique, however, frequent responses must be elicited. Only when a learner is actively involved in the learning can the child be effectively assisted in mastering the skill.

REINFORCING

The final way to directly assist learning is through reinforcement. Reinforcement goes by many names. Some call it reward, others bribery. As teachers, we too often view the condition of reward as an intrinsic state where success at the task is internalized; the student learns for the sake of learning. This is fine for the successful learner who has developed such a reward system, but, unfortunately, many children come to school never having learned what it means to be praised for doing something well. The poor learner has not yet learned how to accept reinforcements. Your first task in using reinforcement, consequently, is to judge each child individually and to choose reinforcers that are appropriate to that child's system (see Chapter 11).

At the lowest level, these reinforcements are physical—an apple, a token that buys a toy plane at the end of the week, some candy, and so on. This looks like bribery but can be the start of developing an intrinsic reward system.

The next step above physical rewards is a touch or movement reward. Here you pat a shoulder or shake a hand when the learning is properly mastered. At a still higher level, you gradually replace the touch or movement with a word or two of verbal praise.

Your objective here is to help the learner find satisfaction in the learning task, moving through the levels of reinforcement as he or she progresses. As this happens, you gradually get rid of the lower rewards, replacing them with words and gestures. To learners who ultimately develop sophisticated reinforcement systems, a smile or a nod on your part is sufficient reward. In any case, the reward or reinforcement must be appropriate to the learning and to the learner's reward system.

A second, and equally important consideration, is to provide the reward immediately following the correct response. Delayed rewards work only after the child has *learned* to delay them. At the early stages of learning especially, children need immediate feedback on their successes for, just as the response is a teacher's primary indication of the learner's understanding, the reinforcement is the learner's primary indication of success.

Reinforcement, then, entails providing a reward for the learner when he or she makes the desired response. The reward must be appropriate to the learning and to the learner's reward system. You should utilize levels of reinforcers with the intent of moving learners from extrinsic to intrinsic rewards and should immediately follow the correct response with the reward to provide the learner with feedback. Such reinforcement, when used skillfully, directly assists the child in attempting to learn the skill.

SUMMARY

Teaching is different from testing because you do not directly assist the learner during a test but do provide such assistance during teaching. In this section, six techniques have been provided for directly assisting the child in learning. In every skill lesson, the teacher should insure that the difficulty of the task is acknowledged, that the learner's attention is directed to the task to be learned and to its salient features, that these salient features are highlighted for the learner, that the highlighting is gradually diminished as the learner begins to respond correctly, that there is frequent opportunity for the learner to respond, and that the learner receives immediate reinforcement appropriate to that child's particular reward system.

THE ROLE OF PRACTICE

Because a skill has been taught does not necessarily mean that it has been mastered or that the learner is ready for a posttest. The teaching act itself only takes the child to the point where he or she can perform the task independently on a particular day. Practice is necessary before we can be sure that the child will remember the skill in the future.

Practice consists of numerous repetitions of the task. Its purpose is to help the learner solidify the skill responses so that they become habitual. In many ways, practice exercises are similar to tests in that they require frequent response to a task without any directed assistance from the teacher. A typical example of such practice would be a workbook page or Ditto exercise.

Practice is essential to effective learning because a child will retain what was learned only by frequent repetitions in performing the task. In fact, when children are taught a skill and seem to know it one day but are not able to do it two days later, the difficulty can almost always be traced to not having enough practice. The more practice a child receives, the easier it is to remember the skill when he or she needs it.

Practice does not necessarily have to be boring or a rote exercise. There are many lively ways to provide a learner with multiple repetitions of a task. The creative use of games, audiovisual materials, reading machines, and various kits and workbooks are just some ways in which practice can be made enjoyable. The only limit to innovative practice is the degree of creativity and commitment you are willing to bring to the task.

Regardless of whether you choose to use creative practice or more mundane activities such as workbooks and Ditto sheets, you must ensure that the practice meets certain minimum criteria. First, the practice exercise must provide multiple repetitions of the skill taught and not of some other skill. For instance, a practice activity in which children write new –at phonogram words would not be appropriate following a lesson on *pronouncing* such words when they appear in print. If the skill taught was pronouncing –at phonogram words encountered in print, then the practice exercise would require multiple repetitions in reading and pronouncing these words.

Second, the practice activity ought to be completed independently. That is, when the instruction is over and the child has been taught *how* to do the task, you give him or her the practice activity to complete at the desk or some other location without supervision. This frees you to spend your valuable instruction time with another learner.

Finally, as much as possible, the practice activity should be self-checking. Because the student is doing the activity independently, you are not available to constantly correct and check. Consequently, there is a danger that the child may complete an entire practice activity incorrectly, thereby making a habit out of the wrong response. By providing a way for your learners to check themselves and by directing them to complete the activity only if they are making the correct responses, you are sure that the learners are solidifying the correct, rather than the incorrect, response.

Practice, then, is an integral part of the total instructional process. Without it, the learner may not remember the skill when he or she needs it. Practice is not, however, synonymous with teaching because it does not provide the learner with directed assistance. Consequently, you must insure that the learner can do the skill before being given practice, and you should avoid assigning practice materials (such as workbooks, worksheets, games, and so on) as teaching devices unless these materials provide directed assistance.

SUMMARY OF HOW TO TEACH A SKILL

In their totality, the instructional techniques for teaching reading skills can be described in terms of an hourglass such as the model which follows:

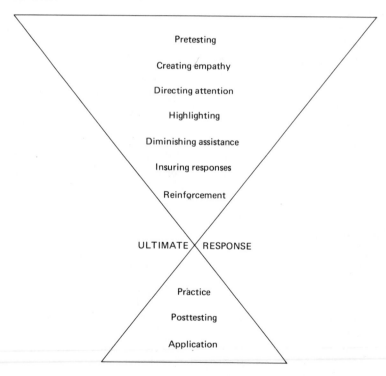

Pretesting

Creating empathy

Directing attention

Highlighting

Diminishing assistance

Insuring responses

Reinforcement

ULTIMATE RESPONSE

Practice

Posttesting

Application

At the top of the hourglass is the pretest where the child is tested on ability to perform the skill. At the neck of the hourglass is the ultimate response, the point at which the child can perform the skill without any directed assistance. When a child fails a pretest, you directly assist him or her in mastering what is not known. Thus, the upper part of the hourglass, excluding the pretest, represents the teaching activity. Once the skill has been taught and the learner can perform it unassisted, the focus moves to the bottom of the hourglass where practice is provided, the posttest is administered, and guidance is given in applying the skill in actual reading situations.

TEST YOUR KNOWLEDGE

1. The key difference between testing and teaching is that teaching calls for directed _____ from the teacher while testing does not.
2. By acknowledging the difficulty of the task, you make it possible for the student to respond without endangering his or her

   _____.
3. A first step in creating attending behavior in learners is to state specifically what the student is to _____.
4. A second step in directing attention requires that you direct the learner to the _____ of the task to be learned.
5. _____ is the teacher's way of dramatizing for the learner the crucial aspects of the task to be learned.
6. Highlighting is a type of crutch and, like all crutches, must be gradually _____.
7. The teacher knows that highlighting can be diminished by noting the quality of the learner's _____.
8. When a teacher elicits responses through a modeling technique, the child is basically being asked to _____ the teacher.
9. The discovery technique, while also making use of the principles of attending and diminishing highlighting, differs from the modeling technique because the teacher tries to set conditions so that the learner can _____ the principle by herself or himself.
10. Children can be encouraged to learn more quickly if we offer suitable rewards or _____.
11. The skill response becomes habitual as a result of _____.

SIMULATION ACTIVITIES

To be an effective skills teacher, you must be able to use the instructional principles described in this chapter. At first, this is a complex and difficult task, particularly when we are dealing with cognitive skills as we are in reading. It may be easier to start with a physical skill such as tying a shoelace. Assume that you are working with a preschool child and you want that child to be able to tie his or her shoes.

1. In setting the stage for the learning, you will want to create a learning set; you will want to acknowledge the difficulty of the task for the child. How might you accomplish this when teaching a child to tie his or her shoes?

2. After you have told the child what is to be learned and have established a learning set, you must direct attention to the salient features of the skill. What specific aspects of shoe tying would you direct
the child's attention to?

3. After directing the learner to the salient features of the task, you
would highlight those features as a means of maintaining attention.
How might you highlight the salient features in shoe tying?

4. After deciding upon your highlighting, you must determine how you
will elicit responses from the learner. You can do this using either a
modeling or a discovery technique. Which of these two techniques
would be most appropriate in teaching a preschooler to tie shoes?

5. Once you have elicited responses from the learner with the salient
features highlighted, you must diminish the crutch. How might you
gradually diminish the highlighting you are using when teaching the
child to tie shoes?

6. As an integral part of your instructional strategy, you must decide
how you are going to reinforce the learner. Let's assume that the
child is eager to learn how to tie shoes. What kind of reinforcement
might be most appropriate for this child?

7. Now let's assume that the child is *not* an eager learner but is instead
reluctant about learning to tie shoes, and you are trying to encourage
the child to learn this task at this time for practical reasons. What
kind of reinforcement might be most appropriate for this child?

8. Now let's assume that the child is able to tie shoes without assistance
from you and without any highlighting. However, you want to give
practice in tying shoes so that the skill will become habitual. How
would you provide for such practice?

9. Once the practice is completed, the skill lesson is over. However, you
will not know whether your instruction has been successful until you
see the child applying the skill. How will you know when the child
has completed the application stage of learning?

10. Let's assume the child does not successfully apply the skill. The
instruction has been a failure, and you will have to reteach the skill.
It is fruitless to repeat exactly the same procedures you used the first
time. Instead, you should look for ways to direct attention more
specifically. How would you more specifically direct attention if this
child had to be retaught how to tie shoes?

SUGGESTED FIELD EXPERIENCES

Observation. When observing in schools, watch teachers when they
teach skills of any kind. Do they create a learning set? Direct attention?
Highlight? Diminish crutches? Elicit responses with either the modeling
or discovery techniques? Provide reinforcement? Give practice?

Teaching activities. When you teach children any kind of skill in
any area of the curriculum, you should use the principles of creating a
positive set for learning, directing attention, highlighting, diminishing
assistance, responding, reinforcing, and practicing.

Client impact. If you use the instructional principles well, your learners will be directly assisted in learning the various curricular skills, making it unnecessary for them to "psych out" the situation either in terms of what is to be learned or how to learn it.

FOR CLASS DISCUSSION

Examine the following statement and be prepared to discuss it with your instructor.

> This chapter has described an instructional strategy in which the teacher controls and directs the learning situation through the principles of attending, highlighting, diminishing assistance, reinforcing, and so on. Some educators, such as some proponents of the "free school" movement, condemn any school situation which "controls and directs" children's learning.

How would you justify the principles in this chapter to such a free school advocate?

ANSWER KEY
  1. assistance
  2. self-concept
  3. do
  4. salient features
  5. highlighting
  6. diminished
  7. responses
  8. mimic
  9. discover
 10. reinforcements
 11. practice

TEACHING THE PREREQUISITE SIGHT-WORD SKILLS

OVERVIEW

This chapter provides you with techniques for teaching the readiness skills of visual discrimination, visual memory, visual sequencing, and naming symbols, all of which are prerequisites to learning to instantly recognize words at sight. Specific and practical suggestions for testing, directing attention, teaching, reteaching, practicing, and applying are provided for each skill. The ultimate objective is:

> Given pupils who need instruction in visual discrimination, visual memory, visual sequencing, and naming symbols, you will teach these skills using the instructional principles described in Chapter 14.

KNOWLEDGE BACKGROUND

In Chapter 5, we learned that the word identification skills can be divided into two streams of skills—the sight-word (or visual) stream and the analysis (or auditory) stream. Both streams contain numerous skills which the child must master to be proficient in the two roles of word identification—recognizing many words instantly and figuring out those words not known at sight.

Our focus here is the sight-word stream. This chapter specifies the prerequisites to learning words at sight, while the following chapter deals with the sight-words themselves once the readiness skills have been mastered.

While there are many individual skills which the child must learn before being able to identify words at sight, these can be categorized into four types: visual discrimination, visual memory, visual sequencing, and naming of visual symbols. Each type of skill is taught many times, first at a very simple level and then again at more complex levels. For instance, in visual discrimination, the child first learns to discriminate among grossly different symbols and is led gradually through succeeding levels of finer and finer discrimination until that child is noting very small differences between words. Each of these tasks is different because each requires a higher level of proficiency, but the type of task—visual discrimination—remains the same from level to level. A similar simple-to-complex sequence is followed for the skills of visual memory, visual sequencing, and naming of symbols. Hence, there are a large number of prerequisite sight-word skills, but there are only four different kinds of skills to be taught.

This chapter provides you with techniques for teaching each of the four types of prerequisite sight-word skills. It does not, however, provide the sequential listing of the various levels of each skill. For this information, we recommend that you consult the skill sequence provided in such texts as *Systematic Reading Instruction*.

VISUAL DISCRIMINATION

Visual discrimination is the first of the major types of prerequisite sight-word skills. Much of a reader's success depends upon skill at spotting the visual characteristics which make one letter or word different from another. Hence, the prerequisite visual discrimination tasks are designed to help the learner visually examine symbols and efficiently note the characteristics which set one symbol apart from another.

PRE- AND POSTTESTING VISUAL DISCRIMINATION

Since the focus in visual discrimination is on noting visual differences, the pre-and posttests should be set up to determine whether the child makes such discriminations. An efficient way to do this is to provide four visual symbols, three exactly alike and one different, and ask the learner to point to the one that is different.

A low-level visual discrimination test would be one such as the following, in which the child is asked to look at sets of geometric figures and point to the one that is different in each row:

At a slightly higher level, the child would be asked to look at sets of grossly different letters and point to the one that is different in each row, as follows:

SET I	t	t	T	t		SET VI	v	b	b	b
SET II	b	b	b	i		SET VII	l	l	l	m
SET III	u	u	j	u		SET VIII	y	e	y	y
SET IV	r	d	r	r		SET IX	a	s	s	s
SET V	c	c	c	x		SET X	w	w	q	w

At a still higher level, a similar procedure would be followed in determining whether a child can visually discriminate among letters that look much alike, as follows:

SET I	q	q	g	q		SET VI	o	o	o	c
SET II	o	a	a	a		SET VII	p	q	p	p
SET III	m	n	m	m		SET VIII	w	w	w	v
SET IV	v	v	v	u		SET IX	l	l	h	l
SET V	b	d	b	b		SET X	i	i	j	i

Finally, you would ask a child to visually discriminate among words that are similar in appearance, as follows:

SET I	dog/dog/cat/dog		SET VI	look/book/look/look
SET II	girl/boy/girl/girl		SET VII	like/lake/lake/lake
SET III	to/to/to/on		SET VIII	box/dox/box/box
SET IV	ten/ten/net/ten		SET IX	chair/chair/chair/char
SET V	fox/box/box/box		SET X	saw/was/was/was

DIRECTING ATTENTION

If the child fails to note the visual differences at any level, you must teach him or her to do so. Such instruction will require that the learner have a concept for *different* and that the lower-level visual discrimination tasks which preceded this one have been mastered. Once these conditions have been insured, you will direct the learner's attention to the specific elements to be noted in order to perform the task well. Since visual discrimination is a discrimination task, you will direct the learner to the specific visual differences which set one symbol apart from another.

For instance, if you want a child to note the differences between circles and squares, you would direct that child to look at the corners on the squares and the absence of corners on the circles, highlighting these features as a means of focusing on the crucial features. In helping the child discriminate between a lower-case t and an upper-case T, you would highlight the point where the letter is crossed and the curl at the bottom of the lower-case t. In directing children to the finer differences found in the d and b, you would highlight the relationship of the stick to the ball, while in helping them to note differences in similar words such as **box** and **fox**, you would highlight the first letters.

It is crucial that you direct the learner's attention accurately and precisely. You must analyze the discrimination task to determine what differences the child must note in order to make the discrimination, and you must then highlight those differences in a way which will help the child *see* the differences when examining the symbols.

TEACHING VISUAL DISCRIMINATION

You can use either a modeling technique or a discovery technique when teaching visual discrimination. If you choose a modeling procedure, you might start by drawing enlarged forms of two of the letters or words on a plain piece of paper, highlighting (with color or in some other way) the visual characteristics which set one symbol apart from the others in a set. Say, "These two figures are different. Watch me while I show you how I know that they are different." Point to each symbol in turn, direct the learner to the highlighting which emphasizes that symbol's unique visual characteristic, and say, "This one is different because it has (visual characteristic) but this one does not." Have the learner mimic your actions and words with the first two symbols and with two new symbols which have the distinctive visual characteristics highlighted. If the response is correct, continue the process with other letters or words, diminishing the amount of help you provide and the amount of highlighting with each sequence until the learner can respond successfully without any assistance.

If you use a discovery technique, you will try to develop the principle that printed symbols have distinguishing visual characteristics which allow us to discriminate one from another. Draw enlarged forms of the figures (or letters or words) on a plain piece of paper, highlighting (with color or in some other way) the visual characteristics which set one symbol apart from the other. Point to the two symbols in turn and ask the question, "Does this look like this?" When the response is "No," say, "Look at each figure in turn and at the highlighting I have added and tell me *why* one is different." If the response is correct, continue this questioning process with other symbols included in the test, diminishing the amount of highlighting with each sequence until the learner can respond successfully without any assistance. If the response is incorrect at any point, emphasize more directly the highlighting which distinguishes the visual forms and repeat the questioning process.

RETEACHING VISUAL DISCRIMINATION

If you teach a visual discrimination skill and the child is still unable to perform the task at the end of the instructional period, you should first check to make sure that that child has a concept for *different* since some children will be unable to perform the task simply because they do not know what you mean when you ask them, "Which one is different?" Next, you should check to make sure that the child has mastered any previous visual discrimination skills, that he or she can note differences at a lower level. If neither of these conditions is the cause of the child's difficulty in learning the task, you must reteach the skill, being more specific in directing the learner's attention and insuring that your high-lighting is an adequate guide to the distinguishing visual characteristics which set one symbol apart from others.

PRACTICING VISUAL DISCRIMINATION

Once the child can perform the skill with you, practice activities should be provided in which the task can be performed many times as a means for solidifying the skill. The following activities are illustrative.

1. Have the learner match geometric forms, letters, and words. The learner draws a form, letter, or word from a grab bag and matches it with individual cards he or she has in front of him or her.
2. Provide simple puzzles of forms, letters, or numerals or provide for experiences in assembling blocks to duplicate symbols.
3. Make up a jigsaw puzzle in which the pieces to be fitted are commonly confused forms, letters, or words. The learner must match the pieces to the appropriate places in the jigsaw puzzle.
4. Forms, letters, or words can be written on the chalkboard in arrangements similar to the following:

    b   b b d b

    The learner is asked to find the one in the set that is different from the solitary one on the left, and then to verbalize the way in which it is different.
5. The same activity as described in question 4 can be varied by using different mediums for the activity. For instance, alphabet blocks, sandpaper letters, tagboard letters, etc., can be used to give the learner the use of the tactile, as well as the visual, sense in assessing the differences which exist in the letters.
6. Using two frequently confused forms, letters, or words, list them on the chalkboard in this fashion:

was	saw
saw	was
saw	saw
was	was
was	saw

    Direct the learner to circle all the words in the two columns which are just like the first word in the left-hand column and to draw a line under each word which is just like the first word in the right-hand column.
7. Use a list of words such as the following and direct the learner to draw a line under all the words in the list which are exactly alike except for the first letter:

    cola   take   cook   make   sake   rake   fade

8. In an exercise similar to that in question 7, use a list of words such as the following and direct the learner to draw a line under all the words that are like the first word except that the letter at the end is different:

   him   hat   hit   have   his

9. Have the learner find in a written series the form, letter, or word that is unlike the other elements in the series and verbalize how it is different.

x	x	x	c
○	△	○	○
dog	dog	dog	cat

10. Provide the learner with two parallel columns of words, letters, or forms in which the same words, letters, or forms are used but in a different order. Direct the learner to draw lines connecting the like words, forms, or letters in the two columns.

△	○	b	n	is	on
○	□	d	b	at	it
□	◇	m	d	it	is
◇	△	n	m	on	at

APPLYING VISUAL DISCRIMINATION

The learners will be applying these skills in the more complex visual discrimination and visual memory tasks with which they will be working as they progress through the skills hierarchy. However, in addition to these applications, you should insure that this visual discrimination skill is used during the routine daily activities of the classroom. Some suggested techniques are:

1. Have play blocks cut in the shape of forms, numerals, and letters, and, as the learner plays with these, ask him or her to pick out the different block from among a group he or she is playing with.
2. During art period, have the learner work with paper cut in the shape of geometric forms, letters, or numerals and require that he or she pick out the different form from a group of forms.

VISUAL MEMORY

Visual memory is the second type of prerequisite sight-word skill. This skill focuses on remembering because the successful reader carries word images in his or her head and remembers what words look like. Visual memory builds upon previously learned discrimination skills—the learner first learns that one symbol is different from another and then learns to remember the symbol. At later stages, both the discrimination and the memory skills are used in combination as the child learns to remember words and to identify them instantly.

TEACHING VISUAL MEMORY

Visual memory is usually best taught using a modeling technique. Start your instruction by using simpler forms and manipulative materials. For instance, use a one-line figure instead of a three-line figure and make the figures from clay, blocks, or some other three-dimensional materials. Say, "I am going to look at this figure and try to remember its shape so that I can draw it when it is taken away. Watch me while I show you how I will remember this form." Point to the symbol's unique visual characteristic and say, "I am going to hold a picture in my mind of this form, remembering particularly that it has (say the visual characteristic)." Then close your eyes, trace the form, and say out loud what it is about the form that you are trying to remember. Have the learner mimic your words and tracing actions using the same figure. Then have the learner go through the same process with a different symbol. Repeat this process with additional symbols, each symbol becoming a little more difficult. As the child begins to respond successfully, gradually replace the manipulative materials with symbols that have visual characteristics highlighted with color. As the student continues to respond successfully, diminish the color highlighting until he or she can remember the form without any assistance.

While the discovery technique is difficult to apply to visual memory, you can use questions to help the learner find a way to remember symbols. Start with the simpler symbols and manipulative materials described above. Say, "I am going to show you this figure (or letter or word), then I will take it away, and I will ask you to draw it from memory. What will have to be remembered about this symbol in order to draw it from memory?" If the child is unable to respond, direct attention to the visual characteristics of the form through the use of highlighting. Repeat the process as the learner proceeds from simple to more difficult figures, gradually diminishing the amount of highlighting and introducing two-dimensional figures until the child is able to do the task as it is presented in the pretest.

RETEACHING VISUAL MEMORY

Visual memory is an extremely difficult skill for some young learners to master, and, as such, it is a skill that will have to be retaught to some youngsters. Whenever a child has difficulty with visual memory, your first step should always be to insure that the previous visual discrimination skills have been thoroughly learned; a child who cannot discriminate differences when seeing them will have great difficulty in recalling such figures from memory.

If the prerequisites have all been met, you will need to reteach the skill lesson. The best technique here is to simplify the early steps of instruction even more than you did the first time, while simultaneously increasing the amount of highlighting on the distinguishing visual characteristics of the form to be remembered. Only by simplifying and increasing the highlighting can the learner's attention be increased to the point of accomplishing the task.

PRACTICING VISUAL MEMORY

Once the child shows that he or she has learned to hold a visual image in the mind, you should plan practice activities which will provide multiple opportunities to perform the task as a means of habituating it. The following activities are illustrative.

1. Play a game with the learner in which you touch one object; he or she then touches that object and one more; the next learner touches both previous objects and one more; and so on with each learner touching all the objects that were previously touched before adding a new object.
2. Play a game somewhat like television's Concentration in which figures, letters, or words are placed on a table and covered up. The learner draws a card containing a figure, letter, or word from a box in front of him or her and must remember where the matching pair is located on the table. Begin simply by using just a few possibilities, adding other figures, letters, or words as the learner becomes more proficient.
3. Place a group of figures, letters, or words on the chalkboard. Direct the learner to examine these and then to turn away from the board. Erase one figure. When the learner turns back, he or she must reproduce the figure, letter, or word you erased. Start simply by using just two possibilities, increasing the number as the learner becomes more proficient.
4. Using a tachistoscope or flashcards, show the learner a numeral and direct him or her to reproduce it from memory. If he or she can do that, repeat the process using two numerals in a sequence. Continue to increase the number of numerals the learner is asked to reproduce as he or she succeeds at each level.

APPLYING VISUAL MEMORY

The learner will be applying these skills in learning the more complex visual memory tasks with which he or she will be working while progressing through the skills hierarchy. However, in addition to these applications, you should be alert for ways to point out the use of these visual memory skills during the routine daily activities of the classroom. Some suggested techniques are:

1. Make visual memory a part of your art lessons by presenting learners with a visual stimulus (such as a geometric form, a letter, or a numeral) and having them reproduce these from memory using a particular art technique (crayon, paint, paper cut-out, collage, and so on).
2. When returning from a field trip or some other activity, ask the learners

to recall the shapes of what they saw, asking questions such as "How many of you saw something that was shaped like the form I am holding up?"

VISUAL SEQUENCING

The third type of prerequisite sight-word skill is visual sequencing. To read successfully, the learner must be oriented in terms of the direction one follows when reading—from the front of the book to the back, from the top of the page to the bottom, and from the left side to the right side. While such sequencing seems natural to those of us who have been reading for years, children who have never read before must be carefully trained in this skill, particularly as it relates to left-to-right orientation. Inadequate visual training in left-to-right sequence often results in children who identify the letter **d** as **b** and the word **was** as **saw**. These are frustrating and persistent errors which come from looking at letters and words from right to left rather than from left to right, a habit which would never develop if visual sequencing were adequately taught at the very beginning levels of reading instruction.

PRE- AND POSTTESTING VISUAL SEQUENCING

Testing visual sequencing skills is a relatively simple task. It consists of asking the child to point to the beginning and to move his or her finger to the end. If you want to determine whether the child understands the top-to-bottom sequence, give him or her a page of print and ask that child to point to the first word and the last word. If you want to check for left-to-right sequence in word identification, give rows of words and have the child point to the first letter and to the last letter in each word.

DIRECTING ATTENTION

Failure to complete satisfactorily tests such as the above indicates a need for instruction. Prerequisite to such teaching, however, is insuring that the child has concepts for the terminology to be used. For instance, if you are teaching left-to-right orientation, you must insure that the child has a concept for *first* and *last*.

If the child does have the needed terminology, you can turn your attention to the problems of how to highlight the crucial features of the task. In visual sequencing, the crucial feature is usually left-to-right movement of the eyes across the page of print. One easy way to highlight this movement is to point to the first letter in a word and then move your finger in a physical left-to-right sweep under the word until you are pointing to the last letter.

TEACHING VISUAL SEQUENCING

As in visual memory, visual sequencing is usually best taught using a modeling technique. You might proceed as follows: Draw an enlarged form of a word on a plain piece of paper, highlighting (with color or in some other way) the first and last letters of the word and the left-to-right direction to be followed in examining it. Say, "We always look at words in the same way. We start here (pointing to the first letter) and move in this direction to here (pointing to the last letter). Watch me while I show you how my eyes move from the first letter to the last letter and then I'll ask you to do the same thing." After demonstrating in this fashion, have the learner mimic your actions of moving your finger from the left of the word to the right as you point out the first and last letters. In subsequent sequences, gradually diminish the amount of highlighting on the printed form of the word and the amount of verbal assistance you provide until the child is able to point out the first and last letters. In subsequent sequences, gradually diminish the amount of high-lighting on the printed form of the word and the amount of verbal assistance you provide until the child is able to point out the first and last letters without any assistance.

With some adaptations, the discovery technique can also be used when teaching visual sequencing, as follows: Provide the learner with an enlarged form of a word in which the visual sequence has been high-lighted as described above. Say, "In the past when I have written a word on the blackboard, I have always shown it to you by moving my finger under it like this (demonstrate a left-to-right movement). Now look at this word and the way in which I have highlighted certain things. As I say the word, I am going to move my finger under the word in this direc-tion. Can you figure out why I do that?" Your intention here is for the learner, with the help of your questions and the highlighting you have provided, to discover the principle that our eyes move from left to right in visually examining a printed word.

RETEACHING VISUAL SEQUENCING

If a child does not learn the visual sequencing skill adequately on the first try, it will be necessary for you to reteach it. On such occasions, the key lies with developing a highlighting technique which will be "fool-proof" in terms of moving the learner's eyes in the direction desired. One such highlighter is to hold a card over a word and then move the card slowly to the right, exposing the first letter, the second, and so on. Such a device forces the child to view the word in a left-to-right sequence.

PRACTICING VISUAL SEQUENCING

For left-to-right sequencing to become habitual, you must provide prac-tice activities which provide multiple repetitions of the task. Examples of such practice activities follow.

1. Make separate cards for each letter in the learner's name. Scramble these and direct the learner to put them back in the right order to form his or her name saying as he or she does so, "First letter, other letters, last letter."

2. Write a word on a card or on the chalkboard, leaving off either the first or last letter. Direct the learner to print the missing letter in the proper position, saying, "first letter" or "last letter" as appropriate.
3. Use puzzles in which the learner must trace a pattern following numbers or letters. Always have the pattern in such activities move from top to bottom and from left to right to establish the sequencing responses desired.
4. Prepare a set of pictures in which direction is clearly indicated. Direct the learners to find something in the pictures that is at the top, at the bottom, going down, going up, going from left to right, etc.
5. Give the learner sets of pictures in which each picture tells part of a story. Comic books are useful for this activity. Scramble the pictures and then direct the learner to arrange the pictures to tell the story. Insure that the learner has arranged the pictures in a top-to-bottom and left-to-right sequence.

APPLYING VISUAL SEQUENCING

The learner will be using this skill as he or she progresses to the more complex visual skills in the hierarchy. However, in addition to these applications, you should insure that this visual sequencing skill is used during the routine daily activities in the classroom. Some suggested techniques are:

1. Any time there is an opportunity to display art-work or other learner products, place these on the chalkboard starting at the left and moving to the right. When discussing these with learners, discuss the one at the left first and progress to the right, emphasizing that movement with a physical motion of your hand in the left-to-right direction.
2. When placing directions on the chalkboard or when writing charts with learners, emphasize both the top-to-bottom sequence and the left-to-right sequence by pointing these out to the learners. Look for opportunities for eliciting learner responses, such as having them go to the chart to point to the first word, the last word, the first letter in a certain word, the last letter in a certain word, etc.
3. When reading stories to children or when sharing picture books with them, point out the front-to-back, top-to-bottom, and left-to-right directions and look for ways to elicit learner responses to sequencing as they share these stories with you.
4. Make frequent use of a wall pocket chart in which the pockets are arranged in rows. Have children use the pocket chart, insuring that they always begin at the top and move to the right across the rows.
5. Use a calendar to apply the left-to-right system by marking off the days in each week.

NAMING SYMBOLS

The fourth type of prerequisite sight-word skill is naming symbols. This is an association task, since the learner is required to pair a name with a visual form. Naming the visual symbols is not nearly as crucial a skill at this stage as visual discrimination, memory, and sequencing since it is possible for a person to learn how to read without ever having a name for the letters. Naming does, however, have two uses. First, knowing the names of the letters is often an aid in discrimination, and, consequently, in teaching the names you are often helping the learner differentiate among them. Second, communicating with the learner is easier if he or she knows the names of the letters because you can simply name them rather than always having to *show* what you mean.

PRE- AND POSTTESTING NAMING

Testing to determine whether a child knows the names of letters or other symbols is simply a matter of showing a letter card and asking for the name of the form on the card. You keep track of those the learner cannot name and teach those.

DIRECTING ATTENTION

Teaching the symbols the child does not know is a matter of pairing the name with the symbol. Since it is an association task, the child must be able to connect the visual form of the symbol to the name for the symbol. To direct attention, you must highlight both the visual form of the symbol and the sound of the name to which it is to be connected. For instance, if you want the child to learn the name of the letter **a,** you could have him or her look at and trace the letter form while simultaneously saying the letter name.

TEACHING NAMING

Because it is an association task, naming depends largely upon memory and repetition. Consequently, it is often best to teach this skill using a modeling technique. As such, you might use the following procedure: Using wooden block shapes for the letters, tell the learner you are going to teach him or her to remember the name of each letter and that you want him or her to watch and mimic your actions. Then pick up one of the letters, point out its distinguishing visual characteristics (such as the two humps on the letter m) and trace the letter with your finger, simultaneously saying, "This letter is **m.**" Have the learner mimic you, insuring that he or she is looking at the letter while saying its name. This is a matter of rote learning and will require, for most learners, some degree of repetition. At each succeeding response, however, the amount of assistance should be diminished until the learner can do the task with an unhighlighted printed form of the letter and without mimicking your actions. *Caution:* letters that are easily confused (such as the letters **b** and **d**) should be taught initially at widely separate times. If the learner has persistent difficulty with these letters, however, they can then be taught together, using the strategy of highlighting the visual characteristics which set the two easily confused letters apart.

While there is no real principle to be discovered, you can use questions to help the learner determine a way to remember the names of letters. Start with the wooden block shapes described above. Say, "This is a (say the letter). Look at the (say the letter) as I say its name. Can you figure out a way to remember the name of this letter?" As the child responds, direct attention to the visual characteristics of the form through the use of highlighting and be sure that the child simultaneously looks at the symbol and says its name. Move gradually from the wooden block shapes to printed forms of the symbol, diminishing the amount of highlighting until the learner is able to remember the symbol without assistance.

RETEACHING NAMING

Because naming is heavily dependent upon memory, there will always be the need for repetition before the child truly knows the names of the letters you are teaching. However, if he or she does not seem to be learning the names at all or is exhibiting unusual difficulty, you should plan to reteach the skill from scratch. In such cases, your strategy should focus on two elements. First, you should make heavy use of tracing to involve tactile and kinesthetic senses as well as visual and auditory inputs, thereby strengthening the degree of attention the learner brings to the task. Second, you should emphasize more heavily the connection between the visual form of the symbol and the sound of the name since it is this connection which is at the heart of the naming task.

PRACTICING NAMING

While practice plays an important part in learning any skill, it is of particular importance in naming since the strength of the association between the letter and its name depends upon the number of repetitions the learner makes. Some appropriate practice activities include the following:

1. Games such as Climb-the-Ladder can be played, in which each rung has a letter connected to it. The learner "climbs" the ladder rung by rung naming each of the letters in sequence.
2. Similar games can be created which make use of other devices, such as adding cars to a train (each car having a new letter), putting leaves on a tree, etc.
3. A form of Concentration can be played. Prepare duplicate cards of five letters. Mix the ten cards and turn them upside down. The learner turns over a card, names the letter, and tries to match it by turning over the card which is its duplicate. *Caution:* make sure the learner *names* the letter when he or she turns it over.
4. Games can be played in which letters are placed on bowling pins. The learner rolls a ball at the pins, knocking down as many pins as possible. However, only those pins whose letters the learner can name are counted in scoring.
5. Place letter cards on the seats of chairs arranged in a large circle. The

learners march around the chairs in time to music until the music stops. Then each learner must name the letter on the seat of the chair next to where he or she stopped.

6. Seat learners in a circle, with one learner in the middle. Provide each learner with a letter card. The learner in the center calls out the names of two or three letters, and the learners having these letter cards change seats. The learner in the middle also tries to get a seat, and the learner left standing calls the next letter.

7. Make a pocket chart and provide the learners with letter cards. Hold up a card (such as the letter a) and say, "This is the letter a. If you have a letter a, come place it in the same pocket where I put mine, and say the letter name as you do so." When all the pockets of the chart are filled, point to each pocket in turn, have the learners examine the letter in that pocket, and have them name each letter while looking at it.

8. Use the pupils' names to help teach letter names. For instance, place the names of the pupils on the chalkboard and say, "How many of our names have the letter f in them? Who can find a letter f in any of our names?" The learner goes to the board, underlines the letter f in as many names as he or she can find it, and says the letter name each time he or she underlines it.

APPLYING NAMING

The learner will be using this skill as he or she progresses through the skills hierarchy. However, in addition to these applications, you should be alert for ways to point out the use of the names during daily activities of the classroom. Some suggested techniques are:

1. Learners can be provided with letter cards while waiting to be dismissed or while waiting to begin another activity, and they proceed according to who has the letter named by the teacher (" All those who have the letter m should go now.")

2. Use the letters as identifying marks around the room and direct children to these points by naming the letter ("Jimmy, please get my book that has the letter b on the cover," or "Mary, would you bring me the pile of papers that has the letter m on top?").

SUMMARY OF TEACHING THE PREREQUISITE SIGHT-WORD SKILLS

Before a child can develop a large stock of sight-words, he or she must know how to visually examine and remember visual symbols. While the learner is taken through a large number of such visual readiness skills prior to beginning to learn sight-words, these skills can be classified into four categories. Each of these—visual discrimination, visual memory, visual sequencing, and naming of symbols—helps a child look at and remember the letters and words encountered in reading. As such, they are crucial readiness competencies which must be thoroughly learned.

The suggestions in this chapter provide you with a resource for such instruction.

TEST YOUR KNOWLEDGE

1. Visual discrimination requires the child to note _____ among symbols.
2. Visual memory requires that the child _____ what visual symbols look like.
3. Visual sequencing focuses on the _____ one follows when reading.
4. The naming task requires that the child associate a visual symbol with its _____.
5. In teaching visual discrimination, the teacher will provide attenders and highlighting which focus on the _____ among symbols.
6. In visual memory, the teacher's attenders and highlighting focus on _____ a symbol's shape and form.
7. In visual sequencing, the teacher's attenders and highlighting focus especially on _____.
8. In naming, the teacher's attenders and highlighting focus on the _____ between the symbol and its name.
9. When a sight-word skill is not learned the first time, an initial reteaching step is to insure that the _____ skills in the hierarchy have been adequately learned.
10. Another technique for reteaching is to improve or increase the _____ to insure that the child is properly attending to the task.

SIMULATION ACTIVITIES

Let's assume that you are teaching a first grade. Several of your pupils fail the following pretest:

The performance objective. Given three letters that are exactly alike and one that is clearly different, the learner marks the one that is different.

The pretest. Direct the learner to indicate (mark or point to as appropriate) which letter in the following sets is different. Criterion for mastery is 80 percent.

SET I	g	g	w	g		SET VI	x	x	x	c
SET II	S	a	a	a		SET VII	d	r	d	d
SET III	e	y	e	e		SET VIII	o	o	j	o
SET IV	m	m	m	l		SET IX	z	z	z	v
SET V	b	v	b	b		SET X	s	s	S	s

1. What is the response that you want the pupils to be able to make at the end of the lesson that they could not make on the pretest?
2. What kind of prerequisite sight-word skill is this?

3. To what will the pupils be directed in the lesson? What will be highlighted?

The following is a lesson you teach to develop this skill with those pupils who failed the pretest. Examine the various sections of the lesson which are identified by arrows and note in the margin what principle of instruction you are employing at each point.

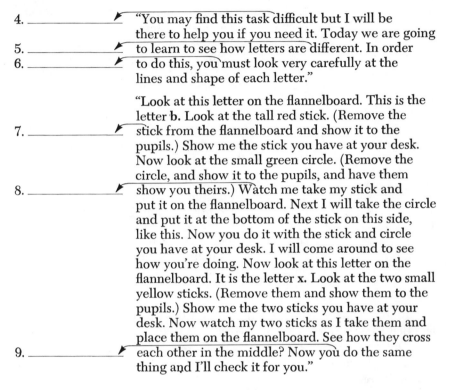

4. _____ ⟋ "You may find this task difficult but I will be there to help you if you need it. Today we are going

5. _____ ⟋ to learn to see how letters are different. In order

6. _____ ⟋ to do this, you must look very carefully at the lines and shape of each letter."

"Look at this letter on the flannelboard. This is the letter **b**. Look at the tall red stick. (Remove the

7. _____ ⟋ stick from the flannelboard and show it to the pupils.) Show me the stick you have at your desk. Now look at the small green circle. (Remove the circle, and show it to the pupils, and have them

8. _____ ⟋ show you theirs.) Watch me take my stick and put it on the flannelboard. Next I will take the circle and put it at the bottom of the stick on this side, like this. Now you do it with the stick and circle you have at your desk. I will come around to see how you're doing. Now look at this letter on the flannelboard. It is the letter **x**. Look at the two small yellow sticks. (Remove them and show them to the pupils.) Show me the two sticks you have at your desk. Now watch my two sticks as I take them and place them on the flannelboard. See how they cross

9. _____ ⟋ each other in the middle? Now you do the same thing and I'll check it for you."

A similar procedure is followed for other letters.

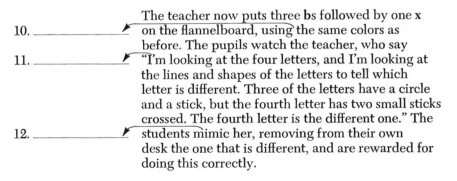

The teacher now puts three **b**s followed by one **x**

10. _____ ⟋ on the flannelboard, using the same colors as before. The pupils watch the teacher, who say

11. _____ ⟋ "I'm looking at the four letters, and I'm looking at the lines and shapes of the letters to tell which letter is different. Three of the letters have a circle and a stick, but the fourth letter has two small sticks crossed. The fourth letter is the different one." The

12. _____ ⟋ students mimic her, removing from their own desk the one that is different, and are rewarded for doing this correctly.

A similar procedure is used with other letters, but the teacher gradually moves away from modeling the process.

13. _____ First, the teacher begins printing the letters on the chalkboard, omitting the color coding.

14. _____ Finally, the students must respond by picking out the different letter when it is printed on a piece of paper.

The pupils practice this skill while working in pairs,
15. _____ independently of the teacher. Each pair of pupils is given a series of tagboard cards. On one side of each card is a series of letters, three that are exactly
16. _____ alike and one that is different. On the back of the card, the same four letters are printed, but the different one is circled. One pupil in a pair holds up a card for the other to see and directs the partner
17. _____ to point to the letter that is different. When the partner does so, the first child checks the response by looking at the correct response on the back of
18. _____ the card. They repeat this procedure, taking turns, for all the tagboard cards.

Ultimately this skill will help the student distinguish one word from another quickly as a step in remembering words by sight. That is a distant
19. _____ application, however. A more immediate application will occur as the skill of visual memory of the same letters is taught. The discrimination skills taught here are used to learn another, more refined skill.

In the same classroom, you administer the following pretest and find that some children cannot perform this task:

The performance objective. Given a few seconds to examine a short word, the learner reproduces the word from memory, to the satisfaction of the teacher.

The pretest. Prepare ten flashcards, each card having one word of the following sequence:

yes   no   and   the   was   in   to   of   my   he

Flash each for the count of three. Then direct the learner to reproduce it. Criterion for mastery is teacher judgment regarding the accuracy of each reproduction. Size is not a criterion.

20. What is the response that you want the pupils to be able to make at the end of the lesson that they could not make on the pretest?
21. What type of prerequisite sight-word skill is this?
22. To what will you direct the pupils in this lesson? What will you highlight?
23. If a child did not learn this skill as a result of one lesson, what would you do differently when you retaught the skill?

Now let's assume that you administer the following pretest and find that some of your pupils are unable to meet the criteria for mastery:

The performance objective. Given cards with the words **yes** and **no** and the student's name printed on them, the learner, when directed, points to the first letter in each of these words and to the last letter in each of these words.

The pretest. Provide the learner with three cards on which are printed the words **yes** and **no,** and his or her name. The learner reads each word and, when directed to point to the first and last letter in each of these words, does so. Criterion for mastery is 100 percent.

24. What is the response you want the pupils to be able to make at the end of the lesson that they could not make on the pretest?
25. What type of prerequisite sight-word skill is this?
26. To what will you direct the pupils in this lesson? What will you highlight?
27. What will the focus of the practice activity be?

Finally, let's assume that you administer the following pretest to your first graders and find some who are unable to perform the task.

The performance objective. Given a random group of lower-case alphabet letters, the learner points to and names each letter in turn.

The pretest. Direct the learner to point to and name each of the following letters. Criterion for mastery is 100 percent, with the rationale being that if the learner can name ten randomly selected letters, the chances are good that he or she knows all the letters. However, if you note that a learner does not know all the letters despite a 100 percent performance on this task, you should test for all the letters of the alphabet and teach those not known.

m   t   w   a   s   e   l   r   o   y

28. What is the response that you want pupils to be able to make at the end of the lesson that they could not make on the pretest?
29. What type of prerequisite sight-word skill is this?
30. To what will you direct the pupils in this lesson? What will you highlight?

SUGGESTED FIELD EXPERIENCES

Observation. When observing in schools, you should note whether nonreaders are provided with instruction in visual discrimination, visual memory, visual sequencing, and naming. How does the teacher direct the pupils' attention to these tasks? How are the tasks highlighted? How are they practiced?

Teaching activities. When working with beginning readers in a classroom setting, you should be able to determine what prerequisite sight-word skills each child has, and you should be able to use the principles of instruction to teach such skills to those pupils who need them.

Client impact. By carefully diagnosing and thoroughly teaching the prerequisite sight-word skills, you will be insuring that your pupils will develop efficient skills of visual examination which will form the foundation for their eventually becoming fluent and efficient sight-word readers.

FOR CLASS DISCUSSION

Teachers faced with pupils who confuse letters and words and who reverse letters and words often turn immediately to phonics, saying that the child's problem lies with not knowing the sounds of the letters. In terms of what you know of the dual goals of word identification (instant recognition on the one hand and analytical problem solving on the other), what would your reaction be to such a strategy?

ANSWER KEY
  1. differences
  2. remember
  3. left-to-right sequence
  4. name
  5. differences
  6. remembering
  7. left-to-right sequence and first-and-last
  8. association
  9. prerequisite
10. highlighting

TEACHING
SIGHT-WORDS

OVERVIEW

This chapter provides you with techniques for teaching children to recognize words at sight. Specific and practical suggestions for testing, directing attention, teaching, reteaching, practicing, and applying are provided. The ultimate objective is:

> Given pupils who do not recognize words instantly at sight, you will teach this skill using the instructional principles developed in Chapter 14.

KNOWLEDGE BACKGROUND

The instant recognition of words is a crucial reading skill for several reasons. First, our job is to develop fluent readers and not ones who must analyze and sound out each word in turn. Fluent readers are readers who instantly recognize words they are reading. Second, many of the words we read in the English language do not lend themselves to sounding out since they do not follow the phonetic principles of the language. The only efficient way to teach such words is to teach the learner to recognize each at sight. Finally, to master the complete phonetic system of English is a laborious process and would take too long if we were to wait until the learners had mastered this system before we let them read independently. By teaching them to read certain words instantly, we are allowing them to independently read many materials at a stage when they would otherwise be unable to do so.

The technique of recognizing words at sight is, simply, a process of memorizing words. If you have seen a word a number of times and either have been told what it is or have successfully analyzed it, you eventually come to know the word—that is, you neither have to be told what it is nor analyze it. You recognize it instantly.

SELECTING WORDS TO BE TAUGHT AT SIGHT

It is neither possible nor wise to have a child learn all words through sight-word recognition simply because there are too many words in the language to memorize each one in turn. Consequently, we must choose which words we will teach the child to recognize instantly. This decision is usually made on the basis of utility and the phonetic consistency of the word. Utility means that the most utilitarian words, or most frequently used words, are taught first, with the less frequently used words taught later. Consequently, we often find words such as **the, in, to** and **it** being taught as sight-words very early in a reading program because they appear so frequently in everyday reading. Phonetic consistency means that nonphonetic words are taught as sight-words since a child would not be able to analyze them independently. For instance, the words **come** and **have** are usually taught as sight-words because they violate phonetic principles and are not pronounced according to the "rules," while words such as **rat** and **bat** usually are *not* taught as sight-words because they can be analyzed and pronounced using the phonetic principles of the language.

Most teachers use source lists for determining what words are to be taught at sight. The most widely known list, and one which has stood the test of time, is the Dolch list.[1] In addition, the basal textbooks found in most classrooms usually specify the words which should be taught at sight, as do most well-developed skills hierarchies.

PRE- AND POSTTESTING SIGHT WORDS

Once we have selected which words the child should know at sight, it is a relatively easy task to determine whether he or she knows them. First, print each word on separate flashcards. Then flash each word to the learner, allowing only a second or less to examine the word. It is crucial that you only show the word for a second since we are trying to find out if the child recognizes the word *instantly* and not whether he or she knows the word if given time to study it. As you go through the list of words, keep track of the ones the child misses, since only the missed

[1] E. W. Dolch, *Teaching Primary Reading* (Champaign,, Ill.: Garrard Press, 1941), pp. 205-207.

words need to be taught. If the child is unable to respond at all when the word is flashed, note that word. If, however, the child responds with the wrong word, note both the correct word and the response given since you will want to teach the two confused words together.

DIRECTING ATTENTION

Learning sight-words is a visual task which draws heavily on the previously taught skills of visual discrimination, visual memory, and visual sequencing. In teaching this skill, then, you must first insure that the learner has mastered the skills described in Chapter 15. If not, it is unlikely that he or she will be able to learn sight-words.

A second important condition to learning sight-words is whether the word being taught is in the child's oral vocabulary. If it is a word which the child does not use in daily speech, it is not likely that the child will remember it as a sight-word. For instance, inner-city children frequently have difficulty learning the sight-word **were** because it is not in their oral vocabulary; they say things like, "We *was* going downtown" and *not* "We *were* going downtown." Such children will have great difficulty learning the word **were** until they are taught to use the word orally.

Because sight-word recognition is a visual task, the teacher must direct the child to the unique visual characteristics of the word. This would include initial and final letters, length, shape, double letters, and so on. If the child is trying to learn the word **dinosaur,** you might highlight the beginning letter and the length of the word, while if the word to be learned is **cow,** you might highlight the beginning letter and the shortness of the word.

TEACHING SIGHT-WORDS

If, on the pretest, the child did not respond at all when you flashed a word, you can assume that that child has no idea what the word is. To teach the child to identify the word instantly when he or she sees it in print, you can use either a modeling or a discovery technique.

If you chose to use the modeling technique, you would follow a sequence somewhat as follows: Once you determine that the learner is familiar with the word and can use it orally, tell him or her that you are going to show a way to remember the word and that he or she is to watch and mimic you. Show the printed form of the word (in which the unique visual characteristics have been highlighted) saying, "This word says (say the word). I can remember this word because it has (specify and point to that word's unique visual form). Have the child mimic you and then show him or her how to connect the visual form to the word by saying, "I am going to look at the word, note its characteristics, and say its name. Now you do the same." Provide for a number of repetitions in which the amount of modeling and highlighting is gradually diminished until the learner is able to recognize the word without assistance.

If you prefer to use a discovery technique, you might follow a sequence somewhat like the following: The principle to be developed in teaching sight-words is that every word has visual characteristics which serve to make it unique from all other words. Using a word which is in the learner's oral vocabulary and which has been printed on a card with the distinguishing characteristics highlighted, ask questions designed to guide the learner to discover independently how to remember each word. For instance, place the highlighted word before the child and say, "This word says (say the word). Look at the word and tell me how you will remember it so that you will know it instantly when I flash it to you." Have him or her describe how he or she will remember, using your highlighting as a guide if the child desires. Then have the child look at each word, note its characteristics, and then say the word. Provide for a number of repetitions in which the amount of highlighting and the number of cueing questions posed by you are gradually diminished until the learner is able to instantly recognize the word without assistance.

TEACHING RECOGNITION OF EASILY CONFUSED WORDS

The child who is being pretested on sight-words does not always say nothing or guess wildly when he or she does not know a word. Sometimes that child will respond with another word which is almost like it. For instance, when presented with the word **there,** the child might respond with **where,** and when presented with **was,** the child might respond with **saw.** You are still faced with a sight-word recognition problem, but your strategy must be altered slightly.

When a child confuses two similar-looking words, it is because of inability to visually examine printed symbols, particularly as they relate to visually discriminating among fine differences and looking at words in the correct sequence (from left to right and from top to bottom). To teach the instant recognition of such words, then, you must highlight the visual discriminator in each pair which serves as the cue for contrasting the words. With the words **where** and **there,** for instance, you must highlight the **wh** in **where** and **th** in **there,** while in the words **was** and **saw** you must highlight the first letter and the left-to-right sequence in each of the words.

You may use either a modeling or a discovery technique when teaching easily confused sight-words. If you use a modeling strategy, you might proceed as follows: Tell the learner that you are going to help him or her remember two words which are difficult to tell apart and that he or she is to watch and mimic your actions. Write each pair of words on a piece of paper, with the discriminator highlighted with color or some other technique. For instance, with **where** and **there** you might circle the **wh** in **where** and the **th** in **there,** while with **was** and **saw** you might circle the first letter and draw an arrow under the word to show the direction to be followed in visually examining the word. Say, "I can tell **where** and **there** apart because **where** begins with **wh** and

there begins with **th**." Then point to each word in turn and say, "This is the word **there** because it begins with a **th**, and this is the word **where** because it begins with a **wh**." Have the learner mimic you, insuring that he or she is noting the discriminator and is looking at the word while saying its name. Repeat the procedure several times, diminishing the amount of highlighting on the discriminating cue until the child can instantly recognize the words without mimicking you and without any highlighting.

If you prefer to use the discovery technique, the procedure would be somewhat as follows: The principle to be discovered is that each of the easily confused words has a visual characteristic which serves as the discriminator for contrasting the pairs. Using the same kind of highlighting as is described above, point to the two words in turn, and ask the question, "Does this word look like this other one?" When the response is no, say, "Look at each word in turn and at the highlighting I have added and tell me why one is different from the other. If the pupil responds correctly, have him or her look at each word and say its name. Continue this procedure with diminished amounts of highlighting until the learner can respond successfully without any assistance. If the response is not successful, emphasize more directly the highlighting which distinguishes the words and repeat the questioning process.

RETEACHING SIGHT-WORDS

If the learner is unable to instantly recognize a word at sight after the first lesson, you must reteach the skill. Your first steps in such reteaching should be:

1. Recheck to make sure that the words are in the learner's oral vocabulary and, if they are not, teach the learner to use the word orally before asking him/her to recognize it in print.
2. Return to previous visual discrimination, visual memory, and visual sequencing skills in the hierarchy to insure that the child possesses the prerequisite skills needed to perform this more complex visual task.
3. Reexamine your analysis of the visual characteristics of the word to insure that you are having the learner note the most helpful visual characteristics.
4. Reteach the skill using a more dramatic form of highlighting to direct the learner more specifically to the unique visual characteristics of the word.

If none of the above strategies prove fruitful and the learner is still unable to recognize the word at sight, you should teach the word using one of the following techniques:

1. Use the *VATK technique* in which the visual, auditory, tactile, and kinesthetic senses are used to help the child remember the word by printing a large form of the word on paper, in sand, or on some other rough material and having the child repeatedly trace the word with his/her index finger while simultaneously saying its name.

2. Have the learner temporarily use the initial sound of the word as a crutch (providing the child has already mastered the sound–symbol connection for that letter) by telling him/her to look at the word and to "get your mouth ready" to say the first sound before actually saying the whole word.
3. If the word has a low association value (such as the words **the, through,** and so on), teach the hard word in combination with another word which has high association value (such as **dinosaur, astronaut,** and so on) by putting both words on a card together in a phrase (as in **the dinosaur**).

PRACTICING SIGHT-WORDS

Once you have taught the learner to instantly recognize the word, you must provide multiple repetitions to insure habituation of the skill. There are many activities which would provide such practice, of which the following are illustrative.

1. Make up racing games in which learners progress by pronouncing at sight the words to be learned. For instance, construct an auto racing course, dividing the track into equal sized squares. Give each learner a toy racing car and provide yourself with a pack of cards upon which are printed the words you want the students to practice. Flash one word to each learner in turn. The learner who pronounces it instantly moves the racing car one square closer to the finish line. If he or she is unable to pronounce the word, the car does not move. The first learner to get the car to the finish line wins.
2. Help learners construct self-help references for the words they find difficult. For instance, each learner can be provided with a three-by-five-inch file box and a supply of file cards. Every word he/she has difficulty learning is written on the file card together with a picture or other memory aid. The learner refers to the file frequently to study the words and to remember what the word is if unable to identify it when reading.
3. Place the words to be practiced on the chalkboard. One learner is sent out into the hall and another goes to the board and points to one of the words. The rest of the class pronounces the word to insure that all the learners know it. Then the first learner is brought back into the room and tries to guess which word has been pointed to. He or she points to one word and says, "Is it (word)?" and continues this way until the word is identified.
4. Construct ladder games in which a paper ladder leads to a place where a reward of some kind is waiting. For instance, the ladder can lead to the upper branches of a paper apple tree which has many paper apples on it. Each rung of the ladder has a sight-word attached to it. The learner must instantly pronounce the word on each rung of the ladder. If successful in reaching the top of the ladder, the learner receives a reward such as a real apple or a check on his or her progress chart.
5. A multitude of games for building sight-words can be devised based

on the idea of a trip. This trip may be a reconstruction of the adventures of some famous story character (such as Peter Rabbit), a trip that the learners are actually going on, or a trip that is completely imaginary (such as a trip to the moon, a trip to a distant city, etc.). In any case, a gameboard is constructed upon which is drawn the path to be followed in reaching the destination, the hazards to be overcome along the way, and so on. Each learner progresses on the trip by correctly pronouncing the words flashed to when his or her turn comes. The first learner to complete the trip wins the game.

6. A fishing game can be played in which the learner is given a pole constructed of a stick and a string with a magnet tied to the end. Paper fish, with the words to be practiced printed on them, are placed in a box or in some other object which will serve as a pond. A paper clip is attached to each fish. Learners drop their line into the pond until the magnet attracts the paper clip on a fish. They pull the fish out and get to keep it if they can correctly pronounce the word printed on its side. The learner catching the most fish wins.

7. Make nine packs of ten cards each. The nine packs represent the nine holes of a golf course, and the words printed on the cards are the words to be practiced. The cards are shuffled and each player puts a pack for the first hole face down on the desk. The player turns each card over in turn, pronounces the word, and goes on. Every time he or she is unable to correctly pronounce a word, a mark is placed on the scorecard, and the number of wrong answers on the first hole (first pack of cards) is the score for that hole. The learner continues in this manner through the nine packs of word cards, trying to get as small a score as possible. You should encourage each child to keep a chart record of the score on this course so that the child can note progress "mastering the course." New courses offering new challenges can be constructed as new words need to be learned.

8. Put the words to be practiced on cards, placing a numerical value in the upper-right-hand corner of each card in accordance with its degree of difficulty in being remembered. For instance, **dinosaur** is a fairly easy word for learners to identify and would only be given a value of 1, but **the** is very difficult for young learners to recognize and would be given a value of 3. Learners take turns drawing the cards, reading the words, and noting their scores. If they pronounce the word correctly, their score is the numerical value noted on the corner of the card. The learner with the most points at the end wins.

9. Play a treasure hunt game in which several packets of ten or more words each are hidden around the classroom. Give the learner the first packet and direct him or her to read each word. The last card will tell where the next packet is hidden. The child goes to that packet and repeats the process. The final packet will direct the child to a spot in the classroom where he or she will receive a prize for having completed the game.

10. A variation of Concentration can be played. Place the words to be learned on cards and put them face down on the table. The learner must remember which two cards are exactly alike and try to pick up

matching pairs. As the player turns over each card, he or she must pronounce the word on the card. If successful in picking up a word which matches the first word, the learner gets another turn. The learner with the most pairs at the end wins.

APPLYING SIGHT-WORDS

Once the child has learned to instantly recognize a word when it is flashed on a card, you should immediately provide for transfer and application of this skill by giving reading material containing the new words he or she has learned. The following examples would be appropriate.

1. Make a class dictionary in which the sight-words are printed in alphabetical order in a large notebook. The learners use old magazines to find pictures illustrating the words and are then encouraged to use this dictionary to look up a word any time they are reading.
2. Make a habit of sending short personal notes to your learners. For instance, when they arrive in the morning, they may find on their desks a note from you saying, "Can you help me at my desk?" or "How do you feel?" or even something as simple as "I like you." In leaving these notes, you should make sure that they utilize words which each learner needs to practice but that no words are used which the learner has never been exposed to. This is a highly motivating device for encouraging learners to master sight-words.
3. Place the learner in a basal textbook having a readability which matches the instructional reading level and have him or her read and discuss the stories. Point out the words the learner has learned at sight and be sure he or she uses them in the contextual setting.
4. Write stories for the learner which feature the child as the central character and which utilize many of the words he or she has learned to recognize at sight. The child reads these stories for purposes specified ahead of time by either the teacher and/or the child and, in the process, uses the sight-words already taught.
5. Encourage much recreational reading using library books, magazines, and other reading matter which is written at the learner's instructional reading level.
6. Make use of "experience charts" in which common experiences of the class are recorded on large chart paper following a sequence of steps such as the following: The learner first participates in an interesting and significant experience and discusses it with the other children and with you. Then you help plan a title, the general content, and the exact sentences for the chart. The learners dictate sentences to you which you print on the chart. Be careful to use either words which the learners have been taught to recognize or which you have adequately identified for them. You then read the chart to the learners, and they each take turns reading the chart alone.

SUMMARY OF TEACHING SIGHT-WORDS

This chapter has presented you with techniques for teaching children to recognize words instantly at sight. Your strategy in teaching sight-words would follow this sequence:

1. Select the words to be taught using one of the sources specified in the chapter.
2. Use flashcards to determine which words the child does not know.
3. If a child does not know a word at all, teach it using the first suggestions provided; if the child confuses one word with another, use the technique of cueing to the discriminator which sets one word apart from another.
4. If the child does not learn the word on the first try, check to make sure that the word is in the oral vocabulary, that the child has all the prerequisites, and that you are directing attention to the appropriate visual characteristics.
5. If he or she still does not learn the word, reteach using either VATK, phonic crutches, or high-association words as your strategy.
6. Once he or she has learned the word, provide practice to habituate the skill.
7. Following practice, posttest to insure mastery, using flashcards as you did in the pretest.
8. Once mastery is insured, help the learner transfer that learning from flashcards to actual reading material.

TEST YOUR KNOWLEDGE

1. If a reader does not have a large stock of sight-words, the reading of textual material will be slow and laborious rather than quick and _____.
2. The first words to be taught at sight are usually those which are most frequently _____.
3. The major prerequisites to sight-word learning are the previously learned skills of visual discrimination, visual memory and visual _____.
4. A child is not likely to learn a word at sight if that word is not in his or her oral _____.
5. Because learning sight-words is a visual task, your attender to the learner will focus on an _____ of the word.
6. To learn a sight-word, it is essential that the child say the name of the word while _____ at the form of the word.
7. If a child does not learn a sight-word on the first try, you would make sure the word is in the child's oral vocabulary, make sure that he or she has the prerequisites, and make sure that you are directing the child to the unique visual _____ of the word.
8. The reteaching technique of VATK directs the child to use four sensory inputs in combination when learning a word. They are _____, _____, _____, and _____.
9. Practice activities for sight-word recognition all require a child to look at the form of a word and to say its _____.
10. Good application activities for sight-word recognition will require that the child identify in _____ the words previously identified on flashcards.

SIMULATION ACTIVITIES

Let's assume that you are teaching a first grade class. You want the pupils to become fluent readers, so you plan to teach them to recognize many words at sight. To determine which words you should teach, you consult a source list and decide that you will start with the following words:

look   on   little   then   after

You pretest your class and find that Joe, one of your pupils, is unable to correctly identify any of the words. He is unable to respond at all when the words **look, little,** and **after** are flashed to him, and he says **no** for **on** and **when** for **then.**

1. One of the first things you should determine is whether these words are in Joe's oral vocabulary. How can you determine this quickly and easily?
2. You also want to be sure that Joe possesses the prerequisite skills for learning sight-words. One of these skills is visual memory. How could you quickly determine whether Joe possesses visual memory without asking him to say the name of a word?
3. In teaching the words that Joe did not know at all (**look, little,** and **after**), you would highlight the unique visual characteristics of the words. What would you highlight in the word **look**? The word **little**? The word **after**?
4. For the confused words **then** and **when,** you must highlight the discriminator which sets one word apart from the other. What would you highlight?
5. What prerequisite skill is most important in preparing children to carefully examine similar words such as **when** and **then**?
6. For the confused words **on** and **no,** what would you highlight?
7. What prerequisite skill is most important in preparing children to avoid confusing words such as **on** and **no**?
8. Assume that in teaching the words **then** and **when,** you underlined the beginning letters of the two words to highlight what Joe had to pay attention to. You find, however, that he still does not learn the words and that you must reteach. How could you increase your highlighting in the second lesson to be sure that he is focusing on the discriminator?
9. In providing practice for Joe to insure that he solidifies his learning of these words, you consider having him copy each word ten times. You discard this suggestion for two reasons. The first is that it is a boring and unimaginative task. What is the second reason for rejecting it?
10. You would not use flashcards when you are helping Joe apply his sight-words. Why not?

SUGGESTED FIELD EXPERIENCES

Observation. When observing in schools, you should note the ways in which teachers help children learn sight-words. What words do they teach? What do they highlight? What do they do differently when words need to be retaught? What kind of practice do they provide? How do they insure that the child will use the sight-words in context?

Teaching activities. When working with children in a classroom setting, you should be able to choose appropriate words to teach at sight, to directly assist children in learning these skills, to provide appropriate practice, and to help them transfer the sight-words from flashcards to contextual settings.

Client impact. By teaching sight-words with the techniques provided in this chapter, your pupils will develop a large stock of words which they recognize instantly, and they will be smooth and fluent readers rather than slow and laborious readers.

FOR CLASS DISCUSSION

Research has indicated that individuals learn through a variety of modalities. Some people are primarily visual learners, others are primarily auditory learners, and a few are kinesthetic learners. Following the logic that some readers will not learn easily through the visual modality, it can be assumed that they may find it difficult to learn sight-words. If you had such a pupil in your class, what would you do? Would you ignore sight-word instruction with that pupil? Would you use particular techniques? Would you focus on the prerequisites? State your position on this problem and be prepared to discuss it with your instructor.

ANSWER KEY
1. fluent
2. used
3. sequencing
4. vocabulary
5. outstanding visual characteristic
6. looking
7. characteristics
8. visual, auditory, tactile, kinesthetic
9. name
10. reading material

TEACHING THE PREREQUISITE WORD ANALYSIS SKILLS

OVERVIEW

This chapter provides you with techniques for teaching children the readiness skills of auditory memory, auditory discrimination, sound–symbol connection, and sound-symbol connection in combination with context. Specific and practical suggestions for testing, directing attention, teaching, reteaching, practicing and applying are provided for each skill. The ultimate objective is:

> Given pupils needing instruction in the prerequisite word analysis skills, you will teach these skills using the instructional principles developed in Chapter 14.

KNOWLEDGE BACKGROUND

In previous chapters, you have learned that good readers have a large stock of sight-words and that this skill requires training in examining accurately and efficiently the visual characteristics of letters and words. As a result, you have been provided with techniques for teaching such visual skills, both at the prerequisite level and at the level of actually learning sight-words. However, it is not possible for you to teach the child to recognize at sight every word he or she will ever need. Consequently, the child must also have skills for identifying words never seen before, for figuring out what an unknown word is. These are the mediating skills, the skills of word analysis.

While sight-word recognition depends entirely upon the child's skills of visual examination, word analysis requires both looking at the symbols and listening to what the symbols say. It is distinct from sight-word recognition, then, because (1) the reader uses the sounds of letters and words as well as their visual characteristics, and (2) analysis takes time rather than being instantaneous. Ultimately, the child should be able to figure out an unknown word either by identifying the various letter sounds and blending these together to pronounce the word (phonetic analysis), by using meaning clues in the sentence and the initial sound to guess what the unknown word is (contextual analysis and sound–symbol connection), or by using the meaning elements of words such as prefixes, suffixes and roots to find pronounceable parts (structural analysis).

These skills do not happen automatically, however. There must first be prerequisite training to get the child ready. These prerequisite skills are the focus of this chapter and fall into four categories: auditory memory, auditory discrimination, sound–symbol connection, and the combination of sound–symbol connection and context (sometimes referred to as sound–symbol–meaning with the meaning coming from the context of the sentence in which the unknown word appears).

Like the prerequisite sight-word skills, the prerequisite word analysis skills are arranged in a spiraling hierarchy from the simple to the complex. Many skills are listed in such a hierarchy, but they tend to be the same four basic types of skills repeated again and again at increasing levels of difficulty. While this chapter will concentrate only on how each of the four types of skills are taught, you will want to consult one of the sources noted in Chapter 10 for a specific ordering of the skills.

AUDITORY MEMORY

Auditory memory is the first of the four types of prerequisite word analysis skills. It is a crucial skill since the child's eventual success as a reader will depend, in part, on ability to remember sounds in a specific sequential order. For instance, the blended sounds of a word analyzed in print will be remembered and produced in a precise sequence from the first to the last sound. Such auditory memory is not always easy for the young child, who must usually be provided with directed assistance in learning.

PRE- AND POSTTESTING AUDITORY MEMORY

Since this is totally an auditory skill, there should be no visual stimulus in the testing. You simply produce the sounds you want the child to remember and ask the child to repeat the sounds for you in the order in which he or she heard them.

For instance, a common type of auditory memory task deals with tapped rhythms. The teacher, using a fist on a tabletop, produces a rhythmic pattern of sounds corresponding to regular Morse code signals (a tap followed by a pause is a dash; a tap without a pause is a dot). After tapping out the rhythm, the teacher pauses and then has the child reproduce what was heard from memory. A similar procedure is followed when the child is tested on remembering ordered sounds and words at higher levels.

DIRECTING ATTENTION

Because this task is auditory, the attender must direct the child to listen for the specific sequence in which the sounds are produced. You can help direct attention by adding physical and voiced cues. For instance, when testing auditory memory of tapped rhythms, you might take the learner's hand and create the rhythm for the child, saying the rhythmic pattern ("dot–dot" or whatever) as you do so.

TEACHING AUDITORY MEMORY

Because auditory memory is a low-level memory skill, it is usually best to use a modeling technique when teaching it. To teach memory for clapped rhythms, for instance, start by directing the learner to watch and listen as you clap your hands in a simple rhythm. Then take the learner's hands and repeat the same pattern, saying "clap–clap" as you do so. Then have the learner repeat the clapping pattern independently. Repeat the process using more complex clapping patterns, and gradually stop holding hands with the learner and saying the pattern as he or she begins to respond successfully. Once the child can remember a sequence of claps, do the same thing with tapping. Assist at first by holding hands and by providing an oral cue as you did for the clapping. Gradually reduce this assistance until the child can reproduce the rhythms without you.

It is difficult to use the discovery technique with this skill. However, you can use a questioning technique to help the learner discover a way to remember the sequence of sounds. Start with the simpler clapping procedure described above and say, "I am going to clap my hands in a certain way and then I will ask you to do the same thing. Watch and listen while I do it once and then tell me what you will have to remember in order to do what I did." If the learner is unable to respond, guide his or her hands in repeating the clapping pattern and then repeat the question. Diminish the amount of physical assistance provided until both the clapping and the tapping can be done unassisted.

RETEACHING AUDITORY MEMORY

If the child does not immediately master the particular auditory memory skill you are teaching, two techniques can be used for reteaching. First, simplify the task at the beginning by giving less to remember and gradually increase what must be remembered until the child is at the criterion level of the pretest. Second, increase the amount of highlighting to help the learner in remembering the patterns. In any case, much repetition will be needed before some children will master this task.

PRACTICING AUDITORY MEMORY

Once the child is able to remember without your help, you must create practice which will solidify the skill as a habit. The following activities are illustrative.

1. Using a tape recorder, record patterns of sounds. When recording each set, first give the pattern, then instruct the child to stop the recorder and to repeat the sound pattern, and then have the child turn the recorder back to where the sound pattern is given and repeated as a self-testing exercise.
2. Play the Airport game with learners, using a gameboard, a toy airplane, and a buffer to give the oral sound patterns to each child in turn. The child who reproduces each pattern correctly moves his or her airplane one space per pattern down the runway. As each plane reaches the end, it may be flown briefly. The same technique can be used in reverse to return the airplanes to the hanger.
3. Play a game in which learners are paired and take turns clapping pairs of sound patterns to each other. The partner must respond to each pattern by identifying it as the same or different. The winner can be determined by either keeping track of the number each child gets right or by adapting the game to a gameboard like the one described in number 2.
4. Play the game "Monkey Hear, Monkey Do," using pairs of players and a gameboard. One child claps or says a sound pattern and the partner mimics it. If the response is correct, the pair moves forward one space on the gameboard.
5. Play a dot-to-dot game using any connect-the-dots picture. Learners are paired; one says or claps a sound pattern and the other mimics. If the response is correct, each pair connects as many dots in the picture as there are sound units in the pattern.
6. Play a memory game in which one learner says a word, the next learner says that word and adds another, the third learner repeats the first two words and adds a third, and so on. Continue until one learner cannot remember the sequence. The object is to develop as long a sequence of words or sounds as possible.

APPLYING AUDITORY MEMORY

The learner will be applying this skill in learning the more complex auditory memory tasks with which he or she will be working while progressing through the skills hierarchy. However, in addition to these applications, you should also be alert for ways to point out the use of this auditory memory and sequencing skill during the routine daily activities of the classroom. Some suggested techniques are:

1. Sing songs with learners which make use of an ever-increasing number of sound units which must be repeated in order. A typical example would be "The Twelve Days of Christmas."
2. Use choral speaking with children, choosing poems which require remembering sounds in a sequence.
3. Play playground games with children, such as rope skipping, which are done to the accompaniment of a repetitive song or chant.

AUDITORY DISCRIMINATION

A second word analysis prerequisite is auditory discrimination in which the learner must distinguish between various beginning, middle and ending sounds. It is a particularly crucial skill since the child's ultimate ability to phonetically analyze unknown words will depend upon success in hearing the various sounds in words.

Auditory discrimination is a purely auditory task. While letters are involved, it is *only* the sound of the letter that is important here and not the shape or name of the letter. Later, the learner must tie the sound to a letter, but, to simplify the learning task, he or she first learns to distinguish one sound from among others.

PRE- AND POSTTESTING AUDITORY DISCRIMINATION

To test auditory discrimination, you simply tell the child what you want him or her to listen for, say it, and ask the child to identify the position (beginning or ending) of the sound or which sound is different. To test whether a child can tell if pairs of words sound the same or different at their beginnings, say each pair of words in turn and ask the child to say yes if the words sound alike at the beginning and no if they are different. For instance, if you want to determine whether a child can distinguish a beginning **t** sound from a beginning **d** sound, say two words, one beginning with **t** and one beginning with **d** and ask the child if the beginning sounds are the same or different.

DIRECTING ATTENTION

To teach a learner to auditorily discriminate, you must first insure that he or she has a concept for *different* as it relates to sounds. Many times, a young child will fail a pretest not because of inability to distinguish the sound but because the child did not understand what you meant by different.

Once the concept of different is grasped, you must direct attention to that part of the word you want the child to distinguish. Since this is an auditory task, you should use auditory highlighting. A good way to do this is by using the say-it-fast, say-it-slow technique in which you say each word twice, exaggerating the crucial sound the first time and saying the word normally the second time. For a word such as **mother,** you would first say **m–m–mother** and then say **mother** to help the child see that it is the first sound of the word that he or she is to attend to. This technique cannot be used with words having a hard sound at the beginning, such as **date, time, boy,** and so on. However, you can achieve the same effect by having the learner get his or her mouth ready to say the sound. This, like the say-it-fast, say-it-slow technique, exaggerates or highlights the sound to be heard and helps the learner attend.

TEACHING AUDITORY DISCRIMINATION

Assume that we are teaching children to distinguish whether two words, such as **mine** and **music,** sound the same or different at their beginnings. A modeling technique for teaching this skill would go as follows: Tell the learner that you are going to say each of the two words twice, once slowly and once in the normal way, and that he or she must listen to the first sound in both words and tell whether they are the same or different. Say, "I'm going to say the first word slowly. **M–m–mine..** Now I'm going to say it fast. **Mine.** Now I'll say the second word slowly. **M–m–music.** Now I'll say it fast. **Music.**" Then ask the learner if the sounds heard at the beginnings of the two words were the same or different. If the child has difficulty, repeat the same procedure using words that differ only at their beginnings, such as **mine** and **line, bake** and **lake,** and so on. For words like **bake,** in which the first sound cannot be said slowly, highlight by telling the learner to watch your mouth as you get ready to say the first sound, and then exaggerate this mouth movement and have the learner mimic your actions. As the learner begins to respond satisfactorily, gradually diminish the amount of emphasis you place on the beginning sound until the learner is able to distinguish the sound differences when you say the words in a normal way.

If you use a discovery technique, the principle to be discovered is that spoken words have distinguishing auditory characteristics which enable us to tell one from another. Using words which differ only at their beginnings and using highlighting, such as the say-it-slow, say-it-fast or "get-your-mouth-ready-to-say" techniques described above, say a pair of words and ask the question, "Do the two words sound the same?" If the response is "no," say, "Listen to the two words as I say them again and tell me where the two words are different." If the learner responds by correctly identifying the beginning sounds as being different, continue this questioning process with other pairs of words, diminishing the amount of auditory emphasis with each sequence until you get a successful response without giving any assistance. If the learner does not respond correctly at any point, emphasize again the part of the word which is to be discriminated and repeat the questioning process.

RETEACHING AUDITORY DISCRIMINATION

If the learner does not learn to discriminate the sounds being taught on the first attempt, you will need to reteach the skill. To do so, first insure that the learner has a concept for *different.* Second, provide for more emphasis on the sound to be distinguished, with the auditory highlighting being emphatic enough to help the learner separate the crucial sound from among the other sounds of the word. Finally, learners having extreme difficulty can be helped by showing them how the sound is formed with the mouth. For example, you can provide the learner with a mirror and let her or him see the difference between how he or she forms the sound heard at the beginning of **fish** as opposed to how he or she forms the sound heard at the beginning of **dish**.

PRACTICING AUDITORY DISCRIMINATION

Once the child can discriminate the sound without your help, you should provide practice to solidify the skill. The following examples are illustrative of suitable practice activities.

1. Have learners bring to class pictures cut from magazines, with each picture or series of pictures showing something which has the same sound at the beginning (or end or middle).
2. Bring in a group of magazine pictures yourself, directing the learner to name what each picture shows and to sort the pictures according to the common beginning, middle, or ending sounds. For instance, all the pictures which begin with the same sound heard at the beginning of **kite** go in this pile, all the pictures which begin with the same sound heard at the beginning of **top** go in this pile, and so on.
3. Paste a number of pictures on a large piece of tagboard. Direct the learner to match smaller pictures to the pictures on the tagboard on the basis of like sounds at the beginning, middle, or end.
4. A form of Bingo can be played which will reinforce the learning of beginning, middle, or ending sounds. For instance the learner can be provided with a bingo-like playing card having pictures in the squares. Say, "Do you have a picture on your card which begins with the same sound you hear at the beginning of **dog?** If you do, you may cover that square with a marker." The first learner to have every picture in a row covered wins the game.
5. A group of picture cards can be placed on the table. Learners take turns matching pairs of pictures that begin with the same sound. Learners having the most pairs win. This activity can also be adapted to ending and middle sounds.
6. Provide learners with an oral listing of words, such as **boy, bat, ball, bingo, tall.** Direct each learner to name the word which has a different sound at the beginning (or end or middle).
7. Spread a group of pictures on the floor. Direct the learner to point to a picture that has the same sound heard at the beginning (or end or middle) of the word you say.
8. Play games with learners that follow this pattern: "I'm thinking of something on your desk which begins with the same sound heard at the beginning of the word **pig.** What am I thinking of?" This activity can also be adapted to middle and ending sounds.
9. Play a fishing game with learners, in which pictures are paper clipped or stapled to paper fish. Give the learner a pole with a magnet tied

to the end. As the learner catches each fish, direct him or her to say, "I caught a fish that begins like (another word with same initial sound)." This activity can also be adapted to middle and ending sounds.

10. Pass out picture cards. Hold up another picture card yourself saying, "Who has a picture whose name sounds the same at the beginning (or end or middle) as the name of my picture?" Direct the learner to hold up any of his or her cards that have such a picture.

11. Recite lines from familiar poems, leaving out the rhyming word in the second line of the couplet. Directions to the learners are, "What word goes here? What other word does it sound like? In what way does it sound like that word?" Then you might say, "Can you think of another word which sounds like these two words at the end?"

12. You can play the game "I am going to Africa." You say, "I am going to Africa and I'm going to take a ring, and I will sing. Who can go to Africa with me?" The learner must respond with something he or she is going to take to Africa and which also ends with the –ing rhyme. For instance, if you are working with ending rhymes, the learner might say he or she is going to take a **swing.** If you are working with the ending –ong sound, the pupil might say he or she is going to take a **song.** This activity can also be adapted to beginning and middle sounds.

13. You say, "Let's play a game with words." Choose a rhyming pattern and say two words, elongating the first sound, and then, have the learner complete the third word, as in "**b** . . . **at, s** . . . **at, c** . . . ." This activity can also be modified for use with both ending consonant sounds and middle sounds as well as with rhymes.

14. You pronounce a word for the learner, who listens and then provides another word which has the same sound at the beginning or middle or end.

15. Construct a shallow box divided into four squares. Place a key picture in each of the top two squares. Provide the learner with a group of pictures, directing him or her to sort the pictures and place them in the square beneath the picture with the same sound at the beginning (or end or middle).

APPLYING AUDITORY DISCRIMINATION

The learner will be applying this skill in more complex word analysis tasks as he or she progresses through the hierarchy. However, in addition to these applications, you should insure that this auditory discrimination skill is also used during the routine daily activities of the classroom. Some suggested techniques are:

1. Direct the learner to point to and name things in the classroom which have the same beginning (or ending or middle) sound as is heard in (choose a word).

2. As learners are waiting to be dismissed or to move to another activity, you can say, "If you can tell me a word that sounds the same as (choose a word) at the beginning (or the middle or the end), you can go."

3. After returning from a field trip or some other common activity, you can direct the learners to name all the things they saw which had the same sound at the beginning as (choose a word). This activity can also be adapted to middle and ending sounds.
4. During Show-and-Tell, you can direct the learner to show something he or she has which has the same beginning (or ending or middle) sound heard in (choose a word).

SOUND–SYMBOL CONNECTION

Sound–symbol connection is the third prerequisite word analysis skill. It focuses on helping a child connect a particular letter to the sound that letter produces. It is a particularly crucial task since a reader's ability to sound out words will depend upon the ability to connect the correct sound to each letter.

Sound–symbol connection always follows auditory discrimination for the same letter sound. First, in the auditory discrimination task, the teacher insures that the child can distinguish the letter sound from among other sounds. Once this is established, the learner can be asked to not only distinguish the sound but to tie that sound to the particular symbol which produces it. As such, sound-symbol connection goes beyond discrimination, requiring that an association be made between a visual and an auditory stimulus.

PRE- AND POSTTESTING SOUND–SYMBOL CONNECTION

Sound–symbol connection can be tested either by giving the child a sound and asking him or her to identify the letter or by giving the child a letter and asking him or her to produce the appropriate sound. In either case, however, you should avoid having the sound produced in isolation since this causes distortion, particularly with the hard consonant sounds. For instance, isolating the sounds of **cat** might well result in "cuh-a-tuh." Instead, you should refer to the sound heard at the beginning of **cap**, or the sound heard at the end of **rot.**

You could illustrate the sound–symbol connection for the beginning consonant **d** by saying some words which begin with **d** (such as **den, dial, dig,** and so on) and having the pupil tell you what letter makes the sound heard at the beginning of each of these words. Another way would be to show the child the letter **d** and have him or her make up a word which begins with that sound. In the latter case, it is best not to have the learner give you a word which has already been learned at sight since he or she might simply recall the word by visual memory without ever noting what sound is heard at the beginning.

DIRECTING ATTENTION

To connect letters and their sounds, the learner must use both visual and auditory skills. He or she must previously have learned to visually discriminate among and name the letters *and* to distinguish the sounds of the letters from among other sounds. Consequently, your first task in teaching sound–symbol connections is to insure that the learner possesses these prerequisites.

Then you direct attention to both the sound heard and the letter it is to be connected with. For instance, if you are teaching the sound–symbol connection for the letter **m**, you would exaggerate the beginning sound as you say the word **men** while simultaneously pointing to the letter **m**. It is crucial that the child both look at the letter and say the sound simultaneously for the desired connection to occur.

TEACHING SOUND–SYMBOL CONNECTION

Either the modeling or the discovery technique can be used to teach sound–symbol connection. If we were trying to teach the sound–symbol connection for the letter **m**, the modeling procedure might be somewhat as follows: Gather together both a series of objects or pictures which have names beginning with the sound of the letter **m** and cutouts of that letter. Direct the learner to watch you and be ready to mimic your words and actions. Take one of the pictures (or objects) which begins with the letter **m**, for example, a mouse, and say, "This is a picture of a **mouse**. I'm going to say the word slowly and then fast so I can hear the beginning sound. **M–m–mouse. Mouse.** Now I'm going to put the picture down, put the letter m to the left of it, and say the name slowly, pointing to the letter m as I say the first sound. **M–m–mouse.** Then I'll say it fast. **Mouse.** The letter I hear at the beginning of **mouse** is **m.**" Then have the learner mimic your actions, insuring that he or she is both pointing to and looking at the letter while saying the beginning sound of the word so that the connection between the letter and its sound will be made. As the learner responds successfully, repeat the procedure and gradually diminish the amount of help you provide until the learner is able to name the letter heard at the beginning of **m** words without either modeling your actions or exaggerating the sound when pointing to the appropriate letter.

If you prefer, the discovery technique can be used. The principle to be discovered is that a particular sound at the beginning of a word is associated with a particular alphabetic letter. Use pictures and cut-out letters as described above. Show several of the pictures and say their names one after another, exaggerating the beginning sounds in the initial stages. Have the learner listen to the beginning sounds and tell you whether all the words begin alike: If the response is "yes," say, "The first word begins with the letter **m**. Watch and listen as I point to the letter m and say the word. **M–m–mouse. Mouse.** If the first word begins with **m** and all the words sound alike at the beginning, what letter do you suppose the other words begin with?" If the learner responds correctly, have him or her say each word in turn, pointing to the beginning letter while saying the beginning of each word. If the response is incorrect, return to the first word, exaggerate again the sound as you point to the letter **m** and say, "The first letter in **mouse** is **m. Man** begins with the same sound as **mouse**. The first letter in **man** is also **m**. Listen to the next word. **Money.** Does it begin like **mouse** and **man?** If **mouse** and **man** begin with the letter **m**, what letter will **money** begin with?" If the response is correct, have the learner say the remaining words while pointing to the letter heard at the beginning.

RETEACHING SOUND–SYMBOL CONNECTION

If the child is unable to connect sound and letter after the initial period of instruction, you should reteach the skill. First, check to insure that difficulty does not lie with a deficiency in previously learned skills of visual and auditory discrimination. If the learner possesses all the prerequisites and is still unable to learn the task, plan a second lesson which emphasizes more heavily the sound of the letter, its shape, and the connection between the two. Usually, the modeling technique is most fruitful for such reteaching.

PRACTICING SOUND–SYMBOL CONNECTION

Once the learner can connect the sound to the letter without your help, plan practice activities which will help solidify the skill. The following suggestions would be appropriate.

1. Make a shutter device out of tagboard in which the opening of the shutter can be controlled by you. Insert a card which has the letter to be learned at the left, followed by a picture of an object which has the sound of that letter at the beginning. Open the shutter to reveal first the letter and then the picture. Direct he learner to form the letter sound with his or her mouth and to blend that sound into the picture name as it is exposed.
2. Use the same device as described in number 1 but this time insert a picture first, then the letter, then the picture again. Direct the learner to say the picture name, then to say the letter sound heard at the beginning of the picture name, and then to blend that sound into the picture name as it is exposed the second time.
3. Use flashcards containing the letters to be practiced. Flash a letter to the learner and direct him or her to respond with a word that begins (or ends) with that letter sound.
4. To help the learner connect the letter and the sound, display pictures of common objects (such as dogs, apples, etc.) with the letter the object begins with printed at the left. Encourage the learner to use these pictures when trying to remember the sound of a particular letter.
5. Make a box and label it with a large printed form of the letter you are teaching. Place in the box pictures and objects whose names begin (or end) with the letter to be learned. Direct the learner to reach into the box, draw a picture or object, name it, and tell what letter the object begins with. Make sure the learner looks at the letter on the box while saying the object's name.

6. For learners who need review on a number of letters and their sound correspondence, you may modify the activity described in number 5 by putting several letters on the outside of the box and by placing objects which begin with all these letters in the box. The learner then draws an object, names it, and points to the letter on the box which begins the object's name.

7. Give each learner a group of pictures, some of which begin (or end) with the letter to be worked on and some of which do not. Hold up a letter card and direct the learner to hold up any picture which begins (or ends) with the sound associated with that letter.

8. Using a flannelboard or a pocket chart, place a letter card to the left and a row of three pictures to the right. Two of the pictures should begin with the sound associated with the letter at the left and one should not. Direct the learner to pick out the two pictures which begin with the sound associated with the letter at the left.

9. Make a bulletin board or a large chart which has the letters to be learned revealed and beside each a flap covering a picture whose name begins with the sound associated with that letter. When the learner cannot remember the sound of **m**, for instance, he or she can go to the bulletin board, look under the flap next to **m** and see that the sound of **m** is what is heard at the beginning of whatever the picture is under the flap.

10. Make a tagboard chart with the letters to be learned listed down one side and pictures beginning (or ending) with the sounds of these letters listed down the other. Attach pieces of string to the letters and direct the learner to connect the string for each letter to an object which begins with the sound of that letter.

11. Provide the learner with a number of letters. Play a game in which you say, "I see a letter whose sound we hear at the beginning of the word **mouse**. What letter do I see?" The learner responds by holding up the proper letter card, looking at it, and saying, **Mouse** begins with the letter **m**."

12. Make a set of picture cards for each letter sound. Teach the learner to play a card game in which several cards are dealt to each player. The learner tries to pair picture cards beginning with the same letter sound. Each player takes turns asking opponents, "Do you have a picture card beginning with the letter **m**?" If they do, they give the picture card to the learner requesting it and then have the opportunity to draw a card from the learner's hand in return. The learner having the most pairs at the end wins.

13. Give the learners a group of letter cards. Each learner takes turns saying, "I have a letter. **Mouse** starts with the sound of my letter. What letter do I have?" The learner who responds correctly is the next one to select a letter.

14. Play a dramatization game with learners in which you hold up a letter card and ask them to act out something that begins with the sound of that letter. The rest of the learners must try to guess what it is that begins with that letter that the actor is dramatizing.

APPLYING SOUND–SYMBOL CONNECTION

The learner will be applying this skill in more complex word analysis tasks. However, in addition to these applications, you should insure that this sound–symbol connection skill is also used during the routine daily activities in the classroom. Some of the suggested techniques are:

1. Have the learner name objects around the classroom and tell what the beginning letter of that name would be.
2. Have the learner tell the beginning sound of a word you write on the blackboard or a word encountered in reading.
3. When new words come up in class discussion, write them on the blackboard and say, "This word is (name the word). It starts with the letter **m** because it has the same sound at the beginning as (name another word which the learner knows begins with **m**)."
4. When the child is reading and sees an unknown word beginning with a known letter sound, encourage the child to get the mouth ready to say the sound of the letter as an initial step in analyzing the word.

SOUND–SYMBOL–MEANING

Sound–symbol connection in combination with context is the last of the prerequisite word analysis skills. This skill recognizes that word analysis should not be limited to simple sounding of letters. Rather, the learner should be encouraged to also use understanding of language patterns and experience to make realistic guesses of what the unknown word might be. By combining syntactic and semantic sense with knowledge of initial consonant sounds, the learner systematizes this guessing, limiting the number of possibilities regarding what the unknown word could be. For instance, let's assume Tommy encounters a sentence such as: "The swimmer dived into the **lzqf**." He has never seen the word **lzqf** so he uses his syntactic and semantic sense to guess what it might be, with the possibilities including **river, pool, lake, ocean, pond, sea,** and so on. He then further narrows his analysis by noting that the word begins with an **l**, meaning that the unknown word must be **lake**. He has successfully used both context and sound–symbol connection of the initial consonant to identify the unknown word.

At the prerequisite stage, sound–symbol–meaning must be an oral task since the children cannot yet read. This oral experience gets them ready for using the same skill in their actual reading in later stages of reading development.

PRE- AND POSTTESTING SOUND–SYMBOL–MEANING

At the prerequisite stage, sound–symbol–meaning should be tested orally. You do this by saying to the child a sentence with one word missing and showing the letter which begins the missing word. For instance, if you want to determine whether the child can use the letter **m** with context to identify an unknown word, you might use the word **money** and say to the learner, "I like to spend _____," showing the letter **m** at the point where the missing word should be.

In testing this skill, care must be taken to insure that the sentence matches the learner's experience background and provides enough meaning clues to complete the sentence. For instance, if the above sentence does not provide enough context assistance, you might alter the sentence in either of the following ways:

We go to the bank to get some _____ (show the letter **m**).

I earn most of my _____ (show the letter **m**) by mowing lawns.

DIRECTING ATTENTION

In order to complete this task successfully, the learner must attend to the three major elements of the task—the letter symbol, its sound, and the meaning clues in the sentence. The sound–symbol connection for the letter used should have been learned in a previous skill. Consequently, your first task in teaching sound/symbol/meaning is to insure that this crucial prerequisite has been mastered.

Then direct the learner's attention to the way sound–symbol connection can be used in combination with meaning clues. Highlight the words in the sentence which provide clues to the identity of the unknown word, the letter which the unknown word begins with, and the sound associated with that letter. For instance, in the example "I like to spend m_____," you might auditorily emphasize the word **spend,** then direct the learner to look at the letter **m** and to get the mouth ready to say the sound of that letter.

TEACHING SOUND–SYMBOL–MEANING

This skill can be taught using either a modeling or a discovery technique. In the modeling technique, the procedure would be somewhat as follows: Tell the learner that you are going to show him or her how to figure out what an unknown word is by using clues in the sentence and the sound of a letter, and that he or she should be ready to do as you do when you are done. Then say the phrase "I like to spend m_____," holding up the **m** letter card when you come to the blank. Say, "I must figure out what the last word in the sentence is. I know it begins with the letter **m** and so the word must sound at the beginning like **monkey, milk,** and other **m** words. I also know that the word must be something that I like to *spend.* So I am going to say the sentence again, think about what I like to spend, and get my mouth ready to say an **m** word when I come to the blank." Say the sentence again, emphasize the word **spend,** exaggerate the get-your-mouth-ready technique, and say the word **monkey.** Say, "I have an **m** word in the blank but it does not make sense because we do not spend monkeys." Repeat the process but put in the word **money.** Say, "**Money** must be the right word because it is an **m** word and it is something that we like to spend."

Repeat the same process with the second sentence, but after you have highlighted the clue word(s), the letter, and its sound, have the learner supply the word to complete the sentence. Continue through subsequent sentences, diminishing the amount of assistance you provide until the learner is able to perform the task without assistance.

In the discovery technique, the priniciple to be discovered is that we can identify an unknown word by using the sense of the sentence and the sound value of the first letter. To help the learner discover this principle, do several of the pretest items for him or her, highlighting the clue word, the beginning letter of the unknown word, and its sound value as you do so. Then ask the learner to discover how you knew what the unknown word was, directing attention with questions such as:

Why did I emphasize this word (the clue word) when I said the sentence?

Why did I look at the letter and get my mouth ready to say its sound when I came to the blank in the sentence?

How did I know the word in the first sentence wasn't **monkey?**

How did I know it wasn't **dollars**?

As the learner responds correctly, provide other examples but gradually diminish the amount of highlighting you provide and the number of questions you ask until the learner can perform the task without assistance.

RETEACHING SOUND–SYMBOL–MEANING

If a child does not learn this skill in the first instructional situation, the problem may lie with one of several prerequisites. First, he or she may not have adequately learned the sound–symbol connection for the letters being used, in which case you should return to those skills and reteach them before expecting the child to use the letter sounds in combination with context. Second, the problem may lie with the content of the sentences themselves, in which case you should alter them to match the learner's experience background. Third, the child may be generally deficient in oral language, in which case you should first provide many sentence-completion activities in which the learner orally finishes thoughts begun by you without using letter–sound clues.

If you are sure the child possesses all these prerequisites, reteach the lesson itself. Alter your strategy to place more emphasis on both the meaning clues in the sentences and the initial letter sound. If the learner still has difficulty, reverse roles and let the child create the sentences, with you responding. As he or she sees how the process works, you can gradually return to the situation where you are providing the sentences again and the child is responding.

PRACTICING SOUND–SYMBOL–MEANING

Following instruction, you will need to create practice activities to help the child habituate this skill. The following suggestions are illustrative.

1. Once the learner develops a sight-word vocabulary, you can use those words to create sentences such as those in the pretest, asking the learner to read the sentence and to provide the missing word. If the learner cannot yet read independently, you can do the same thing as a listening activity, with the sentences put on tape or provided by another learner, an aide, or you.
2. Read a paragraph to the learner. Tell the learner that you will stop reading every once in a while and hold up a letter card. Direct him or her to keep the paragraph in mind, to look at the letter on the card, to think of the sound associated with that letter, and to say a word which both begins with that letter sound and which fits the sense of the paragraph.
3. Play games with the learner which require using both context and sound–symbol connections as part of participation. For instance, direct the learner to listen to a sentence such as, "I went to the store and bought a mouse, a (pause), a (pause), and a (pause)." Hold up a letter card to indicate the beginning letter of the word to fill the missing space. The learner expands the sentence by adding words which begin with the sound associated with the letter you show.
4. Group your learners in pairs. Give each pair a supply of letter cards. Let each child take a turn in making up a sentence in which one word is left out. The child must hold up the beginning letter of the missing word at the appropriate spot in the sentence. The partner uses the sense of the sentence and the sound–symbol connection of the letter card to guess what word goes in the space. If he or she correctly identifies the missing word, it is the partner's turn to make up a sentence.
5. Give learners riddles in which the context supplies only a minimum outline of what the missing word is. For instance, you could provide the sentence, "The swimmer dived into the _____." Elicit learner response, encouraging a variety of answers, such as **water, pool, lake, river,** etc. Then place a letter card (such as the letter **w**) at the left of the blank space and say, "Now what word *must* go in the blank space?"

APPLYING SOUND–SYMBOL–MEANING

This skill should be applied frequently during the daily routine activities in the classroom. During oral activities, you should look for opportunities to start sentences which learners complete, giving as a clue the beginning letter of the word you are thinking of. Once the child begins reading, even at the lowest levels, that child should be encouraged to analyze unknown words by using both the context and the sound value of the first letter to make a calculated guess on the identity of the word.

SUMMARY OF TEACHING THE PREREQUISITE WORD ANALYSIS SKILLS

Ultimately, we want our pupils to know many words at sight and to be able to figure out the rest of the words by themselves. To get them ready for the task of mediating or figuring out unknown words, we must teach them the prerequisite skills of auditory memory, auditory discrimination, sound–symbol connection, and sound–symbol–meaning. These four major types of skills appear many times at the prerequisite stages, with each skill being taught first at a simple level and then again at ever more complex levels. Gradually, as these prerequisites are mastered, the child moves into the actual reading task and is prepared to use these readiness skills in analyzing unknown words.

TEST YOUR KNOWLEDGE

1. The analysis skills are distinct from the sight-word skills because analyzing requires a child to use visual skills in combination with _____ skills.
2. The skill of remembering sounds in a specific order is _____.
3. The skill of distinguishing one sound from other sounds is called _____.
4. The task of associating a particular sound with a particular letter symbol is called _____.
5. When a child figures out an unknown word by using context in combination with sound–symbol connection, it is called _____.
6. The skill of noting a sound and identifying its letter requires that the learner be directed to the letter, its sound, and the _____ between them.
7. Auditory discrimination requires that the learner be directed to the place in the word where the _____ occurs.
8. A major prerequisite to sound–symbol connection is _____.
9. A major prerequisite to sound–symbol–meaning is _____.
10. To help a child learn sound–symbol–meaning, you would highlight the beginning letter of the missing word, its sound and the _____ in the sentence.

SIMULATION ACTIVITIES

Let's assume you are teaching a first grade class. The skill you are teaching is stated as follows:

The performance objective. Given a spoken stimulus word beginning with either the **m** or **d** sound and a group of three other words one of which begins with the **m** or **d** sound, the learner pairs the two words beginning with the same sound.

1. What type of prerequisite word analysis skill is this?

2. How would you pretest to determine whether your pupils possess this skill?

You find that some of your pupils need to learn this skill. You begin teaching the lesson by directing their attention in the following manner:

> You say, "Today we are going to do something that is very hard. In order to do this, you must listen very carefully to the sound you hear at the very beginning of words." To help the learners focus on the listening task, direct them to close their eyes as you pronounce the words.

3. What have you neglected to do in directing your pupils' attention?
4. What would you have said to make your attender complete?

Two attempts at teaching this skill using the modeling technique follow. Examine both presentations carefully.

> Say a single word and ask the learner to repeat the word, saying, "Say this word and listen carefully to what you say at the beginning of the word." When the learner mimics your response, reward him or her and provide another word, repeating the above process without the modeling. Then direct the learner to say other words one after another, saying, "Listen to the beginnings of these words as you say them. Is the sound the same (or different) at the beginning? How can you tell it is the same (or different)."

> Use contrasting pairs of words in which only the beginning sound is different, as in **mate** and **date**. Using the say-it-slow, say-it-fast technique, tell the learner, "Listen carefully as I say this word slowly. **M . . . ate**. Now I'll say it fast. **Mate**." After modeling the activity for the learner in this way, have the learner repeat the task, directing him or her to emphasize, but not to isolate, the beginning sound when saying the word slowly, comparing the sound made at the beginning of one word with the sound made at the beginning of another. Provide other words, gradually reducing the emphasis on the beginning sound and introducing words which are not contrasting pairs.

5. Which of these two presentations is likely to be most effective?
6. What principles of instruction does the second presentation have that are lacking in the first one?

The following is an example of a practice exercise which could be used to solidify the skill with the **m** and **d** (or any letters of your choice).

> Have a large number of magazines in the classroom and direct the learner to cut out pictures that begin with the sound you hear at the beginning of **mouse** or **dog.** A variation of this activity is one

in which the learner is given a number of pictures beginning with the **m** and **d** sounds and is directed to sort them into two piles. All the pictures whose names begin with the sound heard at the beginning of **mouse** are placed in one pile and the pictures the names of which begin with the sound heard at the beginning of **dog** are placed in another pile.

7. Since this is an auditory discrimination task, the learner is dealing only with the sound and not with the letter. If you cannot use letters to identify the piles in which the pictures should be placed, how would you identify them?
8. What device could you use to make this practice exercise self-checking?

Let's continue to assume that you are a first grade teacher and the skill you are teaching is stated as follows:

> Given spoken words beginning with **s** or **h** sounds, the learner identifies the beginning letter as being either **s** or **h**.

9. What type of prerequisite word analysis skill is this?
10. Describe how you would pretest to determine whether your pupils possess this skill.

The following is a step-by-step plan of the way some teachers might present this skill. We suggest that you study each step of this plan and then state an improved way to teach it.

Teacher's plan

STEP 1   Say, "Today we are going to do something that is difficult, but I'm going to give you any help you need to do this work. So pay close attention to me and we'll start working."

STEP 2   "Look at this letter." (holding up a card with a highlighted **m** on it) "What letter is this? What letter comes after **m** in the alphabet? . . . Can you think of a word that begins with **m**?"

STEP 3   "Now watch this." (holding up another card with an **h** on it, but not highlighted) "What letter is this? . . . That's right; it is an **h**."

STEP 4   Go through the other letters the same way.

STEP 5   For practice, ask the children to find the previously taught letters on signs, calendars, books, and so on. Whoever gets the most right gets two candies.

STEP 6   For application, the student will go through an old workbook and underline the alphabet in order.

SUGGESTED FIELD EXPERIENCES

Observation. When observing in schools, note what skills teachers provide for beginning readers to help get them ready for word analysis. Do you see distinct lessons in auditory memory? Auditory discrimination? Sound–symbol connection? Sound–symbol–meaning? Note also the teaching techniques used. What do teachers highlight when teaching each of these skills? Do you notice a difference between when teachers are teaching or directly assisting learners and when they are having learners practice? How do teachers insure that the pupils use the skills once learned?

Teaching activities. When working with beginning readers in a classroom setting, you should be able to pretest to determine what prerequisite word analysis skills need to be taught, you should be able to directly assist children in learning these skills, and you should be able to plan appropriate activities for practicing and applying these skills.

Client impact. By systematically teaching the prerequisite word analysis skills to those who need them, you are enhancing your pupils' chances of successfully learning to analyze and identify unknown words in print when they are actually reading.

FOR CLASS DISCUSSION

Many teachers who plan to teach in the upper grades (grades three through six) in the elementary school frequently express the feeling that they should not have to know anything about the prerequisite skills because they are not relevant to the needs of an upper-grade teacher. React to this on the basis of what you know about the spread of reading achievement one can expect to find in a typical fifth grade, and be prepared to discuss this with your instructor.

ANSWER KEY
1. auditory
2. auditory sequencing
3. auditory discrimination
4. sound–symbol connection
5. sound–symbol–meaning or context and sound–symbol connection
6. association
7. crucial sound difference
8. auditory discrimination
9. sound–symbol connection
10. meaning clues

18

TEACHING
WORD
ANALYSIS
SKILLS

OVERVIEW

This chapter provides you with techniques for teaching children to phonetically and structurally analyze and identify unknown words met in their reading. Specific and practical suggestions for testing, directing attention, teaching, reteaching, practicing, and applying are provided for each skill. The ultimate objective is:

> Given pupils who do not analyze and identify unknown words which they meet in their reading, you will teach this skill using the instructional principles developed in Chapter 14.

KNOWLEDGE BACKGROUND

Chapters 15 and 16 focused on helping a child memorize words so as to be able to recognize them at sight. However, a reader who only knows how to memorize words does not have adequate word recognition techniques. Every day, in everything read, the child will be faced with words not yet memorized—words never seen before—and will have to stop reading and say, "I don't know that one." The reader must have a technique to read those words without having to ask you what they are; he or she must be able to analyze or mediate these words. How to teach such analysis skills is the focus of this chapter.

The first step in helping a child analyze words is to provide the foundational prerequisite skills using the suggestions provided in Chapter 17. These skills, when learned thoroughly, get the child ready to use the analysis skills themselves.

The analysis skills fall into three major categories. The first one—using context in combination with sound–symbol connections—is familiar from Chapter 17. It involves reading a sentence and guessing the identity of an unknown word by using the meaning clues in the sentence and the sound value of the first consonant of the unknown word. The principles for testing and teaching this type of skill at the analysis stage are the same as they were at the prerequisite stage except that the child now reads the sentence rather than having it read. Consequently, because you can adapt your teaching ideas from those provided in Chapter 17, this word analysis technique will not be discussed further in this chapter.

The second major category of word analysis skills is phonetic analysis. This deals with analyzing words by individual letter–sound units and blending the various sounds together to pronounce the unknown word. Many skills of phonetic analysis were discussed as prerequisites in the previous chapter and only three types of skills remain to be discussed. The first is *letter substitution* in which the learner replaces one letter with another in a known phonogram pattern and pronounces the new word, as when **b** is substituted for the **c** in **cat** and the new word is pronounced **bat**. The second is recognizing and using various *vowel principles* in analyzing unknown words, as when the learner recognizes the silent **e** principle operating in the word **lime** and is therefore able to pronounce the word correctly. The final type of skill is *syllabication* in which long words are broken down into shorter sound units as a means of pronouncing them more easily. As mentioned, the prerequisite skills of auditory memory, auditory discrimination, and sound–symbol connection are also part of phonetic analysis, but, because they are skills which get the child ready for the actual task of analyzing words in reading, they are considered prerequisite to the use of phonetic analysis.

The third major category of word analysis skills is structural analysis. This skill, like syllabication, focuses on helping children break long words down into smaller units as a means of pronouncing them more easily. However, while syllabication deals with sound units, structural analysis deals with meaning units, such as prefixes, suffixes, roots, and compounds. For instance, a child will be able to pronounce the unknown word **unhappy** if he or she knows the prefix **un–** and the root **happy**. Because structural analysis focuses on meaning, it is closely related to comprehension, and you will find it discussed again as a comprehension skill in later chapters.

The remainder of this chapter develops techniques for teaching phonetic and structural analysis. Remember that techniques for teaching sound–symbol–meaning are available in Chapter 17.

LETTER SUBSTITUTION

Letter substitution is an important skill for the young reader to learn since it provides great versatility in attacking unknown words. The child who has mastered the skill of substitution can go from the known word **cat** to unknowns such as **bat, cab, chat, chap, cash,** and, ultimately, to the unknown word **cut.** The child examines words for known parts, identifies them, substitutes letters in the initial, final, or medial position, and then pronounces the new word.

In the final analysis, however, the greatest value of letter substitution is that it gives us a means for efficiently teaching letter–sound correspondence for *short* vowels. While letter–sound correspondence is fairly easy to teach with consonants (see the discussion on sound–symbol connection in Chapter 17), the vowels are difficult because the sound the vowel makes is unknown until we see the "neighborhood" in which it lives—that is, the letters that surround the vowel in the word. For instance, the vowel **a** can have many sounds but we cannot identify the correct sound until we see it in a word. In the case of **cat,** we know that the vowel makes a short sound because it is followed by a consonant sound unit. This neighborhood is called the *closed-vowel* neighborhood in which the **at** (or similar **a** plus consonant units) are called *short a vowel phonograms.*

Teaching vowels has plagued teachers for years, leading to such desperate tactics as training children to mark vowels either long or short. The fruitlessness of this technique is evident when you consider that the correct diacritical mark cannot be assigned until *after* the pupil has correctly pronounced the word. The diacritical marking, then, does not help in pronouncing the unknown word but only teaches what mark to assign after the word has been pronounced.

How *should* a child be helped to pronounce the vowels? We would suggest that you first teach a child to auditorily discriminate among the vowel sounds and then to attach the sounds to the appropriate vowel letters, following the same procedures as outlined for consonants in Chapter 16. Then you should teach the letter substitution skill to assist recognition of the various vowel patterns used in English and the way in which letters can be substituted into these patterns to identify unknown words. To illustrate, if you wanted to teach the short vowel **a,** you would first teach the child to discriminate the vowel sound from among other vowel sounds, then to connect the sound to the letter **a,** and, finally, to use the letter substitution skill to pronounce many short **a** vowel phonogram words such as **cat, fat, hat, had, hack,** and so on.

PRE- AND POSTTESTING LETTER SUBSTITUTION

The best way to test a child's letter substitution skills is to provide lists of words containing the vowel elements desired and ask the child to pronounce each word in turn. For instance, if you want to determine whether the child can substitute initial consonants in short vowel phonograms, you might provide the following lists of words for pronunciation:

cat	get	sit	hot	but
bat	met	fit	got	cut
hat	set	hit	lot	nut
stat	chet	vit	fot	chut

Note that some of the words on the lists are nonsense words. You include these because you want to make sure that the learner is indeed analyzing and not simply recognizing the word at sight. By inserting an occasional nonsense word, you are insuring that the child *must* analyze the word since it could not have been previously learned as a sight-word.

DIRECTING ATTENTION

The first step in teaching letter substitution is to insure that the child possesses the necessary prerequisites for both the consonants and the vowels that you expect the child to use. For instance, in the lists provided above, the child must be able to auditorily discriminate and to attach sound to symbol for several single consonants, for the digraphs **sh** and **ch,** and for the short vowels. If he or she cannot do the prerequisite tasks, the child is not likely to have success in mastering the letter substitution task.

Once you have insured that the learner possesses the prerequisites, direct attention to both the vowel phonogram which is common from word to word and the letter sound of the letter to be substituted. In the list of short **a** words above, for instance, you would direct the learner's attention to the **at** phonogram and to the sounds of the various initial consonant units.

TEACHING LETTER SUBSTITUTION

The letter substitution skill lends itself well to either a modeling or a discovery technique. When using the modeling technique, your procedure might be one such as the following: Using a known sight-word which illustrates the vowel pattern being taught, print this word on the chalkboard, asking the learner to read it. Then print underneath it another word having the same pattern, highlighting with color the common vowel phonogram. If you are using **cat** and **bat,** for example, you would then say, "I can read the first word. It is **cat.** I see that the new word has an **at** in it just like the first word. It must sound like the **at** in **cat.** But the second word is not **cat** because it starts with the letter **b.** I'll get my

mouth ready to make the **b** sound and say the new word **b . . . at, bat.**"
Then put up another word of the same pattern, diminish the color cue,
and repeat the procedure as above but with learner participation.
Gradually diminish the assistance on subsequent words until the learner
can complete the process independently.

If you prefer to use a discovery technique, proceed somewhat as
follows: Place a list of words on the blackboard, each having the same
vowel phonogram. Pose a series of questions in which you use the learner's
responses to lead him or her to note that all the words in the list have
the letters **at** in them. *Caution:* While you may provide cues by highlighting the common phonogram, do not tell the learner what you want
discovered. When the learner has noted the visual similarities in the
words, have him or her note the sound similarities by either reading
whatever words in the list the learner can identify or by reading one or
two of the words yourself. Auditory highlighting of similar sounds should
be done at this time so that the learner recognizes the relationship between what is seen and what is heard. Finally, ask questions which
direct the learner to the sound of the first letter in each of these words.
Both auditory and visual highlighting (such as pointing to the key element and directing the learner to get the mouth ready to say this sound)
would be appropriate. If the learner can then pronounce the remaining
words on the list, he or she has discovered the sound of the short vowel
phonogram and the technique of consonant substitution.

RETEACHING LETTER SUBSTITUTION

If you need to reteach the letter substitution skill to some children, you
should first return to the prerequisite vowel and consonant sound–symbol
connection skills to insure that the learner can produce the necessary
sound value for each letter. Once you are certain that the prerequisites
are mastered, alter your instructional strategy to increase your highlighting on the common vowel phonogram and the sound values of the
varying letters to be substituted; where necessary, model the blending
process for the learner and have him or her mimic your actions.

PRACTICING LETTER SUBSTITUTION

Once the learner can substitute letters into the patterns you are working
with and pronounce the new words, you should create practice activities
to solidify the skill. Exercises such as the following are illustrative.

1. A useful device to help learners master this task is the word wheel.
   You can construct word wheels by cutting two circles from tagboard,
   one slightly larger than the other. On the larger wheel, print words in
   which the initial element is missing, starting each about the same
   distance from the center and progressing toward the outer edge like
   the spokes of a wheel. On the smaller circle, cut a slot whose size and
   position will expose only one word ending at a time, printing the consonant letter, blend, and digraph to be used to the left of the slot.

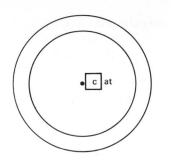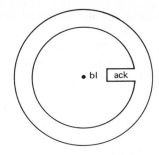

Fasten the two circles together with a paper fastener. As you rotate the lower circle, the letters on the upper circle will make a new word as they are combined with each ending on the lower circle. This same principle can be reversed so that the ending remains constant and the beginning changes.

2. A similar device is the slip card. The phonogram pattern being worked on is written on a wide piece of tagboard and the letters to be substituted are written on narrower cards and attached to the larger piece in a manner which allows one letter at a time to be shown with the phonogram pattern.

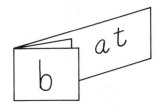

3. Use activities in which you provide the learner with a key word and a sentence in which one word is missing. Direct the learner to supply a word to fill the blank which is *related* to the key word. If the key word is **cat** and the sentence is, "Hit the ball with the _____," then the learner must supply the word **bat.**

4. Play games in which you start with a common phonogram pattern written on the board and the learner must change either the initial or final letter, substitute another, and pronounce the new word. The next learner must change it again and pronounce the new word. The pattern of words might look something like this:

    cat . . . bat
    bat . . . bag
    bag . . . bad
    bad . . . had
    had . . . has

5. Have one learner write on the chalkboard a word illustrating a common phonogram pattern. The learner must then pronounce the word and make up a sentence using that word. The next learner goes to

the chalkboard, changes either the initial or final consonant in the word, pronounces the new word, and uses it in a new sentence. At first you may want to accept any sentence the learners produce. As they become more skillful, however, you can modify the activity by having them produce successive sentences which are related to each other and which tell a story. For instance, the sentence might proceed in this manner:

The **cat** is in the house.
He is sleeping near the **bat.**
A man put the cat in a **bag.**
He must be a **bad** man.

6. Make word cards using words incorporating the common phonogram patterns you have been working on. Include also a number of cards which have the word "changeover" written on them. Deal each learner five cards. One learner starts by laying down any word card and naming it. If the next learner cannot play a word containing the common phonogram element, he or she draws from the deck until picking a word that can be played or until drawing three cards. If the learner has the "changeover" card, he or she can play that and name a word containing a new phonogram element that can be played on it. The first person out of cards wins the game.

7. Play a variation of Crazy Eights by making a deck of forty cards which have printed on them words containing the phonogram patterns you have been working on. Make six cards having the numeral 8 on them. Each learner gets four cards, with the rest of the cards placed in the center of the table. The first learner lays down a card and pronounces the word on it. The next player must play a card from his or her hand which contains the same word element or an 8 card. If the learner has neither a word card that fits nor an 8 card, he or she must draw a card from the deck. The learner who gets rid of all cards first is the winner.

8. A variation of Bingo can be played in which the game card has the common spelling patterns you have been working on printed in the squares. The learner is given a number of consonant letters, blends, and digraphs. The leader holds up a letter card, and the learner sees if he or she has the letter in his or her pile. If so, the learner tries to combine it with one of the spelling patterns on the game card. When all the words in a row have been formed, the learner may call "bingo." If the learner can then pronounce each word formed in the row, he or she wins the game.

APPLYING LETTER SUBSTITUTION

Once the learner has practiced this analysis technique, provide reading material which calls for the use of this skill, and guide the child in applying this technique when meeting unknown words in daily reading. Basal textbooks, library books, language experience stories, magazines, comic books, and any other reading material in which the learner encounters unknown words which can be analyzed through consonant substitution would be suitable.

VOWEL PRINCIPLES

A second type of phonetic analysis skill focuses on vowel principles, such as the silent e principle (as in like, bake, and so on), the two vowels together principle (as in **boat, raid,** and so on), the diphthong principle (as in **oil, boy,** and so on), and others. While the learner *could* learn to pronounce all vowels by looking for patterns and substituting initial consonants (as in **ride, hide, wide,** etc.) as is done in letter substitution, teaching common vowel generalizations has some value. Armed with both substitution skills and generalizations of the major vowel principles, the learner is equipped to analyze most of the vowel patterns likely to be encountered in reading.

PRE- AND POSTTESTING VOWEL PRINCIPLES

As with letter substitution, you can test the child's ability to identify words illustrating vowel generalizations by providing word lists and asking the learner to pronounce each in turn. For instance, if you want to determine whether pupils can pronounce words illustrating the silent e principle, you might ask them to pronounce words such as the following:

ride	cake	hole	nose	smile
hide	dame	shome	note	stone
nive	rope	joke	plate	take

this

Again, as with letter substitution, nonsense words appear in the lists to insure that you are getting a measure of the child's ability to analyze unknown words and not a measure of sight-word vocabulary.

DIRECTING ATTENTION

As with the letter substitution skill, the first step in teaching vowel generalizations is to insure that the child possesses the prerequisite sound–symbol connection skills for each of the consonants and vowels to be used. Once you have insured that the prerequisites have been mastered, you should direct the learner's attention to a three-step progression. The first attender is auditory and directs the child to the sound you want heard. The second is visual and directs the child to the letters you want noted. The third directs the child to examine the pattern from which the generalization is drawn. For the silent e principle, for instance, you would direct attention by first auditorily highlighting the long vowel sound in the middle of the words, then visually highlighting the medial vowel and silent e in each of the words and, finally, modeling the principle itself.

We caution you that all vowel generalizations have exceptions, and you should tell your learners that principles are generally true but not universally true, citing examples to support the point. For the silent **e** principle, for instance, you might illustrate with such common exceptions as **come** and **have**.

TEACHING VOWEL PRINCIPLES

Either the modeling or the discovery technique can be used to teach this skill. Assuming that you were teaching the silent **e** principle, the modeling technique would require rearranging the words in the pretest so that the long **a** words are together, the long **i** words are together, and so on. Start with the **a** words, using the say-it-slow, say-it-fast technique to exaggerate the sound of the medial vowel. Say, "I am going to say a word slowly and then fast, and we should listen carefully to the sound we hear in the middle. Here is the word. L . . . a–a–a . . . te. **Late.** The sound we hear in the middle is **a.**" Repeat this process with other words, gradually diminishing the modeling you do and the exaggeration you provide on the medial sound until the learner is able to identify the sound heard in the middle. Then write on the board the same words you just used, circling the medial **a** and silent **e.** Say, "Here are the word we were just listening to. We said that the sound heard in the middle was **a.** I am going to look at the first word. What letter does it have in the middle? It is an **a.** We heard an **a** sound and the letter in the middle is an **a.** But now let's look at the last letter in the word. The last letter is an **e.** We did not hear an **e** in the word but it has one at the end." Continues this process with subsequent **a** words, gradually diminishing the assistance you provide until the learner is independently identifying the visual pattern of the letters in the words. Then model the principle for the learner, saying, "Let's look at the word we have. In each word, we heard an **a** sound and we saw an **a** letter in the middle and an **e** which did not make any sound at the end of the word. Apparently, a word which ends in an **e** has a middle letter which say its own name, and the final **e** is silent. Let's look at some of the other words to make sure." Repeat basically the same procedure with words having other medial letters, diminishing the assistance you provide auditorily, visually, and in verbalizing the principle. You can go on to practice when the learner can look at a word illustrating the silent **e** principle and accurately predict the pronunciation of the word.

When using the discovery technique, as in the modeling technique, arrange the pretest words according to common medial sounds and start with **a** words. Direct the learners to listen carefully to the middle sounds of the words you are going to say and to tell you what letter sound was heard. Use the say-it-slow, say-it-fast technique to highlight the medial sound, gradually diminishing the assistance as the learner responds correctly. When he or she has established that the sound in the middle is an **a** sound, direct the learner to look at the list of words you have on the board and to tell you what they have in common. You may circle (or otherwise highlight) the medial letter and the final e to direct attention to the visual features you want noted, diminishing such assistance as the child begins to recognize the visual pattern. Then pronounce the first few words for the learner, telling him or her that they are the same words you had been saying earlier. As you pronounce the words, encourage the learner to hypothesize about how to predict the sound of the middle and final letters in each of the subsequent words in the list. Provide as much assistance as is needed initially, gradually diminishing this as the learner begins to see the effect the silent e has on the preceding vowel. Repeat the process with the other lists of words, providing less and less help each time. Once the learner can accurately predict the pronunciation of words illustrating the silent e principle, he or she is ready for practice.

RETEACHING VOWEL PRINCIPLES

If it is necessary to reteach this skill to some children, first establish that they possess the necessary sound–symbol connection skills to produce the sounds needed. Then reteach the skill itself, increasing the amount of highlighting at the auditory, visual, and principle stages to assist the learners in attending to the task. Finally, if some pupils still have diffi-culty reteach the skill as a task of letter substitution, arranging the words according to common final endings (such as **ride, wide,** and **hide**) and using the teaching suggestions provided for letter substitution.

PRACTICING VOWEL PRINCIPLES

Once the learner can pronounce words containing vowel principles without your help, create practice activities to habituate the skill. The following exercises are illustrative.

1. Using pairs of words such as those listed below, play games with the learner which require pronouncing each pair of words and explaining the effect of the silent **e.**

not	Tim	mad	hid	shin	rid	rod	slid
note	time	made	hide	shine	ride	rode	slide

2. Using words such as those listed above, construct a word wheel or a slip card in which a word is first pronounced without the final **e** and then is pronounced with the final **e.**
3. Make up short stories for the learner to read, insuring that each story has many opportunities to recognize and use the silent **e** principle (as in "*Tim* did *not* get the *note* on *time.*").
4. Make up nonsense words which illustrate the principle and have the learner read these, or use nonsense words found in poems such as Lewis Carroll's "The Jabberwocky" and have the learner read lines such as "Twas brillig and the slithy **toves.** . . ."
5. Play a variation of Bingo in which one-syllable words having no

silent **e** are printed in each square. The learner calls out a one-syllable word with a short medial vowel and looks for this word on the card. If the learner has the word *and* can correctly pronounce the new word that is made by adding an **e** at the end, he or she can cover it with a marker. When all the words in a row are covered, the learner can call "bingo." If he or she can then pronounce each word on the card *and* what each word would be if an **e** were added at the end, he or she wins the game.

6. Play a game with the learner using a construction paper spider web (such as the one shown) and a deck of cards which have vowel

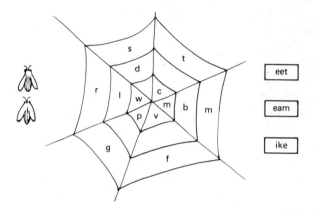

generalizations printed on them. The learner picks a card from the pile, puts the vowel generalization with one of the beginning letters in the spider web, and pronounces the new word. If the word is pronounced correctly, the learner fills that space in the spider web with a paper fly. When the spider web is filled with flies the game is over.

7. Play a form of the card game Go Fish with the learner. Each player is dealt a group of playing cards which have words containing vowel generalizations printed on them. The object is to get rid of all the cards by pairing vowels and correctly pronouncing the words. Each player asks the player to the right for a specific vowel. If that player has the requested card, he or she must give it up, and the first player can use it to make a pair and discard those cards. If a requested card is not available, however, the first player must draw from the pile.

8. Play a variation of a ring toss game with the learner. On each ring, print a beginning consonant letter or combination, and on each hook print an ending which illustrates a vowel generalization. The players throw the rings, attempting to put the rings on the hooks. If successful, the learner gets an additional point for pairing the beginning sound on the ring with the ending on the hook and pronouncing the new world.

9. A variation of baseball can be played with the learner. The batter is

given four examples of vowel generalization (such as **ai** or **oa**). The pitcher "throws" the batter two consonants which the learner must then combine with the vowels and pronounce. For each word completed correctly, the learner receives one base; if all four words are done correctly, the learner gets a home run.

10. Play a variation of Scrabble with the learner in which some of the blocks have vowel letter combinations (such as **oa, ow, ee,** and so on) printed on them and others have consonants printed on them. For each word constructed, the learner must provide an accurate pronunciation in order to receive credit.

APPLYING VOWEL PRINCIPLES

Once the learner has practiced this analysis technique, give him or her reading material which calls for the use of the skill and guide him or her in applying the technique when meeting such unknown words in daily reading. You can use basal textbooks, textbooks, library books, language experience stories, magazines, comic books, and any other reading material in which the learner encounters unknown words which can be analyzed through application of the silent **e** principle.

SYLLABICATION

A reader can sound out an unknown word by using letter–sound correspondence skills with consonants and phonogram units and by using what he or she knows of phonetic generalizations in the English sounding system. However, what does the reader do upon encountering a "big" word? How is a polysyllabic word sounded out?

Much as we did with phonetic generalizations above, we can teach the learner to look for patterns in the way big words are broken into syllables; from this division, we can help the child approximate the pronunciation of such words. This is a crucial task for the reader since many of the words encountered in reading will be long and will require syllabication to break them down into manageable sound units.

While it is crucial to learn, syllabication is also extremely difficult because it is so complex. To accurately pronounce multisyllable words, the learner must be able to isolate each syllable, decide on the correct vowel sound for each, determine where the primary, secondary, and tertiary accent falls, insert a schwa sound where appropriate, and, finally, pronounce the word. For most beginning readers, this is more than can be mastered. Consequently, the recommended strategy is simplified.

To develop syllabication skills, we emphasize only three principles: visually isolating syllables; assigning standard vowel sounds to each according to the arrangement of consonants and vowels; and saying the word with the understanding that the resultant pronunciation will be an *approximation* of the real word which the learner will then have to verify through context and experience. For instance, the learner would approach the unknown word **millimeter** by dividing it into syllables according to the visual pattern of consonants and vowels (**mil/li/me/ter**); pronouncing the syllables by assigning each vowel a short sound if it is followed by a consonant and a long sound if it is the last letter in a syllable; and then pronouncing the word and trying to match that approximation with a word previously heard (for instance, the learner might pronounce it as "mil–lie–me–ter" and then say, "Oh, I know that word. We talked about it in math. It's **millimeter**."). If this first attempt does not work, the learner is encouraged to move the syllable divisions one letter to the right (**mill/im/et/er**) and repeat the process. If neither process results in an approximation which the learner can tie to a word already heard, he or she has no recourse other than asking the teacher to pronounce the word.

PRE- AND POSTTESTING SYLLABICATION

As with the letter substitution and vowel generalization skills, you can test syllabication by presenting children with a list of words illustrating the desired syllable principle and asking them to pronounce these words. Again, a few nonsense words should be inserted to insure that the child is analyzing rather than recognizing the words at sight.

DIRECTING ATTENTION

As with other skills, syllabication has prerequisite skills which must be mastered; the child must know the sound values for all the letters (both consonants and vowels) to be sounded and letter substitution. It will do a child no good to break a long word into syllables if, after having done this, he or she is unable to pronounce the shorter sound patterns which result.

In teaching syllabication, direct the learner's attention by stating exactly what is to be learned and by highlighting first the number of sound units heard, then the vowel-consonant arrangement which signals the syllable division, then the sound value attached to each vowel and, finally, the process of trying the resultant approximate pronunciation to a word the child has experienced in oral vocabulary.

TEACHING SYLLABICATION

If you choose to use a modeling technique in teaching this skill, say to the learner, "I am going to say a word slowly and see if I can tell how many syllables I hear. **Af** . . . **ter.** I heard two syllables, **af** and **ter.** Now I am going to say another word slowly, and you see if you can tell me how many syllables you hear." Say other words for the learner, gradually diminishing the amount of help you provide by saying each succeeding word a little faster until you are saying the words normally. Then, write the words on the board one under another, labeling the vowel-consonant–consonant-vowel arrangement and the syllable division as follows:

246 ●

VC CV
al/most

VC CV
bas/ket

VC CV
pic/nic

Say to the learner, "Look at the first word. It is **al . . . most.** We hear two syllables in the word. We also hear two syllables in **bas . . . ket** and **pic . . . nic.** I have written the words on the board showing the syllable break. I have also labeled an arrangement of vowels and consonants in the word because the syllable division in these words comes between the two consonants. If I see a vowel-consonant–consonant-vowel arrangement like this in a big word, I can divide the word between the consonants and figure out how to say it." Demonstrate this with the three words, modeling the sound of the vowel when it comes before a consonant. Then write another word on the board, highlight the syllable break, the arrangement of vowels and consonants, and the vowel sound, and then help the learner pronounce the word. Repeat with other words, gradually diminishing the amount of help you provide in identifying the syllable break and letter pattern until the learner is able to identify each word without help. As he or she pronounces each word, emphasize that the pronunciation may be an approximation, which will require thinking of a word already known in oral vocabulary that is close in pronunciation. If you wish to use the discovery technique, pronounce each word slowly for the learner, directing him or her to tell you the number of syllables heard. With each correct response, diminish the amount of exaggeration used in dividing the syllables until the child is able to tell you the number of syllables as you say words normally. Then list the words on the board with the same highlighting as is described in the modeling technique. Say to the learner, "Look at this list of words. They are the words we just listened to, but now I have shown you where the syllable division is. Also, I have labeled the pattern of vowels and consonants which appears in each word. Can you look at the arrangement of vowel-consonant–consonant-vowel in each of these words and tell me how you might know where to make the syllable division in other words like these?" Provide whatever additional highlighting is necessary to help the learner see that the division comes between the consonants. Then try this with other words, gradually diminishing your assistance as the learner is able to identify the syllable breaks. Then show the learner that the resultant syllables are like the small words he or she has worked with before in letter substitution objectives and that, when the vowel comes before a consonant, it makes a short sound. Have the learner pronounce each of the words, providing as much help as is necessary until all the words have been pronounced unassisted. While doing this, remind the learner that the pronunciation may only be an approximation, and that the word would then have to be related to a word in the oral vocabulary.

RETEACHING SYLLABICATION

When reteaching is needed, it may be because the learner is having difficulty in identifying the sounds produced by the vowels and consonants in each syllable. In such cases, return to the appropriate sound–symbol connection and letter substitution skills, and insure that these have been mastered before reteaching syllabication.

If there is no difficulty with the prerequisites, reteach the syllabication skill, increasing your highlighting on the sound units heard, on the pattern of vowels and consonants, on the sound produced by the vowel in each syllable, and on tying the resultant pronunciation to a word in the child's oral vocabulary. If the learner has persistent difficulty, it may be necessary to rely heavily on a modeling technique.

PRACTICING SYLLABICATION

Once the learner can pronounce multisyllable words without assistance from you, give practice exercises to solidify the skill. Activities such as the following are illustrative. *for teaching Syllabication.*

1. Provide the learner with a list of multisyllable words similar to those he or she has learned to divide. Have the learner pronounce each word correctly to you or to a fellow classmate who already knows the words.
2. Play games with the learner in which aspects of syllabication must be used. For instance, use a gameboard device in which a learner progresses space by space toward some goal. Progress along the board is dependent upon ability to tell you how many sound units are heard in given words, utilizing one or more of the syllable principles you have taught.
3. Play riddle games with children in which syllabication plays a part. For instance, you could say:

   I am a big animal. I have a trunk and tusks. You see me in the zoo. I have three syllables in my name. Who am I?

4. Play a variation of dominoes with the learner in which the usual rules are used, but the dominoes have printed on them words which illustrate the various principles of syllabication. Each player has several dominoes, places them next to others which illustrate the same syllabication principle, and pronounces the words.
5. Play the Spin-a-Word game with the learner. Construct a spinner by making a circle out of oak tag, dividing it into pie shapes with multisyllable words printed in each section and attaching a spinner in the middle. The student spins the spinner and pronounces the word it stops on. Progress is recorded by moving space by space along a game board.

6. Play a variation of Ball-Toss with the learner. Post a list of multi-syllable words. The player with the ball must pronounce one of the words on the list, then toss the ball to another student who has ten seconds to pronounce another word on the list. If the catcher is successful, the ball goes back to the thrower, who gets another turn.

7. Play the Take-All game. Use a deck of cards which have multisyllable words printed on them. Place all the cards face down on the table. In turn, each player turns over one card and pronounces that word. If correct, he or she keeps the card, but if incorrect, the card is left on the table face up. The next student turns over a new card. If the word is pronounced correctly, the learner gets that card plus all the cards that are face up. If incorrect, the card must be returned to the table face up until someone can take all of them. The person who has the most cards when all the cards on the table are gone is the winner.

8. A variation of a bean bag toss can be played. The materials include six three-by-five-inch cards which are numbered in sequence from 1 to 6, bean bags and cards with multisyllable words printed on one side and the numbers 1 through 6 printed on the other according to the difficulty of the word. The word cards are placed face down in six piles, each pile being a different degree of difficulty. The numbered cards are placed on the floor in a random pattern. The player tosses the bean bag toward the numbered cards on the floor. If it lands on or near a number, the player draws a word from the pile having that difficulty rating and pronounces it. If correct, he or she gets that many points, with the winner being the first player to reach a predetermined score.

9. Play a motorcycle racing game using toy motorcycles, a gameboard, and dice. Each space on the gameboard contains a multisyllable word. Each player in turn throws the dice, moves that number of spaces, and pronounces the word printed there. If the word is pronounced correctly, the player stays; if not, he or she goes back that number of spaces. The first player to get to the end of the gameboard wins.

10. Play a variation of Scrabble in which the wood blocks are syllables and the object is to construct and pronounce multisyllable words. *Stop*

APPLYING SYLLABICATION

Once the learner has practiced a syllabication skill, supply reading material which calls for the pronunciation of unknown multisyllable words illustrating this principle and guide him or her in applying this skill in these situations. Basal textbooks, library books, language experience stories, magazines, comic books, and any other reading material in which the learner encounters unknown multisyllable words would be appropriate.

STRUCTURAL ANALYSIS

The final word analysis skill is structural analysis in which the learner identifies unknown words by looking at word parts or word structure, for instance, identifying the parts in prefixed words such as **un-happy,** in suffixed words such as **back-ing,** in contractions such as **I'll,** and in compound words such as **snow-man.** (*Caution:* Note that this skill is not the same as syllabication, which divides words into parts on the basis of *sound units* rather than on the basis of *meaning units* as is done here.) As such, analyzing by structure is another problem-solving technique the learner can use when meeting a word not known at sight. For instance, if the child is unable to pronounce the word **backing** but already knows the word **back** and the sound produced by the **–ing** ending, he or she can say, "I know that **b–a–c–k** is pronounced **back,** and I know the sound the **–ing** makes at the ends of words, so **back** and **–ing** must say **backing.**" This is a particularly efficient skill since it allows for rapid identification of the unknown word.

PRE- AND POSTTESTING STRUCTURAL ANALYSIS

To test structural analysis, you should provide pupils with lists of words made up of the structural units you wish to teach. Ask each child to pronounce each word and note the errors made; plan to teach any structural element the pupil has difficulty with. For instance, if you want to determine whether children can pronounce words when the structural endings **–s, –ed,** or **–ing** have been added, you would provide lists such as the following:

like	**fish**	**back**
likes	fished	backs
liked	fishing	backed
liking		backing

Note that, in contrast to the phonetic analysis skills, no nonsense words appear on the list. This is because structural analysis deals with meaning units and, therefore, words which have no meanings are inappropriate for use with this skill.

DIRECTING ATTENTION

As with the other word analysis techniques, there are prerequisites which must be met before teaching structural analysis. However, where the prerequisite for phonetic analysis skills tended to always be sound–symbol connection skills, the prerequisites for structural analysis relate both to sight-word recognition and comprehension. Specifically, to use structural analysis well, the pupil should be able to recognize the root word at sight and should know the meaning of the prefix or suffix being added. Both these prerequisites are crucial since the learner will not know when to use structural analysis as a means for breaking unknown words into smaller parts unless able to recognize the known root at sight and unless familiar with the prefixes and suffixes.

Once the prerequisites have been mastered, direct the learner's attention by telling him or her exactly what is to be learned and by highlighting the known root word and the visual and sound components of the new structural ending. With the word **likes,** for instance, you might underline the known root word **like,** circle the unknown structural ending s and exaggerate the ending s sound when pronouncing the word. *Note:* It is particularly crucial that you *do not* tell learners to "look for the little word in the big word" since this process is not helpful in analyzing many words. For instance, it is of little help to look for the little word **at** in **boat** or the little word **fat** in **father.**

TEACHING STRUCTURAL ANALYSIS

When using a modeling technique to teach a structural analysis skill, first print the root on the board and make sure the child is able to pronounce it. Next, directly underneath the first word, print the word again, adding the structural ending. Underline the root word and circle or otherwise highlight the structural element. Next, point to the first word and say, "I know that this word is **like** because I have seen and pronounced it before. When I look at the word directly underneath it, I see that it has **like** in it (point to the underlined root word), and I see that it has an s ending (point to the circled s)." Then pronounce the new word, using the say-it-slow, say-it-fast technique as a means for auditorily highlighting the sound value of the structural ending. Have the learner model your behavior. Repeat this procedure with other words, gradually reducing the modeling and highlighting assistance until the learner can pronounce the words independently.

If you prefer the discovery technique, place a list of word pairs on the blackboard, each pair having a root word and each root word having a common structural ending (for instance, you might use the words **like** and **likes, back** and **backs,** etc.). Pose a series of questions in which you lead the learner to note that all the words in the list have the s ending. While you may provide cues by highlighting the common structural element, do not tell the learner what you want him or her to discover. When the learner has noted the visual similarities in the words, have him or her note the sound similarities by either having that child read whatever words in the list he or she can identify or by reading one or two of the words yourself. Auditory highlighting of the common structural elements should be done at this time, using the say-it-slow, say-it-fast technique since this directs the learner to say the familiar root word and to add the ending. As he or she begins to respond correctly, you may diminish the amount of assistance provided by gradually removing the highlighting on the root word and structural element and by diminishing the amount of auditory highlighting on the sound value of the structural element.

RETEACHING STRUCTURAL ANALYSIS

When it is necessary to reteach structural analysis, first insure that the child recognizes each of the root words at sight and that he or she has a meaning for the prefixes and/or suffixes being taught. If these prerequisites are there, reteach the skill, highlighting more dramatically the root word and the visual and sound components of the affix.

PRACTICING STRUCTURAL ANALYSIS

Once the learner can analyze words according to their structural elements, you should plan practice activities to solidify the skill. The following exercises are illustrative.

1. The word-wheel and word-slip techniques can be adapted for use in teaching the blending of structural elements in known words. A description of the construction and use of word wheels and word slips is contained in the storehouse of suggestions provided in this chapter.
2. Context activities can be used to develop this skill. Provide the learner with sentences in which one word is missing, giving a choice of a root word or a root and its structural ending to fill the space. For instance, a sample sentence might be, "The two (boy, boys) went to the store." The learner chooses the correct word to fill the blank, pronounces it, and tells why that word is the correct one. *Caution:* The successful use of this technique presupposes that the learner already knows orally the correct form of the word. Certain dialects will not contain many of these inflected and derived forms of words. Teach these as oral responses prior to this activity.
3. It is sometimes helpful to reverse the process described in the model teaching activity. That is, ask the learner to *create* words having prefixes or suffixes, or words which are compound. In such a case, you should print the known words and word parts on separate cards, scramble them, and have the learner choose one. Then the learner must choose another word card which would go with that word, making it either a prefixed word, a suffixed word, or a compound word. Be sure, however, that you have the learner pronounce the word created.
4. Make a chart or a worksheet in which root words or parts of compound words are listed down the left side, and suffixes or the other parts of the compounds are listed down the right side. Attach strings to the words in the left-hand column and direct the learner to connect the string with the suffixes or the other parts of the compounds listed at the right so as to make a new word.
5. Make up crossword puzzles in which only compound words and/or prefixed and suffixed words can be used as answers.
6. Play a card game in which each player is dealt cards having root words written on the cards. The deck, containing just prefixes and/or suffixes is placed in the center of the table. The learners take turns drawing cards from the deck and trying to match the drawn card with one of the root words to form a new word. Whoever can do so lays the two cards down together and pronounces the new word. If the player draws a card he or she cannot use, it goes back on the bottom of the pile. The first player to get rid of all his or her cards is the winner.
7. Give context experiences in which the learner must complete a series of sentences using the same root word in each. For instance, you might

provide the root word **play** and tell him or her to use it together with suffixes to complete these sentences (see *Caution* in activity number 2):

He is a baseball _____.
He is _____ in the game.
Yesterday, he _____ football.
When he _____, he is happy. *Stop*

APPLYING STRUCTURAL ANALYSIS

Once the learner has practiced the structural analysis skill, provide reading material which calls for the use of the skill and give the child guidance in applying this technique when meeting words containing the structural elements. Basal textbooks, library books, language experience stories, magazine, comic books, and any other reading materials in which the learner encounters words which contain the structural elements would be appropriate.

SUMMARY OF TEACHING WORD ANALYSIS SKILLS

You now have techniques for teaching the three primary word analysis techniques: sounding, structuring, and the use of context. A pupil who can use these skills to identify an unknown word is well on the way to mature reading skills. All that must be done now is to apply these skills at appropriate times on appropriate words. Some words will sound easily, but context is no help. Others will yield their pronunciations to structural attack faster and more easily than to either of the other techniques. The good reader internalizes the reading code, both the graphemic and the syntactic/semantic components, and uses the analysis techniques singly or in combination to identify words not yet memorized.

TEST YOUR KNOWLEDGE

1. The word analysis skills can be categorized into three groups: sound–symbol–meaning, phonetic analysis, and _____.
2. The category of phonetic analysis contains three major types of skills: letter substitution, vowel generalization, and _____.
3. Phonetic analysis is different from structural analysis because the first deals with sound units and the second deals with _____ units.
4. A major value of the letter-substitution skill is that it gives us a means for efficiently teaching letter–sound correspondence for

   _____.
5. To use the phonetic analysis skills well, a pupil must first master the prerequisite skills of auditory memory, auditory discrimination, and

   _____.
6. Nonsense words should occasionally be used in testing phonetic analysis skills to insure that the child is analyzing and not identifying the word at _____.

7. Before a child can substitute initial consonants in short vowel phonograms, he or she must first be able to discriminate the _____ for the short vowel.

8. In practicing letter substitution, it would not be effective to ask the pupil to write lists of words illustrating the pattern since this activity requires that the child use spelling skills rather than _____ skills.

9. The skill of vowel principles requires the pupil to make use of common phonetic _____ or rules.

10. In teaching both vowel generalizations and syllabication, you would follow a three-step sequence in which you first highlight the sound heard, then highlight the _____ pattern, and finally ask the learner to generalize.

11. Because syllabication is so complex a task, in the early stages we only teach the pupil enough to get to an _____ pronunciation of the word.

12. A reader knows where to divide words into syllables by noting the patterns of vowels and _____.

13. Structural analysis is an appropriate analysis technique only when the unknown words are composed of affixes or are _____.

14. Pupils should be helped to apply their analysis skills in their daily _____ so that skill instruction is not isolated drill exercises.

SIMULATION ACTIVITIES

1. Assume that you are teaching a third grade child named Kathy to substitute initial consonants in common short vowel phonograms. She does well with the short **a** phonograms (**cat, bat, rat,** etc.), with the short **o** phonograms (**got, rot, lot,** etc.), and with the short **u** phonograms (**but, mug, tug,** etc.). However, she has great difficulty with short **e** words and short **i** words (**get, set, met** and **sit, fit, lit**). The difficulty seems to lie with the vowel sounds themselves since she interchanges the short **e** and short **i** in these words (saying **get** as **git, sit** as **set,** and so on). What instruction would you plan for Kathy?

2. Assume that Tom is in the same skill group. He pronounces all the words correctly except the nonsense words (for instance, he will correctly pronounce **cat, bat,** and **rat** but will make no attempt to pronounce the nonsense word **zat**). What do you suppose the difficulty is and what instruction would you plan for Tom?

3. You are teaching structural analysis to Sam as a means for identifying the word **snowman.** After instruction, he successfully analyzes and pronounces the word. The next time he meets it in print, he again analyzes it. He does the same thing the third time he meets the word, and the fourth time, and the fifth time. If he continues to analyze the word on the sixth and seventh times, what would you do?

4. Bart is a second grader, and he has been moving easily through the hierarchy of reading skills. He has failed the pretest on pronouncing multisyllable words illustrating the vowel-consonant–consonant-vowel pattern, so you attempt to teach him that skill. You notice that he is

truly confused, so your approach is to model and highlight this skill as much as possible. You begin by highlighting the sound units of a word by saying **un . . . done, cel . . . ery, pic . . . ture,** and so forth. You ask Bart to mimic you. Then you give him a list of words he knows at sight and do the same activity. You say **bas . . . ket** and Bart mimics you. Then you take the same list and go through the same activity, this time drawing lines between the syllables. You again ask Bart to mimic you. Then you present Bart with a list of nonsense words like **aptod, tacbit, wonsis,** and so on. Again you model the spoken behavior of saying **ap . . . tod,** plus you draw a line to separate the syllables and ask Bart to mimic you. Then you give Bart a posttest and find that he can't do the skill unless you help a little. What has gone wrong here?

5. Assume you are working with Mary, a fourth grader. You determine through your pretesting that she needs help with the vowel principles for the silent **e,** two vowels together, and diphthongs. You teach each of these skills in turn, following each lesson with practice exercises. Two weeks later, you listen to Mary read a paragraph written at her instructional reading level, and you note that she still cannot pronounce words which illustrate any of the three vowel principles. You administer the posttests again and she indicates mastery of each of the skills. What has gone wrong with this instruction and what would you do to eliminate the problem?

6. Assume that you are working with Christopher and that he has mastered all the prerequisite word analysis skills. In listening to him read, you note that he misses the following words: **fireside, chopped, slave, kitchen,** and **flat.** Which of the word analysis skills would be most useful in teaching him to analyze *each* of these words?

7. Assume that you want to teach John to analyze and pronounce words by substituting consonant letters in the final position, as in **bit, big, bid,** and **bib.** What will you tell John that he is to learn today? What will you highlight for John when you teach this lesson?

8. Assume that you want to teach Denise to pronounce multisyllable words illustrating the vowel-consonant–consonant-vowel principle of syllabication. You know that there should be three stages to this instruction. What would you highlight during the first stage of the lesson? What would you highlight during the second stage of the lesson? What principle do you hope she will be able to use at the conclusion of the lesson?

SUGGESTED FIELD EXPERIENCES

Observation. When observing in schools, you should note the analysis skills taught and the way in which they are taught. Do teachers clearly differentiate between identifying words at sight and analyzing them? Do teachers make it clear that analysis is a temporary skill which the reader uses until he or she has seen the word enough to remember it as a sight-word? Do teachers direct attention and highlight appropriately when teaching the various kinds of word analysis skills?

Teaching activities. When working with children in a classroom setting, you should be able to teach them to analyze words through phonetic analysis, through sound–symbol–meaning, and through structural analysis.

Client impact. As a result of your instruction, your pupils will be able to figure out those words which they do not know at sight, thereby giving them the ability to read material without stopping to ask you the pronunciation of the occasional unknown words they encounter.

FOR CLASS DISCUSSION

Many people would consider use of the dictionary as a type of word analysis skill since a reader who is unable to pronounce an unknown word can look it up and use the dictionary's phonetic key to pronounce it. Why do you suppose that we have not included use of the dictionary as a word analysis skill to be taught prior to the achievement of functional literacy? At what point do you think such dictionary skills should be taught?

ANSWER KEY
1. structural analysis
2. syllabication
3. meaning
4. short vowels
5. sound–symbol connection
6. sight
7. sound
8. reading
9. patterns
10. visual
11. approximate
12. consonants
13. compounds
14. reading

TEACHING ORAL LANGUAGE AS READINESS FOR COM- PREHENSION

OVERVIEW

This chapter describes the relationship between oral language and reading, particularly as it affects instruction in comprehension. It includes instructional techniques for teaching oral language generally and for developing comprehension readiness by teaching thinking skills in listening settings. The ultimate objective is:

> Given pupils who need instruction in oral language, you will develop such skills as they are needed.

KNOWLEDGE BACKGROUND

So far, a major part of this book has been devoted to word identification. This is because, in actual reading, word identification is the first step— the printed page cannot be understood until the printed symbols have been identified. However, comprehension is the ultimate goal in reading, and it now becomes the focus of our attention.

Reading comprehension is the ability to understand what the author has stated in print and is synonymous with thinking. Of course, children begin to think long before they come to school and in areas other than reading; they think while they listen, speak, use nonverbal language, and interpret nonverbal language. When they learn the skills of reading and writing, they expand their thinking into those language areas. In order to teach reading comprehension, one must understand the relationship between language generally and the specific skills of thinking.

Our thinking is expressed either by verbal, nonverbal, or printed language, and we receive another person's thinking through that person's use of verbal, nonverbal, or printed language. Communicating and understanding the communications of others depends on language. Language—verbal, nonverbal, and printed—is the channel for expressing thoughts. Thinking skills, however, are the tools used to create and interpret communications at various levels of difficulty and in varying degrees of abstractness. Our examination of oral language, therefore, focuses first on language generally (in the sense of whether the child's communication channel is adequate for the task) and then on the specific thinking skills (in the sense of whether the child possesses the tools for creating and interpreting thought).

LANGUAGE: THE CHANNEL FOR EXPRESSING THOUGHTS

Since language is the channel for communication, each person's language must be adequate enough for thoughts to be expressed and understood. Prior to reading instruction, the learner expresses thoughts only through oral and nonverbal language. It is important that these language channels expand so that the learner can continue to express thoughts through a known language channel and so that the printed words met in reading will already be familiar to the learner in oral language. In this way, the learner recognizes in print only what is already known orally, and reading becomes "talk written down."

To promote this language expansion, teachers need to focus on and make the children aware of five general language concerns: the interaction and interrelation of the communication skills (oral—speaking and listening, printed—writing and reading, and nonverbal), the functional use and pleasure that can be gotten from written materials, the acquisition and understanding of new language styles where appropriate, the matching of the learner's oral language style with the school's oral language style, and acceptance of the learner's oral language style.

THE INTERACTION AND INTERRELATION OF THE COMMUNICATION SKILLS

The first concern is to assist the learners in their awareness of the interrelation and interaction of the areas of communication. Most children come to school with the ability to speak and listen, that is, to give and receive information which has been a part of their background experience. Many children have an awareness of how these skills interrelate and interact. However, few children come to school aware of how reading and writing interrelate with each other or how these areas reflect oral language, and these understandings must be developed.

At one level, you must help children see oral language as an abstraction of thought which contains the components of listening and speaking. Listening is the component that brings in information, and speaking is the component that gives others information. It is important that learners understand that speaking is verbalizing thoughts and listening is hearing someone else's verbalized thoughts.

Further, you should help children perceive that printed language is an abstraction of speech and that it includes both writing and reading. Writing is the component that gives others information and reading is the component that brings in information. Writing is someone's verbalized words put into print and reading is understanding what someone else has verbalized in print. Consequently, reading is a way to gain information just as listening is.

Nonverbal language is also an expression of thought and also has the dimensions of giving information and of understanding information given by others. One can give nonverbal information by body movements, body stance, and facial expressions; learners can understand nonverbal language by interpreting those signals.

These language areas all relate in that they are ways of getting and giving information. Learners come to school using and understanding verbal and nonverbal language. Teachers expand these skills and teach two additional ways to express and receive thoughts—reading and writing.

GETTING INFORMATION AND PLEASURE FROM PRINTED LANGUAGE

The second concern focuses on providing a bridge from oral language to printed language and on helping children understand the functional use and pleasure provided by books and other reading materials. Most children have been listening to others for years before they come to school, and many have had stories told to them or read to them. However, the teacher must make them *all* aware that they can get information and pleasure from reading materials. Listening to the teacher read books and stories aloud develops a bridge between oral and printed language while instilling a purpose for learning to read. Learners see again that printed words are talk written down and that eventually they can obtain new information and stimulation entirely on their own through printed language.

ACQUIRING AND UNDERSTANDING VARIOUS LANGUAGE STYLES

The third concern is to help learners acquire new language styles and to understand the flow of these new language styles. Most adults have several language styles, a formal style for formal occasions, informal styles for informal situations, and perhaps a dialect style used in geographical regions or cultural areas. The number of language styles is unimportant. What is vital is knowing *when* to use a given style.

The schools play a major role in teaching learners how to decide what style to use. The teacher should help the child learn and use several language styles in the classroom and should provide opportunities for practicing these various language styles. This helps to prepare the child for reading by showing that although reading is talk written down, there are several styles of "talk," and only one of these is found in most standard children's books.

MATCHING ORAL LANGUAGE AND "LISTENING" LANGUAGE

As implied above, the oral language used in the classroom should approximate the listening language of the learners, and the initial language style read should approximate the one used in speech. Obviously, understanding will be impaired if these are significantly dissimilar. This may require the teacher to provide an initial listening channel that does not reflect the standard speech taught in most schools; initial instruction will be in the learners' language style. Gradually, however, the new school language will be introduced, and the children will learn to communicate in the school language as well as in their own styles. At this point, the children can begin to receive formal reading instruction since they will have an oral background for the language used in most books.

ACCEPTANCE OF THE LEARNERS' ORAL LANGUAGE STYLE

The last concern relates to the learners' basic oral language style. Failure to learn to read can result not only from lack of ability but from anxieties about self-worth. Since children beginning school normally have only oral and nonverbal language as the means of expression, their language style is a reflection of themselves. When the learners' language style and the school's language style do not match, you must exercise extreme caution. If learners feel that their language style is somehow unacceptable, they feel that they are unacceptable too. This creates anxieties about self-worth that can lead to failure in school generally and in reading particularly. Each teacher should be very aware of this when introducing new language styles and should help all learners feel that their language style is acceptable.

SUGGESTIONS FOR DEVELOPING GENERAL ORAL LANGUAGE

There are many ways to make learners aware of the interaction of the modes of communication and to develop oral and nonverbal language as a basis for printed language. Ongoing activities that develop oral and nonverbal language can be incorporated into any part of the school day. These include speaking and listening activities such as direction-giving (the teacher gives directions and verifies that they are understood) as well as traditional oral activities such as Show-and-Tell.

A variety of oral and nonverbal language can also be built into the content areas. Puppets can be used to discuss information in content areas such as social studies, science, math, language arts, and so on. Pantomime can also be used as a method to give and receive information. Learners can act out activities such as the different roles played by community helpers (policemen, firemen, postmen) or act out how characters feel in different stories, such as how Mike or his steam shovel felt in *Mike Mulligan and His Steam Shovel* by Virginia Burton (Boston: Houghton Mifflin, 1939). Art and music activities can be acted out before they are applied. Movement to music or rhythm is an excellent way to develop nonverbal or verbal expression.

Activities which help learners become aware of the interaction of oral and nonverbal language with printed language are also numerous and can be adapted to any content area during the school day. These include:

1. *Experience charts,* where the students speak and the teacher writes.
2. *Student dictation,* where the student dictates a letter and the teacher writes.
3. *Student-made books,* where learners tell a story and the teacher or an assistant helps make a book of the story to add to the class library.
4. *Word-card files,* where a list of words chosen by the children can be compiled for each learner and put on individual cards.
5. *Field trips or walking tours* of the school neighborhood, which can be used to generate oral discussions and written stories.
6. *"Orff,"* where words, spoken or sung, can be tied to rhythm by use of musical instruments such as bells, blocks, cymbals, tambourines, and xylophones. Usually the teacher sings or says the words as the students express those same words orally and in rhythm.
7. *Creative dramatics,* where situations can be provided which develop nonverbal language and can highlight the interaction and interrelation of nonverbal and oral language channels.

As the learners acquire language skills and an awareness of their relationships, application situations should be created to keep these skills current and active. Many of the activities cited above can be adapted here; variety within the activities and content areas is endless.

SUMMARY
Oral and nonverbal language is the basis for reading comprehension. Every teacher needs to make certain all learners have an adequate oral and nonverbal language base and then build an awareness in each learner of how these languages interact and interrelate with the printed modes. Only when a child has a firm oral language foundation can reading instruction begin.

THINKING SKILLS FOR COMMUNICATION

As the language channels for communication are developing and expanding, skill instruction in the thinking areas can begin. Thinking ability as it relates to reading instruction can be divided into three major categories—information gathering skills, manipulative skills, and evaluative thinking skills. These, of course, are the same major areas of comprehension as described in Chapter 6. The thinking skills do not change—whether one is thinking in oral language or in written language, the same skills can be used. Therefore, one of the major ways to develop readiness for comprehension is to teach the thinking skills in an oral setting until the child develops enough word identification skills to use the thinking skills in reading comprehension.

The thinking skills should be developed in a spiraling hierarchy similar to the one in word identification. Information gathering, manipulative thinking, and evaluative thinking skills are learned in a sequence at increasing levels of difficulty. This means that some information gathering skills are learned, some manipulative thinking skills are learned, some evaluative thinking skills are learned, and then the process repeats itself at a more difficult level and more skills within the three categories are learned. This simple-to-complex structure continues until the thinking skills have been acquired.

Since beginning readers do not yet know how to identify printed words, the development of the thinking skills must be done initially in listening situations. Such instruction can begin as soon as the child starts school and should be developed and expanded until the learners have enough word identification skills to read. At that point, thinking skills can be taught in the reading setting as *reading comprehension*. The important thing is that the thinking skills be developed, whether it be through listening situations or reading situations. The activities used to develop these skills in oral language are the same as those described in chapters 20, 21, and 22—except that at the prereading or readiness stage, the activities would be adapted to listening situations rather than reading ones.

SUMMARY OF TEACHING ORAL LANGUAGE AS READINESS FOR COMPREHENSION

Oral language is a crucial prerequisite to reading generally and to reading comprehension particularly. It can be developed in two ways—through general language development, which focuses on language functions and usage, and through the development of the specific thinking skills that are the tools of comprehension. Teachers—particularly those working with primary children—should be prepared to create activities in both general oral language development and in the use of specific oral thinking skills as a means for readying children for reading instruction.

TEST YOUR KNOWLEDGE

1. Thinking skills can be taught in both _____ and
   _____ situations.
2. Thinking is communicated by _____, _____, or
   _____.

3. _____ is the channel for expressing thought.
4. _____ are the tools used to create and interpret communication.
5. Body movements, body stance, and facial expressions are ways to give _____ information.
6. _____ is "talk written down."
7. It is important to know _____ to use different language styles.
8. Oral language in the classroom should match the learner's _____.
9. Anxieties about oral language styles can lead to _____.
10. The three areas of thinking skills are _____, _____, and _____.
11. At the early stages of comprehension, thinking skills should be taught in _____ situations.

SIMULATION ACTIVITIES

José is a new student in your first grade. He has lived in the United States all his life, but his parents speak only Spanish at home and his older brothers and sisters speak English only on occasion. He is very shy and will sit quietly all day doing nothing if allowed. What would be your concerns in developing his language channels? How would you begin to develop his language channels? When would you start to teach thinking skills?

SUGGESTED FIELD EXPERIENCES

Observation. When observing in schools, note how the teacher provides activities for general language development and thinking skills. Are all the channels for communication developed? Are the channels interrelated? Are the early thinking skills taught orally? Is there a system for the development of the thinking skills?

Teaching activities. Select an activity from those listed in this chapter and teach that activity to a group of students who need it.

Client impact. If you are aware of the need for developing oral language and of its interaction and interrelationship with the other channels of communication and the thinking skills, and if you can teach oral language development and thinking skills, you are directly assisting learners in their preparation for becoming functional readers. The impact will be noted in your students' ability to express themselves and understand others, be it through oral, printed, or nonverbal means.

FOR CLASS DISCUSSION

Dr. James Moffett is a strong believer in language performance. In his book, *A Student-Centered Language Arts Curriculum, Grades K-13: A Handbook for Teachers* (Boston: Houghton Mifflin, 1968), he states:

A long list of mental activities that any psychologist would consider general properties of thinking that occur in many different areas of human experience have somehow or other all been tucked under the skirts of reading. "Recalling," "comprehending," "relating facts," "making inferences," "drawing conclusions," "interpreting," and "predicting outcomes" are all mental operations that go on in the head of a non-literate Aborigine navigating his outrigger according to cues from weather, sea life, currents, and the positions of heavenly bodies. Not only do these kinds of thinking have no necessary connection with reading, but they have no necessary connection with language whatever.

Do you agree or disagree with Dr. Moffett? Which statements do you agree with? Which statements don't you agree with?

ANSWER KEY
  1. oral, written
  2. writing or printed language, speaking or oral language, and nonverbal language
  3. language
  4. thinking skills
  5. nonverbal
  6. reading
  7. when
  8. listening language
  9. failure in school
 10. information gathering, manipulative thinking, evaluative thinking
 11. oral

TEACHING
INFORMATION
GATHERING
SKILLS

OVERVIEW

This chapter provides you with techniques for teaching the comprehension skills of information gathering, including word meaning, signalers of relationships, contextual prediction, and factual recall. Specific and practical suggestions for testing, directing attention, teaching, reteaching, practicing, and applying are provided. The ultimate objective is:

> Given pupils who need instruction in word meaning, signalers of
> relationships, contextual prediction, and factual recall, you will
> teach these skills using the instructional principles described in
> Chapter 14.

KNOWLEDGE BACKGROUND

In Chapter 6, we learned that the comprehension skills can be divided into three streams—information gathering, manipulative thinking, and evaluative thinking. Each stream contains numerous oral language and reading comprehension skills which the child uses to understand what is read.

Our focus in this chapter is on the first of the streams: information gathering. This stream includes four types of skills which have in common the literal aspect of language: word meaning, understanding how relationships are signaled, making contextual predictions, and recalling the words and phrases which answer factual questions.

Each of the four types of skills appears many, many times in a simple-to-complex progression. For instance, the easier, more frequently used word meanings are taught first, and the harder, less frequently used words are taught later. This chapter provides you with techniques for teaching each of the four types of skills.

WORD MEANING

Word meaning is the first information gathering skill. You will remember from Chapter 6 that content words are words having a referent in our culture, as opposed to function words which exist to signal grammatical relationships among content words. Since the ultimate goal of reading is obtaining meaning, and since the content words are the foundation upon which meaning is built, we will focus on content words in this section.

PRE- AND POSTTESTING CONTENT WORD MEANING

You should select the words to be tested from among the words which appear in the basal textbook, in stories you are reading orally to the class, or in a particular content area such as social studies. Testing should be done orally since a child should not be asked to identify in print words whose meanings may not be known. The best way to find out whether a child knows the meaning of a word is to say the word and ask the child to make up a sentence or to send you a message using that word. If the child can do so, he or she knows the meaning of the word; if not, then you should teach the meaning. Of course, if you know from your personal experience with the child that he or she uses the word meaningfully in oral language, it is not necessary to test.

DIRECTING ATTENTION

To teach content word meaning, you must direct the learner's attention by (1) providing either actual or vicarious experience to form the basis for the concept, (2) identifying the characteristics of that concept, and (3) connecting the concept with its word label. To teach the word **dog**, for instance, you would show the learner a real dog, a model of a dog, or a picture of a dog; list the characteristics of "dog-ness" which form the concept; and help the child connect this concept with the verbal label *dog*. For words having multiple meanings, you must additionally direct the learner to the context in which the word is found. For instance, contextual setting becomes an important cue in the sentences, "The *dog* was looking for his bone" and "The soldier decided he would *dog* it for the rest of the day."

TEACHING CONTENT WORD MEANING

You can use either a modeling technique or a discovery technique when teaching content word meaning. In either case, the first step is to select an appropriate experience or set of experiences. The more direct the experience, the better the learning will be, although vicarious experiences must necessarily be used when it is impossible to provide direct experiences.

In using modeling to teach the meaning for the word **dog**, you would refer to an experience the learner had previously had with dogs, or bring a real dog or a model or a picture of a dog to class. Using the experience as a basis, identify the characteristics of "dog-ness" for the learner, having him or her mimic or otherwise attend you. Say, "This is a *dog*. I know it is a *dog* because it is an animal, it has four legs, it is larger than a cat but smaller than a horse, it makes a barking noise, (etc.)." Then connect this concept to the word label by saying, "This animal is called a *dog*." You should then repeat the process several times with different kinds of dogs. This will enrich and broaden the understanding of the concept *dog* while also allowing you to gradually diminish the amount of modeling as the learner becomes more confident of the concept. When the learner is using the new word comfortably in oral language, you can assume he or she has learned its meaning.

If you use the discovery technique, the basic frame of the lesson remains the same ; the major difference lies in the way you handle the second step—identifying the characteristics of "dog-ness." Rather than being highly directive in specifying the characteristics for the learners as when modeling, you encourage them to use their observation skills to identify the characteristics themselves. Consequently, the dialogue might proceed as follows: "This is a *dog*. I know it is a *dog* because of certain things it has and does. Can you look at it and guess how I know it is a *dog?*" As the learner responds, you encourage and direct the child to certain characteristics which he or she may be overlooking. After examining one example of a dog and listing its characteristics, the child should be shown another example, directed to list its characteristics, and helped to consolidate these observations into a solid concept of *dog*. As before, when the learner is using the new word in oral language, he or she has learned its meaning.

RETEACHING CONTENT WORD MEANING

If you teach a content word and the child still does not understand its meaning, reteach the word using a more relevant and direct experience. For instance, if a vicarious experience such as a picture had been used to teach the word **dog**, you might want to bring in a real dog for the reteaching.

If you are certain that the quality of the experience is not the difficulty in learning the content word, provide more direction and assistance in highlighting the characteristics of the concept, insuring that you are not using unknown words to explain the meaning of another unknown word. For instance, do not characterize a dog as being "smaller than a horse" unless the learner already knows the meaning of both *horse* and *smaller*.

Once the child knows the meaning of the content word, you should provide practice activities in which the new word can be used. Activities such as the following are illustrative.

1. Use exercises in which words are replaced with synonyms. Each learner can be encouraged to supply another word that "means about the same thing." Appropriateness to the concept can be judged by discussion of the group.
2. Teach word opposites. One way to discriminate a concept is by knowing not only what it is but what it is not. It is most appropriate at all stages of reading development to play word games in which learners supply words which are opposites in meaning.
3. Encourage learners to associate content words with mental pictures of that concept. Let each learner draw or describe his or her mental picture.
4. Have learners note on three-by-five-inch cards the word meanings learned and the key characteristics and/or synonyms created. In this way, you not only build meaning vocabulary but also a synonym source for use in writing assignments.
5. Combine known simple words to create either real compound words or new compounds, and discuss the new concepts which are created when two simple words are made into one compound word.

APPLYING CONTENT WORD MEANING

Once the child has learned the meaning of the new content words, make sure he or she uses those words in contextual settings during the routine daily language activities in the classroom. A good way to do this is to use the words yourself in conversation with the children and to ask questions in which they will have to use the new words in their responses. Finally, of course, the learners should ultimately be taught to identify the word in print and to use it in reading.

SIGNALERS OF RELATIONSHIPS

Once a child knows the meaning of the content words in a message, he or she must then be able to determine the relationship between and among those content words. These relationships may be positional, cause–effect, compare–contrast, and so on and are normally signaled by function words. The instructional emphasis in the relationships category, then, is on function words and the relationships they signal.

PRE- AND POSTTESTING RELATIONSHIPS

To test whether a child understands relationships, the teacher must ask the child to respond in terms of the meaning being signaled. For instance, if the relationship is one of position, as signaled by function words such as **in, to,** and **on,** the teacher might give the child a hollow tube and a small block, asking him or her to complete oral directions such as:

1. Put the block **in** the tube.
2. Bring the tube **to** the block.
3. Put the block **on** the tube.

At a higher level where the relationship is one of chronology or cause–effect, the teacher may have the child read a passage and state what happened first, second, and third or tell what caused an event to happen. In any case, the test consists of asking the learner to respond in terms of the relationship being signaled.

DIRECTING ATTENTION

Information gathering in the English sentence results from a partner-ship between content words and function words. In any sentence, the learner must know both the concepts associated with the content words used and the relationship between those content words as signaled by function words. As such, function words are as important, much more subtle, and less definitive than content words.

Teaching function words meaning is more difficult than teaching content words because the relationships signaled by function words are difficult to visualize. To teach these relationships, you must direct the learner's attention by emphasizing the function word as it appears in oral context, while simultaneously demonstrating the relationship sig-naled. For the function word **in,** for instance, you could say, "I will put the block *in* the tube," emphasizing the word **in** as you simultaneously place the block in the tube.

TEACHING RELATIONSHIPS

You can use either a modeling technique or a discovery technique when teaching relationships. In either case, you must use the word in a sen-tence, while simultaneously demonstrating its relationship. To model the function word **in,** for instance, you could put the block in the tube as you say, "I'm putting the block *in* the tube," emphasizing the word as you say it. The learner watches you and mimics both your actions and your words. In subsequent sequences, you would provide less modeling and fewer manipulative demonstrations until the learner is using the function word comfortably in daily language.

In using the discovery technique, you would substitute questioning procedures for the mimicry found in the modeling technique. For in-stance, you might use two contrasting sentences such as:

Put the block **in** the tube.
Put the block **on** the tube.

You would say each sentence in turn, emphasizing the function words, while simultaneously demonstrating the relationships. Then say, "What did I do differently in each case? What word tells you where to put the block in the first sentence? In the second sentence?" In subsequent sequences, you would provide less auditory emphasis on the function word and fewer manipulative demonstrations until the learner is using the function word comfortably in daily language.

RETEACHING RELATIONSHIPS

If you teach a function word meaning and the child is still unable to respond in terms of the relationship being signaled, reteach the skill, providing greater assistance to the child. For instance, you might increase the number of oral language activities in which the function word is used, provide more tangible manipulation of the relationship being signaled, and emphasize the function word more clearly to insure that the learner is attending to the correct word in the sentence.

PRACTICING RELATIONSHIPS

Once the learner understands the meaning of the relationship being signaled, provide practice activities which call for the use of the relationship. Activities such as the following are illustrative.

1. Give children oral sentences and ask them to identify words that answer questions you pose, such as:

   > Which word tells where the boy is?
   > Which word tells when the event happened?
   > Which word tells who "she" is?

2. Put on the chalkboard words that signal certain relationships and have the learner think up sentences using these function words.
3. Play games in which you provide a partial sentence which begins or ends with a function word. The learner completes the sentence, using words appropriate to the relationship signaled by the function word. For instance, you might provide sentences such as:

   > The book is on _____.
   > In school, Tommy was _____.

4. Using paragraphs such as the following, have learners specify the different relationship meanings of each paragraph and identify the function words which signal these relationships in each.

   > During our visit to the museum, we saw a collection of old silverware, an absorbing display of old-fashioned wedding gowns, a room filled with Indian relics, and the first Stars and Stripes ever carried in battle.

   > During our visit to the museum, we saw the first Stars and Stripes ever carried in battle; after that we enjoyed a collection of old silverware, later wandered into the room filled with Indian relics,

and finally found ourselves absorbed in a display of old wedding gowns.

During our visit to the museum, we enjoyed seeing the first Stars and Stripes ever carried in battle and the absorbing display of old-fashioned wedding gowns much more than we did the room filled with Indian relics and the collection of old silverware.[1]

APPLYING RELATIONSHIPS

Once the child understands the relationship being signaled, insure that he or she uses the skill in the routine daily activities of the classroom. At the early stages, this is best accomplished by using the function words in your oral language interaction with the child, requiring response with the appropriate behavior or action. Later, when the child begins reading, ask him or her to read the function words in print and to respond by identifying the information being conveyed by that function word or series of words.

CONTEXTUAL PREDICTION

A child's ability to obtain information from a passage depends greatly upon use of English grammar to predict what words and ideas will follow other words and ideas. The child uses an understanding of language patterns and personal experience as a language user to make guesses about the information the author is trying to convey.

This is a fundamental reading skill in both comprehension and word recognition. In comprehension the learner uses the skill to predict what information should be gathered; in word recognition he or she uses the same skill to predict what an unknown word might be. (See sound–symbol–meaning in Chapter 17.)

As can be seen, contextual prediction is a broadly utilitarian skill which appears in many forms. For the purpose of illustration here, however, it will be discussed from the standpoint of its use in predicting unknown word meanings in sentences such as the following (in which the meaning of the word **biplane** is unknown):

A **biplane,** an airplane with two wings, flies very fast.

PRE- AND POSTTESTING CONTEXTUAL PREDICTION

To test whether the child can use contextual prediction to identify the meaning of an unknown word such as **biplane,** tell him or her that you will use the word in a sentence which gives a clue to the word's meaning; after stating the above sentence, ask the child to draw a picture of the word, point to a picture of the word, or otherwise identify it.

---

[1] O. S. Niles, "Comprehension Skills," William K. Durr (ed.), in *Reading Instruction: Dimensions and Issues,* Boston: Houghton Mifflin, 1967, pp. 130–31.

DIRECTING ATTENTION

In determining word meaning through context clues, the learner makes use of several previously learned comprehension skills. For instance, he or she must know the meanings of the words around the unknown word to be able to use them as clues, and he or she must know the relationships that are signaled. In teaching this skill, then, you must first insure that the learner has mastered the prerequisite comprehension skills and then direct attention to the unknown word, to the commas which set off the explanatory phrase, and to the words within the phrase which explain the meaning of the unknown word. In the illustrative sentence, for example, you would direct the learner's attention to the word **biplane,** to the commas after **biplane** and **wings,** and to **airplane** and **two wings** within the phrase.

TEACHING CONTEXTUAL PREDICTION *clues*

Start

You can use either a modeling technique or a discovery technique when teaching contextual prediction. In either case, you could show the highlighted sentence such as the following:

A **biplane,** an airplane with two wings, flies very fast.

You could then model by saying to the learner, "If I do not know the meaning of **biplane** in this sentence, I could figure out its meaning by looking for clues in the sentence. There are two kinds of clues. The commas are the first clue and tell me that the author is providing me with extra information. When I see commas setting off words in this way, I want to examine the words between the commas for clues. Certain key words are the second kind of clue. In this case, I find the words **airplane** and **two wings** between the commas. These words help me understand that a biplane is an airplane with two wings." In subsequent sentences, ask the learner to assume more and more of the description of the thinking process while you provide fewer and fewer clues in the form of underlining, circling, and drawing arrows. When the learner is able to determine independently the meaning of unknown words in such sentences, you can assume that the skill has been learned.

In the discovery technique, you could still make use of a sentence in which the clues have been highlighted with circles, underlines, and arrows, but instead of directly modeling the thinking process you could direct the learner's attention with questions. For instance, you could direct the learner to the commas and say, "Why do you suppose the author added the words within the commas? What words within the commas give us clues to the meaning of the word **biplane?**" In subsequent sentences gradually diminish both the highlighting and the questioning until the learner is able to use this type of context clue without assistance. *Stop*

RETEACHING CONTEXTUAL PREDICTION

If you teach a contextual prediction skill such as the above and a child cannot figure out the meaning for the unknown words, first make sure the prerequisites are there and then provide additional highlighting on the commas and the words within the commas which provide clues.

PRACTICING CONTEXTUAL PREDICTION

Once the child understands how to make contextual predictions such as the above, provide practice to solidify the skill. The best way to do this is to give exercises which offer multiple opportunities to use the skill. Ditto sheets, workbook pages, and similar activities would be appropriate.

APPLYING CONTEXTUAL PREDICTION

After learning to use contextual prediction, be sure the child uses the skill in daily classroom activities. For instance, provide context clues each time you orally introduce new words in content area lessons, or, once the child develops an instructional reading level, give reading in which similar contextual clues provide assistance in determining meanings of new words.

FACTUAL RECALL

The final information gathering skill is factual recall. Once the child knows the word meanings, the relationships signaled, and the predictions which can be generated from context, he or she must identify the important information and remember it. As such, factual recall typifies the end product of the information gathering stream.

PRE- AND POSTTESTING FACTUAL RECALL

To test recall of factual information, simply give the child a passage and ask factual questions about it afterwards. The number of correct responses will indicate the child's mastery of this skill.

Factual recall can be tested in both oral and written form. If the child does not yet have an instructional level, you should read the passage and orally ask him or her to answer the questions; once the child can read, you can supply written passages commensurate with instructional level.

DIRECTING ATTENTION

Factual recall is more a task of *remembering* than thinking, more a function of memory than of cognition. The learners must note and remember those words or phrases which answer questions posed. They will remember best when they have meanings for the words used and when they know what you are looking for. So, to teach factual recall, you must insure that the learner knows the meaning of the words in the passage, and you must direct attention by asking specific questions which serve as cues for what to note and remember (For example, the questions to be asked should be posed *before* the child listens to the passage.).

?

TEACHING FACTUAL RECALL

Either the modeling technique or the discovery technique can be used to teach factual recall. In illustrating both strategies, the following paragraph and questions will be used as a sample:

> Every morning a boy and his friends went to a high, grassy hill.
> Every morning the boys jumped and skipped to the top of the hill.
> When they got to the top, they ate their lunches until they were full.
>> Where did the boys go?
>> How did they get to the top of the hill?
>> How long did the boys eat?

After insuring that the learner knows the meaning of each word, say, "To answer questions about details and facts in a story, you must first know what the questions are and then you must find and remember the words which answer the questions." Show the learner the sample paragraph but alter it by putting the first question ahead of the paragraph, underlining the phrase *high, grassy hill,* and drawing an arrow from the question to the underlined phrase. Say, "The first question asks where the boys went. In the first sentence of the story, it says the boys went to a high, grassy hill. So, to answer the first question, I must remember the phrase *high, grassy hill.*" Repeat the same procedure with subsequent questions in this and other paragraphs, gradually diminishing your modeling, the highlighting arrows, and the underlining until the learner is able to recall factual information at this level without your assistance.

The procedure for the discovery technique is basically the same, but you substitute questions for modeling. For instance, still using a paragraph which has been altered as described above, ask questions such as, "Why do you think the question to be answered is put first? Why are the words *high, grassy hill* underlined? Why is there an arrow pointing from the question to the underlined phrase? What must you try to do when you have to answer questions about details and facts in a story?" This procedure should be repeated with other questions and other paragraphs, gradually diminishing your questioning and highlighting devices.

RETEACHING FACTUAL RECALL

If the learner still cannot recall factual information after instruction, provide additional help, incorporating suggestions such as the following:

1. Insure that the learner knows the meaning of each of the words being used in the selection.

2. Reteach the skill using simplified material in which the answers to questions are more obvious.
3. Highlight more clearly both the question posed, the answer in the selection, and the connection between them.

PRACTICING FACTUAL RECALL

Once the learner is able to recall details and factual information, give plenty of practice to solidify the skill. Activities such as the following would be appropriate:

1. Before reading a selection from a textbook or reader, put the following purpose-setting formula on the board:
   Who? Where? When? How many? What happens?
   Ask the learner to use this formula as a guide in reading. Such a guide invariably will produce the details of a selection.
2. Before directing a learner to read a selection, set a purpose by asking to see how many things he or she can learn during reading. Direct the learner to make a tally mark on a paper as he or she reads, each mark standing for something learned while reading, usually a factual detail in the selection.
3. Before assigning a reading lesson, list key words from the selection on the board. Set the purpose by directing the learner to "find information about these words."
4. Prior to assigning a specific reading task, list several factual questions on the chalkboard as purpose setters. Direct the learner to find the answers to these specific questions as he or she reads.
5. Teach the learner how to set purposes autonomously while reading by asking his or her own questions. In a pretest selection on the Monarch butterfly in Chapter 27, for example, train the learner to anticipate factual information by listing some questions that he or she thinks he or she should be able to answer after having read the selection. At the conclusion of this reading, the reader checks to see how many of the questions he or she can answer, how many were not answered by the selection, and how many facts had not been anticipated in the questions.
6. Teach the learner to use the SQ3R technique. This is a systematic purpose-setting study technique that is particularly effective with content textbooks. The five steps are: *Survey, Question, Read, Recite,* and *Review.* Before beginning to read, the learner is taught to *survey* a chapter or selection to get an idea of what it is about; then to examine the material, particularly the headings and subheadings, and pose *questions* for himself or herself, which should be able to be answered when he or she has finished reading; then to *read* to answer the questions; then to *recite* to see if he or she is now able to answer the questions; and finally, *review* to find information relative to any question not answered. The first two steps in this technique, survey and question, are particularly appropriate to purpose setting because the learner is actively involved in determining what he or she is trying to learn, and in setting the goals. The learner's own questions guide the reading.

Stop?

This creates a relevance for learning that can be missing from other types of purpose setting.

APPLYING FACTUAL RECALL

In this case, practice and application are often synonymous since in both cases the child can be reading or listening to actual materials to gather actual information. You should insure that such reading and/or listening is done frequently after teaching this skill so that the child sees the utility and relevance of what he or she has learned to do.

SUMMARY OF TEACHING INFORMATION GATHERING SKILLS

Gathering information is one of the primary goals of reading. To be able to do this, however, the child needs skills in several areas. The content word meanings should be known, the relationships among and between the content words should be understood, predictions should be made from context, and the important facts should be noted and remembered. With children who have difficulty gathering information from their reading, you should provide assistance similar to that described in this chapter.

TEST YOUR KNOWLEDGE

1. The four types of skills in the information gathering stream are _____, _____, _____, and _____.
2. _____ words are words that have a referent in our culture.
3. The best way to determine if a learner knows the meaning of a word is to _____.
4. You should direct the learner's attention in teaching content words by using the following three steps:
   a. _____
   b. _____
   c. _____
5. Function words signal relationships between and among _____.
6. It is difficult to teach function word meaning because _____.
7. To teach relationships you should use the word in a sentence while simultaneously _____ its relationship.
8. A learner uses knowledge of language patterns and personal experience in contextual predictions to _____ about unknown words.
9. In order to make contextual predictions, a learner must know the _____ of the words around the unknown words and the _____ that are signaled.
10. _____ is the ability to identify important information and remember it.

SIMULATION ACTIVITIES

You should be ready to apply your knowledge of information gathering skills. Read the following situations and answer the questions.

1. Elementary school children will comprehend best those selections which deal with words such as **dinosaur, owl, submarine, helicopter,** and **pollution.** They will have greater difficulty with words such as **bacteria, peace, justice, professional,** and **self-reliance.**

   a. Why will children have greater difficulty with the second group of words?
   b. If you *had* to use the second group of words with children in the elementary school, how would you teach them? Illustrate with the words **bacteria** and **justice.**

2. You are using this story problem to practice relationship thinking skills with a group of five students.

   > A car dealer has 16 new cars on his lot. Furthermore, he has 11 used cars. A new shipment of new cars is coming soon. He had ordered 9 more cars, but the company can only send part of his order. After the new order came in he has a total of 31 cars on his lot. How many cars came in on the order?

   Four of the five learners catch on quickly, while one child, Billy, is unable to do the task. You know it is not because of his math ability because he has the necessary skills of addition and subtraction. It would appear that the problem rests with his comprehension of the written problem.
   a. What function words might be causing a problem here?
   b. What is the relationship being signaled in this problem?
   c. How would you help children comprehend this relationship so they can do the thinking needed to complete the problem successfully?
3. The following is a sample pretest for a comprehension skill.
   The pretest. State the unknown word, telling the child that you are going to use the word in a sentence which will give a clue to the word's meaning. After stating the sentence, ask the child for the meaning of the word. Criterion for mastery is 80 percent.

biplane	A **biplane,** an airplane with two wings, flies very fast.
jester	The **jester,** a man who tried to make people laugh, was very old.
escalator	An **escalator** is like a moving staircase and is fun to ride.
larder	The **larder,** a storage place for food, was large and cool.
figs	The king was eating **figs,** a sweet fruit grown in faraway lands.

a. What type of skill within the manipulative stream is this pretest assessing?

b. In teaching this skill, what would your attenders be?

4. One way to determine whether children lack comprehension skills is to ask them questions about what they have read. Read the following paragraph and list the questions you would ask to test comprehension.

> The ruler (Khedive) of Egypt engaged in extravagant expenditures on public works and private pleasures. Needing money, he was forced to sell his Suez Canal stock to Britain and to borrow huge sums at interest rates as hight as twenty-five percent. His inability to pay his debts led to British and French interferences in Egypt's government. This brought about a nationalistic revolt in 1882.

List three factual recall questions you might ask.

SUGGESTED FIELD EXPERIENCES

Observation. When observing in schools, you should note how teachers assess, teach, evaluate, and apply information gathering skills. Are word meaning skills included? Are signalers of relationship skills included? Are contextual prediction skills included? Are factual recall skills included?

Teaching activities. When giving instruction in information gathering skills, assess learners to determine who needs the skill, teach the skill to those who need it, posttest, and provide application situations. Be careful to include a set for the skill, attenders, directed assistance, diminishing of that assistance, and practice for each skill presented.

Client impact. By teaching information gathering skills, you are giving your learners knowledge of the basic skills in thinking. This will prepare them for using these skills in reading and for the higher-level streams of manipulative and evaluative thinking.

FOR CLASS DISCUSSION

An observer in an elementary school classroom was watching a teacher work with students on word meanings. The observation report was critical, stating that "the teacher explained the words but didn't teach them." What do you suppose the observer meant by this comment? Is this a common practice in word meaning lessons? How would a teacher *teach* a word meaning, rather than *explain* it?

ANSWER KEY

1. word meaning, understanding how relationships are signaled, making contextual predictions, factual recall
2. content

3. say the word and then ask the learners to make up a sentence or to send you a message using the word
4. a. provide a direct or vicarious experience
   b. identify the characteristics of the concept
   c. connect the concept to its word label
5. content words
6. they have no referent, are difficult to visualize
7. demonstrating
8. make guesses
9. meanings, relationships
10. factual recall

TEACHING
MANIPULATIVE
THINKING
SKILLS

OVERVIEW

This chapter provides you with techniques for teaching the comprehension skills of manipulative thinking, including classification, main
idea, and inferential reasoning. Specific and practical suggestions for
testing, directing attention, teaching, reteaching, practicing, and applying are provided. The ultimate objective is:

> Given pupils who need instruction in classification, main idea, and
> inferential reasoning, you will teach these skills using the principles
> described in Chapter 14.

KNOWLEDGE BACKGROUND

Chapter 20 described strategies for teaching information gathering skills.
That stream of skills, while important in its own right, also serves as a
crucial foundation for the other two streams of comprehension skills—
manipulative and evaluative thinking.

Manipulative thinking is where a child uses the information he or
she has gathered to *think*, that is, to structure or restructure, categorize
or recategorize, or otherwise *manipulate* the basic information of a
passage to gain new insights. Such manipulation, however, cannot be
done in a vacuum. There must be information (in the form of facts, con-

cepts, or ideas) to be manipulated. In this sense, information gathering is prerequisite to manipulative thinking—the child must be able to locate the facts before manipulating them.

Once the basic information is there, however, the depth of comprehension is increased if the child can do three basic kinds of manipulative thinking: classification, main idea, and inferential reasoning. How these three skills are taught is the focus of this chapter.

CLASSIFICATION

Classification is the first manipulative thinking skill. It focuses on finding meaning relationships between and among words, facts, concepts, and ideas. For instance, one might classify **cat** and **dog** together because both are animals. When a learner can classify, he or she is able to group together (or categorize) various concepts according to some common trait.

Classification skills help the learner observe and label the world not as disconnected and mutually exclusive objects and events but as realities related to other realities, as experiences which can be grouped according to selected similarities or excluded because of some unacceptable contrast. This skill helps the child grasp the relationship of the part to the whole or the whole to the part and, as such, is prerequisite to extracting the main idea from paragraphs and selections.

PRE- AND POSTTESTING CLASSIFICATION

Classification thinking, like all comprehension, develops in a simple-to-complex sequence. At the earliest stages, the child classifies one-word concepts which he or she has directly experienced, while later he or she categorizes groups of words or abstract ideas.

Whatever the level, the testing procedure remains basically the same. The concepts or ideas to be classified are presented to the child, who is asked to group them according to common traits or their relationship to each other. As the teacher, you must remain flexible since there is seldom only one acceptable relationship. For instance, you may expect a child to classify **cat** and **dog** together because they are both animals, but the child who groups them together because they are both pets is also correct.

DIRECTING ATTENTION

To teach classification, first insure that the learner has meaning for each of the words and concepts used. Then, direct attention by highlighting the concepts and/or traits associated with each item to be categorized and the common denominator which allows them to be classified together. For the words **cat** and **dog**, for instance, first list the concepts associated with each word and then show that some of these concepts are the same for both words, thereby making the words related.

You can use either a modeling or a discovery technique when teaching classification, but, in either case, you must first insure that the words or ideas to be categorized are part of the learner's meaning vocabulary. Then, to model the words **cat** and **dog,** for example, write the words on the board and say to the learner, "Each of these words describes something I know about. For instance, I know that a *cat* is an animal, is a pet, meows, and humps up its back when it is mad. A *dog* is an animal, it is a pet, it barks, and it is sometimes used for hunting." As you say each characteristic, write it beside the word on the board. Then say, "I can look at the things I know about each word and I see that some of the things are the same for both words." As you say this, draw lines between the common elements, as shown below:

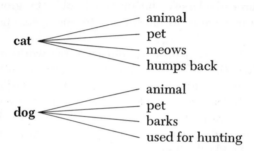

Now say, "We can say that the words **cat** and **dog** are related because they are both pet animals. They would both fit together in a box labeled 'Pet Animals.' Dogs and cats are different in some ways and alike in other ways. The ways they are alike are the ways in which they are related." With subsequent pairs of words, diminish the amount of modeling and decrease the amount of chalkboard highlighting until the learner is classifying without assistance from you.

When using the discovery technique, proceed in generally the same fashion, substituting questioning and learner response for the directed modeling used above. For instance, after listing the word **cat** and **dog** on the board, ask the learner to supply the characteristics to be listed for each word. Then ask him or her to inspect the characteristics and find any common concepts, highlighting these by drawing lines between them as necessary. When the child has identified the common concepts, ask him or her why these words are related. Repeat the same procedure for subsequent pairs of words, gradually diminishing the listing and lines until the child can relate the words without relying on such highlighting. At this point, the learner should have the ability to use the process of relating and classifying with other known words or phrases.

RETEACHING CLASSIFICATION

If you teach a classification skill and the child is still unable to categorize, you will have to reteach the skill. First, check the child's understanding of the words being used. If you are sure the words and concepts to be categorized are in the learner's meaning vocabulary, provide more highlighting to emphasize the ways the concepts are related. If the idea of classification itself is not understood, create an analogy between words that are related and family members, noting that the words, like the family members, are different but are tied together by something they have in common.

PRACTICING CLASSIFICATION

Once the learner understands how to classify, provide practice activities to solidify this skill. Activities such as the following are illustrative.

1. Play games with learners in which you say words or show objects and the learners must tell how they are alike or which one does not belong.
2. Put pictures and/or words into a container. The learner classifies all the pictures and/or words and tells what each category has in common.
3. Create sentences like, "Jack collects many things, such as butterflies, rocks, matchbooks, model airplanes and arrowheads." The learner classifies *butterflies, rocks, matchbooks, model airplanes* and *arrowheads* in a category titled "Things Jack Collects."
4. Play a bingo-type game in which squares on the board contain content words and one of the learners calls out other content words. Players but markers on words which can be related to the word called by the leader.
5. Play games in which one learner calls out a category (such as *groceries*) and another learner supplies as many things that go in that category as he or she can.

APPLYING CLASSIFICATION

Once the child has mastered the classification task, insure that he or she uses this thinking in the routine daily activities of the classroom. A good way to do this is to look for opportunities to ask questions such as, "How are these two things alike?" Or, "Of the things we have talked about, which one is different and why?"

MAIN IDEA

Teachers are quick to acknowledge the importance of having children determine the main idea of a paragraph, an appropriate title for a selection, or the theme of a particular book. All three tasks can come under main idea thinking. This task is similar to classifying since both require the learner to find the common focus of a group of words or concepts; both require that the learner use a categorizing procedure to extract the common denominator. The major difference between the skills of classification and main idea is that main idea thinking is much more complex, requiring the simultaneous grouping of several categories. Main idea is a crucial comprehension skill since it allows the learner to listen to or read hundreds and hundreds of words about a subject and identify the point of it all when finished.

PRE- AND POSTTESTING MAIN IDEA

Main idea thinking is usually tested by having the child select an appropriate title after reading a paragraph or selection. At the prereading stage, main idea thinking is tested by having a child listen to a selection and choose an appropriate title, while mature readers do the same basic thinking when deciding upon the theme of various kinds of written materials.

DIRECTING ATTENTION

To teach main idea thinking, be sure that the topic reflects the learner's background experience, that he or she knows the meaning of each word in the selection, and that he or she has mastered the prerequisite classifying skills. Then direct attention to the facts in the paragraph, to the common denominator of these facts which allows them to be categorized together, and to the single idea which reflects this category.

TEACHING MAIN IDEA

Either modeling or discovery can be used to teach main idea. In using modeling, provide the learner with both a paragraph in which the key facts have been highlighted and several title choices. Say to the learner, "The facts of the paragraph are (list the facts). If I were to put all these facts together, I could say they are all related because they all have something to do with (say the category). Therefore, the best title would be one that says (choose the title that best fits the category)." Repeat the procedure in subsequent paragraphs, gradually reducing the amount of highlighting and modeling until the learner is doing the main idea thinking independently.

If you wish to use the discovery technique, retain the paragraph with highlighted facts but substitute questioning for modeling, as follows. Say, "Look at the facts of the paragraph. Using your previously learned classifying skills, how would you group these facts together? How would you label the category in which all these facts fit?" Once the learner has decided upon a category, have him or her examine three possible titles, saying, "Now look at the titles you must choose from. Which of these describes a category that is almost the same as the one you described?" Repeat this procedure with other paragraphs, gradually reducing the highlighting on the facts and the amount of direction you provide through questioning until the learner is able to do the thinking independently.

RETEACHING MAIN IDEA

If it is necessary to reteach this skill, first check to make sure that the learner's difficulty was not caused by lack of prerequisite experience, word meanings, or classifying skills. Then teach the skill using a simpler paragraph in which the main idea is more easily identified, and increase the highlighting of both the facts and the way they can be cataloged to form the main idea.

PRACTICING MAIN IDEA

Once the child understands how to determine the main idea, provide practice such as the following to solidify the skill:

1. Select a well-written informational paragraph. Put the paragraph's individual phrases on the chalkboard, then direct each learner to examine each phrase and use classifying skills to select his or her own phrase that expresses the main idea.

> *Example:*   Brushing teeth regularly
>   Bathing frequently
>   Eating well-balanced meals
>   Getting enough rest
>   Getting regular exercise

> The main idea might be "Good Health Habits."

2. Using the "telegram" technique, direct your learners to read the paragraph and decide what words could be omitted without losing the meaning. Explain that they are going to send the paragraph as a telegram and will have to pay for each word. What is left will be a selection of the main idea and essential supporting details.
3. Make "stand-up" paragraphs. They can be fun and they can practice main idea–detail skills. Select a learner to stand in front of the class and think up a key topic sentence. (This might have to be "planted" at first.) Other members of the class think up details that elaborate on the topic sentence. As each adds an important detail, he or she stands behind the learner who made the topic sentence. The paragraph becomes a row of learners starting at the front of the room. When all the "sentences" have taken their places, have them repeat their sentences one after the other and then construct the paragraph. Don't be afraid to have sentences rearranged or even omitted if they do not belong.
4. Ask a question that requires an answer and the reasons for that answer; for example, "Did you have a good time over the weekend?" Answers should be either oral or written, reasons listed one, two ,three, and so forth. The sentence that answers the question is the main idea, and the listed reasons are the supporting details.
5. Teach learners to anticipate where the main idea is likely to occur. For example, at the lower reading levels, the main idea is invariably the first or last sentence. If the structure of such paragraphs is analyzed and graphically illustrated for learners, they will have a strategy for finding the main idea. That is, the learners will look at the first and last sentences and see if they communicate the point of the paragraph. One good way to graphically illustrate paragraph structure is to compare paragraphs to triangles; paragraphs with the main idea first are structured as $\triangle$ and those with the main ideas last are structured as $\triangledown$.

APPLYING MAIN IDEA

You should insure that main idea is used as a thinking tool during all the routine daily activities of the classroom. Encourage the children to identify the main idea in all reading and listening they do. For example, in social studies you might say, "There are three important ideas in this section of your textbook. See if you can use main idea thinking to find them as you read."

INFERENTIAL REASONING

The final manipulative thinking skill is inferential reasoning. This skill teaches the learner to infer information, understandings, and outcomes implied in a passage. All information worth obtaining is not necessarily stated literally; much valuable data are found "between the lines." That is, the author may imply certain things without stating them explicitly. It is important, therefore, that the learner be able to do inferential thinking.

There are many times when inferential thinking is a crucial comprehension skill. For instance, the child uses inference when predicting a conclusion to a story, when identifying factual data implied in a passage, and when drawing conclusions about the personality traits of various characters in a story. Many times, full comprehension is possible only when the child can identify implied meanings.

PRE- AND POSTTESTING INFERENTIAL REASONING

To test for inferential thinking, you must examine the material to determine what information is implied. Once identified, inferential questions can be posed to determine whether the child comprehended the implied ideas. At the earliest stages, of course, this testing would be done in a listening situation and would involve the simpler and more concrete kinds of inferential thinking.

DIRECTING ATTENTION

In teaching inferential thinking, three important points must be remembered. First, inferential thinking is based on the concepts, relationships, and facts found in the passage. Second, the learner cannot do inferential thinking about concepts or ideas not yet experienced. Third, the learner is not likely to do inferential thinking unless prodded by questions which force him or her to think between the lines. Consequently, to teach inferential thinking you must be sure that the learner has had a related background experience and knows the prerequisite skills of word meaning, factual recall, relationships, and classifying; you must pose questions which require the learner to examine what is implied; and you must direct the learner's attention to what the facts say and what personal experience has taught the child about such concepts and ideas.

TEACHING INFERENTIAL REASONING

You can use either a modeling or a discovery technique to teach inferential thinking. To model inferential thinking, first highlight the inferential question itself to determine both what is being asked and that the answer is not stated explicitly. Then highlight the facts contained in the passage. Relate these facts to an experience common to the child to show how experience background can be applied to these facts to determine implied information.

If you decide to use a discovery technique, the procedure remains the same, except that you ask questions rather than having the learner model your thinking. For instance, you might ask, "What does the story say is happening? What is the problem? Have you ever had a similar experience or have you ever seen anyone else have a similar experience? How was it solved in the other experience? Could you use that idea to solve the problem in this situation?" Repeat the procedure with subsequent examples, but gradually diminish the assistance you provide until the learner is able to answer the question without assistance.

RETEACHING INFERENTIAL REASONING

If the child still cannot do this thinking after instruction, first insure that he or she has the prerequisite comprehension skills and that he or she has had experience with concepts similar to those in the material being used. If the prerequisites are there, direct the child more explicitly to the connection between the facts in the story and the related experiences which can be applied to this situation. One good way to do this is by following the inferential question with other questions which guide the learner to apply his or her experience to the problem. The idea is to help the child do inferential reasoning by leading, with questions, through a step-by-step sequence in which he or she uses related experiences to guess what is happening between the lines.

PRACTICING INFERENTIAL REASONING

Once the child understands how to do the inferential reasoning, provide multiple opportunities to solidify this skill. Such practice can take the form of games in which learners must supply implied answers in order to achieve the goal, or workbook pages and Ditto sheets which offer numerous inferential reasoning problems similar to the type taught.

APPLYNG INFERENTIAL REASONING

You should make sure that the child's skill at reading inferentially is transferred to the daily activities in the classroom. The best way to do this is to include inferential questions among those you ask during lessons in social studies, science, and other content areas.

SUMMARY OF TEACHING MANIPULATIVE THINKING SKILLS

Once a child has gathered the basic factual information in a passage, he or she should then be able to manipulate that information to glean meanings which go beyond simple factual recall. Such manipulative thinking involves the use of classification, main idea, and inference. To teach these skills, the teacher should first insure that the child possesses the prerequisite information gathering skills and then use the techniques described in this chapter to develop such thinking in children.

TEST YOUR KNOWLEDGE

1. Manipulative thinking is where the learner uses the information gathered to _____.
2. The three skills in manipulative thinking are _____, _____, and _____.
3. When a learner can classify, he or she can group according to a _____.
4. Main idea can be tested by _____.
5. Main ideas are commonly found at the _____ or _____ of a paragraph.
6. Inferential reasoning is the skill of understanding the meanings that are _____.
7. Inferential reasoning includes skills such as _____, _____, or _____.
8. Inferential reasoning requires thinking about concepts or ideas that the learner _____.
9. The types of questions used in teaching inference skills should require the learner to think _____.
10. Inferential thinking involves the prerequisite skills of main idea and classifying in manipulative thinking and the skills of _____, _____, _____, and _____ in the information gathering stream.

SIMULATION ACTIVITIES

You should be ready to apply your knowledge of the manipulative thinking skills. Read the following situations and answer the questions.

1. The following is a sample pretest for a comprehension skill. Read it carefully and answer questions a and b.
   The pretest. Direct the learner to read the list of words below and to divide them into three categories, labeling each category. Then tell him or her to select one title which would fit all three categories from the four provided. The three categories should be *farm animals, wild animals,* and *pets.* Criterion for mastery is 100 percent.

cows	pigs	cats
dogs	goats	squirrels
deer	raccoons	sheep

Possible titles:

> At the Zoo
> Animals We Know
> In the Woods
> What We See in the Woods

    a. What type of skill within the manipulative thinking stream is this pretest assessing?
    b. In teaching this skill, what would your attenders be?
2. Examine the following selection from a sixth grade social studies text:

> Would you say that people giving a play are a group? According to sociologists, two or more people make up a group when four things can be said of them. First, people in a group interact. That is, the behavior of each member of the group affects the behavior of the other members. Second, the members of a group depend on each other. Members, then, are interdependent. Third, members of a group share common goals. Fourth, they share meanings. In other words each member knows and understands the values and goals of the other members. Each member understands the rules of the group. And he knows how he and the other members are expected to behave.
>
> Now can you give reasons why people giving a play are a group? Can you give reasons why the people in each of the pictures are a group?

The point to this selection, its focus, its main idea, is *group*. Can you list some content words you could highlight to develop this main idea through classifying?
3. A man is standing in the middle of a street in which many cars are rushing by. He calls across the street to the officer, "Officer, can you tell me the quickest way to the hospital?" The Officer responds, "Just stand right where you are."
    To most fully comprehend the meaning of this passage, the reader must rely on what thinking skill? How would you teach a child to comprehend this passage?

SUGGESTED FIELD EXPERIENCES

Observation. When observing in schools, you should note how teachers assess, teach, evaluate, and apply manipulative thinking skills. Are classifying skills included? Are main idea skills included? Are inferential reasoning skills included?

Teaching activities. When giving instruction in manipulative thinking skills, assess the learners for those who need the skill, teach the skill to those who need it, posttest, and provide application situations for the skill. Include a set for the skill, attenders, diminishing directed assistance, and practice for the teaching episode.

Client impact. By teaching manipulative thinking skills, you are giving your learners knowledge of the basic skills in thinking. This prepares them for comprehension in reading and for the higher-level stream of evaluative thinking.

FOR CLASS DISCUSSION

1. In ancient Greece, Socrates used a method of asking questions as a basic technique for teaching. We have used in this book the *discovery method* or *inductive teaching* as a strategy to use in teaching. Think about this strategy and be prepared to discuss with your instructor its strengths and limitations as a total instructional strategy. Be particularly prepared to explain how Socrates was teaching and not testing.
2. It has been stated that inferential thinking has prerequisite skills. What are those prerequisite skills? Do those prerequisite skills have any prerequisites?

ANSWER KEY
1. think (or categorize or structure or recategorize or restructure)
2. classification, main idea, inferential thinking
3. common trait
4. having the learner select an appropriate title
5. beginning, end
6. implied (or inferred)
7. predicting the outcome, drawing conclusions, identifying implications
8. has experienced
9. between the lines
10. word meaning, signalers of relationships, contextual prediction, and factual recall

TEACHING EVALUATIVE THINKING SKILLS

OVERVIEW

This chapter provides you with techniques for teaching evaluative thinking, including specific suggestions for testing, directing attention, teaching, reteaching, practicing, and applying this comprehension skill. The ultimate objective is:

> Given pupils who need instruction in evaluative thinking, you will teach these skills using the principles described in Chapter 14.

KNOWLEDGE BACKGROUND

The two previously discussed categories of comprehension—information gathering skills and manipulative thinking skills—might be described as purely receptive; the reader is simply trying to determine what message the author is conveying. However, the final category of comprehension, evaluative thinking, goes beyond simply receiving a message and requires the reader to make a judgment, to say, "I believe" or "I don't believe" what was read.

Evaluative thinking is comprehension of the highest order. It not only requires sophisticated use of the previously learned information gathering and manipulative skills but also requires the reader to react in terms of personal experience and value system. The child must perform both self-examination and examination of the material being used in order to do evaluative thinking.

Two kinds of skills help a child become an evaluative reader. The first focuses on evaluating the content of the material in terms of its consistency with the reader's view of reality. The second helps the reader examine the author's word choice as a means for detecting bias or propaganda.

JUDGING THE CONTENT VALIDITY OF MATERIAL

A major part of evaluative thinking is learning to judge whether what is written really happened or could have happened; whether it is fact, opinion, or fancy; whether the content is valid in terms of reality. This skill combats the tendency to believe something simply because it appears in a book.

PRE- AND POSTTESTING CONTENT VALIDITY

Like all comprehension skills, the validity of content can be tested as listening comprehension or reading comprehension, depending upon the pupil's stage of reading development. In either case, the material used should reflect concepts and experiences familiar to the child since it is impossible to judge the validity of something irrelevant to personal experience.

A typical test might use phrases or stories, some factual and some fanciful, with the learner directed to decide whether what is described could really happen. A yes or no for each statement will be sufficient. Keep in mind that such decisions may often depend upon the rationale of the learner.

DIRECTING ATTENTION

To teach the difference between factual and fanciful statements, direct the learner's attention to whether the event could happen or not by using material that reflects the learner's background experience. For instance, if you want the learner to judge if *a turtle sitting on a rock* were fact or fancy, that learner could only decide it was a fact if he or she had seen or heard of such an event. Likewise, if the learner were to judge whether *a dog making cherry pies* were fact or fancy, he or she could decide it was fancy on the basis of never having seen or heard of a real dog that makes cherry pies.

TEACHING CONTENT VALIDITY

You can use either modeling or discovery when teaching this skill. A modeling technique could be quite simple. For example, the learner is asked to judge whether the phrase *sisters who look like each other* is a fact or a fancy. You would say, "This phrase is a fact since I've seen two sisters who look alike." The learner then mimics your decision. Repeat this procedure with other statements, diminishing the modeling as the learner gains confidence. Once the learner is successfully judging the content of the material, you can assume mastery of this skill.

The basic frame of the lesson remains the same for discovery, but, rather than being highly directive in specifying the decision of fact or fancy as you would in modeling, you allow the learner to discover the reasons for the factual or fanciful statement. For instance, the phrase could be *a kitten who puts on rubbers to go out in the rain.* The dialogue could be:

TEACHER: "Have you ever seen or heard of kittens wearing rubbers?"
STUDENT: "No, I've never seen or heard of a kitten who can do that."
TEACHER: "So is it fact or fancy that a kitten can put rubbers on?"
STUDENT: "It is fancy, since kittens can't put rubbers on."

Repeat this procedure with other phrases, gradually diminishing your use of questions as the learner provides his or her own until the learner can make the judgment independently. At this time, you can again assume that the learner has mastered the skill.

RETEACHING CONTENT VALIDITY

If a child does not catch on to this skill immediately, the best reteaching strategy is to select material which reflects the child's experience more directly. In other words, ask him or her to react to the validity of statements about things directly experienced before moving to more subtle judgments which may relate only to vicarious experiences.

PRACTICING CONTENT VALIDITY

To practice this skill, provide multiple opportunities for the learner to react to statements similar to those taught. Ditto sheets and workbook pages containing such statements can be used, games utilizing such statements can be created, and children themselves can create and exchange such statements.

APPLYING CONTENT VALIDITY

Make sure that the learner uses this skill in judging content during the regular school activities. One way to do this is to read literature to children frequently, occasionally asking them whether a particular incident, story, or poem is factual or fanciful. Another valuable technique is to use reading matter that is considered factual, such as newspapers, magazines, copies of speeches, and so on, and direct the children's attention to those printed sections which tend to be more fancy than fact.

JUDGING WORD CHOICE

A second important evaluative thinking skill is teaching the learner to assess word choice for clues to an author's position on a topic. Good readers can detect bias through an author's use of emotion-laden words, words that create bias or stereotype, mood words, or other elements of word choice. Evaluation of word choice is an important thinking skill since it is a major way to make judgments about the validity of what is read.

PRE- AND POSTTESTING ASSESSMENT OF WORD CHOICE

Since the author's choice of words is the major focus of this skill, a good test must focus on word choice. One effective way to do this is to create sentence pairs in which the two sentences are exactly alike except for a single word change. The following examples are illustrative:

> The **excited** boy ran to his mother.
> The **frenzied** boy ran to his mother.
>
> The **new** gadget was on the table.
> The **newfangled** gadget was on the table.

Direct the pupil to read each sentence pair and then to react in terms of how the differing word choice from sentence to sentence reflects a different attitude on the part of the writer.

DIRECTING ATTENTION

To teach this skill, first insure that the learner understands that various people can have various views on a given topic and that authors, too, have biases which are reflected in their writing. Then direct the learner's attention to the key word which signals the author's position and to the connotation associated with that word. In the first pair of sentences above, for instance, you would highlight the word **frenzied** and the aura of panic which is often associated with that word.

TEACHING ASSESSMENT OF WORD CHOICE

Either modeling or discovery can be used, with the modeling procedure looking somewhat as follows: Using the first pair of sentences from above, write them on the chalkboard one under another. Highlight the different word. Orally describe a scenario from the learner's experience background in which lines such as the sample sentences might be used. Say, "An author has opinions and feelings about things just like everyone else. When writing, the author often signals personal opinions and feelings to us by using certain words. For instance, in the first pair of sentences, the writer would use the word **frenzied** to let us know that the person was not very cool (or was a bit panicked), and the author would use **excited** if he or she felt either neutral or more positive about the situation." Create another pair of sentences using the same words and have the learner model your thoughts in describing how the key words reflect an author's feelings. Repeat the same procedure with other sentences and other key words, gradually diminishing the highlighting and the amount of modeling until the learner is able to judge an author's position by examining the choice of words.

In the discovery technique, use the same type of sentences with the key word highlighted, and create a scenario to provide an experiential context for the sentences. Then ask questions which lead the learner to discover the significance of the single variant word. Such questions might include: "Do you suppose an author sometimes has feelings regarding the topics written about? How might a writer reveal those feelings? Looking at the two sentences on the chalkboard, why might a writer use **frenzied** instead of **excited** in that sentence? What does the writer's use of **frenzied** tell you regarding the author's opinion?" Repeat the process with other sentences and other words, gradually diminishing the highlighting on the key word and the amount of questioning until the learner is able to determine an author's feelings through choice of words.

RETEACHING ASSESSMENT OF WORD CHOICE

Two options are available for helping the pupil who does not immediately master the idea that certain words provide clues to the author's position on a topic. The first is to use sentences which more directly reflect the child's personal experience so that he or she can bring more concrete meaning to the task. The second is to use role playing, with its emphasis on oral language, intonation patterns, and nonverbal language to help the child see the emotion that is attached to certain key connotative words.

PRACTICING ASSESSMENT OF WORD CHOICE

Once the child understands how word choice can provide clues to an author's position on a topic, provide the pupil with practice to solidify the skill. The following three examples might be useful.

1. Create practice exercises similar to the pretest which offer multiple opportunities for the learner to make judgments about key words used by the author.
2. Play games in which one learner creates a sentence and another changes one word or phrase to indicate a change in emotion.
3. Create Ditto exercises in which the learner fills in a blank with a word signaling a negative position on the part of the writer.

APPLYING ASSESSMENT OF WORD CHOICE

Ensure that the learner uses the skill of judging material on the basis of word choice during the routine daily activities of the classroom. You can do this by pointing out the way the learners use connotative words in their own encounters and the way in which connotative language is reflected in the daily reading they do in newspapers, magazines, and so on.

SUMMARY OF TEACHING EVALUATIVE THINKING SKILLS

Teaching evaluative thinking involves two quite different types of skills. The first—judging the validity of content—is taught primarily by directing the child to match what he or she reads with his or her experience and value system. The second—assessing word choice for clues regarding an author's position—is taught by focusing a child on key words and the emotional connotations implied in these words. Both are crucial skills which, when used together, help a reader make judgments in reading.

TEST YOUR KNOWLEDGE

1. Evaluative thinking requires the learner to use previously learned comprehension skills as well as personal _____ and _____.

2. The two types of skills involve judging _____ and _____.

3. In judging content validity, the learner must be directed to decide whether the event is _____ or _____.

4. If the learner does not succeed in the content validity skill when a vicarious situation makes up the instructional episode, the teacher should use a more _____ situation.

5. Judging word choice includes such skills as detecting _____ or _____.

6. Judging word choice depends on the learner's ability to select key words that signal _____.

SIMULATION ACTIVITIES

You should be ready to use your knowledge of evaluative thinking skills. Read the following situations and answer the questions.

1. The attender for making evaluative judgments about what is read is often key words. For instance, examine the following paragraph and note the emotion-laden words used.

> In a recent speech to a private group, Mr. Smith analyzed with precision and force the government's position in the war. His statement is the most complete and convincing argument that has been made for continuing the war. He went to the very heart of our nation's interests as the basis for his position and wisely ignored the carping of those who lack his vision.

   a. On what would you teach pupils to focus in order to make an evaluative judgment about this passage?
   b. What words are the attenders?

2. Although some key words signal bias, others signal fact and opinion. By attending to key words, the pupil can often make an evaluative

judgment regarding the factual validity of a statement. Examine the following statements and identify them as fact or opinion.

> Probably most of the pans and cooking utensils in the kitchens of our homes are made from aluminum.

> The great forests of the north may someday be a valuable resource.

> The people of Switzerland have succeeded in overcoming their handicaps and in making the best possible use of the advantages they have.

    a. On what would you teach pupils to focus in determining whether to believe these statements as fact?
    b. Is this the same as an attender?

3. Assume you are trying to teach a group of upper-elementary students to make evaluative judgments by focusing on key words. Using the following three hypothetical news dispatches from a war front, describe an instructional episode to teach evaluative thinking. Be sure to include diminishing directed assistance.

> The forces of the Blue army savagely attacked the Greens again yesterday. Following the battle, the Blue army withdrew its front lines into previously prepared positions.

> The forces of the Blues vainly threw themselves against the solid lines of the Green army yesterday. Following the battle, the Blues hastily withdrew in disordered retreat.

> The forces of the Blue Army clashed with those of the Green army yesterday. Following the battle, the Blue army returned to the position it had previously held.

4. Assume you are going to teach learners how to make judgments regarding content validity using *"Goldilocks and the Three Bears."* What would you direct the learner's attention to? What elements would you highlight?

SUGGESTED FIELD EXPERIENCES

Observation. When observing in schools, you should note how teachers assess, teach, evaluate, and apply evaluative thinking skills. Is judging of content validity included? Is judging of word choice included?

Teaching activities. When giving instruction in evaluative thinking skills, assess learners for a need for the skill, teach the skill to those who need it, posttest, and provide application situations for the skill. Include all parts of the instructional episode.

Client impact. By teaching evaluative thinking skills, you are giving your students knowledge of the highest-level thinking skills in functional literacy. This will help them make judgments about their reading.

FOR CLASS DISCUSSION

When teaching evaluative thinking you must be aware that your role is not that of an evangelist seeking converts. As the teacher, you must be aware that your personal bias does affect your pupils' decisions. Keep this in mind whenever you discuss issues that require evaluative thinking. You could, of course, use only relatively "safe" topics, such as pollution, conservation, or traffic violations. However, there are many current issues that, although potentially explosive, do indeed require evaluative thinking. Should you as the teacher sidestep issues such as war, politics, freedom, justice, or pacifism?

ANSWER KEY
1. background experience, value system
2. content validity, word choice
3. fact, fancy
4. concrete
5. bias, mood
6. the author's position

SUGGESTED ADDITIONAL READINGS FOR SECTION FIVE— TEACHING THE SKILLS

ALLINGTON, RICHARD. "Using Visual Highlighting To Teach Discrimination and Patterns." *Reading Horizons,* Summer 1975.

———. "Cue Selection and Discrimination Learning." *Academic Therapy,* Spring 1974.

DUFFY, GERALD G., AND SHERMAN, GEORGE B. *Systematic Reading Instruction.* 2d ed. New York: Harper & Row, 1977.

ENGELMANN, S. *Preventing Failure in the Primary Grades.* Chicago, Ill.: Science Research Associates, 1969.

FERNALD, GRACE M. *Remedial Techniques in Basic School Subjects.* New York: McGraw Hill Book Co., 1943.

GAA, JOHN P. "Goal Setting: Review of the Literature and Implications for Future Research." ERIC Ed 050413.

HARING, NORRIS. *Attending and Responding.* San Rafael, Calif.: Dimensions Publishing Co., 1968.

OTTO, WAYNE, AND KOENKE, KARL (EDS.). *Remedial Teaching: Research and Comment.* Boston: Houghton Mifflin, 1969.

STAATS, ARTHUR W. AND CAROLYN K. *Complex Human Behavior* (Chapter 4). New York: Holt, Rinehart & Winston, 1964.

SIX
INSURING TRANSFER AND APPLICATION OF SKILLS

USING THE
BASAL
TEXTBOOK
FOR GUIDED
APPLICATION

OVERVIEW

The previous chapters have focused on teaching the skills needed for functional literacy. However, teaching is not accomplished until the skills are being used; they cannot be taught in isolation and then forgotten. Instead, they must be transferred to the reading act—they must be put to work in books. This chapter provides suggestions for helping children use the skills they have learned in reading the basal textbook. The ultimate objective is:

> Given a child who has mastered one or more of the skills of word recognition and comprehension, you can systematically guide the child to put the skills to work in reading basal textbooks.

KNOWLEDGE BACKGROUND

The biggest danger in emphasizing skills is that we may become so busy with skills teaching that we neglect to develop readers; that is, we may produce learners who can perform the skills in isolation but who cannot or do not use them in reading. To combat this eventuality, we must provide a balance between skills instruction and meaningful reading activities, avoiding polar positions such as saying on the one hand that skills are the answer to everything, or, on the other, that children "learn to read by reading" and that skills should not be allowed to clutter things up. As discussed in Chapter 2, a balanced view recognizes that children need both the skills and many reading activities where their skills can be put to work. Our task, then, is to create learning situations in which children receive needed skills instruction while also using their skills in their reading.

There are two ways to help children transfer learned reading skills from the skill lesson to the reading of books. One involves teacher assistance and is called *guided application*. The other involves independent reading and is called *independent application*. This chapter focuses on the former, and the next chapter provides suggestions for the latter.

In guided application, the skill is taught in a skill lesson, and once it is mastered the child is given a specific piece of reading material in which the skill must be used. When giving the child this material, you direct attention to the skill he or she ought to apply. In some instances, particularly for those children who have difficulty making the transfer from the skill lesson to reading, you might even highlight certain sections, thereby directing the learner's attention to the fact that this is an opportunity to put the newly learned skill to work. As the learner becomes more proficient, of course, this highlighting would be gradually diminished until he or she could apply the skill unassisted.

The most useful material for guided application is the basal reading textbook. It has the advantages of being found in most classrooms, of containing a variety of stories which are graded in difficulty, and of having a teacher's guide which often provides clues about the skill demands of particular stories. As such, it is an extremely valuable source for guided application.

When using the basal text for guided application, first divide your instructional time into periods for skills teaching and periods for application. In the early grades where two separate periods are frequently allocated for reading, use one for skills and the other for application. At the later grades, you may wish to devote one day's reading period entirely to skills teaching and another day's to guided application. In any case, during the time set aside for guided application, group your learners according to reading level and meet with each group in turn.

The purpose of the basal text group should be clear to both the teacher and the students. In fact, the teacher should introduce the lesson by stating, "We are reading this story so you can put to use some of the reading skills you have recently learned." In this way both the teacher and the pupils are clear about the purpose of the activity, and the first step in transferring the learned skill to context has been made.

Once the pupils know what skills they are expected to use, progress through the following sequence of steps:

1. Introduce the story by providing background information and brief descriptions of what the story is about.

2. Identify any new words which may appear in the story, insuring that the learners know both the words as they appear in print and their meanings.
3. Specify with each child exactly what skills he or she is expected to apply and how he or she will know when to apply them.
4. Set any other appropriate purposes for reading the story.
5. Have the child read the story silently (or, in the very early stages of reading development, orally).
6. Discuss the content of the story to insure that the children comprehended.
7. Check with each child to insure that the previously learned skill was applied.

This format enhances the transfer process, particularly for the child who finds reading difficult. First of all, the child is not asked to use skills which have not already been taught. Second, the skill to be used, which to the child often seems to be hidden among all the words and sentences of contextual passages, is clearly identified. Finally, once the child sees the place where the skill can be used, he or she is given assistance in using it. In this way, transfer is not left to chance and the skills learned are put to work to help the child become a better reader.

SUMMARY OF USING THE BASAL TEXTBOOK FOR GUIDED APPLICATION

Effective reading instruction does not end with skills instruction. In fact, instruction is clearly a failure if children can perform the skills in isolation but are unable or unwilling to apply them. Consequently, a good reading program must include provisions for helping children put learned skills to work in context.

A good place to provide such assistance is in the basal textbook. While this is an excellent source for such application, other material could be used. For instance, many publishing companies produce kits and booklets of graded reading material which are excellent for use as guided application material. One widely used example of such material is the *SRA Reading Laboratory*, a multilevel kit of short appealing stories with accompanying exercises which are graded in difficulty. Whether or not the exercises are used, the stories are useful places to help children put learned skills to work.

Whatever kind of guided application is used, you will want to identify those learners who have the greatest difficulty in making the transfer from skill instruction to application since they will need the greatest amount of guidance. While many children apply the learned skills quite easily, it will be necessary to directly assist some children, sometimes even to the extent of modeling the application process and having the learner mimic your actions. However, once children get the idea that the skills are not being learned for their own sake but for their utility in improving reading, they will begin to make the transfer more readily. It is at this point that they are ready for independent application.

TEST YOUR KNOWLEDGE

1. The purpose of application activities is to help the child use learned skills when _____.
2. Guided application means that the child applies the skill with help from the _____.
3. In introducing a basal text story, the purpose should be clearly specified as _____.
4. The teacher can help the child who is having trouble identifying where the skill appears in the basal story by _____.
5. While many children learn to apply skills quite easily, others need systematic and directed _____.

SIMULATION ACTIVITIES

Examine a basal text story and determine what skills of comprehension and word identification are required when reading the story. Describe how you would use this story for guided application.

SUGGESTED FIELD EXPERIENCES

Observation. When observing in schools, note whether a basal textbook series is used and whether this use exemplifies the suggestions provided in the chapter. If the basal text is used differently, determine the rationale for its use and analyze this rationale.

Teaching activities. When teaching elementary reading, teach a child a skill and then use the basal textbook to insure that he or she can use the skill in context.

Client impact. As a result of using guided application activities, you will be minimizing the chances that your pupils might learn a skill in isolation but never be able to use it in context.

FOR CLASS DISCUSSION

Examine a popular basal textbook series. Note the suggested format for teaching reading lessons and the suggestions in the teacher's guide. Discuss the relative merits of the particular basal text series and compare its suggestions for using the basal with those proposed in this book.

ANSWER KEY
1. reading
2. teacher
3. application of learned skills
4. modeling application of the skill
5. assistance

INDEPENDENT APPLICATION THROUGH RECREATIONAL READING

OVERVIEW

Chapter 23 emphasized techniques for directly assisting learners in their efforts to transfer learned skills from the isolated instructional setting to the act of reading. While this is an important task, it is not the only application situation. The true test of reading instruction is whether children use their learned skills when the teacher is *not* providing guidance—whether children read books on their own. Developing this crucial aspect of reading instruction is the focus of this chapter. The ultimate objective is:

> Given a child who has the necessary reading skills, you can
> encourage him or her to be an enthusiastic and independent reader.

KNOWLEDGE BACKGROUND

In independent application, the learner applies the reading skills to library books and other recreational reading materials without teacher assistance. Because the development of voracious readers who automatically use their skills in pursuing genuine and meaningful reading tasks is the ultimate goal of skills instruction, such recreational reading is a crucial part of good reading instruction.

Recreational reading is just what its name implies—reading for the fun of it. As such, it must be structured to make reading enjoyable. It should be presented as a respite from the rigors of the regular school day, as relaxation, and as an activity having inherent value for the learner. It should never take on the connotation of "work" nor should the learner ever be put in the position of reading a book simply to complete a book-report assignment.

Implementing a recreational reading program as a vehicle for independent application requires conscious effort and commitment on your part. You must find the time, provide the materials, structure a supportive environment, and plan related activities. We shall discuss each of these and then answer some of the questions frequently asked about recreational reading.

FINDING THE TIME

Time is always a factor. There are so many things to teach, and there is only so much time in the school day. However, we always find time for the important things, and providing for independent application certainly is one of them. Consequently, we must "steal" the time, if necessary. A good way to do this is to schedule recreational reading first thing in the morning so that you *know* you will have time for it. Another technique is to use recreational reading as one of the independent activities which learners do when they are not working directly with you during the skills instruction period. However, you must always be careful not to relegate recreational reading to the status of "something you do when all your other work is done" since this implies that everything else is more important.

In any case, recreational reading must occur frequently. While the time periods devoted to it can be short, they should be part of the regular schedule so the learners can anticipate them. Avoid the traditional practice of confining recreational reading to the last period on Friday when the learners are fidgety, and do not view the recreational reading period as something you schedule only when you need to complete your attendance register or other pressing paperwork.

PROVIDING MATERIALS

For independent application to succeed, there must be something to read. Library books are obviously your major source of materials, but you should not confine yourself to books. Magazines, newspapers, comics, brochures, pamphlets, and any other printed matter having any interest to your learners should be provided. The collection should reflect a wide range of interests and abilities consistent with the assortment of individuals with whom you are dealing. Room libraries, consisting of books borrowed from the school library or the local public library, should be on constant display in the room, with one collection of books frequently replacing another. Fiction and non-fiction books should be used in the subject matter areas, with other related fictional and informational books being available. All this reading material is of little value, however, if the learner never has time to use it. Consequently, you must frequently encourage the learners to browse through and read the material being displayed.

Obtaining reading materials is frequently a problem. Schools rarely have the money these days to purchase them, so you must find alternate ways. The most obvious of these is the library system in your local community. While librarians are a frequent target of abuse, it has been our experience that most are anxious to help, and when informed of what you are trying to do, they will gladly provide you with books. Another source is the paperback book clubs which provide learners with the opportunity to purchase some of the best children's books at a very low cost. You can then encourage each child to leave his or her books in the room library to share with other readers. Another source is local newsstands, which frequently save torn copies of paperback books, magazines, and comics and willingly donate these on request. The learners themselves can be involved in gathering materials by soliciting book and magazine donations from the neighborhood; by running cake sales, paper drives, or other fund-raising projects in which the proceeds are used to purchase reading materials; by contributing the books they have at home to the room library, and by contributing the books they have authored, illustrated, and made. Finally, you must be a beggar, a borrower and a saver yourself, collecting reading materials from any source available and storing them in your classroom for use by your learners. In providing materials, the best guide is, "I can never have too much."

STRUCTURING THE ENVIRONMENT

The classroom environment plays a crucial role in independent application. It should reflect the focus on books in many ways. Bulletin boards, for instance, should present recommended book lists, books on a single theme, information on the winners of book awards, authors' backgrounds, children's art depicting book scenes, and children's evaluations of books they have read. Films and recordings of fables, folk tales, poetry, picture books, and so on should be available for use. Finally, a place should be designated in the classroom for relaxed reading, as we mentioned in Chapter 12 under *safety valves*. This can be a corner of the room where you have laid an old secondhand rug, scattered about some throw pillows, and perhaps placed an old easy chair or rocker. The intent is to provide an appealing place in the room where children can relax with a book.

In the final analysis, however, the most important element of a supportive environment is *you*. If you want your learners to be readers, you must constantly seek to convey this attitude to the class. You should become familiar with all kinds of children's books, make frequent references to children's literature in your teaching, and show that it is important to you that learners enjoy their reading. Most important of all, however, you should make obvious your own enjoyment of the act by reading a book of your choice when the learners are themselves engaged in recreational reading. Nothing will impress your learners more than your eagerness to "practice what you preach" about recreational reading.

PLANNING ACTIVITIES

The reading habit can also be developed through book-related activities. Two of the most profitable activities are your reading aloud to the students and their telling about or sharing the books they have read. The daily activities of all reading classes should include your oral reading of children's literature since such reading, especially when it emphasizes highly recommended books the learners are unlikely to read by themselves, is probably more effective than any other single technique in building a love of literature and in starting learners toward the reading habit. This activity requires some preparation on your part, however, since you must be familiar with the book and practice reading it aloud if you are to read it well. It should be emphasized, also, that this activity is designed to be enjoyable. Any discussion following the oral reading should be casual and nonintimidating, not a testing session.

Book sharing by the learners also creates interest in reading and stimulates independent application. The emphasis, however, must be on sharing and not on reporting, since reporting has a coercive connotation we want to avoid here. Consequently, the decision to share a book with others should be left to the learner. When the child reads a book he or she really enjoys, encourage the child to share it as a means of getting a peer interested in reading it. Such sharing may take the form of book talks, audience reading, book fairs, puppetry, dramatization, book want ads, or any other activity in which learners discuss a book with the intention of interesting others in it.

COMMON QUESTIONS

Teachers rarely question the value of independent application itself. They do, however, frequently pose questions about particular aspects of recreational reading. Some of these are answered below.

1. *What kind of book should we encourage the learner to use for independent application?*
   There are really only two considerations in terms of the kind of book a learner should read. The first is, does the child want to read it? That is, does the book interest the child? The second is, can the child read it? That is, is the child ready to apply the reading skills necessary to handle the book, or is it too hard? If the child *wants* to read the book and is *able* to read it, it is a good book for that child.

2. *How do we involve the very slow reader in independent application?*

Because a learner is unable to read does not mean he or she cannot participate in the recreational reading program. The child can be provided with picture books and picture magazines which are interesting and which he or she is able to handle. You can also make booklets out of interesting material cut from old editions of *My Weekly Reader, Jack and Jill, Children's Digest,* and other sources containing material commensurate with ability. Comic books are another source for such learners. Using such easy material, the child can read for relaxation in the same manner as more advanced learners and will not feel like a "dummy," unless your attitude *makes* him or her feel that way. If you accept the reading material as being worthwhile, so will the child.

3. *Should we outlaw comic books in the classroom?*

As has been implied in the statements above, we are not opposed to comic books per se. For children having much difficulty with reading, it is better that they read comic books than nothing at all. However, it is doubtful that comics help develop the reading habit, and learners should be weaned away from them and guided to books as soon as they have the skills to handle a book. These first books should have the same characteristics of low readability, adventure, action, and colorful pictures that attract children to comics in the first place. It is helpful to remember also that the most effective way to eliminate the appeal of comics is to make them readily available. As soon as you ban them, they attain the aura of "forbidden fruit," and their appeal soars.

4. *Should we be concerned about the learner who just reads Dr. Suess stories or who just reads horse stories?*

In independent application, our primary concern is that of applying learned skills and developing the reading habit. Initially, any book will do as long as it calls for the use of previously learned skills and as long as the child *wants* to read it. Once the reading habit has become established, however, you may wish to encourage learners to vary their interests and enrich their tastes.

5. *Should we have contests in our classroom to see who can read the most books?*

Definitely not! In the first place, we want to encourage children to read because it is an enjoyable and rewarding act in itself, not because it will win a prize. Secondly and more important, however, such contests motivate only those who need no motivating, while frustrating those who need to be encouraged the most, since only the good readers have a chance to win the prize. If you feel that some form of reward is needed to encourage learners to begin reading books, make it a personal thing between you and the learners rather than a competition.

SUMMARY OF INDEPENDENT APPLICATION THROUGH RECREATIONAL READING

The focus of independent application is recreational. By making reading a fun activity, we painlessly show the reader that the skills being learned have an immediate payoff. This payoff represents the ultimate goal of reading instruction—developing learners who not only are *able* to read but who *do* read.

TEST YOUR KNOWLEDGE

1. Independent application requires children to apply learned skills without teacher _____.
2. Independent application should focus on reading for _____.
3. Independent application will not occur unless children are given the _____ to read independently.
4. The materials to be read independently should not be limited just to _____.
5. The classroom environment should reflect the emphasis on _____ reading.
6. It is important that the classroom teacher model _____ for the students.
7. Children should be encouraged to _____ their books, but required reporting should be minimized.
8. The two questions to ask about what books a child should read independently are, does the child _____ to read it and _____ he or she read it.
9. Comic books can be used as a first _____ toward developing the reading habit.
10. The focus of independent application is the development of children who _____.

SIMULATION ACTIVITIES

1. Imagine that you are teaching a third grade and you have your class organized according to the principles developed in Chapter 12. How could you use independent application as a rich source of independent activities and safety valves?
2. Personalized reading was one of the major approaches to reading instruction discussed in Chapter 2. How could you incorporate the characteristics of personalized reading with the concept of independent application?

SUGGESTED FIELD EXPERIENCES

Observation. When observing in schools, note the extent and flavor of classroom programs of independent application. Are children encouraged to develop an interest in reading?

Teaching activities. When working with children in a school setting, you should provide the time, the support, and the activities which will encourage children to develop an interest in reading and to use their learned skills in an actual reading situation.

Client impact. By consciously including independent application in your reading program, you are insuring that your pupils will develop positive values about recreational reading.

FOR CLASS DISCUSSION

Most teachers and prospective teachers are required to take a course in children's literature. Discuss the way the content of a children's literature class contributes to building an effective reading program.

ANSWER KEY
1. assistance
2. enjoyment
3. opportunity
4. books
5. recreational
6. reading a book
7. share
8. want, can
9. step
10. want to read

SUGGESTED ADDITIONAL READINGS FOR SECTION SIX– INSURING TRANSFER AND APPLICATION OF SKILLS

ALLINGTON, RICHARD. "Attention and Application: The Oft Forgotten Steps in Teaching Reading." *Journal of Learning Disabilities*, April 1974.

BRUTON, RICHARD. "Individualizing a Basal Reader." *The Reading Teacher*, October 1972, p. 59.

DUFFY, GERALD G. "Developing the Reading Habit." *The Reading Teacher* 21, December 1967, pp. 253–256.

FADER, DANIEL, AND MC NEAL, ELTON. *Hooked on Books: Program and Proof.* New York: Berkeley Publishing, 1968.

PAGE, BARBARA. "Instill a Love for Reading." *Instructor*, December 1974, p. 13.

SEVEN
WHAT TO TEACH BEYOND FUNCTIONAL LITERACY

CONTINUED SKILLS INSTRUCTION

Reading instruction does not end with functional literacy. Your learners must also master skills which allow them to use reading as a tool for satisfying interests and for reaching goals. Achievement of these skills leads to maturity in reading and is the focus of this chapter. The ultimate objective is:

> Given students who have mastered the basic word identification and comprehension skills, you can plan instruction in study skills and skills of literary understanding.

KNOWLEDGE BACKGROUND

Functional literacy is the major goal of reading instruction in the early grades. When functional literacy has been achieved, however, what is the next step? Is functional literacy enough for all students? What do you teach the child who is beyond functional literacy? What skills go beyond functional literacy?

Reading, when considered in its totality, consists of four major skill areas as follows:

THE READING SKILLS

Grade	Word recognition	Comprehension	Efficient study	Literary understanding
K				
1				
2				
3				
4				
5				
6				
7				
8				
9				
10				
11				
12				

The first two streams of word identification and comprehension are the fundamental skills needed to achieve functional literacy and receive heavy emphasis in the early grades. As the child moves through school and masters the basic skills, however, he or she goes beyond functional literacy and into the skills of *efficient study* and *literary understanding*.

The functional literacy skills are prerequisites to the skills of efficient study and literary understanding. For instance, it is not possible for the child to do a study skill such as looking up words in the dictionary until having first mastered the functional literacy skill of recognizing the letters of the alphabet. Similarly, we cannot expect a child to recognize different types of humor in literature if unable yet to comprehend the main idea in a simple paragraph. At the early stages of reading instruction, the emphasis is on learning *how* to read; beyond functional literacy, the focus changes to learning to use these skills in an efficient and insightful way. This chapter will discuss how to organize, diagnose, and teach these more advanced skills.

ORGANIZATION OF THE SKILLS

The skills of efficient study and literary understanding are organized much like the word identification and comprehension skills. Each is made up of streams of skills, and each stream contains subcategories of skills similar to those we encountered in word identification and comprehension.

Efficient study includes three streams of skills: *locational skills* (directions, dictionary skills, reference skills, library skills, and graphic skills), *organizing skills* (study techniques, outlining, note taking, and summarizing), and *reading rate skills* (using flexible and varying rates according to purpose). Similarly, literary understanding includes two streams of skills: recognizing and interpreting *informational and persuasive techniques* and recognizing and interpreting *literary characteristics.*

The structure of the skills beyond functional literacy, therefore, can be represented as follows:

Efficient study			Literary understanding	
Locational	Organization of information	Rate	Recognizing and interpreting informational and persuasive techniques	Recognizing and interpreting literary characteristics

SPECIFYING THE SKILLS OF EFFICIENT STUDY

The diagram illustrates graphically the three streams of skills which lead to efficient study. Each of these contains specific skills which should be developed.

Locational skills. The locational stream focuses on helping children locate information quickly and accurately. The skills to develop in this stream are:

1. Following oral or written directions
2. Using the dictionary as an aid in pronunciation (demonstrating ability to interpret phonetic spelling and diacritical marks)
3. Using the dictionary to check spelling
4. Using the dictionary to determine the word meaning appropriate for the context
5. Using the dictionary to locate synonyms or antonyms
6. Using a card catalog as an aid to locating books and nonbook materials (newspapers, magazines, audiovisual aids, vertical files)
7. Using the Dewey decimal book classification system for locating
   a. Books; fiction, nonfiction, reference
   b. Nonbook materials; see number 6
8. Finding information in an encyclopedia and selecting the specifics applicable to the purpose
9. Finding information in a dictionary
10. Finding information in almanacs, atlases, telephone books, and other general references
11. Finding information using indexes
12. Finding information in nonbook materials (see number 6)
13. Using various parts of a book, including:
    a. Preface, foreword, and/or introduction
    b. Table of contents
    c. List of illustrations

d. Figures and maps
e. Chapter, section, and subsection headings
f. Glossary
g. Index
14. Using maps and globes, including:
    a. Locating desired information
    b. Interpreting key and map symbols
    c. Using map scales
    d. Interpreting directions
15. Using graphs, tables, diagrams, and other pictorial materials

Organizational skills. The organizational stream focuses on helping children use and remember information once it has been located. The skills to develop in this stream are:

1. Using a systematic technique, such as SQ3R (see page 275), for reading study materials in which the child:
   a. Surveys the materials: in approximately one minute, reads the headings and summary paragraph of the material, states or writes the main ideas around which the reading will center
   b. Questions: constructs questions from each heading
   c. Reads: reads to answer the questions constructed
   d. Recites: writes or states the answers to each question without referring to the written material
   e. Reviews: checks answers, reviews any section where recitation was either incomplete or incorrect
2. Taking notes when both listening and reading
3. Using notes to construct an outline
4. Summarizing information from:
   a. a paragraph
   b. more complex selections
   c. several sources

Reading rate skills. The final stream of skills for efficient study focuses on reading rate. Here the child should be instructed in using various reading rates according to the purpose of the reading material, its difficulty level, and the child's own experience background relative to the content being discussed.

The four different reading rate skills to be developed are:

1. Using a skimming rate to locate information.
2. Using a fast rate for recreational and/or easy material
3. Using a study rate for content material which is to be retained
4. Using a slow rate for highly exact or extremely difficult materials

For instance, if the students' purposes are just to locate information, they would use the rate of skimming; if they are reading to retain information, they would use a slower, more concentrated rate; and if they are reading for enjoyment, they would use an average or rapid rate. The chart below gives the rates, their definitions, and their uses.

READING RATES

Rate	Purpose	Kind of material
1. Skimming	To locate information	Directory, dictionary, any material which will yield a specific answer
	To survey or get an overview and raise questions the selection can answer	Study material, difficult material, material that must be organized, textbooks, technical articles
	To skim for the main idea or to find out what happens next	Simple materials, news-papers, magazines, fiction
2. Speeded reading (fast)	To read rapidly for certain details or main ideas	Any material in which main ideas and supporting facts are to be picked up—news-papers, magazines, stories, easy texts, etc.
3. Study reading (slow)	To read with maximum understanding using the SQ3R technique	Textbooks; technical articles; any material read in detail to organize, present to others, or retain
4. Careful and reflective reading (slowest)	To follow directions as, for example, how to bake a cake or perform a chemistry experiment; to reflect on content; to evaluate; to enjoy; to read aloud to share an aesthetic experience	Directions; any work which contains complex thoughts; reports of current events; editorial pages of news-papers; poetry, drama, etc.; descriptive material; any-thing read orally.

SPECIFYING THE SKILLS OF LITERARY UNDERSTANDING

The area of literary understanding is divided into two streams, each of which contains specific skills to be developed. The first focuses on recognizing and interpreting informational and persuasive techniques, and the second deals with recognizing and interpreting characteristics of literature.

Recognizing and interpreting informational and persuasive techniques. The first stream—recognizing and interpreting informational and persuasive techniques—focuses on an author's choice of words and use of logic in developing the topic, and the authenticity with which the piece is written. The specific objectives for this stream are:

1. Classifying words as vague or precise

2. Determining the author's purpose (to inform, to persuade, to entertain, to evoke feelings)
3. Recognizing the elements of validity (conclusions following premises, unstated premises and conclusions)
4. Evaluating the validity of a written selection
5. Recognizing elements of reliability (soundness of premises and conclusions, fallacies, illogical reasoning)
6. Comparing information gathered from various sources

Recognizing and interpreting literary characteristics. The second stream—recognizing and interpreting literary characteristics—focuses on distinguishing between various forms of literature; interpreting components of literature such as character development, story plot and so on; and understanding the author's use of literary devices such as symbolism, humor, metaphor, and so on. The specific objectives for this stream are:

1. Recognizing various forms of literature (biography, historical fiction, realistic fiction, etc.)
2. Recognizing various forms of poetry (lyric, limerick, haiku, etc.)
3. Recognizing the ways an author uses dialogue, character thoughts, and character development
4. Recognizing the structure of literary material (episodic, accumulative, parallel, etc.)
5. Tracing the development of plot in terms of sequence and climax
6. Recognizing the author's use of special techniques (foreshadowing, flashback, etc.)
7. Interpreting the theme
8. Evaluating the author's writing style
9. Recognizing and interpreting the author's use of symbolism
10. Recognizing and interpreting the author's use of various devices of humor (slapstick, irony, satire, etc.)
11. Recognizing and interpreting the author's use of metaphors and other descriptive techniques

DIAGNOSING THE SKILLS

The skills listed above, when taught systematically, can lead the child who has mastered the skills of functional literacy to the point where he or she reads with efficiency and insight. However, knowing what the skills are is not enough. You must also diagnose to determine which child needs which skill.

You can accomplish this most efficiently by adapting the system of pretesting which was developed in Chapter 10. The system can be applied with the skills of efficient study and literary understanding much as it is with word recognition and comprehension. By referring to the specific objectives listed earlier in this chapter, you know what skills a child must master. You then must build pretests for each of these skills and use them to determine which students need help with any particular skill. Illustrations of how you can do this with selected skills follow:

Efficient study

1. *If you want to determine whether a child can use the dictionary as an aid in pronunciation:* Give a list of ten unfamiliar words, have the child look them up in a dictionary, and listen to him or her pronounce each; if he or she can pronounce nine of them accurately, that child already knows how to use the dictionary as a guide to pronunciation.
2. *If you want to determine whether a child can use the card catalog to locate a book:* Give a list of books and have the child use the card catalog to locate them in the library; if he or she quickly locates all ten books, that child already knows how to use the card catalog.
3. *If you want to determine whether a child can find information in a book by using the index:* Give five specific topics and tell the child to use the index to locate the pages on which the topic is discussed in the book; if he or she can find these pages, the child already knows how to use the index.
4. *If you want to determine whether a child varies rate of reading according to purpose:* Give three selections of equal length; time the child as you have him or her read the first one "for the fun of it," the second one to remember the major points and details, and the third one to find a single piece of information; if he or she takes longest when reading to remember the major point and details and goes fastest when reading to find a single piece of information, that child is varying reading rate appropriately.

Literary understanding

1. *If you want to determine whether a child can distinguish between vague and precise words:* Give ten words and have the child categorize them as being either precise or vague; if nine are done correctly, that child already knows how to distinguish between vague and precise words.
2. *If you want to determine whether the child can use story dialogue to determine character development:* Give a section of story dialogue and ask the child to tell you what kind of person might have said that; if he or she can do this correctly on three different dialogues, the child already knows how to use dialogue to determine character development.
3. *If you want to determine whether the child recognizes and interprets the author's use of symbolism:* Give a short piece of writing which contains symbolism, and have the child find and interpret the symbols; if he or she correctly recognizes and interprets most of them, the child already knows how to recognize and interpret symbolism.

Pretests such as those described above should be constructed and administered to each child. The results should be recorded in a notebook, and you should teach each child the skills he or she has not yet mastered, starting with the simplest and working up to the most complex.

TEACHING THE SKILLS

As in word identification and comprehension, your instruction in the skills beyond functional literacy will succeed only if you can direct the students' attention and highlight effectively. To do this, you must identify the salient features of the task. Illustrations of how you do this with selected skills follow:

Efficient study
1. *If you want the child to use the dictionary as an aid to pronunciation:* Direct attention to the phonetic symbols and to the sounds associated with each, providing the child with directed assistance in remembering both the symbols and their associated sounds.
2. *If you want the child to use a systematic study technique such as SQ3R:* Direct attention to each of the five steps in the process, providing the child with directed assistance in performing each step correctly.
3. *If you want the child to use a skimming rate of reading to locate specific information:* Direct attention to the key words to look for when skimming, providing the child with directed assistance in both finding the key words and in moving the eyes faster across the page.

Literary understanding
1. *If you want the learner to recognize elements of validity in writing:* Direct attention to the author's premises and the degree of relationship which exists between these and the conclusions drawn, providing directed assistance in recognizing the degree of logic present.
2. *If you want the child to recognize and interpret various metaphors:* Direct attention to both the metaphors used by the author and what is being described, providing directed assistance in helping the child see how the author's image helps us picture the way the author perceives what is being described.

Once you have determined the salient features of the task, plan lessons which incorporate the principles of creating a set, attending, directing assistance, diminishing, practicing, and applying as described in Chapter 14.

SUMMARY OF CONTINUED SKILL INSTRUCTION

A child's reading instruction does not stop when functional literacy has been achieved. Good instruction insures that each child goes beyond this minimal level to achieve efficiency and insightfulness as a reader.

Just as functional literacy can be described as a group of skills, so can the area beyond functional literacy. However, rather than emphasizing skills in word identification and comprehension, the emphasis shifts to efficient study and literary understandings.

Under the area of efficient study, there are three distinct types of skills: those relating to the location of information, those relating to the organization of information, and those relating to reading rate. Similarly, the area of literary understanding has two distinct types of skills: those relating to informational and persuasive techniques and those related to literary characteristics.

The skills in both areas should be taught using the same principles of systematic instruction as prescribed for the skills of word identification and comprehension. Pretests and posttests should be built to insure mastery, and instruction should be characterized by the principles of skill teaching developed in Chapter 14.

TEST YOUR KNOWLEDGE

1. The skills instruction for a child who has mastered all the functional literacy skills shifts to the skills of _____ and _____.

2. The category of efficient study contains three streams of skills. They are: _____, _____, and _____.

3. The category of literary understanding includes two streams of skills. They are recognizing and interpreting both _____ and _____.

4. The skill of using an atlas would fall into the major category of _____ and into the substream of _____.

5. The skill of note taking would fall into the major category of _____ and into the substream _____.

6. The skill of recognizing the reliability of persuasive materials would fall into the major category of _____ and into the substream of _____.

7. The skill of interpreting the theme of literary material would fall into the major category of _____ and into the substream of _____.

8. Generally speaking, the teacher in the primary grades would expect most students to need reading instruction in _____ and _____, although some would be ready for instruction in efficient study and literary understanding.

9. The teacher in the middle grades, on the other hand, would expect to have some students who needed instruction in the functional literacy skills of _____ and _____ and others who needed instruction in the skills beyond functional literacy.

10. In planning instruction in the skills beyond functional literacy, the teacher would use the six-step model of _____, _____, _____, _____, _____, and _____ as was used with the skills of functional literacy.

SIMULATION ACTIVITIES

You should now be able to diagnose and teach reading skills that carry the students beyond functional literacy. Assume that you are a fifth grade teacher and want to determine if your students possess certain reading skills beyond functional literacy. State how you would diagnose whether or not your students possessed the following skills:

1. The student recognizes various forms of literature, such as biography, historical fiction, and realistic fiction.
2. The student determines the author's purpose (i.e. to inform, to persuade, to entertain, to evoke feelings).
3. The student finds information in a dictionary.

Once you know how to diagnose for skill needs, the next step involves the development of directing the learner's attention and, subsequently, highlighting elements for directed assistance. For each of the following examples, state how you would direct the learner's attention and highlight effectively:

4. The student identifies the type of humor as slapstick.
5. The student uses a slow reading rate for extremely difficult material.
6. The student determines the author's purpose.

Throughout this chapter the skills have been discussed in terms of their final usage. All of the skills need to be broken into smaller manageable units for instruction which moves the students from the simple examples to the more complex examples of each skill. Examine the following data on instruction for index usage.

> Mrs. Williams assessed five of her students and found that three of them could not use the index to locate page numbers of specific topics. When preparing a number of specific skill lessons designed to eventually prepare the students to use an index, the following example entries were selected. Organize these index entries into a simple–to–complex sequence.
> Road, Roman, 91–93, 95, ill. 97, 100, m. 102
> Rollo, 139, ill. 139
> Rights, in American colonies, 284, 287–289, 302, 305–314; in Chile, 349; in England, 154–155, 160, 162, 184, 209–210, 250, 295; in feudal systems, 302; in France, 170, 173, 182–183; in Greece, 80, 81–83, 91–92; in Middle Ages, 301, 309; in Rome, 142–146, 153, 161, 173, 175; in Switzerland, 309. *See also* Citizenship; Democracy; Freedom
> Puritans, 304
> Luther, Martin, 116–119, 121, m. 125
> Slavery, in America, 382, ill. 383, 388, 391–394; in Egypt, 41; in Greece, 77, 83, 88; history of, 289; in Rome, 143–145; trade in, 401–402

SUGGESTED FIELD EXPERIENCES

Observation. When observing in schools, note how the teacher assesses for specific skill needs beyond functional literacy. How is the attention of the students directed for this skill instruction? What type of directed assistance is used?

Teaching activities. Diagnose a small group of students for a reading skill in the areas beyond functional literacy. Teach that skill to those who need it. Remember to teach the skill initially with the simplest examples and to use attenders and diminishing directed assistance.

Client impact. By being aware of the skills beyond functional literacy and by being able to diagnose for and teach those skills, you are directly assisting students in their development as mature readers. The impact will be noted in your students' ability to satisfy their reading interests and to use study tools as they become mature readers.

FOR CLASS DISCUSSION

Use of the dictionary is an important study skill. The smaller units of instruction in this skill are many. Develop the subskills, moving from the simple to the complex, which comprise the skill of using the dictionary.

ANSWER KEY
1. effective study, literary understanding
2. locational, organization of information, rate
3. informational and persuasive techniques, literary characteristics
4. efficient study skills, locational skills
5. efficient study skills, organization of information
6. literary understanding, recognizing and interpreting informational and persuasive techniques
7. literary understanding, recognizing and interpreting literary characteristics
8. word recognition, comprehension
9. word recognition, comprehension
10. creating a set, attending, directed assistance, diminishing, practicing, applying

CONTENT AREA
READING

OVERVIEW

This chapter specifies the variables which cause difficulty in reading content area material and provides techniques for insuring comprehension in such material. The ultimate objective is:

> Given a content area lesson to teach, you control the variables which influence comprehension to insure that each child learns the content.

KNOWLEDGE BACKGROUND

As the child moves beyond the foundation skills of functional literacy, the child becomes more and more involved with textbooks, especially in content areas such as social studies and science. This change of emphasis requires that you—the teacher—insure that the child *can* learn from reading such textbooks. You must know what variables influence a child's comprehension of textbook material and how to give him or her control of these variables.

The variables that affect reading comprehension are word identification barriers, comprehension barriers, interest and purpose variables, and the experience background of the students. Accounting for these variables while planning a content area lesson can insure that all students understand the material.

WORD IDENTIFICATION BARRIERS

The first condition necessary for understanding textbooks is adequate word identification skills. Obviously, the student who cannot identify the words on a page will not understand what the words are saying. Pause for a moment and picture a fifth grade social studies class with five students who have an instructional reading level of second grade. How can they be asked to understand their social studies material when they have not yet mastered the skills for identifying the words on the page? The answer, of course, is that they cannot. We must find other ways for them to learn the material.

One way is to substitute books of lower readability level which cover the same information. Libraries and book publishers have lists of such lower readability materials. The second way is to eliminate the need for decoding by having another person read the material to the child or by taping the material and having the child listen.

The wisdom of eliminating the word identification barrier is illustrated by a recent elementary classroom experiment in which students were given two identical tests, except that the first was given in written form and the second was put on tape. The good students did well on both tests, but the poor students did significantly better on the tape-recorded test, indicating that the poor readers knew the material but were penalized by their inability to decode the written questions on the first test. If we really want children to comprehend, we must insure that the textual material we assign is written at their instructional reading level, or we must allow them to listen to the material.

COMPREHENSION BARRIERS

The second condition necessary for understanding textbook material is possession of the basic comprehension skills. Students who cannot read for meaning will not understand the content. Looking again at our fifth grade social studies class, we may have students who have not mastered the basic skills of information gathering, manipulative thinking, and evaluative thinking, as well as students who have word identification problems. Even if a child can pronounce each word on the page, the child will be unable to learn content material if the basic comprehension skills are lacking.

The best way to help students who lack these basic thinking skills is by using study guides. A study guide is just what its name implies—it guides the students in studying the material. These guides can range from relatively simple outlines to elaborate, highly detailed devices. Whatever their form, the study guides help the students comprehend the material. For instance, a study guide might identify the meaning of new terminology, it might highlight the main ideas or the central events, and/or it might direct students to specific sections of the textbook where crucial information can be found. The intention is that the guide will do some of the spadework for the child, thereby insuring that he or she will not be unduly penalized because of lack of prerequisite comprehension skills.

INTEREST AND PURPOSE VARIABLES

The third condition that influences comprehension is pupil interest and/or purpose. Most students do not have a built-in interest in a particular content. We know, however, that comprehension is improved if the child is interested in what he or she is learning. Consequently, your responsibility as a teacher (and as the person who knows why the content is taught) is to create interest. You can do this by using the principles of relevance, excitement and variety, and personal purpose setting.

Let's assume you are teaching a social studies unit on ancient Egypt. The principle of relevance demands that you let the students know why it is important for them to study this particular topic. Why should they learn about pyramids and pharoahs? What good is it going to do them? If you can answer these questions adequately, you will be creating an interest in the topic and will enhance their comprehension. If you cannot, however, then either the unit should not be studied or you should find someone who can explain why the content is important.

A second way to create interest is to make use of varied and exciting learning activities. Students tend to be bored when you follow the same instructional procedures day after day. They tend to be interested, however, when a variety of activities are used (such as movies about Egypt, simulation activities and role playing of events in ancient Egypt, pyramid-building projects, and so on).

The most powerful technique for creating interest, however, is the deceptively simple device of involving pupils in the purpose-setting activities of a study. Once again, pretend you are teaching a unit on ancient Egypt. Interest may be low because the entire purpose for reading is beyond the child's control; either the teacher or the author of the textbook says, in effect, "Learn this because I say so." Shouldn't the pupils' purposes be part of the learning situation? The answer, of course, is yes. The more a student reads to find answers to his or her own questions, the greater interest will be and the more thorough comprehension will be.

Hence, you are involving pupils in purpose-setting activities when you let them ask their own questions. Suppose, however, that you ask a class, "What do you want to learn about the pharaohs of Egypt?" and they respond with, "We don't want to learn anything about it." What can you do then? Your job is to entice the class into creating purposes. Consider the following example:

Go to the board and write **Egypt, pyramid,** and **pharoahs.** Turn to the class and say, "Can anybody read all three of these words?" When somebody reads them out loud, say, "Hey, that's good! Let's everybody say these three words," and in unison the pupils say the words as you point to them. Are they turned on by this? No. Has a purpose been set? No. But you have done the first step in creating purposes for this assignment. Now say, "Ok, class. These three words are the key ideas in the section of your history book between pages 61 and 65. I wonder if anybody can, with only these three words, figure out a question that you think will be answered in those four pages. Now, this is hard and maybe you can't do it. After all, you only have three words as clues. Does anybody want to try?" You will always get at least one person to respond to this challenge. Someone in class will suggest a question. As soon as one question has been posed—good or bad—you must positively reinforce the pupil's behavior: "Great! I really didn't think anybody could come up with a question with so little help. Can anybody else come up with a question?" It is unlikely that you will ever have a situation in which other pupils will not respond in an attempt to match the behavior of the first student. As these questions are being asked, write them on the chalkboard. Any question is a good question at this point. But be sure that you do not destroy the pupils' purpose in your desire to restate any poor questions as you write them on the board.

Once the questions are posed and noted on the board, have the students read the textbook to answer the questions. In this way, students are reading to answer their own questions and they are, consequently, more likely to be interested.

EXPERIENCE BACKGROUND

The final condition necessary for understanding content material is the background experience of the students. If you have students whose backgrounds have been so limited in kind and quality that they are unable to relate to the content in the textbook, you must alter the tasks to account for this lack of experience.

Assume you are preparing for a social studies lesson about desert tribes of Africa in your third grade class in the inner city of Detroit. The students are all products of the urban ghetto. They have no previous knowledge for desert tribes of Africa, so they need background experience first. One way to neutralize such experience deprivation is to relate the unknown concepts in the study to the students' previous experience. Using the lead-in question "What do we really mean by this word?" the concepts of **desert** and **tribe** could be explained in the following way:

Some land is so poor that people and things can't live on it. It is too hot or too cold, too dry, or too barren. This is a **desert.** Can you think of a place in our neighborhood that is a desert? How is it like an African desert? How is it different?

Sometimes people join together in clubs and make rules for the club and run projects. These clubs are like **tribes.** Do you know of a club? Why do people join this club? How are tribes like clubs? How are they different?

You are overcoming the experience deficit by teaching word meaning, by helping students relate a concept common to them with a new concept. It is once again a process of using the known to solve the unknown; you are teaching by analogy or by comparison.

A limited experience background can also impede the students' ability to answer questions about the topic, particularly if the questions are abstract. For instance, it would be rare for a child of limited experience to give an immediate answer to the question "Why are most desert tribes of Africa **nomadic?**" However, by providing concrete examples from the students' own experience and by moving gradually from this concrete level to the abstract, such students can answer the questions. For instance, the question about why desert tribes of Africa are nomadic could be broken down into smaller steps. Rather than immediately asking about African tribes, you might begin by saying.

Nomadic means to move around frequently. Can you think of any reasons why people might be nomadic here in Detroit? Why might city people move around frequently? Do you think people in the desert move around for the same reasons? Why might desert tribes be nomadic?

By carefully using questions which lead the student from the known to the unknown, we can compensate for experience deprivation and insure greater comprehension in the text areas.

SUMMARY OF CONTENT AREA READING

Individual differences do not disappear when the child moves beyond functional literacy and into reading content area textbooks. If anything, the problem of controlling individual differences becomes *more* complex because you must be sure that each student is not impeded by:

1. a textbook containing words he or she is unable to identify
2. a textbook requiring thinking processes he or she has not yet mastered
3. a lack of interest or a failure to understand the purpose for the study
4. limited experience relative to the particular topic being studied

If you account for each of these variables when using textbooks, you can be confident that your students will comprehend in the content areas. Failure to account for these variables, however, unjustly penalizes the children and deprives them of the opportunity to learn.

TEST YOUR KNOWLEDGE

1. If a child does not adequately learn the material in a content area such as social studies or science, it may be because the teacher is not controlling the _____ which influence comprehension in textbooks.
2. When a child is unable to pronounce the words encountered in a textbook, the teacher has failed to control the _____ variable.
3. When a child can say the words on the page but is unable to answer certain kinds of questions, the teacher has failed to control the _____ variable.
4. When a child is bored or sees no viable reason for learning the material in a content area textbook, the teacher has failed to control the _____ variable.
5. If a child does not learn textbook material because of unfamiliarity with the terminology and/or the concepts, the teacher has failed to control the _____ variable.
6. If a child cannot identify the words in the textbook, the teacher can control this variable by giving _____ books to read.
7. If a child cannot find the answers to certain kinds of questions when reading textbooks, the teacher can control this variable by providing a _____.
8. If a child is bored with the material in a textbook, the teacher can control this variable by allowing the child to share in setting _____ for the study.
9. If a child is unfamiliar with the terminology and/or concepts used in a textbook, the teacher can control this variable by creating analogies using concrete examples from the students' immediate _____.
10. To control, the variable which influence comprehension in textbooks, the teacher must be just as aware of individual _____ as when teaching functional literacy.

SIMULATION ACTIVITIES

You should now be able to apply your knowledge of how to insure comprehension in content textbooks to a hypothetical teaching situation. Assume that you are a third grade teacher and the class is studying a unit on Indians. Pages 30–45 of the social studies text have descriptive material on Indians which you want all your pupils to experience. You know, however, that some pupils are deficient in areas which influence comprehension. Consequently, they would probably have difficulty with the assignment unless it is adjusted to meet their specific needs. How would you adjust the assignment to ensure that each of the children described below comprehends the material on pages 30–45?

Sam has difficulties with word identification skills and is unable to pronounce many of the words.

Joan has difficulty with the basic comprehension skills. Specifically, she has not yet learned to draw conclusions from inferential information, a skill which is required in order to understand the material.

Mary has a very limited meaning vocabulary. She knows only a few of the terms used.

Joe comes from a large metropolitan area. He lacks experience with many of the concepts discussed, particularly the more abstract ones that are required to understand this material.

Joan enjoys housework and domestic chores. She has little interest in Indians and sees no need to learn about them.

Marvin's mind seems to wander constantly. He does not concentrate on the material and just seems to slip through the textbook purposelessly.

The variables that influence textbook comprehension should be used in selecting textual material. Consider this hypothetical situation: You have taken a teaching job as a fourth grade teacher. Your principal has appointed you to serve on the textbook selection committee. The committee's first task is to select a new social studies series for grades 4 through 6.

1. What would you look for in a new textbook to help minimize the problems your students might have in identifying words?
2. What would you look for in a new textbook to help minimize problems in doing the thinking which is required?
3. What aids could a textbook provide to create interest?
4. What aids could a textbook provide to create purpose?
5. What aids could a textbook provide to minimize terminology problems caused by limited experience backgrounds?
6. What aids could a textbook provide to help students handle abstractions in this content area?

Note: It would be rare for a textbook to supply all these aids. As a teacher, you must be able to use the aids offered in the text and supplement the text with additional techniques of your own.

Attending to all the variables which influence textbook comprehension is difficult to manage. How can you account for all these differences in a single social studies or science period? The following strategy might be helpful:

1. Set general purposes for the entire class (purpose-setting questions).
2. Group pupils according to the variables which need attention.
3. Have pupils read or listen to the textbook material in the small groups, with you providing the groups with the special help needed.

4. Have the entire class then discuss what they found out in their respective groups about the purposes set at the outset.

Let's assume a hypothetical situation in which the above strategy is used. You are teaching a sixth grade social studies class. The topic is "Various Forms of Government." Your "textbook" is a special booklet you ordered from the U.S. Government Printing Office. You have a copy for each of your twenty-five students. However, five of your pupils cannot read the booklet because of word identification barriers, three others cannot read the booklet because of barriers relating to the basic comprehension skills, and eight other children lack experience with many of the words and, consequently, do not have any grasp of meaning. The remaining nine pupils can read the booklet without assistance although they, like most of the others in the class, are not particularly interested in either studying about forms of government or in reading the booklet. You decide to follow the four-step strategy described above.

1. At the start of the period, you meet with the whole class to set purposes. You elicit from the students many questions which they feel they should be able to answer in reading the booklet. What variable are you controlling when you do this?
2. You break the class up into four groups, one for those who can read the booklet without help and one for each of the groups having some kind of difficulty. What will your directions be to the nine students who can read the booklet without help?
3. What will you do with the group of five pupils whose reading is impeded by word identification barriers?
4. What will you do with the group of three students whose reading is impeded because they have not yet learned the necessary fundamental comprehension skills?
5. What will you do with the group of eight students whose reading is impeded because they lack experience with the terminology?
6. When, toward the end of the period, you meet with the class as a whole, what will the discussion focus on?

SUGGESTED FIELD EXPERIENCES

Observation. When observing in schools, you should note how teachers prepare for and teach textbook lessons. Is the word identification variable controlled? The basic comprehension skill variable? The interest/purpose variable? Are the backgrounds of the students related to the topic?

Teaching activities. When teaching content area textbook lessons, you should control the variables that influence comprehension. Be sure to set purposes. Individualize by grouping for special needs. Be ready to present material visually or auditorily as needed. Plan for some means of determining what your students learned.

Client impact. By controlling the variables that influence textbook understanding, you are removing the barriers that hinder learning of the content material. Your students are then able to learn the content material without floundering with decoding problems, basic comprehension problems, lack of interest, and inadequate background. The impact will be noted in your students' enthusiasm, participation, and retention of learning in the content areas.

FOR CLASS DISCUSSION

Assume that you are teaching in a rural school system where the social studies and science achievement test scores are extremely low. The state department of education, in an attempt to raise the level of achievement, awards you a grant of $5000 and instructs you to spend the money to improve social studies and science achievement. Considering the variables which influence reading comprehension, what could you buy to increase comprehension by controlling word identification problems? Basic comprehension skill problems? Interest and purpose problems? Experience background problems?

ANSWER KEY
1. variables
2. word identification
3. comprehension
4. interest and purpose
5. experience
6. easier
7. study guide
8. purposes
9. environment
10. differences

TEACHING COMPREHEN- SION SKILLS IN CONTENT AREA TEXTBOOKS

OVERVIEW

This chapter provides you with techniques for helping children use thinking skills when they are reading from content area textbooks. The ultimate objective is:

> Given a content area lesson to teach, you will directly assist students in using comprehension skills while reading from the assigned textbook.

KNOWLEDGE BACKGROUND

Teaching your learners to think about and understand what they read requires imagination and flexibility. You must accurately assess both what your learners need to know in order to understand a selection and what kinds of thinking operations they must use.

In the first instance, you want your learners to know and understand the content of the selection. If they are reading a history book, you want them to know history. Consequently, part of your effort is directed toward teaching history. In the second instance, however, you want your learner to think. Now the history book becomes the vehicle; the content assumes a secondary importance, while the process of thinking becomes the focus.

To accomplish the dual goals of understanding content and thinking, follow a five-step sequence in planning and teaching content area lessons as follows:

1. Determine what content is to be learned. If the lesson focuses on the Revolutionary War, what is it you want your students to know about the Revolutionary War? If the lesson focuses on ecology, what do you want your students to know about ecology? Specify this learning by stating one or more objectives which describe what the students will know or do as a result of completing the content lesson.
2. Examine the reading material and determine what the student must do in order to comprehend. This requires that you account for the variables of word identification, comprehension, interest and purpose, and experience as specified in the previous chapter. If you are to achieve the dual goals of understanding content and thinking, it is particularly crucial that you know what thinking skills are required.
3. List questions you want the students to be able to answer. If you want them to learn certain content and to use certain thinking skills, devise questions that will be appropriate.
4. Specify how you will help students to do the required thinking. Devise ways to help students use comprehension skills while reading and thinking about the content.
5. Organize your content area lesson to facilitate differentiation of instruction. If you have some students who need extra help, devise ways to structure the classroom to give them the extra attention they need.

To illustrate this procedure, let's use the following three-paragraph selection about whales, typical of most fourth or fifth grade science books, to teach a content lesson in which the students learn about whales while also doing specified kinds of thinking.

The Largest of All Animals [1]

The largest of all land or water animals is the whale. The great blue whale is sometimes over one hundred feet long and weighs as much as one hundred and twenty-five tons. Our largest elephants do not often weigh more than six tons, so the largest whale weighs more than twenty times as much as the largest elephant. Not all whales are as large as the great blue whale, however. The smallest whale, or dolphin, is seldom over four feet long.

The whale can grow to such great size because it lives in water. The water supports its great weight and provides plenty of food for it. As the whale swims through the water, it sweeps bushels of food into its mouth at one time.

Although the whale is shaped like a fish, it is really a mammal.

[1] *Atomic Submarine Book*, Building Reading Skills, Wichita, Kansas: McCormick-Mather Publishing Co., 1965, p. 72.

Its young feeds on the mother's milk. It has lungs instead of gills. It breathes air. The whale usually comes to the top of the water every five or ten minutes, but it can stay under water for forty-five minutes. When it comes to the top of the water, the whale blows stale air from its lungs and takes in a supply of fresh air. Often when fishermen see the cloud of water vapor and air which the whale breathes out, they say, "There she blows."

DETERMINING THE CONTENT TO BE LEARNED

A multitude of objectives could be generated from this selection, depending upon the teacher's goals. For the sake of illustration, however, we will use the following three objectives for the selection:

1. The students will be able to list three facts about whales (*factual thinking*).
2. The students will be able to explain why whales don't live on land (*inferential thinking*).
3. The students will be able to take a position for or against continued hunting of whales by whale fleets (*evaluative thinking*).

ASSESSING THE DEMANDS OF THE CONTENT

From the previous chapter, you know you must account for the variables which influence comprehension of textual material. Specifically, you must examine the material to determine whether all your students can identify the words in the passage, whether they have an interest in the material or a purpose for pursuing it, whether they have experience with the fundamental concepts, and whether they have the thinking skills necessary for completing the objectives.

For instance, if you apply the Fry readability formula,[2] you find that the selection is of approximately a sixth grade difficulty level. Consequently, students who have an instructional reading level of less than sixth grade will have difficulty reading the selection, and you will have to find easier material on whales or give then the content as a listening situation.

Similarly, the interest and purpose variable must be considered. While some students may be very interested in learning about whales, others will not find this content interesting. For these students, you must use one of the techniques described in Chapter 26 to create interest.

The experience variable is also crucial in dealing with this selection. Many of the fundamental concepts, such as *one hundred feet, one hundred and twenty-five tons, mammal, gills, lungs,* and *water vapor* require some previous experience. Students lacking such experience will need

---

[2] Described in Emerald Dechant, *Improving the Teaching of Reading*, 2nd ed., Englewood Cliffs, N.J.: Prentice-Hall, 1970, pp. 279-280.

extra help in achieving the objectives of the lesson. Examples of the way some of these terms could be developed follow:

One hundred feet: Not one fifth grader in a hundred has an accurate estimation of the linear measurement of 100 feet. Because size is so important to an understanding of this selection, you would need to devise a teaching tactic to clarify this value. You might have your learners measure the length of the classroom and picture whatever number of rooms it would take to make 100 feet. It might be even better to measure a hall that is at least 100 feet long, or even to pace this distance off on the playground. Some learners might also grasp this concept by directing them to picture a football field in their minds, with 100 feet roughly the distance from the goal to the 35-yard line.

One hundred and twenty-five tons: This is another measurement that needs some kind of description if it is to be understood. You might make an approximation of this weight by directing your learners to the fact that a car weighs about 3,000 pounds. One hundred and twenty-five tons is 250,000 pounds. How many cars piled on top of each other would equal one great blue whale? This could even be extended to the weight of the learners in your room. How many rooms of fifth graders would it take to balance the weight of one blue whale?

Gills and lungs: A fish drawing or model would illustrate what gills are and where they are located. Their function would be explained as similar to lungs. Again, a human model or demonstration of breathing would illustrate what lungs are, and the comparison would be clear.

Water vapor: To develop the concept, you could ask your learners what happens when they breathe out on a cold winter morning. The warm air from the lungs is condensed by the cold, and we see it in the form of water vapor. This also happens when a whale expels air after diving deep in the cold ocean water.

Finally, assessing thinking skills is especially crucial if you are to help students use these skills when reading the selection. Consequently, you must look at each of the objectives and determine what kind of thinking the child must do while reading (or listening to) the material. For instance, the first objective requires the child to list three facts about whales; since the facts are explicitly stated, factual thinking is required. The second objective requires the child to explain why whales don't live on land; this information is not explicitly stated in the passage but is implied and calls for inferential thinking. The final objective asks the child to take a position on the continued commercial hunting of whales; this requires a judgment and calls for evaluative thinking. Students who have a firm grasp of these three types of thinking skills and who have previously demonstrated an ability to use them in reading will have little difficulty in reading the selection. Students who have not yet mastered the use of these skills, however, will need assistance.

ASKING APPROPRIATE QUESTIONS

Whether your instruction reflects information gathering, thinking, or a combination of these depends upon the purposes you set for pupils. Purposes are communicated by the kinds of questions you ask. If you ask only factual questions, then you are a knowledge gatherer, a "funnel teacher" who perceives teaching as funneling facts into students. The other extreme asks pupils only speculative questions when they have no facts as a basis for their thinking. The good teacher steers a middle course.

To steer such a course, however, you must ask different kinds of questions. If you want students to think in terms of the facts, you must ask questions which focus the children on the factual information specified in a passage. Such questioning is illustrated in the following sample paragraph:

> In the spring and early summer, butterflies appeared as if by magic. Most of them emerged from cocoons that were attached to weeds and bushes during the last year's fall. However, one of the most colorful butterflies, the Monarch, didn't spend the cold winter in a cocoon. Instead it migrated, like the birds, to warm southern California and there spent a cozy winter. In the spring it flew north, again bringing spring color to signal the end of winter.

Sample factual questions:

1. Which butterflies migrated to the north in spring?
2. Where did this butterfly spend the cold winter?
3. When did the butterfly return to the north?
4. To what are cocoons usually attached?
5. What besides the butterfly migrates south for the winter?

Many times, however, you want the learner to think beyond the literal meaning found in the material, "What do the facts suggest? What do I know from my experience about these facts? What implications are possible?" Questioning which elicits this kind of thinking is illustrated in the following sample paragraph:

> Annie took her little kitty out to play. "We will play here," she said. "We will have fun." Then the little kitty saw a robin hopping on the grass. He ran to play with it. "Silly kitty," said Annie. "Birds do not play with kittens. You come back and play with me."

Sample inferential questions:

1. What will Annie do next?

2. Which of the following sentences might be true according to the story?
   a. Annie's kitty is black and white.
   b. Annie has a pet robin.
   c. The robin flew away.
3. Why was the robin hopping on the grass?
4. Why did Annie play with her kitty?

While many content objectives require only factual and inferential thinking, there are times when you want the child to make judgments about either the author's credibility or about the child's own position on the topic. Objectives of this kind require evaluative thinking. For instance, evaluative thinking would be required when you ask students to read about gun-control laws and to then take a position on whether such laws would be good or bad. Similarly, evaluative thinking would be required when asking students to identify the bias of an author such as the one who wrote the following selection, also used in *Simulation Activities*, Chapter 22:

> In a recent speech to a private group, Mr. Smith analyzed with precision and force the government's position in the war. His statement is the most complete and convincing argument that has been made for continuing the war. He went to the very heart of our nation's interests as the basis for his position and wisely ignored the carping of those who lack his vision.

Effective questioning, then, is a crucial part of the good teacher's repertoire. To focus the learner on the facts, ask factual questions. To have students read between the lines, ask inferential questions. To have students make judgments, as evaluative questions. Without good questions, students will not do the thinking desired, or, at best, will do it only by chance.

While good questions serve the important function of directing the learner to specific aspects of the content, they do not in themselves insure comprehension. This is because asking questions is basically a testing, rather than a teaching, device. The true test of a good teacher is what he or she does when, after asking a student a good question, the child responds, "I don't know" or "I can't remember."

DIRECTLY ASSISTING LEARNERS IN THE THINKING TASK

When children are unable to answer the questions you pose, you will need to provide specific assistance in using comprehension skills. In the lesson on whales, for instance, you might ask the following questions as a means of directing the students to the three objectives of the lesson:

1. How large does the great blue whale become (*factual*)?
2. Why can't whales live on land (*inferential*)?

3. Do you think commercial hunting of whales should be abolished (*evaluative*)?

A simple way to help a student answer question 1 and other factual questions would be to provide a copy of the selection in which the factual information is highlighted. Such a paragraph might look like this:

The size of the largest whale	The largest of all land or water animals is the whale. The great blue whale is sometimes over one hundred feet long and weighs as much as one hundred and twenty-five tons. Our largest elephants do not often weigh more than six tons, so the largest whale weighs more than twenty times as much as the largest elephant. Not all whales are as large as the great blue whale, however. The smallest whale, or dolphin, is seldom over four feet long.
The size of the smallest whale	
How the whale grows so big	The whale can grow to such great size because it lives in water. The water supports its great weight and provides plenty of food for it. As the whale swims through the water, it sweep bushels of food into its mouth at one time.
How the whale is different from a fish	Although the whale is shaped like a fish, it is really a mammal. Its young feeds on the mother's milk. It has lungs instead of gills. It breathes air. The whale usually cames to the top of the water every five or ten minutes, but it can stay under water for forty-five minutes. When it comes to the top of the water, the whale blows stale air from its lungs and takes in a supply of fresh air. Often when fishermen see the cloud of water vapor and air which the whale breathes out, they say, "There she blows."

Devices such as this or any others that you might create will directly assist the student in finding the facts requested in your questions. As the child becomes more proficient in locating facts, gradually diminish such assistance until he or she can perform the task without any help from you.

To help students with inferential thinking, you must either relate the problem with an experience the child has previously had or create such an experience in the classroom. To determine why whales can't live on land, your dialogue with the students might go like this.

TEACHER: Can whales live on land?
CLASS: No, whales can't live on land.
TEACHER: Why not? They are mammals, they breathe air just like we do.

CLASS:	They need the water to keep their skins wet.
TEACHER:	All right. I'll water the whale with a fire hose and keep it wet. Now can it live on land?
CLASS:	No. How would it eat?
TEACHER:	I'll trap tons of food for the whale and pump the food into its mouth and down its stomach. Now can it live on land?
CLASS:	No. Whales just can't live on land.
TEACHER:	Well, why not?

Although this looks like a stalemate, if you push hard enough and refer the class back to the word **supports** in the second sentence of the second paragraph, some learner will grasp the implication of this word, and the dialogue will then continue like this:

CLASS:	A whale can't live on land because the water supports it, but land doesn't.
TEACHER:	What do you mean by **supports** it?
CLASS:	Well, a whale is so heavy that it just collapses on land, while in the water it doesn't collapse.
TEACHER:	Why not?
CLASS:	Water supports whales.

Once again you need to direct the class to a key concept, that of buoyancy. You could do this with a series of questions such as these:

TEACHER:	How many of you can swim? How many of you can float? What happens when you float? What does the water do?

With a little planning, you could have a pail of water, a spring scale (fish scale), a brick, and some cord on hand to provide a simple demonstration of the effect of buoyancy on the weight of the brick. This would illustrate the concept, and you could conclude in the following manner:

TEACHER:	Why can't a whale live on land?
CLASS:	Land won't support its great weight. It probably wouldn't be able to breathe. Its great weight would just squeeze it together and it would die.
TEACHER:	Why can it live in the water?
CLASS:	It has lots of food available, and it can catch food in the water. The water also supports its great weight; it doesn't weigh so much in the water [buoyancy]. Water allows it to breathe.

The area of evaluative thinking, like inferential thinking, frequently requires that the child draw upon additional experiences or information.

To discuss whether commercial hunting of whales should be abolished, the child must have background information about both the possible extinction of whales through indiscriminate hunting and the value of whale by-products. Once the child has both pieces of information, encourage taking and defending a position. You can help by setting up a "Pro and Con Chart" regarding whether commercial whale hunting should be abolished, listing under the "pro" column all the reasons the child can think of for why such hunting should be abolished and listing under the "con" column all the reasons why it should be allowed to continue. Have the child choose a position and allow him or her to use the chart in defending it.

ORGANIZING FOR DIFFERENTIATED INSTRUCTION

It is obvious that effective content area instruction calls for attention to many different variables. In any one classroom you are likely to have some students who need little or no assistance in achieving the objectives and others who will need help with one or more of the variables of word identification, interest and purpose, experience, and/or thinking skills. The question that remains to be answered is how you can structure your classroom to give each child the help he or she needs.

One way is to make use of an intraclass grouping pattern such as in the following chart.

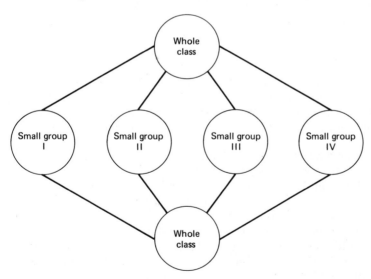

At the beginning of the class period, work with the whole group, setting purposes for the lesson and giving specific directions for various groups. During the heart of the period, have the small groups, formed on a basis of common needs, work on various tasks prescribed by you. One group of five children could listen to a tape of the teacher reading a textbook selection they cannot decode themselves; another could read independently because they need no special help from you, another could use the textbook and a study guide to answer specific factual questions; while you could provide the fourth group with directed assistance in answering inferential questions. In the final part of the period, bring the whole class together again to share the information obtained from various sources, achieve the objectives set at the outset, and determine the goals for the next period.

This plan, then, requires that you work directly with some children while others work independently. Such instruction requires efficient management of those students not directly under your supervision. The principles of classroom organization and management, described in Chapters 12 and 13, can be applied to accomplish this goal.

SUMMARY OF TEACHING COMPREHENSION SKILLS IN CONTENT AREA TEXTBOOKS

Helping pupils use comprehension skills in context textbooks is a complex task. Rather than simply specifying the content you want learned, you must also ask good questions, assess the textbook to determine what special skills are demanded, differentiate your instruction to provide assistance where it is needed, and organize your classroom so that specialized assistance can be provided. Such instruction is difficult to accomplish, but, with patience and diligence, it can result in successful content area teaching.

TEST YOUR KNOWLEDGE

1. The first step in planning a content area lesson is to specify what _____ is to be learned.
2. After you have specified the content objectives, you would assess the reading material to see what _____ are demanded of the students.
3. The next step would be to decide upon _____ which will serve to focus the students on the content.
4. Your next step would be to provide help, for those who need it, in doing the _____ required in the reading.
5. Finally, you must decide how you will _____ your class to provide each reader with the particular kind of help he or she needs.
6. In helping children whose reading level is less than the readability of the text, you must either provide _____ reading material or give them the content in an _____ situation.
7. For those students who are unfamiliar with the basic terminology used in the content assignment, you must provide instruction using the principles developed in the chapter on _____.
8. In helping children do inferential thinking in the content area, your highlighting must help the student relate his or her previous _____ with the topic.

9. Effective organization of content area lessons calls for the use of both large and small _____.
10. To use grouping effectively in the content area, you will have to make use of the _____ principles described in Chapters 12 and 13.

SIMULATION ACTIVITIES

The following selection, entitled "The Monarch Butterfly," is a typical fifth grade science selection. Assume that you are teaching a fifth grade class of twenty-five students and that you want to teach them from this selection to develop the following content objectives:

1. Enable them to list the parts of a monarch butterfly's body and the three stages of a monarch butterfly's life. (factual)
2. Enable them to state what plant is found as far north as the Hudson Bay. (inferential)
3. The students will be able to take a position regarding whether monarch butterflies should be tagged as a means for determining their migration routes. (evaluative)

The Monarch Butterfly [2]

The male monarch is one of the most beautiful of all the butterflies. He is not only neat looking and pretty, but on each hind wing he carries a little pocket of perfume to help get the attention of the female monarch. She is as brilliant as he but lacks the perfume pockets. Birds do not like to eat monarch either as adults or as larvae, probably because the monarch feeds on the milkweed which is a distasteful plant.

The monarchs are great travelers. They travel north during our growing season but must go back south when we have winter. In the early spring, the mother butterfly flies north as far as she can find milkweed growing and lays her eggs on the milkweed plant. These eggs hatch and the larvae soon become adults and fly farther north because later in the summer the milkweed will be growing still farther north. Sometimes monarchs are found as far north as the Hudson Bay. When cold weather comes, these butterflies gather in great flocks and move back south. It is impossible for us to know how flocks of butterflies are guided in their migration. The monarch is the strongest flyer of all the butterflies. He has been seen flying out over the ocean five hundred miles from land.

The monarch butterfly, like other insects, breathes by means of a system of air tubes through the sides of his body. The body is divided into three parts: the head, the thorax, and the abdomen. He has one pair of antennae, three pairs of legs, and two pairs of wings. He has two large compound eyes but no single eyes. The monarch

[2] Source unknown.

has sucking mouth parts to draw the honey out of flowers, for example, but he cannot bite.

There are four stages in the monarch's life: egg, larva or caterpillar, chrysalis or pupa, and adult. When the egg hatches into a larva, the larva is very small. This larva molts, just as grasshoppers do, before it becomes as large as it will get. After molting out of its skin four or five times, the larva spins itself a cocoon and in about two weeks hatches out of the cocoon as an adult monarch. The adult monarch is a beautiful brown with the border and veins black and with two rows of white spots on the outer borders. If the adult does not meet with an accident, it will likely live for from five to six years.

1. What is the readability level of this selection?
2. If you have five students who read at the third grade level, five that read at the fourth grade level, ten who read at the fifth grade level, and five who read at the sixth grade level, how many children will be unable to read this selection?
3. How would you get the content on the monarch butterfly across to those students who could not read the text?
4. It is not likely that all your students will be inherently interested in studying about the monarch butterfly. How could you make such a study relevant to those students who are not interested?
5. How could you use the principle of question asking to help your students establish a purpose for reading the selection on the monarch butterfly?
6. In the process of having the students pose questions as a means for generating a purpose for reading, you could also pose questions of your own to direct students to the specific objectives specified above. What are two factual questions you could ask?
7. What is one inferential question you could ask to get at the second objective?
8. What is one evaluative question you could ask to get at the third objective?
9. This selection has a heavy load of terminology. Look at the title and first paragraph. Which three words might have to be taught to some of the students in your class?
10. Using the principles developed in Chapter 19, can you briefly describe how you might help a student develop an understanding for the term monarch butterfly?
11. If you have students in your class who cannot independently do factual thinking, what kind of highlighting could you do to direct their attention to the answers to the two questions you posed in number 6 above?
12. What kind of directed assistance could you provide to help students answer the question you posed in 7 above?
13. What kind of directed assistance could you provide to help students answer the question you posed in 8 above?

14. Let's think about how you would organize the content lesson to manage the various kinds of help needed. If you met with the whole class for the first ten or fifteen minutes of the period, what kinds of things would you do during that time?
15. Let's say that you plan to have four groups meeting during the middle thirty minutes of the content lesson. While all four groups would be working to achieve the content objectives you establish in the first ten minutes of the period, each of the groups would be organized for a particular reason. How would each of the four groups be different?
16. At the end of the period, you would meet with the whole class again. What kinds of things would you do with the class during that period?
17. While the above-mentioned organizational scheme can be used during a regular class period, it can also be adapted and used over longer periods if you have greater amounts of content to cover. For instance, you could use the same strategy for a weekly period rather than a daily period. If this was the case, what would you do on each of the days of the week?

SUGGESTED FIELD EXPERIENCES

Observation. When observing in schools, you should note whether content area lessons have specified objectives, whether the planning accounts for the various demands of the material, whether the teacher poses a variety of questions which reflect the objectives, whether students are directly assisted in doing the thinking, and whether the classroom organization and management facilitate individual help from the teacher.

Teaching activities. When working with children in a content area, you should insure that you specify the content objectives, that you assess the material to determine what is demanded of students, that you ask a variety of questions, that you give assistance in doing the thinking where such assistance is needed, and that you organize the classroom to accommodate individual assistance.

Client impact. By carefully planning your content area lessons according to the principles developed in this chapter, your students will more regularly and completely achieve the objectives which you consider important in that content area.

FOR CLASS DISCUSSION

Content area specialists in the upper grades and the middle school are often confused about their role in terms of reading. Some people adhere to the slogan "Every teacher is a teacher of reading," while others say that no content area teacher can be expected to be an expert in both reading and content. The authors of this book feel that if you are teaching students to think, you are teaching comprehension; if you have them read a textbook, you are working in the area of reading comprehension. What is your position on the content area teacher's role in reading?

ANSWER KEY
 1. content material
 2. thinking skills
 3. questions
 4. thinking
 5. differentiate
 6. easier, oral
 7. information gathering
 8. experience
 9. groups
10. organization

SUGGESTED ADDITIONAL READINGS FOR SECTION SEVEN— WHAT TO TEACH BEYOND FUNCTIONAL LITERACY

DUFFY, GERALD G., AND SHERMAN, GEORGE B. "Improving Achievement Through Differentiated Instruction." *Reading in the Middle School.* Edited by Gerald Duffy. Newark, Del.: International Reading Association, Inc., 1974.

EARLE, RICHARD, AND SANDERS, PETER. "Individualizing Reading Assignments." *Journal of Reading*, April 1, 1973, 550.

HERBER, HAROLD. "Classroom Diagnosis of Work Study Skills." *Progress and Promise in Reading Instruction.* Edited by Donald Cleland. A Report of the Twenty-second Annual Conference and Course on Reading, University of Pittsburgh, 1966.

HERBER, H. L. *Teaching Reading in Content Areas.* Englewood Cliffs, N.J.: Prentice-Hall, 1970.

ROEHLER, LAURA. "Techniques for Improving Comprehension in Social Studies." *Reading in the Middle School.* Edited by Gerald Duffy. Newark, Del.: International Reading Association, Inc., 1974.

WALKER, JAMES E. "Techniques for Developing Study Skills." *Reading in the Middle School.* Edited by Gerald Duffy. Newark, Del.: International Reading Association, Inc., 1974.

EIGHT
WHERE TO GO
FROM HERE

CONTINUED PROFESSIONAL GROWTH

OVERVIEW

Becoming a good teacher of reading is a difficult and complex task. No single book or course of study can provide you with all the answers you need. In recognition of that, this chapter suggests ways to continue your professional growth beyond the foundations provided by this book. The ultimate objective is:

> Given the opportunity to teach in the elementary school, you will
> use a variety of professional sources to continue improving your
> instruction.

KNOWLEDGE BACKGROUND

One veteran of the "teaching wars" has said that some old-time teachers have thirty years experience and others have taught the first year thirty times. The difference between the two is that the former group of teachers continued to grow professionally after beginning their teaching careers, while the latter stopped growing once they got their first jobs. The most effective teachers, of course, are those who continue learning and improving.

Continuing your professional growth requires that you retain an open attitude, that you keep informed, and that you carefully evaluate emerging programs and approaches. This chapter provides suggestions on these.

RETAINING AN OPEN ATTITUDE

Those teachers who get better with the years are the ones who are open and receptive to change. It is vital that you possess such a willingness to change since elementary education generally and reading instruction particularly will encounter dramatic forces during the course of your career. As has always been the case, some of these forces will represent wise and reasoned suggestions for change, while others will represent pure opportunism, commercialism, and gimmickry. Most, however, will be somewhere in the middle; the new program, package, idea, or philosophy will probably contain the germ of a good idea which should be included as part of your total program but which should not replace all aspects of your program.

To deal effectively with these forces, you will need to be receptive to new ideas but not gullible. You will need to be analytical, using the professional sources you will have available to determine how emerging innovations can be adapted to your ongoing reading program.

KEEPING INFORMED

While it is vital to be open and sensitive to innovations in reading instruction, you must know where to look for such changes. How can you, as a teacher, keep up-to-date about recent developments in reading instruction?

An easily accessible source is the reading consultant for your building, your school district, or your county district. This person will be able to introduce and explain many new developments as they emerge. Another source is your professional reading organization and the local and state reading conventions it sponsors. In most cases, such organizations are affiliates of the International Reading Association and can provide many current sources. Still another major source is the graduate courses and workshops in reading offered by many universities. You should make use of such opportunities for advanced training as a means for keeping up to date. Your local school district will also sponsor in-service activities designed to upgrade the quality of instruction in the school district. You should participate in the planning for such in-service days and insure that at least some of the time is devoted to recent developments in reading instruction. Finally, professional journals are a major source. You should plan to subscribe to at least one or two of the following:

Elementary School Journal, University of Chicago Press, Chicago. Eight issues yearly.
Journal of Reading, International Reading Association, Inc., Newark, Del. Six issues yearly.
Language Arts, National Council of Teachers of English, Champaign, Ill. eight issues yearly.
Learning, Education Today Company, Inc., Palo Alto, Calif. Nine issues yearly.
NEA Research Bulletin, National Education Association, Washington, D.C. Quarterly (February, May, October, December).
Psychology Today, Ziff-Davis Company, New York, N.Y. Monthly.
Reading Research Quarterly, International Reading Association, Newark, Del.
The Reading Teacher, International Reading Association, Inc. Newark, Del. Eight issues yearly.
Review of Educational Research, American Educational Research Association, Washington, D.C. Five issues yearly.

EVALUATING EMERGING PROGRAMS

New commercial programs are constantly being published, and the accompanying "sales pitch" always seems to imply that the new product is the panacea which will solve all our problems in reading. As a prospective buyer, you must be able to realistically evaluate such programs.

For instance, let's imagine that a new diagnostic kit is on the market; you have examined it and found that it consists of graded oral reading paragraphs, sight-word lists on word wheels, and a special chart which tells you how to determine instructional reading levels. On the basis of this information, you decide not to purchase this kit since you already have graded oral reading paragraphs, sight-word lists, and a formula for computing instructional reading levels. The kit is inadequate in terms of your situation.

You can usually make such judgments by asking the right questions of the sales representative to your school. For instance, according to the salesperson, another new product has a test which forms the basis for skill grouping, has self-checking workbooks that teach the skills, and allows for individualization and self-pacing of the students. Before buying this material, you should ask questions such as the following:

1. You have been told that individualization and self-pacing are part of the new materials, but how are they provided? How are organization and management enhanced? Is it through workbooks, ideas, activity files, etc.?

2. One test supposedly provides a basis for all skill grouping. Does this procedure allow for flexible grouping based on individual growth in skills, or does it lead to inflexible grouping? In addition, can a one-time

testing situation be expected to reliably provide such information? Finally, if there is only one test, how does the teacher know that the students have learned all the individual skills?

3. This program claims that workbooks teach the skills. While some students of higher ability may learn reading skills without being taught, many students need directed assistance. Do these workbooks direct attention with highlighting and then gradually diminish it as the student responds correctly?

4. Finally, you should determine what reading skills are included and what type of hierarchy is developed. Do the authors of this program have a balanced view of the reading process, or are they emphasizing just one or two types of skills?

The more complicated new programs require a more systematic way of evaluating their worth. The following sample checklist is one example of such a device which can guide you when you are evaluating such programs.

1. Will this program enhance my sensitivity to my students by
   a. giving me more time?
   b. giving me better ways to be aware of students' needs? my needs?
   c. giving students better ways to be aware of others' needs?
2. Will this program give me opportunities for more individualization during
   a. diagnosing?
   b. teaching?
   c. evaluation?
   d. application of skills?
3. Will this program provide a better diagnosis of each student's
   a. rate of learning?
   b. reading skill levels?
      (1) word recognition?
      (2) comprehension?
      (3) study skill?
      (4) literary understandings?
   c. reading levels?
      (1) independent?
      (2) instructional?
      (3) frustrational?
   d. recreational reading interests?
   e. content area reading?
4. Will this program further assist me in identifying the skills of word identification and comprehension by
   a. listing the skills?
   b. providing a balance among all types of skills?
5. Will this program improve my current instruction in
   a. word identification?
   b. comprehension?

c. study skills?

d. literary understandings?

6. Will this program help pupils apply reading skills in

a. commercial reading materials?

b. content area materials?

c. recreational areas?

d. student-made materials?

7. Will this program enhance my classroom organization in terms of

a. environment for learning?

b. record keeping?

c. scheduling instruction?

8. Will this program enhance my management during the reading period for

a. routines?

b. directions?

c. instruction?

d. diagnosing?

e. evaluating?

f. application?

g. independent activiteis?

h. safety valves?

To illustrate how this checklist might work, let's assume you have just attended a state-sponsored reading meeting where a new reading plan has been introduced. Research and films of actual classrooms using this plan proclaim its worth. Several experts unanimously agree that the plan has value. You are impressed and investigate further. You find that the basis of this plan rests in expectancy of learning rate. A formula researched and standardized in twenty states establishes an expectancy for each child. The expectancies for learning rate are measured in early June so that class lists can be compiled and teachers can begin planning for the school year throughout the summer. The teacher assigns students to a group based on this expectancy and then only has to prepare lessons for each group during the school year.

Using the above checklist as a guide, the following statements can be made:

1. a. This program may help me in effective use of time, but more information is needed.

b. It does not make me more aware of student's needs; it probably covers them up by dealing only with expectancy.

c. It does not help students become more aware of other students' needs.

2. The only individualization that occurs is during the establishment of the expectancy for the rate of learning.

3. This program may help in a better diagnosing of the expectancy learning rate, but it apparently ignores other diagnostic areas.

4. This program gives the teacher no assistance in teaching the skills of word identification and comprehension.

5. While a better expectancy for each child may effect skill instruction, more information is needed.
6. There appears to be no assistance in application of reading skills.
7. There appears to be assistance in grouping based on expectancy, but classroom organization is much more complex than this.
8. There is no assistance for management of the reading class beyond expectancy grouping.

A checklist such as this can help you make decisions about the worth of a program, helping you decide whether the strengths of the program will create a better learning situation in your room and whether it can be modified to fit your classroom.

SUMMARY OF CONTINUED PROFESSIONAL GROWTH

This chapter has presented basic information about where to find information on recent developments in reading instruction and how to evaluate these developments. Armed with sensitivity, openness to change, and your understanding of reading instruction, you should now be ready to evaluate the new materials, techniques, management plans, instruction, and research which we know will become available. Change will occur in teaching; as a teacher, you must be prepared to adapt, adjust, and grow with it.

TEST YOUR KNOWLEDGE

1. One way to remain current in reading instruction is to keep an _____ attitude about reading innovations.
2. Three ways for keeping informed are to _____, _____, and _____.
3. List three professional journals
   a. _____
   b. _____
   c. _____
4. As you evaluate new materials, your evaluation should be based on a _____, such as the one found in this chapter.
5. In the years ahead, the only thing you can be certain of is _____.

SIMULATION ACTIVITIES

Read the following situation and answer the questions that follow:

Imagine that your school district has the option of using the new SWING program (Start with Individual Needs and Go). As a fourth grade teacher in a suburban district, you are very interested, especially in the individual needs aspect. Brochures include a rationale which strongly advocates individual differences. Closer examination shows that this will be true during reading assessment and that that assessment will be the basis for grouping for a semester. In February another assessment will be made for individual differences in reading, and this information will be the basis for grouping until June. Reading levels which include content areas and recreational reading areas will be established from the assessment.

According to the research completed by the SWING staff, auditory discrimination is the key to reading, so all instruction centers around that. The group of teachers in your district that were evaluating this program found on provision for sight-words except when words were explained during the background of the story in the individualized basal readers. The program has a set of materials which includes a basal, a workbook, and an enrichment book for each group, with six groups per grade level, making a total of 36 sets. A huge loose-leaf notebook filled with lists of books and magazines keys the teacher to additional reading when a basal is finished. In order to provide further individualization, the students keep their own records by taking tests (pretests, posttests, and review tests) and then by correcting and recording the results. The teacher need only to periodically check the records. The teacher's manual has a whole section on learning stations: how to set them up, where to get the materials, and how to keep then current.

1. How would you decide whether or not to adopt this program in your classroom?
2. If a consultant were available, what questions would you ask?

SUGGESTED FIELD EXPERIENCES

Observation. When observing in schools, note how the teacher keeps an open attitude toward reading innovations. Note how he or she keeps informed and how new materials are evaluated.

Teaching activities. Discuss with the classroom teacher how he or she decided on the latest material adopted. Volunteer to evaluate any new set of materials using the eight principles in the checklist as a basis.

Client impact. By your awareness of perpetual change and knowledge of the eight principles of program evaluation, you are putting yourself in the position of effectively handling reading innovations. The impact will be noted as your students receive the best possible reading instruction from you.

FOR CLASS DISCUSSION

Assume that recent research in child development indicates that any child having difficulty in telling time by the age of seven will not be able to read at grade level throughout the elementary school years. A group of parents and school board members want to test all second graders on telling time in order to place any students who fail in special groups for intensive remedial training. You, by being opposed to this proposal, have found yourself the leader of a group that plans to debate the issue at a school board meeting. What will be your defense for not adopting the proposed plans?

ANSWER KEY
1. open
2. attend conventions, consult the reading specialist, read professional journals
3. (any of the ones listed on page 357)
4. systematic checklist
5. change

SUGGESTED ADDITIONAL READINGS FOR SECTION EIGHT— WHERE TO GO FROM HERE

GIBSON, ELEANOR, AND LEVIN, HARRY. *The Psychology of Reading.* Cambridge, Mass.: MIT Press, 1975.

GREER, MARY, AND RUBINSTEIN, BONNIE. *Will the Real Teacher Please Stand Up?: A Primer in Humanistic Education.* Pacific Palisades, Calif.: Goodyear 1972.

GUSZAK, FRANK. *Diagnostic Reading Instruction in the Elementary School.* New York: Harper & Row, 1972.

HARRIS, LARRY, AND SMITH, CARL. *Reading Instruction Through Diagnostic Teaching.* New York: Holt, Rinehart & Winston, 1972.

HOLT, JOHN. *How Children Fail.* New York: Pitman, 1964.

KOZOL, JONATHAN. *Free Schools.* Boston: Houghton Mifflin, 1972.

LEONARD, GEORGE. *Education and Ecstacy.* New York: Dell, 1968.

SILBERMAN, CHARLES. *Crisis in the Classroom.* New York: Random House, 1970.

SMITH, HENRY, AND DECHANT, EMERALD. *Psychology in Teaching Reading.* Englewood Cliffs, N.J.: Prentice-Hall, 1961.

WALLEN, CARL. *Competency in Teaching Reading.* Chicago: Science Research Associates, 1972.